To Elena Charvátová, my mother

PETR CHARVÁT

SIGNS FROM SILENCE
UR OF THE FIRST SUMERIANS

CHARLES UNIVERSITY
KAROLINUM PRESS 2017

KAROLINUM PRESS
Karolinum Press is the publishing department of Charles University
www.karolinum.cz

Designed by Jan Šerých
Set by DTP Karolinum Press
Printed in the Czech Republic by Karolinum Press, Prague
First edition

Cataloging-in-Publication Data is available from the National Library
of the Czech Republic

ISBN 978-80-246-3130-1
ISBN 978-80-246-3134-9 (pdf)

The manuscript was reviewed by Bertrand Lafont (French National Centre
for Scientific Research) and Mitchell Rothman (Widener University, U.S.)

CONTENTS

FOREWORD

This is a book on the early history of ancient Mesopotamia, describing the story of the Sumerian city of Ur before the well-known "Royal graves" of the 27th pre-Christian century (c. 3000–2700 B.C.).

All through my career in Assyriology and Oriental Archaeology I have been fascinated by the phenomenon of the "Royal graves" of Ur. It goes without saying that I was not alone in this; such distinguished names as Leonard (later Sir Leonard) Woolley, Max Mallowan, Agatha Christie, Sidney Smith, Hans-Jörg Nissen, Susan Pollock, Roger Moorey, Richard Zettler, Holly Pittman or Gianni Marchesi all belong to personages that were, in one way or another, involved in the excavation and interpretation of this unique source for the early history of Sumer, and at the same time fascinated by the light that these treasures of the past shed on the early history of mankind.

Only very recently did I realize with some amazement that my investigations of Early Dynastic Ur have begun more than thirty years ago (*Charvát 1979; Charvát 1982; Charvát 1993; Charvát 2002; Charvát 2011b*). However, good fortune showered mercy on me, and brought me the chance to obtain deeper knowledge of all the problems of early Ur, only after the year 2000 A.D.

My stay in the U.S., where I worked in the University Museum of Archaeology and Anthropology of the University of Pennsylvania at Philadelphia precisely on the Ur materials in 2003–2004 as a John William Fulbright fellow, opened me the door to a closer study of the Ur finds, including a firsthand experience with items from the "Royal graves" and some of the household articles that Her Majesty, Lady Puabi (or Puabum, as my learned friend and colleague Gianni Marchesi would have it) took with her on her voyage to eternity. In Philadelphia, I had the occasion to profit from the friendliness and kind help of Richard Zettler and Shannon White, of the Near Eastern Section of the abovementioned Museum. My daily *pied-à-terre*, however, was the Tablet Room of the Babylonian Section of the said Museum, and here I must with gratefulness acknowledge the amity and heartfelt assistance of Barry Eichler, then Director of the Babylonian Section, Steve Tinney, its present Director, Philip Jones, Fumi Karahashi, Richard Palmer, Ann Guinan and especially my very dear colleague and friend Erle Leichty.

I owe a great deal of gratitude to Holly Pittman, who spared no effort to be of assistance to me at Philadelphia, and who put me in contact with Sara Jarmer Scott, another personage to which I feel bound by gratitude. Sara has put very generously at my disposal her doctoral dissertation on the SIS sealings of Ur, in which she treated all the currently accesible materials from Ur in Philadelphia and London.

I feel deeply convinced that the key to the unravelling the mystery of the "Royal graves" phenomenon lies in our understanding of the society that produced them, and that in its historical dimension. What was this society like? Did it enjoy an assured subsistence level, or were its members living on the brink of starvation? What social structures did this society build? How did it make its decisions, who were the persons and/or institutions of authority? Did the Ur kingdom (for at that time I conceived of it as of such) merit the designation of "Oriental despotism"? What role did religion play in the public life of archaic Ur? Not until we know more about all this can an attempt to solve the mysteries guarded so well by those who went down into the "Royal graves" of Ur be succesful.

In the endeavour undertaken in this book, my attention focuses particularly on the mass of seal impressions found in what Leonard Woolley called the "Seal Impression Strata" (henceforth abbreviated as SIS) of Ur, comprised between the so-called "Jamdat Nasr cemetery" as a lower chronological margin and the extensive burial ground containing the "Royal graves" as the upper chronological margin. These sealings constitute historical sources of unique character. Their reverses supply much precious archaeological information. Bearing inscriptions, they also give historical evidence, and the images carved in them present a priceless source material of iconographic character.

Having resolved to find as comprehensive answers to these questions as can be put forward, I managed to obtain materials in Philadelphia with the help of which I intended to tackle the whole complex of problems. As I proceeded with the study, it became clearer and clearer that an important source group will have to be addressed – namely the inscriptions on the SIS sealings. This necessitated one more trip to Philadelphia, where I spent the summer of the year 2005 thanks to a grant from the American Philosophical Society, working in the Tablet Room to see through the skeleton information supplied by the inscriptions on SIS seals.

All the necessary materials being then at my disposal, I looked forward to sit down to work on them. The fate, alas, decided otherwise. Turbulences of practical life induced me to leave the Oriental Institute of the Academy of Sciences of the Czech Republic at Prague, where I had been working until the end of 2005, and to seek employment in a new and dynamic University of West Bohemia at Pilsen, which offered me a post thanks to the obligingness of the then Head of the Depatment of Anthropology, Ivo Budil. After 2005, Prague reserved for me a half-post at the Faculty of Education of Charles University, and a fraction of a post in my research base of yore where I had spent my formative years as a scholar, the Archaeological Institute of the Academy of Sciences of the Czech Republic, v. v. i. I am sorry to say that this link with the "cradle" of my academic career came to an end in 2011. Putting into operation a new series of university courses, and settling down to new tasks and routines, commanded more of my time and energy than I had thought previously. Nevertheless, I could at least initiate, and bring to an end, two research projects focusing on ancient Mesopotamian history after 2005. In these we concentrated on the relations between rulers and deities of ancient Mesopotamia (*Šašková-Pecha-Charvát 2010*), and on connections between the rulers and the ruled in the antiquity of the Land of Two Rivers (*Charvát-Maříková Vlčková 2010*). At this point I have to render deeply felt thanks to my learned colleagues and friends who made all this possible by exercising themselves, often to the utmost: Lukáš Pecha, Kateřina Šašková, Petra Maříková Vlčková, and Jana Mynářová.

At a point where I nearly despaired over the heap of Ur materials lying still on my shelves, the *Internationales Kolleg MORPHOMATA* of the University of Cologne, Germany, appeared on the scene as if prompted by a superior force. Having been asked whether I would have anything to contribute to the *MORPHOMATA* research programme – *Genese, Dynamik und Medialität kultureller Figurationen* – I suddenly realized that here was a fair chance to rescue my Ur evidence from oblivion, and to bring my efforts, which had by then extended over eight years, finally to fruition. The project which I submitted was kindly approved by the *Beirat* of *MORPHOMATA*, and so I could happily dedicate myself to research on Ur in the hospitable and friendly ambience of the *Kolleg*, situated in a quiet neighbourhood abounding in greenery within the justly famous city of Köln am Rhein. Having seen the tombstones of Roman soldiers of African and Indian origin in the *Römisch-Germanischen Museum* of Köln, I feel sure that I have been preceded by other Oriental or Orientalist personages at Colonia Claudia Ara Agrippina. Yet, I must say that during the year 2011–2012, support extended to me by the *MORPHOMATA* helped me to write this book in which I render account of my efforts aimed at deepening our knowledge of the emergence, and stabilization, of statehood in human history. Again, I have to declare my debt of gratitude both to *MORPHOMATA*, especially in the persons of its both Directors, Dietrich Boschung and Günther Blamberger, as well as to my friends at home who kindly took it upon themselves to bear the burden of extra work due to my absence from Pilsen. This goes especially for *Spectabilis* Pavel Vařeka, Dean of the Philosophical Faculty of the University of West Bohemia at Pilsen, and to Daniel Křížek, my faithful Deputy Head at the Department of Near Eastern Studies of the Philosophical Faculty of the University of West Bohemia at Pilsen; I must not forget Eva Fürbachová and especially Iveta Nocarová, the indefatigable Secretaries of our Department.

I feel obliged to thank at least three of my *confratribus consororibusque pro Oriente Antiquo militantibus*, though I owe much to many of these. Walther Sallaberger of the Ludwig-Maximilan-Universität München was always ready to help myself and all the Pilsen team by going to Pilsen to lecture our students, by giving expert advice and, most obligingly, by admitting us to study in the perfectly furnished Library of his Institute at München. Jean-Marie Durand of the Collège de France has kindly consented to my study visits to the Library of the Cabinet d'Assyriologie upon the venerable Mont-Sainte-Geneviève in the Quartier Latin, where so many wise men and women made their contributions to the world of learning. Giacomo Benati of the University of Turin has been kind enough to read the archaeological part of this book and add a number of valuable comments, for which I am most grateful to him.

It is right and proper that an Orientalist publication should render homage to those next-of-kin to the author. My thanks go to all my family, my sons Jan and Ondřej, daughters-in-law Lenka and Eva, grandsons Antonín, Kryštof, Václav and granddaughters Nora and Markéta. Before all, however, I am obliged to Kateřina, my wife, who had so often patiently suffered the absences of my mind from her side due to the voyages of my imagination into the third pre-Christian millennium.

I wrote this book with help from many who have shown goodwill and amity. All the errors and inconsistencies are, of course, mine.

Acknowledgements

I was fortunate enough to be able to inspect the collections of the Near Eastern Section of the University Museum of Archaeology and Anthropology (University of Pennsylvania, Philadelphia, PA, U.S.) in 2003–2004 during my study stay in the USA, financed by a grant from the Prague establishment of the John William Fulbright Foundation (No. 2003-28-02, Fulbright No. ME659), and in 2005 thanks to a Franklin grant conferred on me by the American Philosophical Society, as well as to that of the Grant Agency of the Academy of Sciences of the Czech Republic (grant No. A8021401). For permission to study in the collections and to refer to the materials discussed above, as well as for manifold help and support, I am deeply obliged to Richard Zettler and Shannon White of the Near Eastern Section of the said University Museum of Archaeology and Anthropology, as well as to to Holly Pittman, Curator of the Near Eastern Section of the said University Museum of Archaeology and Anthropology.

This contribution could not have been written without the generous support which I received in the academic year 2011–2012 as a Fellow of the Internationales Kolleg MORPHOMATA (Universität zu Köln, Germany). I am profoundly grateful to MORPHOMATA, to their Directors Dietrich Boschung and Günther Blamberger, and to the capable and friendly staff of this major institution of interdisciplinary research.

Cologne on Rhine and Prague, in 2012–2014.
Petr Charvát

The central precinct of the Sumerian city of Ur,
with excavation pits of the Leonard Woolley expedition

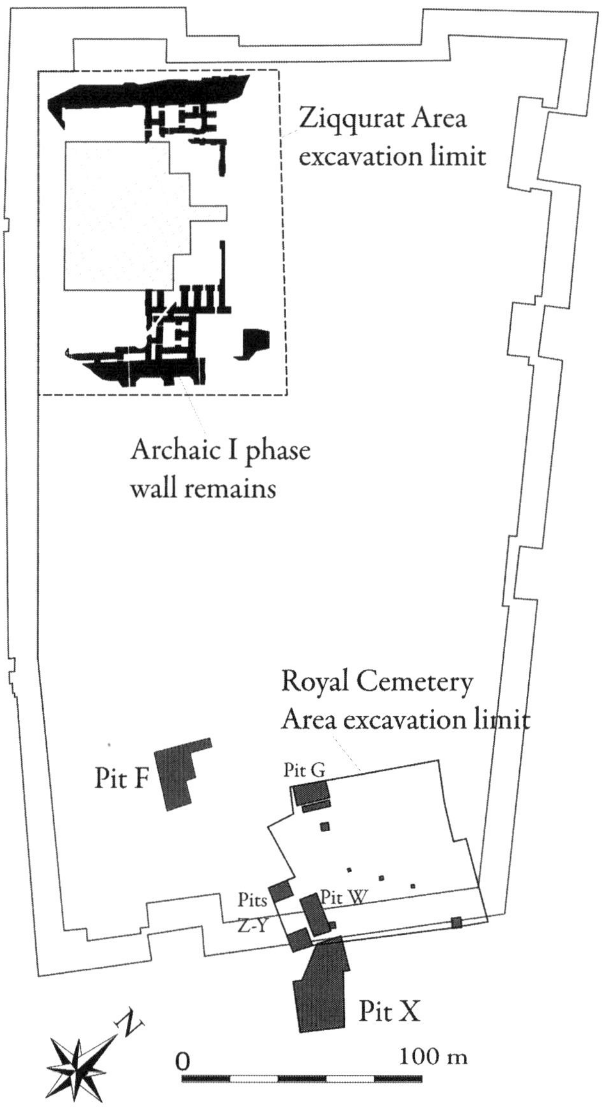

Benati 2015, Fig. 2 p. 4.

I. ARCHAEOLOGY: LIGHT OUT OF THE SHADOWS OF PAST AGES?

The formation of "primary states" during the 4th millennium BC (or Late Uruk period) is a key time for societal change in southern Mesopotamia. The onset of the 3rd millennium BC offers evidence of different socio-economic dynamics that, however, remain largely unknown.

The site of Tell al-Muqayyar, ancient Ur, in southern Iraq, is best known for its late Early Dynastic "Royal Cemetery" (ca. 2500–2350 B.C.) but it had already been a political center at the onset of the 3rd millennium (Early Dynastic I period, ca. 2900–2700 BC). Due to the rich archaeological evidence at our disposal, Ur is an ideal test case for analysis of the stabilization of the freshly formed Mesopotamian statehood for this specific time period. This book addresses the internal economic and political organization, as well as spiritual orientation and achievement, of archaic Ur. Emphasis is placed here upon the interplay between economic and socio-cultural actions, analyzed on the basis of three main lines of evidence: archaeology, written sources and iconographic data.

Excavating within the central sacred precinct of the city, the Leonard Woolley expedition (1922–1934) explored also the archaeological strata below the famous "Royal Cemetery", but above the so-called "Jemdet Nasr cemetery" (see below). These strata have yielded alternate layers of both domestic and administrative refuse including numerous find groups of seal impressions on clay, referred to as "Seal-impression strata" (SIS).

The seal-impression bearing strata constitute an ideal source category for the investigation of economic, administrative, social and spiritual structures streamlining the life of one of the major successor states of the Uruk-age culture. The analysis of the inscriptions borne by the sealed surfaces will give fairly instructive data for the use and socio-economic context of the relevant seals. On the other hand, impressions which the sealed objects left behind on the reverses of the clay sealings will reveal the type of seal carrier, and thus provide first-rate evidence of social and administrative practices of the relevant period. Inscribed seal impressions excavated from reasonably well-dated contexts will thus offer a historian the best possible material for studies of the socially engineered goods-exchange practices available.

Any qualified assessment of the find context of the early Ur sealings (published as *UE III*, on the find context see Woolley, in *UE III* pp. 1–2, and *Woolley*

1955, passim; for recent revisions of the situation see *Sürenhagen 1999* and *Dittmann 2006*) must begin with the review of their stratigraphic situation. This is what must be examined at first.

The best-informed source is, of course, the author of the excavation himself, Leonard Woolley. Let us hear what he has to say:

The upper levels containing graves of the Royal Cemetery age had been dug away by us in 1926; in them there was no stratification[1]*, owing to the disturbance of the soil by the grave-diggers,and our work has always stopped short at a stratum – the first recognisable as such – of red burnt brick earth and broken brick, pottery, etc. This is SIS 4-5, the stratum rich in clay jar-stoppers with archaic seal-impressions* (Ur Excavations, Vol. III) *which underlies much of the cemetery and is invaluable as giving a terminus post quem for the graves* (v. Ur Excavations, Vol. II p. 222).

Below this the strata, sloping sharply down with the fall of the rubbish as dumped here from the town, are remarkable well defined.
A band of light earth,
one of dark soil,
a grey belt containing much lime,
light earth,
dark again and
light succeed one another;
then comes a belt of red burnt earth containing seal impressions and pottery, and
a lime belt also rich in seal-impressions and broken sherds, labelled on the section as SIS 6;
a heavy bed of black mixed rubbish in the upper part especially of which there were more seal-impressions is SIS 7.

Another layer of burnt earth separated this from the next rubbish-mass which thanks to the presence of liberal admixture of burnt matter was itself rather red in colour; it contained very few seal-impressions (SIS 8) but was really distinguished by the common occurrence of clay goblets of the peculiar type JN.25 which were not normally found above this stratum of below it; at the same level were found (in a black streak running through the red) part of a "mixing bowl" of rough clay, Type RC.1, a clay disk with a hole towards one edge, a rough clay figurine of an animal,

1 Here my learned friend and colleague Giacomo Benati of the University of Turin, who had been kind enough to read the manuscript version of this publication, adds a note of caution. In his opinion, the excavators fully understood the stratification of the cemetery only during the 1930–1931 field campaign, looking at the exposed sections (see *Woolley 1934*, Pl. 9a). This must have been due to the excavation methods of the time. However, the examination of the original records allows the observation that strata were often recognized and distinguished even during the excavation of the tombs. Giacomo Benati is now working on these details with the aim of building a better stratigraphy of the cemetery.

part of a limestone bowl, Type JN.11, and a rubbing-stone,; at 7.50 m was a clay goblet of Type JN.25 (Woolley 1955, 79–80).

Leonard Woolley obviously included the SIS 8-4 into the earlier stage of his *Planoconvex Brick Period* and ascribed the accumulation of SIS 5-4 to the time of building layer E in his Pit F, assigning the underlying building layer F to his *Jamdat Nasr Period*. In general, he seems to have supposed that this whole band of strata came into being over a relatively short time (*Sürenhagen* 1999, 180), a proposition to which Dietrich Sürenhagen agrees (*Sürenhagen* 1999, 207).

Dietrich Sürenhagen observes, probably with reason, that the SIS 4-5 stratum probably represents rubbish layers dumped from a higher-lying settlement, and that from NW to SE and to NE. He has also noticed that SIS 7 is directly overlying SIS 8, the latter documented only in Pit Z where it tapers off (*Sürenhagen* 1999, 180).

Except the above-cited publications and comments, several other authors have recently commented on the finds of the sealings of archaic Ur of the incipient third millennium B. C. and their archaeological context. These include Richard Zettler (1989), Reinhard Dittman (2006, 38–39), and Nicolò Marchetti (2006, 71–83, esp. pp. 72–76; the book is now available in English as *Marchesi-Marchetti* 2011, as Giacomo Benati tells me). Their assessments bring arguments for dating the SIS 8, (and possibly also SIS 7?), layers into the early ED-I; indeed, all the SIS 8-4 strata have been recently dated into ED-I (*Marchesi-Marchetti* 2011, 54, reference courtesy Giacomo Benati). Layer(s) SIS 7 and 6 are supposed to relate to the latest graves of the "Jemdet Nasr cemetery", still within the ED-I age. Dietrich Sürenhagen argues that the SIS 7 underlies these interments (*Sürenhagen* 1999, 186), and that the SIS 6 accumulated over them (*Sürenhagen* 1999, 236, and Conclusions, 242–243). The SIS 6 may thus possibly belong to the early ED-II period (*Sürenhagen* 1999, summarizing table on p. 250). It is then proposed that after an interval, comprising obviously a prolonged period of time, the SIS 5-4 strata were deposited (expressedly *Sürenhagen* 1999, table on p. 208). Dietrich Sürenhagen has dated these into the ED-II–ED-IIIa transition period (*Sürenhagen* 1999, summarizing table on p. 250).

On the other hand, Richard Zettler, who has investigated the pottery profiles impressed into the jar sealings of the SIS 8-4 layers, suggests a date in ED-I and/or ED-I–II (*Zettler* 1989, esp. p. 379).

The question is obviously a tricky one, and poses a challenge to anyone wishing to obtain more information on the archaeological context of the SIS strata[2]. Let us see what can be done to elucidate the problems concerned.

2 Again, Giacomo Benati observes that large quantities of pottery fragments from the SIS strata were not properly registered and therefore never published and discussed.

WOOLLEY'S PIT F AND THE SIS

As for the Pit F, brought into connection with the SIS by Leonard Woolley, the abovementioned layer E is the very first in which planoconvex bricks[3] do appear at Ur, following the earlier predominance of rectangular bricks (*Sürenhagen* 1999, 190). The general plan of the building layout, two structures set apart by a narrow lane, is not, however, affected in any manner, continuing from at least the time of stratum H (*Woolley* 1955, Pl. 75; *Sürenhagen* 1999, 205). A similar change from rectangular to planoconvex bricks has been observed in the case of two phases of a "house" between the terrace wall of Woolley's Pit G and RT 777, which clearly represent the earliest phase of structures built within the gradually accumulating rubbish strata (*Woolley* 1955, Pl. 72; *Sürenhagen* 1999, 207). In other words, with the onset of SIS 4-5 we are moving within an (how?) early phase of ED-I[4].

The hallmark of the incipient Early Dynastic pottery tradition, the solid-footed goblet, appeared as early as stratum H here (*Sürenhagen* 1999, 192), though Reinhard Dittman, leaning on the original assessment of Leonard Wooley, puts the *floruit* of the solid-footed goblets to the local layer G (*Dittmann* 2006, 34). In layer E it was already missing[5], with reserved-slip ware and occasional occurrence of items with haematite-coloured slip, of black ware and of pottery decoration by deep triangular notches (*gashed ornament*) and by rope-moulded ridges on shoulders (*Sürenhagen* 1999, 205). The pottery vessels with fenestrated (openwork) ornament found here do nevertheless show that we are still moving within the solid-footed goblet phase of Early Dynastic pottery (*Sürenhagen* 1999, 207).

Dietrich Sürenhagen has also noticed parallels among the finds from SIS 8-4 and Pit F. The mass presence of solid-footed goblets in SIS 8 implies a correlation with terminal stratum H and stratum G of Pit F. Bored diorite lids of black diorite and pottery rattles link SIS 7-6 with Pit F stratum F, possibly even with stratum G (*Sürenhagen* 1999, 207).

Reviewing the evidence of the Ur Pit F, Reinhard Dittmann sees the peak occurrence period of the solid-footed goblets in the local strata H and G (and in SIS 8), equalling these layers with Nippur Inanna XI-X. For him, SIS 7-6 then fit into the time of F and E layers in Pit F and Nippur Inanna X-IX. In their turn, the SIS 5-4 (with the archaic texts of Ur) fall within the stage

3 Giacomo Benati notes that brick types are no longer considered a period marker. But my other learned friend and colleague, Martin Sauvage (CNRS, France), believes that they have not lost their chronological value altogether. Here I leave the decision to the discretion of my readers.

4 Giacomo Benati thinks that SIS 4-5 represent a very late ED-I phase, and that Harriet Martin may be right in dating part of the SIS 4-5 to the ED-II on stylistic criteria.

5 The revision of the Ur records has led Giacomo Benati to the conclusion that solid-footed goblets turned up both in Level H and G, being no longer present in Level F.

delimited by Pit F layers E or D, i.e. perhaps to the terminal period of Nippur Inanna IX (IXB: *Dittmann 2006*, 39).

Dittmann also notes that the Ur and Nippur pottery evidence imply that ED-I pottery style survived longer in the south than in the north; in Ur and Nippur, ED-I style lasted for most of the period characterized by ED-I and ED-II styles in the Diyala sites (*Dittmann 2006*, 38). Dittmann observes that while most of the SIS impressions have been dated into early ED-II (in the Diyala sequence), it cannot be excluded that at least some of the motifs are older (early ED-I, and even before? *Dittmann 2006*, 39).

This author then puts the date of the earlier SIS 8-4 into ED-I–ED-II (*Dittmann 2006*, Tab. 1 on p. 36; see also *Matthews 1993*, 43–44, 46–47, and 49, reference courtesy Giacomo Benati).

WOOLLEY'S *JAMDAT NASR CEMETERY* (JNC) AND THE SIS

The group(s) of burials referred to as *Jamdat Nasr Cemetery* by Woolley (henceforth JNC) give(s) us a *terminus post quem* for the SIS strata, and must thus be taken into consideration as well. The author of the excavations takes notice of the fact that strata SIS 8 (in Pit Z) and SIS 7 (in Pit W) lie above the layer containing burials belonging to this cemetery (*Woolley 1955*, 76, Pls. 77 and 82). This superimposition is direct in Pit W, while a layer containing solid-footed goblets reportedly intervenes between the JNC stratum and SIS 8 in Pit Z[6]. Woolley goes on to say that the NE end of SIS 7 was disturbed by digging of graves which, however, he distinguished from the JNC, with a remark that they are later in date and consequently likely to postdate the deposition of SIS 7; according to him, most of the other JNC graves *were dug before the SIS 7 stratum was formed and are necessarily older than it* (*Woolley 1955*, 76). Pit Y has yielded information to the effect that the SIS 5-4 layer lies directly over the JNC stratum here (*Woolley 1955*, Pl. 82; *Sürenhagen 1999*, 210).

Dietrich Sürenhagen applies a considerable effort in attempting to prove that the NW sector of Pit X contains graves dug into the SIS 7, and thus postdating its deposition (*Sürenhagen 1999*, 210). The relevance of this interpretation depends on the identification of the SIS-7 demarcation in the SW (right-hand) side of Woolley's Pl. 77 with the bundle of thin strata running

6 On the strength of observations of Giacomo Benati, solid-footed goblets occurred in SIS 8, not in the layers above. He says that the thin black layer depicted within the stratification of SIS 8 contained remains of at least one bowl of type RC.1, found elsewhere in Mesopotamia in association with solid-footed goblets and some other finds. However, it is puzzling that Woolley talks about a solid-footed goblet found at 7.50 m. This would mean that at least one example of solid-footed goblets was found in SIS 7 (?, *Woolley 1955*, 79–80).

parallel to one another in the NE (left-hand) side of the same Plate, left of the "staircase" in its centre, which I view as by no means certain.

On the other hand, Dietrich Sürenhagen is probably right in attributing the "SIS IV–V" designation to the stratum bundle in the SW (right-hand) side of Woolley's Pl. 78 to an error and identifying this bundle with a tripartite layer sequence documented in the NE (left-hand) side of Woolley's Pl. 77. We owe him thanks for the hint that sealing *UE III*: 560, whose unmistakably Fara style has not escaped scholarly attention (*Otto* 2010, 22), might have been deposited later and its original archaeological context disturbed by grave-digging of the subsequent ED-IIIa period (*Sürenhagen* 1999, 210).

What follows out of this is that while an overwhelming majority of the JNC is superimposed by SIS 8, 7 and 5-4, a part of SIS 7-6 has been disturbed by grave-digging postdating the main JNC period (*Woolley* 1955, 76).

As to the overall chronology, Dietrich Sürenhagen puts the functional period of the JNC at about 120 years, that is, a space accommodating roughly four human generations (*Sürenhagen* 1999, 232). He also notices that the structuring discernible in material appurtenances of the JNC graves display a great deal of continuity and coherence (*Sürenhagen* 1999, 224, and 236), and opts for dating within ED-I (*Sürenhagen* 1999, 243, see also *Forest* 1983, reference courtesy Giacomo Benati).

SO WHAT?

For our purpose it is of relevance to know the length of the time period during which rubbish layers including the SIS had been dumped. The published find report offers no direct evidence on this and any conclusions can be reached by inferences only. As already observed, Woolley included the SIS 8-4 into the earlier stage of his *Planoconvex Brick Period* and ascribed the accumulation of SIS 5-4 to the time of building layer E in his Pit F, assigning the underlying building layer F to his *Jamdat Nasr period*. In general, he seems to have supposed that this whole band of strata came into being over a relatively short time (*Sürenhagen* 1999, 180), a proposition to which Dietrich Sürenhagen agrees with some hesitation (*Sürenhagen* 1999, 207).

Later authors tend to envisage a longer accumulation period for the whole sequence (*Sürenhagen* 1999, 181). This position has been argued at length by Dietrich Sürenhagen (1999, esp. pp. 182–184), who proposes dating of the SIS into the interval between ED-I and incipient ED-IIIa (*Sürenhagen* 1999, 250, Tab. 54). His opinion may be taken to conclude that

- SIS 8 and SIS 7 fall within the ED-I period, while

- SIS 5-4 are to be situated within the same period of time, but into a somewhat later subphase characterized by the transition from rectangular to planoconvex bricks, and the immediately following time[7].

I must, however, frankly confess that I am sometimes at a loss to follow Sürenhagen's reasoning. Chiefly, it is not clear to me in what manner are the situations encountered in Woolley's Pits D and G to be conceived as shedding light on the SIS of Pits W, Y and Z. I find it difficult to heed at least one of Sürenhagen's stratigraphic interpretations, the one asserting that the terrace wall of Pit G is later than the houses between it and RT 777. Dietrich Sürenhagen uses this proposal to extend the sequence of stratigraphic events which he inserts between the *Jamdat Nasr Cemetery* (defining a *terminus post quem* of the SIS), and the SIS themselves. Stratigraphically speaking, the terrace foundation reaches roughly to the same depth as that of the earliest house, and layers covering the ruins of this house abut the terrace masonry (*Woolley* 1955, Pl. 72). Moreover, we should take into consideration the fact that finds from this area appear to have been substantially mixed, with a considerable quantity of them reaching back to the Ubaid-culture period (*Sürenhagen* 1999, 184).

In addition to this, Woolley's idealized section of this excavation sector (*Woolley* 1955, Pl. 72) gives limited information on the position of particular finds, especially those of epigraphic or sphragistic character. In view of the fact that we do not know whether this "terrace wall" of Pit G (*Woolley* 1955, Pl. 72) was built on ancient surface or whether its lowest parts were sunk into a foundation trench[8], it is next to impossible to assess the dates of the "tablet" recorded in Woolley's Pl. 72 in a layer abutting the foundation of terrace wall, and the "tablets"recorded there between PG 1237 and PG 1332. Supposing that no foundation trench was sunk, the tablet by the terrace wall should precede in date the 1237–1332 tablets, deposited, as it would seem, long after the terrace wall vanished under the heavy rubbish strata. Yet, as we do not know precisely the history of the deposits abutting the terrace wall, I find it difficult to give any unequivocal opinion.

In general, I cannot help seeing in all these stratigraphic data the remains of a series of "houses" (if these flimsy structures deserve such a name), of which Woolley has suggested that they may even have been *store-rooms*

7 Probably still within late ED-I (or incipient ED-II?), see above (*Marchesi-Marchetti* 2011, 54), as Giacomo Benati tells me.

8 Giacomo Benati would consent to this assumption, but adds that according to the original records, most of the Pit-G finds have never been properly published. He feels confident, however, that a review of these materials will allow him to shed more light on the stratification of this Pit.

of a temporary nature (*Woolley* 1955, 71)[9], having been built, used and deserted over short periods of time within an area of dumping rubbish, with both processes running simultaneously. As we shall see, Woolley's notion of improptu structures of short-term use will be of some relevance to the research results presented below. It is probably of relevance that very few of these "houses" supplied evidence of longer-term occupation layers. Having been active within a dump area, their builders are also likely to have disturbed the layers on which they were erecting their structures, and thus I find it difficult to base any reliable conclusions on the position of small finds vis-à-vis the immovable structures. Another aspect likely to be of consequence is the fact that the "house" remains are not directly superimposed over one another, but their stratigraphic position is defined by their situation over the dumped-rubbish strata, of which we do not know the pace at which they kept accumulating[10]. Here it must be pointed out that Dietrich Sürenhagen himself believes that the period of ten years would be sufficient for the emergence of a stratigraphic event. Commenting on Leonard Woolley's assumption that at least ten years must have elapsed between the deposition of an earliest and latest grave in a series of superimposed burials, during which the position of the earliest grave must have been forgotten, he finds this time length *sehr plausibel*, and notes that … *sich die Gelände durch Schuttablagerungen ständig veränderte* (*Sürenhagen* 1999, 231 fn. 183). Admittedly, however, there is very little waterproof information to go by, and a great deal of interpretation must needs involve assumptions of speculative character.

My own impression is that of a series of shelters built within the rubbish sttrata, and in the course of their deposition, deserted within short periods of time, with the ruins of the earlier of them gradually covered by the garbage accumulations. In other words, instead of Dietrich Sürenhagen's stratigraphic sequence (earlier structures – later structures – administrative discards, each phase following the preceding one) I propose to view the stratigraphic record as evidence for a continuous sequence of building structures[11], their abandonment and dumping rubbish, all these goings-on taking place more

9 Giacomo Benati would agree with this, suggesting that the fact that these structures yielded remarkable bulks of administrative materials allows us to think of official buildings.

10 This is only partly true according to Giacomo Benati. He observes that there is evidence of superimposed reconstructions. Notably, the houses lying between PG 777 and Pit G show at least two building phases. This situation appears to be confirmed by the remains excavated near tombs PG 800 and PG 1237, characterized by two construction phases. In particular the house remains near PG 800 produced more than 2.00 m of stratification (*Woolley* 1955, 70).

11 Giacomo Benati is inclined to see this as plausible, going on to say that according to Woolley's account (*Woolley* 1955, 70), some of these structures were built before the accumulation of SIS 4-5, at some point covered by it, reconstructed above it, and then cut by Royal Cemetery tombs. This let us suppose a lifespan considerably long, roughly speaking between the ED-I and the late ED III.

or less at the same time, or in very short temporal stages. I would therefore tend to place the whole SIS sequence within the ED-I (south) period of time.

Giacomo Benati has now provided us with a first review of his findings (*Benati 2015*). Here are his own *ipsissima verba*:

“Building remains were identified in three excavation areas: Pit F, Pit G, and in the strip comprised between Pit G and the southeastern limit of the RC Area. In Pit F – located to the back of the Royal Cemetery (in the following RC) area – a pottery production area with kilns, in use during the late 4th millennium, was converted into a dwelling area at the turn of the 3rd millennium. Large mud-brick compounds lying at about 10m above sea level (in the following asl) in both Pit F and Pit G, suggest that this part of the mound was an urban area with courtyard houses, alleyways and a thick boundary wall during the first quarter of the 3rd millennium (cf. Woolley 1956: pl. 73). Evidence from these soundings indicates that houses were often refurbished, and at intervals rebuilt following similar layouts. As indicated by the stratigraphy of the houses, the first building phase was destroyed by a fire and rebuilt shortly afterwards. A major landscaping episode consisted of the expansion of the built-up area of the town through the construction of new house lots in an open area seemingly located at the brink of the settlement.

Conversely, the strip comprised between Pits Z-Y and W – occupied by steeply sloping rubbish heaps – remained in use as a midden for a long period. The debris excavated in the Royal Cemetery Area were seemingly cast out from an upper terrace lying at ca. 10m asl, into a low-lying area used as burial ground since the late 4th millennium (the so-called “Jemdet Nasr Cemetery”). The debris of SIS 8-4 formed a slope following a northwest/southeast direction, suggesting that the throws originated from the area lying immediately to the back of Pit Z. Repeated episodes of garbage deposition gradually filled the gap between the terrace and the lower ground, and formed a rubbish heap in the area comprised between Pits Z-Y, W and X.

This short-lived quarter was then abandoned (the upper building phase was depleted all over), as was the whole slope (*Benati 2015*, 2–4).

Archaeological data allow us to identify three organizational phases for this settlement:

- Phase 1: the debris of Pit G (1-5), Pit F household remains (Levels K-I), and part of the Jemdet Nasr cemetery burials.
- Phase 2: SIS 8-6 debris, Pit F household remains (Levels H-G), part of the JN cemetery burials.
- Phase 3: the assemblages from SIS 5/4 and connected waste layers, the “administrative quarter” and Pit F household remains in Levels F-E (*Benati 2015*, 12).”

A final note: it may be legitimately asked why this book omits the testimony of coeval cylinder seals actually found at Ur (*Legrain 1951*). The reasons for this are very simple.

First and foremost, very few of the cylinder seals belonging, on grounds of style, to our period of time have reliable find contexts (if any; see *Legrain 1951*, pp. 11–13, Pls. 2–6). Of these, seals Nos. 30 and 31 (*Legrain 1951*, p. 11; see also *Sürenhagen 1999*, 200–201, 284 sub # 47, 286 sub # 79, Taf. 55: 10, 57: 7) turned up in the levels 8.00 and 7.80 m of Pit F, belonging thus to Woolley's *kiln stratum 4*, dated by Reinhardt Dittmann (2006, 28–29) into the *ausgehenden Späturuk-Zeit*. Two of them occurred in Jemdet Nasr-age graves, explored in the extended excavation of the Royal-cemetery area designed as PJ (*Legrain 1951*, 12 # 73, 13 # 88). Still other two items came to light in the filling of the Ziggurat Terrace, dated by Woolley into his Archaic I (*Legrain 1951*, 13 # 84, in SW courtyard, and 13 # 90). But all the other items either do not possess any find context at all, or come from later deposits, frequently from "Royal-Cemetery period" graves. It might be speculated what happened to these seals between the dates of their manufacture and of their deposition in earth, but hardly any safe conclusions might be reached that way, I fear.

In this connection, let us also notice a recently published cylinder seal displaying a Fara-style contest scene and bearing an inscription which might be read E_2 AN ŠEŠ (e_2-^{d}nanna?), possibly from Ur, but collected in Mesopotamia in early nineteenth century (*Thorn-Collon 2013*, 137, # 116). Another ED-I cylinder seal from Uruk has just been published (*Lan 2012*).

Second, to whatever use the bearers of the ED-I cylinder seals from Ur put them, they definitely avoided the engineered-exchange sphere employing the seals which left behind impressions culled from the SIS strata. None of the actual cylinder seals found at Ur matches any of the SIS impressions, and their actual significance thus lies open to doubt. Again, speculations on the meaning of this may be multiplied *ad libitum*. At least one of the possibilites could perhaps be mentioned – that of the matrices of the SIS sealings of Ur having been made of perishable materials like bone, wood or clay[12]. However, under these circumstances I am convinced that the finds of early cylinder seals from Ur do not yield any information which could be used for historical research.

---

12 Documented in Syria: *Mazzoni 1992*, 191 – a wooden cylinder seal from Ebla, TM.75.G.729, and Tav. XLIII: 8. Another example is the "Marcopoli cylinder", an ivory cylinder seal from the collections of the *Ecole Biblique de Jérusalem*: *Thalmann 2013*, 279 Fig. 25. See also *Benati 2015*, 15 fn. 23 for the possibility of clay cylinder seals.

II. INSCRIBED SEALS FROM ARCHAIC UR

The seals and sealings from the SIS strata of Ur constitute historical material of first-rate importance for the reconstruction of the city's history in the crucial period of emergence and first stabilization of the local variety of ancient Mesopotamian statehood. Capable of giving valuable archaeological evidence of the common everyday culture of their users, their importance for the "pictorial language" of the early elites of Ur cannot be overestimated, as we shall see subsequently, the more so as other ED textual material was hardly ever sealed (*Andersson* 2012, 20).

But nowhere does the significance of the SIS seals and, before all, sealings, strike our eyes more forcibly than in the area of the historical evidence which they are capable of supplying. Unlike the cuneiform texts, giving invaluable information but shedding light on few spheres of Sumerian public life only, sealings furnish evidence of a triple kind: in addition to archaeological data on materials and structures sealed, and to iconographical evidence yielding insight into the manner in which the elites of Ur perceived their own roles within the world as they knew and imagined it, inscriptions on sealings supply historical data. In conjunction with the two previously named source categories, these yield a unique insight into the process by which early Mesopotamian statehood sank its roots into the fertile soil between the Euphrates and Tigris rivers.

This was the reason for which I decided to include interpretation of those inscriptions on the SIS seals capable of being deciphered, and shedding light on the historical processes involved. In fact, I have to say at the very beginning that I have concentrated primarily on the impressions from SIS 8-4, which fulfil the condition of depicting the very earliest goings-on in the city state of Ur, just after 3000 B. C., as has been argued in the first chapter. Sealings found in later SIS – those numbered 3, 2 and 1 – are taken into consideration only rarely, especially in those cases when the findspot of the sealing in question cannot be established with precision and the possibility of later origin must be seriously weighed.

The reader will have remarked that entries for the one-hundred and forty eight sealings treated in the following text do differ, falling into two categories. The more extensive descriptions, coming from myself, are based on the study of the materials that went through my hands in the course of my stay at the University Museum of Archaeology and Anthropology of the University of Pennsylvania at Philadelphia in 2003–2004. The shorter entries, which nonetheless supply all the information that we need for an analysis of early Ur society, all come from the publications of Roger Matthews (*Matthews 1993*) and Sara Jarmer Scott (*Scott 2005*). I cannot be grateful enough to both of these authors who substantially facilitated my task and took great care to collect information most useful for all students of the history of incipient Mesopotamian statehood.

It will be apparent that I am trying to include all the information available to me. The sequence in which the sealings are arranged here follows the order in which they appeared in Leon Legrain's publication (*UE III*, my first column from left to right). I give museographical information comprising the excavation number beginning with U (second column), and sometimes also what appears to be the division number, denoting presumably items, despatched after final division to a particular institution (third column, optional, a three-digit number). The fourth column identifies the museum number (starting with the letters UM) and the fifth one the archaeological context.

Data obtained from the museum catalogue follow next, accompanied by references to the treatments by *Matthews 1993*, *Scott 2005*, and to the CDLI files (http://cdli.ucla.edu)[13], where applicable. Verbal descriptions of the reverse and obverse of each sealing describe what can be seen on the item presently. In descriptions of the obverse, I am giving Legrain's rendering of the signs, where available, and also the first attempts of mine, which can differ from the full sign treatment that follows. I have, however, judged it advisable to leave these "first impressions" as they are, in order to offer clues for possible variant readings. As to the description of the reverse traces, and especially imprints of cords and ties of all kinds, I am following the procedure proposed by Roger Matthews (*Martin-Matthews 1993*, esp. p. 37; *Matthews 1993*, 44–46). In measurable cases, my tables give cord thickness (CT), strand thickness (ST), strand interval (SI) and cord spin (Spin). Interpretation of the respective inscriptions then follows after the archaeological data, organized traditionally according to lines and columns in which the signs are identified and their interpretation – in many cases admittedly tentative – is given. I am mostly trying to read from the upper left side to the lower right side, in lines and then in columns. Many of the inscriptions will be found to consist of a kind of shorthand, of which the reading presents enormous difficulties and in some instances I am offering more or less educated guesses. The final parts of interpretation of the inscriptions subsume the effort in an overall "translation" or rather characteristics of content of the inscription.

13 Cuneiform Digital Library Initiative, A joint project of the University of California, Los Angeles, the University of Oxford, and the Max Planck Institute for the History of Science, Berlin.

My references to items published by Matthews and Scott identify the citation from their works (from left to right, first column). Data in the second column give evidence on the object or structure sealed, with the third column adding data on possible counter-marking or counter-signing apparent on the sealing. Finally, the *regest* of the inscription fill in the fourth column, with interpretation of individual signs given below the table where necessary. Wherever the findspot is not given, the item comes from SIS 4-5.

I do hope that my interpretation of inscriptions on sealings from the earlier SIS strata at Ur will do some service.

* * *

1. *UE III*: 1	U 18 490	876	UM 33-35-465	Pit W, Jamdat Nasr Grave Level

See *Scott 2005*, 215, and http://www.cdli.ucla.edu/cdlisearch/search_beta/search_results.php?SearchMode=Text&order=ObjectType&SealID=S006310& [accessed February 13, 2014]. Catalogue: "Ur PG. PIT W. SIS IV–V, Found in Storage 1989". Obverse: signs of writing. Reverse: impression of concentric strands of a basket lid. Individual strands coiled around with bast fibres, the orifice displays impressions of a soft tissue tied over with a string. Strands of the basket-work: r = 32 mm, 27 mm and 22 mm. Maximum basket-strand thickness measurable = 5.5 mm. Cord:

CT = 2.7 mm	ST = 1.7 mm	SI = 6.9 mm	Spin Z

Red-brown clay without visible admixtures.

Inscription:

I: 1:

X

I: 2:

ŠIDIM = *ZATU* No. 524 p. 286 = *MSVO 1* p. 146 = *UET II*: 381 (a dignitary). *MEA* No. 440 p. 199: "to build", "to create". In Abu Salabikh, šitim = "architect" (*Krebernik-Postgate 2009*, 20, register). In ED Lagaš, ŠIDIM = "Baumeister" (*Selz 1995*, 58).

<u>E_2</u> = *ZATU* No. 129 p. 196 = *MSVO 1* pp. 98–99, see *Steinkeller 1995*, 700 sub No. 129 on reading. In Šuruppak, E_2 can also refer to a cluster of arable fields, "agricultural district" (*Pomponio 1987*, 298). *Alster 1974*, 46–47, comments on the lines 207–208 of the Instructions of Šuruppak with the very famous Šuruppak proverb:

ša$_3$ ki-aga$_2$ nig$_2$-e$_2$ du$_3$-du$_3$-u$_3$-dam
ša$_3$ hul-gig nig$_2$-e$_2$ gul-gul-lu-dam,

that is, "a loving heart builds houses, and a heart full of hatred pulls them down". In ED personal names, E_2 could stand for the god Ea (*Krebernik-Postgate 2009*, 15 s. v. E_2).

A less likely variant reading would be UR_3 = *ZATU* No. 591 p. 305, missing in *MSVO 1*. *MEA* No. 255 p. 131: "roof", "terrace". For Thomas Balke (*Balke 2006*, 125 fn. 531), ùr = *mašāru* = "über etwas hinweggehen", "to elevate". *Alster 1991–1992*, 25, comments on line 60: the UR_3 sign turns up at Abu Salabikh, šu__ur$_3$ = *pašāṭu, kapāru* = "to wipe off". *Biggs 1974*, 54, 112: appears in the za$_3$-mi$_3$ hymn collection with an Umma deity, ^{d}Šara. Name of a temple? *Selz 1995*, 218: UR_3 = *sapānu* = "niederwerfen". In Abu Salabikh, ^{giš}GANA$_2$-ur$_3$ = "harrow" (*Krebernik-Postgate 2009*, 19). *Huber 2000*: guru$_7$-a im-ùr-ra = "plaster the guru$_7$ with clay; close, seal the guru$_7$ (most probably a granary)".

I: 3:

X (too broken).

II: 1:

<u>NUN</u> (= AGARGARA, ERIDU) = *ZATU* No. 421 p. 260, *MSVO 1* p. 131. See *Steinkeller 1995* p. 706 sub No. 421. The lexeme NUN occurs in Fara-age personal names, but in one single instance (*Visicato 1997*, 76). *Selz 1995*, 285: ^{d}ur$_2$-nun-ta-e$_3$-a = "Die aus dem Schosse des Fürsten hervorgegangene" = one of the septuplet daughters of the goddess Baba, lukur priestesses, venerated in the Gudea-period ^{d}lama-ša$_6$-ga temple of Lagaš. Seven lukur priestesses are known as early as ED Lagaš where they were nin ensi$_2$-ka. *Szarzyńska 1992*, 282 fn. 24: NUN may turn up alone, elsewhere it refers to the gods Enki, Enlil, Nannar, Ninurta. This term denotes a special rank of the deity mentioned. See also *Charvát 2006*.

<u>PAP = PA$_4$</u> = *ZATU* No. 427 p. 263 = *MSVO 1* pp. 133–134. *Selz 1995*, 272: Maurice Lambert says that the Fara texts have a simple PAP = munus instead of PAP.PAP, translating the term as "La Fertilisatrice"; Selz proposes here "die wachsen lässt, grosszieht", a form possibly identical with the nominal form bulug$_3$ = PAP.PAP = *rubbû(m)*, read currently most often as munu$_4$. "She who fosters growth?" But this sign may also refer to an "unfinished, open transaction" (*Selz 1993*, 186, "Archivvermerk", on this also *Selz 2011a*, 277, and *Schrakamp 2012a*, 146 sub # 1). See also *Krebernik 2004* (ED: "Personennamen… lassen sich hinsichtlich ihrer Aussagen gut auf die Königin [von Lagaš, *pch*] beziehen"; in later lexical tradition "eine weibliche, der Muttergöttin oder Ištar nahestehender Gestalt").

BULUG$_3$ = DIM$_4$ = MUNU$_4$ = *ZATU* No. 62 p. 183, missing in *MSVO 1*. DIM$_4$ = *MEA* No. 60 p. 63, a sense of "big", "to be big", as well as *leqû* = to take. The lexeme occurs in Fara-age personal names (*Visicato 1997*, 122). In Fara-age texts, munu$_4$-mú = "malster" (*Martin-Pomponio-Visicato-Westenholz 2001*, 40 *ad* text 35). *Rosengarten 1960*, 71: BULUG$_3$ = "green malt", sprouting, which, dried in an oven, is turned into BAPPIR. MUNU$_4$ = "Malz" (*Bauer 1989–1990*, 81)

II: 2:

DUR$_2$ = *ZATU* No. 127 p. 195 = *MSVO 1*, p. 98 = *UET II*: 384c. *MEA* No. 536 pp. 221–223: "to sit", "to settle", "to reside". *George 1992*, 291: dúr = *markasu* = "bond". *Rosengarten 1960*, 391–395 on díb = DAB$_5$ = "prendre en main, entreprendre, recevoir". *Bauer 1989–1990*, 80: DAB$_5$ = "ergreifen", "setzen", transitive TUŠ = "sitzen", "sich setzen". *Selz 1995*, 81 fn. 336 on DAB$_5$ = "übernehmen". *Zgoll 1997*, 405–406: dab$_5$ = "packen". On the DUR$_2$ sign also *Alster 1991–1992*, 17 on line 155, and 19 on line 199, also pp. 29–31: érin DI.KUD = DÚR.DÚR di kud = (when) you judge (your) people, out of which it follows that érin = DÚR.DÚR, sedentary people; line 199: sikil ki-dúr-me nu-mu-da-gi$_4$-gi$_4$ = "a girl will not return into our house" (as she will marry an outsider), so again dúr = to reside permanently. In ED Lagaš, DUR$_2$ = dúr = tuš = "weilen" (*Selz 1995*, 182 fn. 832). In Ur-III texts DUR$_2$ = "Standfläche, Standring (von Gefäßen)", and, in general, base of any object; the texts distinguish between UR$_2$ = "Schoß" and DUR$_2$ = "buttocks"; in descriptions of vessels, UR$_2$ = those with figural decorations inside, DUR$_2$ = only if the lower part of vessel is of a different material (*Paoletti 2012*, 147). Cf. also *Gelb-Steinkeller-Whiting 1991*, 55; *Biggs 1966*, table on p. 77, 77–78, fn. 37.

One sign of two lunate curves (a numeral?).

Two illegible signs.

A list of dignitaries, the written agenda of whom was deposited in the sealed basket?

"Builder of houses, one who makes Eridu fruitful (or malster of Eridu?), a resident (or sedentary population)..."?

* * *

2. *UE III*: 9 (= *Matthews 1993*, No. 65 = *Scott 2005*, No. 82), found in SIS 8	Reed matting package	No counter-mark	URI$_3$+AB?? Delivering agency?

See http://www.cdli.ucla.edu/cdlisearch/search_beta/search_results.php?SearchMode=Text&order=ObjectType&SealID=S006251& [accessed February 13, 2014].

Inscription:

URI$_3$ = *ZATU* No. 595 p. 306 = *MSVO* 1 p. 161. *Steinkeller* 1995, 710 sub No. 595: the sign is ŠEŠ, has also a value /nanna/. Also *Szarzyńska* 1992, 281 fn. 12: in archaic Uruk, ŠEŠ is Nannar, not Ur. Also *Michalowski* 1993, 120–121 (Ur is ŠEŠ.AB). *Pongratz-Leisten* 1992, 306, s. v. URI$_3$.GAL: the sign ŠEŠ is to be understood as URI$_3$ since Uruk III; depicts a standard that can be planted into earth, such standards may stand in pairs flanking doors.

* * *

3. *UE III*: 14 (= *Matthews 1993*, No. 78 = *Scott 2005*, No. 84), found in SIS 8	pot with covering	No counter-mark	KAM = tu$_7$ = liquid food?

See http://www.cdli.ucla.edu/search/search_results.php?order=ObjectType&SealID=S006264 [accessed February 18, 2014].

Inscription:

TU$_7$ = not in *ZATU* but related to a group of signs HI × DIŠ, HI × AŠ, KAM and KAM$_4$ (*Steinkeller-Postgate* 1992, table on p. 16). Piotr Steinkeller points to the occurrence of this sign in a text of archaic Ur (*UET II*: 18: iii: 3) and interprets its meaning as "soup". Also, KAM = tu$_7$ = *ummaru* = "eine Suppe oder Fleischbrühe" (*Bauer* 1989–1990, 86), "soup" (*Gelb-Steinkeller-Whiting* 1991, 293). "Eintopf(gericht)" according to *Brunke* 2011, 382–383. In later ED Ur, a receptacle called HI × AŠ = sùr sometimes assumed gigantic proportions, as no less than 500 minas of copper were needed for its production; the lexeme also denoted a gigantic and cumbersome weapon there (*Alberti-Pomponio* 1986, 97 ad text 44). The identity of TU$_7$ = "soup" and "a kind of bread, cake or bun" at Ebla (*Bonechi* 2003, 86–88) implies the possibility that (also?) for transport purposes, Sumerian cooks boiled their potages down to solid "instant" soups, similar to the "pocket soups" of the early modern age of Europe and the U. S. (*Wilson* 1991, 224)[14].

* * *

4. *UE III*: 24	U 18 550	740	UM 33-35-478	Pit W, SIS 6-7

See *Matthews* 1993, 79 = *Scott* 2005, 227, and http://www.cdli.ucla.edu/search/search_results.php?order=ObjectType&SealID=S006265 [accessed February 17, 2014]. Catalogue: "Ur PG. PIT W. SIS VI–VII, Found in Storage 1989". Obverse: signs of writing. Reverse: a cylindrical object coiled around by a cord. The conically expanding end of the object consists of parallel segments. Was this a bale wrapped in reed matting? Cylindrical object: r = 12 mm, thus d = 24 mm. Widths of the terminal segments: 11.4 mm, 10.1 mm and 9.4 mm. Cord: only the CT = 5.9 mm can be measured. Traces of fine parallel grooves, perpendicular to the axis of the cord, are visible on the surface of the cord impression. Red-brown clay without visible admixtures.

Inscription:

Column I:

<u>ŠA</u>$_3$ = *ZATU* No. 503 p. 280, frequently with field plots, = *MSVO 1* p. 142. In Ur-III texts, $^{(tu9)}$ša$_3$ = "Futter (z. B. von Stiefeln)", of textile or wool (*Paoletti* 2012, 174).

An alternative reading would be

14 The relevant passage is well worth citing in full: "With the vogue [late 17th century] for thin soup based on chicken or veal broth came a new invention. Its earliest name was ‚veal glue', and it was the forerunner of the bouillon cube. Strong veal stock was slowly stewed for many hours, strained and simmered again, allowed to set, scrapted free of sediment, and then gently cooked. It was a great deal of work for such a small output. But veal glue, its name later changed to ‚pocket' or ‚portable' soup, continued in demand all through the eighteenth century. Jam or beef or sweet herbs were now often boiled with the veal, to give a tastier flavour."

TU$_7$ = see above, # 3. "Soup".

Does this refer to some form of container?

The following sign is very difficult to decipher. Could it be

KUŠU$_2$ = *ZATU* 305 p. 234, missing in *MSVO 1* and *MSVO 4*?. Piotr Steinkeller (1995, 703 sub No. 305) believes that the identification of this sign as KUŠU$_2$ is erroneous but offers no alternative solution. Might there be a connection with the site GIŠ.KUŠU$_2$.KI, of which a king named Aka dedicated a lapis-lazuli bead to Inanna, discussed by Gebhard Selz (2003, 506–511)? Jeremiah Peterson now identifies KUŠU$_2$ as an aquatic animal other than turtle (*Peterson 2007*, 213–217). Another possibility could be

SUKUD = *ZATU* 493 p. 278, in *MSVO 1* only the double form on p. 141.

ŠA = *ZATU* No. 500 p. 279 = *MSVO 1* pp. 141–142. ŠA = na$_5$ = *pitnu* = in lexical lists "box, chest" (*Krispijn 2008*, 178–179).

Column II:

X

X

"(Delivery of) seafood in containers"?

***

5. *UE III*: 25	U 18 550	706	UM 33-35-469	Pit W SIS 6-7

See *Matthews 1993*, 116 = *Scott 2005*, 219, and http://www.cdli.ucla.edu/search/search_results.php?order=ObjectType&SealID=S006302 [accessed February 17, 2014]. Catalogue: "Ur PG. PIT W SIS VI–VII, Found in Storage 1989". Obverse: signs of writing. Reverse: a peg protrudes from a "wavy" (irregular) surface. No traces of cord. Peg: r = 12 mm, thus d = 24 mm. What is being sealed here? Red-brown clay without visible admixtures.

Inscription:

Column I:

I: 1:

This is a very difficult sign. Two possibilites may be valid:

GISAL = *ZATU* No. 222 p. 215, missing in *MSVO 1*, *LAK* 483 = "ein Feldgerät". *Gelb-Steinkeller-Whiting 1991*, 54 on the sign *LAK* 483, possibly identical with the sign GISAL but its reading is uncertain;

RU = *ZATU* No. 435 p. 265 = *MSVO 1* p. 135 = *UET II*: 204 = *LAK* 281. A similar sign is the RU of Jemdet Nasr-aged NI + RU = *MSVO 1* pp. 128–137 (on this now *Monaco 2004*, 3, fn. 4). Texts presumably from Jemdet Nasr, and possibly from Larsa, feature the clause 1N$_{14}$ Še$_{a}$ RU, where RU specifies both barley and emmer (*Monaco 2007*, 118, CUSAS 1, 077, O0103, with a parallel of *MSVO* 4, 54, possibly from Larsa). *Gelb-Steinkeller-Whiting 1991*, 104: the sign group AN.RU may also be an abbreviated form of ^{d}Sud$_{3}$ (SU.KUR.RU). This seems more likely to me. For ^{giš}RU = *tilpānu*, "(shooting) bow", see *Wilcke 1991*, and *Waetzold 2001a*, 110–111 (= giš-šub-ba "Los, das Los werfen"; ein Wurfholz, eine Art Bogen, Kurzspeer, Wurfspeer?). Karin Rohn (*Rohn 2011*, 14, sub # 1, p. 106 fn. 874 translates "Wurfwaffe", Gebhard Selz (*Selz 2011b*, 229 sub # 3:1) refrains from a *verbatim* translation.

I: 2:

GA$_{2}$ × NAGAR = this sign combination remains unattested. GA$_{2}$ = PISAN = *ZATU* No. 162 p. 203, *MSVO 1* p. 104, NAGAR = *ZATU* No. 382 p. 251, *MSVO 1* p. 127. No corresponding sign in *UET II*. *Selz 1993*, 397: ĝá = "Gebäude", auch pisan = "Behälter", ĝanun = "Speicher", GA$_{2}$ × GI = "Rohrkorb". *Selz 1995*, 28, fn. 75: GÁ = "Gebäude". The same general sense is assumed by Mark Cohen: gá-udu-ur$_{4}$ = "sheep-plucking shed", attested to from Uruinimgina to Old Babylonian (*Cohen 1993*, 61). "Un type d'enclos", "... où se tiennent souvent des bovins et des ovins" (= "Stall, Gehege" = *Attinger-Krebernik 2005*, 73 sub # 254'). GA$_{2}$ = "outbuilding, shed, barn" (*Andersson 2012*, 136 fn. 763). The orthography of the divine name Zababa in the newly discovered Kish plaque suggests an early reading /ba/ for GA$_{2}$ (*Steinkeller 2013*, 134).

The NAGAR sign seems to have carried a host of meanings in the third millennium B.C. A group of archaic texts from Jemdet Nasr and Umma includes the sign group NAGAR$_{a}$ ZI$_{a}$ SANGA$_{a}$ (*Monaco 2007*, 4). In the Fara texts, it occurs either as an abbreviation of the name of ^{d}Nin-ìldu (IGI.NAGAR.BU), denoting Enki as a carpenter, or as the divine name ^{d}E (also Ištar), a god from whose blood mankind was created, with reading ^{d}Alla (*Krebernik 1998*). Moreover, the reading ^{d}NAGAR = ^{d}illa and ^{d}alla may point to a deity known as vizier of Ningišzida, to a divine figure called Hayya (^{d}NAGAR = ha-a-a-u) and to a (later?) pair of "pristine" divine beings killed in order to create human beings

(*Krebernik 2002a*, esp. pp. 293–297). The Fara-age divine name ^{d}Alla-pa-è, "Alla soars in splendour", belonged to an underworld deity identified with Dumuzi (*Mander 1986*, 53; *Cohen 1991*, 167–168 ad No. 7). The NAGAR = Alla reading held on through the Akkad period (*Steinkeller-Postgate 1992*, p. 62 ad ii 14) until the Ur III age (ibid.). On NAGAR = "carpenter" see *Krebernik-Postgate 2009*, 19, register.

The Akkad period brings the first references to "a mysterious entity" named DUB.NAGAR, which consumed food and appeared in the same category as the highest civil dignitaries (king and ensi$_2$, *Westenholz 1987*, 96). A similar meaning is expressed for Ur-III texts by Hans Neumann (*Neumann 1993*, 111 fn. 610 and 203). At Ebla, the DUB.NAGAR was obviously an arts-and-crafts establishments since it disposed of "Meissel, Stemmeisen und Beitel" (*Waetzold 1995*). In an Ur-III text from the fifteenth year of king Ibbisuen (*UET III*: 1498), Marc van de Mieroop translates é-DUB.NAGAR as "ateliers of the sculptors", receiving wax, ivory and wood for the production of luxury items (*Van de Mieroop 1999–2000*, 112–113). Finally, the noun níĝ-nagar^{SAR} denotes an edible substance (*Civil 1982*, 15–16).

The overall impression seems to be one of a notion referring to the vegetation- and fertility symbolism, and to the outcomes of engagement of supernatural fertility forces. A translation of "storage space for (edible?) substances of organic origin" may not be entirely off the mark. Something similar may be implied for a much earlier period by a cylinder-seal impression from tomb U-153 of Abydos in predynastic Egypt, dating to the Naqada IId period (3580–3480 BC, *Hill 2004*, 21, fig. 11. b on p. 37 and fig. 18: e on p. 44).

I: 3:

An alternative explanation will involve the reading bala-bulug$_4$, "contribution of the border regions"?

<u>NAM$_2$ LA</u> = NAM$_2$ is *ZATU* No. 384 p. 251 = *MSVO 1*, p. 127. LA = *ZATU* No. 306 p. 234, with attestation of a lexical unit nam$_2$-la; it is missing from *MSVO 1*, as well as from *MSVO 4*. Both these sign forms from Ur seem to be close to signs from Abu Salabikh peculiar to the *ductus* of those texts: *Biggs 1966*, table on p. 77 and fn. 37 on pp. 77–78. In ED Lagaš LA = syllabic la in suffixes (*Meyer-Laurin 2011*, 55). A dignitary?

Column II:

II: 1:

<u>NIMGIR</u> = *ZATU* No. 399 p. 255 = *MSVO 1* p. 130. In the Fara texts, the NIMGIR was in charge of uru-DU = foreign workers probably coming to the city (*Pomponio 1987*, 33) and of the nu-su personnel. He received 1 gur of barley monthly and must have been a rather high official, as only 24 of them are attested to in the Šuruppak texts (*Alberti-Pomponio 1986*, 108; *Pomponio 1987*, 33, 57). In Abu Salabikh, nigir = "herald" (*Krebernik-Postgate 2009*, 20, register). In Early Dynastic Lagaš, the NIMGIR (= nigir) publicly announced sales

of houses. For the publication of field sales, another official, the dub-sar lú gán-gíd-da, was responsible. The NIMGIR also carried out the kag___dù and ì___ag ceremonies, consisting of driving a nail into the house wall and smearing its head with oil (*Gelb-Steinkeller-Whiting 1991*, 238 and 241). We know this official also from Early Dynastic Nippur (*Alberti-Pomponio 1986*, 109) and his title appears as component of a host of Early Dynastic, Akkadian and Ur-III personal names (*Alberti-Pomponio 1986*, 109–111). For the later ED Ur cf. *Alberti-Pomponio 1986*, 107–111 (ad text 48), and, in general, *Krispijn 2008*, 183, with ref.

II: 2:

This most obscure sign may perhaps be interpreted as $\underline{\text{LU}_2}$ = *ZATU* No. 332 p. 239 = *MSVO 1* p. 122.

II: 3:

Again, this mysterious sign presents great difficulties. At the risk of moving on the verge of the possible, I suggest a reading $\underline{\text{UZ}}$ = *ZATU* No. 611 p. 309, also a tribute. Missing from *MSVO 1* and *MSVO 4*. The lexeme occurs in Fara-age personal names, but only once (*Visicato 1997*, 104). For "uz- und u_5 am Anfang der Namen von Wasservögeln" see *Keetman 2012*, 33. UZ = *ūsu* = duck, other than *paspasu*, Old Akkadian (*Steinkeller-Postgate 1992*, 57). Jeremiah Peterson now translates "goose" (*Peterson 2007*, 49). In later ED Ur, sundry ducks were actually registered upon delivery (*Alberti-Pomponio 1986*, 86–88 ad text 35). On the later e_2-uz-ga see *Dahl 2006*, 83, and *Allred 2006*, 72–80.

The other fragment of this sealing, not joining the former one, displays traces of two columns with two lines:

Column I:

I: 1:

X

I: 2:

X

Column II:

II: 1:

$\underline{\text{LA}_2}$ = *ZATU* No. 307 p. 235, also an official, = *MSVO 1* p. 121. This sign denotes (also) a particular textile product, a furry skirt often appearing in textile accounts (*Szarzyńska 1996*, 239). Text *MSVO 1* No. 234, a damaged account of unclear contents, probably a list of (deliveries to?) personal names or office designations, displays the two signs linked in our sealing (LA_{2a} SA_a, *MSVO 1* p. 121).

$\underline{\text{SA}}$ = *ZATU* No. 436 p. 266 = *MSVO 1* p. 135. Text *MSVO 1* No. 234, a damaged account of unclear contents, probably a list of (deliveries to?) personal names or office designations, displays the two signs linked in our sealing (LA_{2a} SA_a, *MSVO 1* p. 121). An offering ceremony ní-sa-ka, "ripe comestibles"(?) is known from later ED Ur (*Alberti-Pomponio 1986*, 44–46).

A dignitary?

II: 2:

KISAL = *ZATU* No. 295 p. 231, also an official = *MSVO 1* p. 119 = *MSVO 4* p. 61, but the form $KISAL_{b1}$ of both *MSVO 1* and *MSVO 4* differs from our sign, reproducing the earlier Uruk device (*ZATU* No. 295 p. 231 sub a). The *ZATU* entry probably combines several signs, of which only the b-form can be identified as KISAL, while the a-form (ours) is "almost certainly a separate sign" (*Steinkeller 1995*, sub No. 295 p. 703). A group of archaic texts from Uruk, Jemdet Nasr and Umma(?) includes the sign groups KU_{6a} $KISAL_{b1}$ (in texts relating to barley and products thereoff, thirteen times) and SI $KISAL_{b1}$ (*Monaco 2007*, 4, 7–8). For a parallel on an ED-II cylinder seal, see *Buchanan 1981*, No. 253, pp. 99 and 443. Is this to be read $gipar_x$ (*Selz 2011b*, 233 sub # 1: 3)? Not always: *Andersson 2012*, 158 fn. 912. On gipar see also *Lion 2009*, 179; *Westenholz 2013*, 254–256.

Probably a closure of a storage complex used by public institutions, officials and (for?) personnel.

* * *

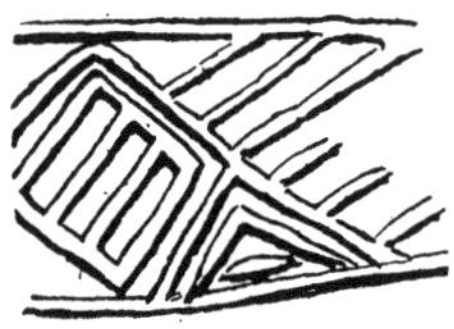

6. *UE III*: 26	U 18 550	720	UM 33-35-474	Pit W, SIS 6-7

Catalogue: "Ur PG. PIT W. SIS VI–VII, Found in Storage 1989 ". Obverse: a geometrical composition of parallel lines, a triangle and a GAN_2 (?) sign. Reverse: a peg coiled around with a cord protrudes from a "wavy" (irregular) surface with a dense breakage structure. Peg: radius = 16 mm, thus d = 32 mm. Cord:

CT = 4.5 mm	ST = 2.5 mm	SI = 8.8 mm	Spin S

Red-brown clay without visible admixtures.

Inscription:

NAM_2 = *ZATU* No. 384 p. 251 = *MSVO 1* p. 127. This sign form from Ur seems to be close to the sign from Abu Salabikh peculiar to the *ductus* of those texts: *Biggs 1966*, table on p. 77 and fn. 37 on pp. 77–78. Also see below, my # 122.

* * *

7. *UE III*: 34	U 18 550	702	UM 33-35-467	Pit W, SIS 6-7

See *Matthews 1993*, 76 = *Scott 2005*, 217, and http://www.cdli.ucla.edu/search/search_results.php?order=ObjectType&SealID=S006262 [accessed February 18, 2014]. Catalogue: "Ur PG. PIT W SIS VI–VII, Found in Storage 1989". Obverse: an AB sign with a spiral. Reverse: impression of a container of cylindrical shape, the surface of which is strewn with tiny particles of an organic matter (chaff?). The orifice seems to have been closed by soft tissue and tied over with a cord. The radius of the container = 22 mm, thus d = 44 mm. Was this a cup? Cord:

CT = 3.2 mm	ST = 1.7 mm	SI = 6.5 mm	Spin S

Matthews 1993: door peg. Red-brown clay without visible admixtures.

Inscription:

AB + $AŠ_2$ = *ZATU* No. 9 p. 170, missing in *MSVO* 1. A city? *Steinkeller 1995*, 696 sub No. 9 and 11: interchanges with AB.gunu in an Uruk-age city list, and replaces AB.gunu in *SF* 23 iii 7. *Gelb-Steinkeller-Whiting 1991*, 234–235: AB + $AŠ_2$ = *šībum* = "elder, wittness". Gelb ascribes this sign to the northern, Kiš tradition, and says that it turns up first in Old Akkadian written materials. *Alberti-Pomponio 1986*, 29 on text 2: obv.: iv: 1 = AB + $AŠ_2$ = "elder, wittness", supposed to be one of the earliest occurrences of this sign.The Fara-age texts include one instance of DUMU.AB as a professional designation (*Visicato 1997*, 112). The sign occurs at Abu Salabikh (*Biggs 1966*, table on p. 77).

"(Delivery of a) City So-and-so"?

"(Delivery of) elders of a city"?

Note: Another related seal occurs in *UE III*: 172, (= my # 30) cf. infra.

* * *

8. *UE III*: 35	U 18 550	739	UM 33-35-477	Pit W, SIS 6-7

See *Scott 2005*, 226. Catalogue: "Ur PG. PIT W. SIS VI–VII, Found in Storage 1989". Obverse: shelters from plaited organic fibres? Reverse: a peg protrudes from uneven surface with traces of organic materials (fibres, stalks). The exterior of the peg base shows traces of spiral ribbing. No traces of cord. Peg: radius = 7 mm, thus d = 14 mm. Was this a door sealing? Red-brown clay without visible admixtures. Are the cracks on the obverse original, or did they arise in the museum collections?

Inscription:

This is most difficult to guess, but the least improbable rendering may be that of a variant of the NAM_2 LA_2 title cited above:

<u>NAM_2 LA_2</u> = see above, # 5 and 6; a dignitary?

* * *

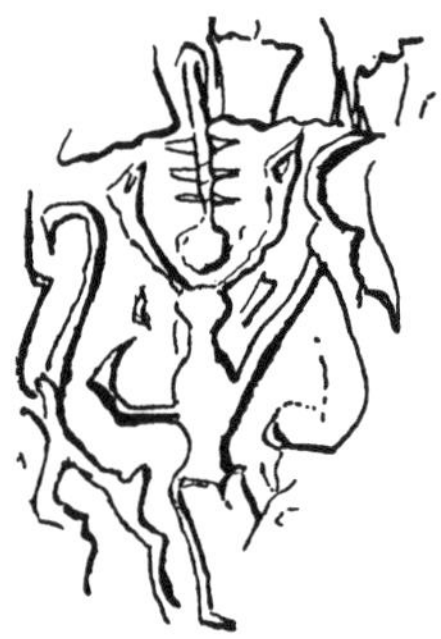

9. *UE III* : 43	U 14 643	UM 31-16-673	SIS 7

Catalogue: "Ur SIS 7". Obverse: An unclear dancing(?) figure with a sign on the head. Reverse: Impression of a rim, neck and shoulders of a vessel. The rim bears impressions of a pliable substance (leather or a diaphragm of some kind?). Rim: r = 23 mm, thus d = 46 mm. Neck below rim tied around with cord:

CT = 1.8 mm	ST = 1.5 mm	SI = 4.4 mm	S-spin

Red-brown clay without visible admixtures. Impressions of fine fibres on cord imprints. The neck may bear an impression of a diaphragm or leather. Cut away with a blade of some kind when the clay was still wet.

Inscription:

(1'): <u>TUR</u> (= DUMU, $BANDA_3$) = *ZATU* No. 562 p. 296, *MSVO 1* p. 153. May appear in the Uruk-III City List (*Johnson 2014a*, 46, *Cities* 31). A group of texts possibly from Uruk, Jemdet Nasr, Umma(?) and Uqair(?) features the sign group ŠU TUR (*Monaco 2007*, 8). In the same texts, TUR = "a type of bread of the smallest size" (*Monaco 2007*, 157). In Šuruppak, DUMU is also a person dependent on somebody else, who may be denoted either by a personal name or by a professional designation, or even on an institution (*Pomponio 1987*, 63; *Visicato 2000*, 2 fn. 5). In early land-sale documents, dumu-gana$_2$ = "sons of the field", relatives of vendors of landed property entitled to material compensation for their consent with the transaction, also indicating a detachment from a purely kinship denomination (*Gelb-Steinkeller-Whiting 1991*, 227). In Abu Salabikh TUR = "child, young (person)" (*Krebernik-Postgate 2009*, 21, register). The PSD, in http://psd.museum.upenn.edu/epsd/nepsd-frame.html [accessed September 27, 2014], s. v. tur, has = "(to be) small; to reduce, diminish; to subtract; (to be) young". But see also TUR = "coral" (*Waetzold 2001*, 41).

(2'): <u>NUN</u> (= AGARGARA, ERIDU) = see above, # 1. "Noble", "Noble (= Enki)"? = "The city of Eridu"?

"Son of a noble or Noble (= Enki)".

* * *

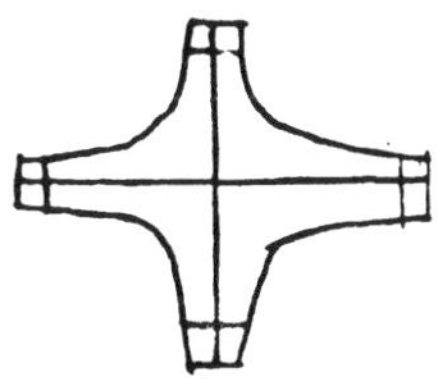

10. *UE III* : 77 (ms)[15]	U 18 394	UM 33-35-263	SIS 4-5, Pit W

Catalogue: "Ur PG. Pit W, SIS IV–V. Found in storage". Obverse: a Greek cross and a cylinder-seal impression with standing and running legs and a tail(?). The cross is incised over the cylinder-seal impression. Reverse: a peg coiled around with cord. Peg: r = 17 mm, thus d = 34 mm. Cord:

CT = 3.15 mm	ST = 2.95 mm	SI = 5.7 mm	S-spin

Red-brown clay without visible admixtures. Impressions of fine fibres on cord imprints. Fingerprints.

Inscription:

The large cross sign could be <u>KIB</u> = see http://psd.museum.upenn.edu/epsd/nepsd-frame.html [accessed September 27, 2014] s. v. šennur = plum or ULUL. Consignment of fruit?

15 This abbreviation (ms) means that the inscription on the sealing is written by hand.

KIB or ŠENNUR = *ZATU* No. 290 p. 230, referring also to a profession. KIB = šennur = *šallūru*, *MEA* No. 228 p. 125, *CAD* Š pp. 253–254: a kind of a fruit tree and its fruit. Also *Civil 1987*, 149–150, KIB = šennur = *šallūru*, a kind of fruit, a plum? *Lafont 2008*, 6, col. D: 17: šennur = "prune" (Word List C, Ur-III period). The lexeme ^{d}KIB.NUN occurs in Fara-age personal names (*Visicato 1997*, 51). On the sign cf. also *Gelb-Steinkeller-Whiting 1991*, 107 (= *LAK* 278). Or is this

KIB.NUN (NA) = Euphrates? Absent from archaic Ur texts but probably identical with the ^{d}KIB.NUN of Fara (*Woods 2005a*, 10–12); see also ^{d}UD. KIB^{ki} = Sippar at Abu Salabikh (*Woods 2005b*) . See also http://psd.museum .upenn.edu/epsd/nepsd-frame.html [accessed September 27, 2014] s. v. kib = an object.

Storage of fruit? Delivery from Sippar?

* * *

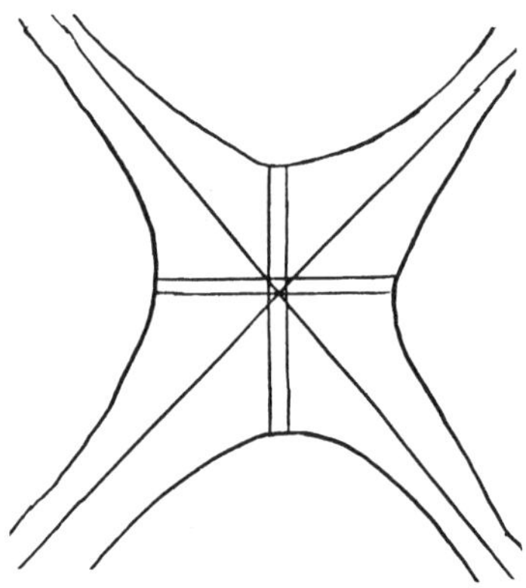

11. *UE III* : 78 (ms)	U 18 394	895	UM 33-35-278	Pit W, SIS 4-5

Catalogue: "Ur PG. PIT W SIS IV–V, Found in Storage 1989". Obverse bears an incised likeness of a large cross. Reverse: This is another jar stopper, of a diameter = 90.1 mm.. Two cords cross each other at right angles on its reverse. One of them:

CT = 2.5 mm	ST = 2.2 mm	SI = 6.45 mm	S-spin

Of the other cord, only the CT = 2.0 mm can be measured. The cords seems to be running over a wrapping of fine textile. On the edge of the stopper zigzag impressions, likely to have been left by an item of reeds, the plaiting of which was arranged in a stair-shaped manner, are visible. This plaiting displays a strand width = 4.9 mm. Segments of the smooth area of the stopper inside bear impressions resembling tiny bubbles, round and globular. Red-brown clay withou visible admixtures. Fingerprints. A bale of goods?

Inscription:

The large cross sign is polyvalent; but it could be KIB = see http://psd.museum.upenn.edu/epsd/nepsd-frame.html [accessed September 27, 2014] s. v. šennur = plum or ULUL. Consignment of fruit?

KIB or ŠENNUR = see above, # 10, a kind of fruit; or

KIB.NUN (NA) = Euphrates, again see above, # 10.

Storage of fruit?

* * *

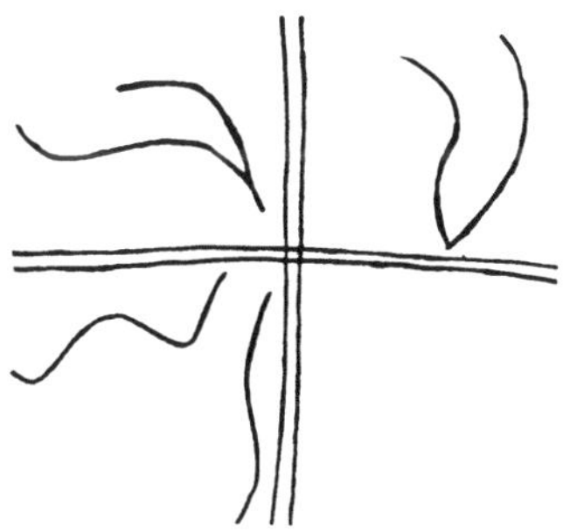

12. *UE III* : 79 (ms)	U 18 394	834, 838 (?)	UM 33-35-267	SIS 4-5, Pit W

Catalogue: "Ur PG. Pit W, SIS IV–V, found in storage 1989". Obverse: divided into four quadrants, three of which contain signs. UR$_2$, and possibly GI, as well as a third sign. Reverse: impressions of organic particles. Jar stopper, d = 91.8 mm. Red-brown clay without visible admixtures.

Inscription (from right to left):

UR$_2$ = also URUM(?), *ZATU* No. 588 p. 304, *MSVO 1* p. 160. In an archaic text from Umma(?), marked in summary as UDU, it turns up as UR$_2$ AN (*Monaco 2007*, 5, 93: CUSAS 1: 053: 00105b). The sign group UR$_2$ AN ŠA$_3$ appears in other texts: MS 2900/07 (allocations of fields), and HJN 28A (with KU$_{6a}$ KISAL$_{b1}$), where it associates with EN$_a$ GA$_{2a1}$ DU ŠU, qualified as SANGA; this last person(?) shows up in texts CUSAS 1: 105, 149 and 153 (*Monaco 2007*, 93). Text CUSAS 1: 105 is summarized with GU$_7$, while the summaries of both CUSAS 1: 149 and 153 bear the signs HAL AL (*Monaco 2007*, 149). UR$_2$ = *sūnu* = "thigh", *MEA* No. 203 p. 117. Also, in general, "human body from the waist down", "lap", "foundation", but also "to sleep" and "to fecundate" (*rehû*). *Sūnu*: *CAD* S pp. 386–388, "lap", "crotch", "sexual organs". On UR$_2$ see *Peterson 2007*, 567–571, and http://psd.museum.upenn.edu/epsd/nepsd-frame.html [accessed September 27, 2014] s. v. ur$_2$. The lexeme occurs in Fara-age personal names

(*Visicato 1997*, 101). In Instructions of Šuruppak, ÚR.AŠ may be a honorific epithet of Šuruppak (*Alster 1974*, 25, and now *Chen 2013*, 9–10, 132–135). *Westenholz 1987*, 43, refers to a binary lexeme A_2 + UR_2, attested to in Agade-period texts, probably a_2-ur_2 = *mešrêtu* = limbs, described as "right" and "left". This seems to allude to limbs of the human body above, and below, the waist, most probably to arms and legs of statuettes produced separately from the bodies. Cf. also *Alster 1991–1992*, 19 and 21, ad ll. 192–193 (ur_2-sikil = "a girl's lap"), and *Mander 1986*, 96 ($^{d}ur_2$ = "il dio delle fondamenta"?).; *Selz 1995*, 285 ($^{d}ur_2$-nun-ta-e_3-a = "Die aus dem Schosse des Fürsten hervorgegangene"), interprets this name (= rain cloud, a fertility symbol) as that of one of the septuplet daughters of the goddess Baba, lukur priestesses, venerated in the Gudea-period ^{d}lama-$ša_6$-ga temple of Lagaš. Seven lukur priestesses are known as early as ED Lagaš where they were nin $ensi_2$-ka. In Ur-III texts DUR_2 = "Standfläche, Standring (von Gefäßen)", and, in general, base of any object; the texts distinguish between UR_2 = "Schoß" and DUR_2 = "buttocks"; in descriptions of vessels, UR_2 = those with figural decorations inside, DUR_2 = only if the lower part of vessel is of a different material (*Paoletti 2012*, 147).

The *gunnû*-form of the UR_2 sign (UR_2 × TAG_4), probably linking up with sign *LAK* 289, later evolved into the UMBIN sign, denoting a kind of vessel or receptacle. One UMBIN may equal 2 $SILA_3$. A similar case is UR_2 × GAR, attested to in the Old Babylonian period (*Gelb-Steinkeller-Whiting 1991*, 54). Is the UR_2 delivery a reward for the holding of the TAG_4 ceremony, supplied in hollow measures?

BAD? = see http://psd.museum.upenn.edu/epsd/nepsd-frame.html [accessed September 27, 2014] s. v. bad = be open, thresh grain. See *ZATU* No. 41 p. 178. Cf. *MEA* No. 69 p. 67 for this exceptionally polyvalent sign. The dominants sememes are "to open", "to attain peace", "to be finished", "to be closed", "to be complete", also "to be old" and "to be dead", one of the sememes being also "blood". *Steinkeller 1981*, p. 22, "to open", first in texts of archaic Ur. *Englund 1990*, 134–136: ba.BAD "eine Art Fischer, nicht 'gestorben' ". In Šuruppak, šu-bad = "to enter into possession", "to take" (*Pomponio 1987*, 178–179, fn. 56). In Instructions of Šuruppak, bad = *rêqu* (*CAD* R 266) = "to withdraw", "to go away", "to depart", "to become lost", "to keep something away", "to remove" (*Alster 1974*, 157). In one of the ED texts from Umma, Josef Bauer translates šè-til as "Die Angelegenheit zu diesem (Vorgang) ist erledigt" (*Bauer 2012*, 69). Here the third-millennium sources, in which BAD = *bēlum* (*Steinkeller 2004*, 12–13), may be more relevant than BAD = sun = *labīrum*, "assignment to a specific kind of labour" (*Charpin 1987*). Does this refer to the nature of deposit (grain?). But see # 46 = *UE III*: 315 for a more probable meaning of "processing grain".

$NINDA_2$ = *ZATU* No. 401 p. 256, *LAK* 95 = *MEA* No. 176 p. 111, "part of a plough", "a kind of fish", and GUR_9, a hollow measure.This sign may be used for the designation of fractions; ^{giš}nindá = in later periods gur$_9$ = "measuring vessel", as in Standard Word List D (*Civil* 1982, 5).

A volume of goods (threshed grain in a pot) for "complete fecundation", or "opened (= activated) fecundation"?

* * *

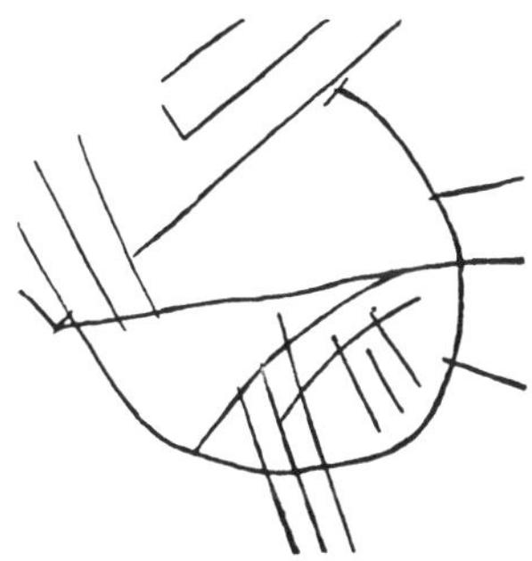

13. *UE III* : 80 (ms)	U 14 878	UM 31-16-680	SIS 4

Catalogue: "Ur A = SIS 4 (?)". A jar stopper. Obverse: incised circle intersected by two axes perpendicular to each other, and other incisions. Reverse: roughly smoothed, impressions in the directions of the four cardinal points. Red-brown clay without visible admixtures.

Inscription:

BU + BU + NA$_2$ = this could be BU + BU + NA$_2$, = *ZATU* No. 58 p. 182. Appears in the Uruk-III City List (*Johnson* 2014a, 46, *Cities* 14). Other occurrences include an Uruk-III sealing from Jemdet Nasr, and an ED-age version of *Cities*. *Monaco* 2009, 151: text W 20236, 1 shows a late and simplified form of the BU$_a$+BU$_a$+NA$_2$ sign from the "Cities" lexical list, hitherto unknown from ED-I texts. Most probably to be interpreted as ARINA$_X$, and equated with ARINA$_X$ or ERINA$_X$, = MUŠ + MUŠ (*Steinkeller* 1995, 699 sub No. 58).

The Fara-age text *SF* 1 has a series of names composed with the NA$_2$:

iv: 1 = NAP (AN.AN)-ná

v: 10 = ^{d}nin-NÁ

vi: 5 = ^{d}nin-NÁ.KI

ix: 19 = ^{d}BU × BU × NÁ.

Furthemore, CT 24 47, ii: 13 = ^{d}lugal-giš-ná-a, and

CT 25 22 34 = ^{d}giš-ná-a (*Mander* 1986, 94).

It would thus seem that the NA$_2$ act (see *Charvát* 1997, 10–12, 22, 57–58) was presided over by special deities, AN and NIN, and that even an office of a "lord of the holy bed" did exist. EN and NIN thus do not appear to have performed the NA$_2$ ceremony as incarnations of divinities, but as mere human carriers of a divine mission and divine will. (At least) the NIN apparently carried out a procedure called NÁ.KI. Or is this

KA = *ZATU* No. 271 p. 226, *MSVO 1* p. 116? This is an alternative solution, with an unidentified subscript with two lobes.

(Possibly a combination of KA with an emblem of the delivering, or consuming, entity.)

A city name?

* * *

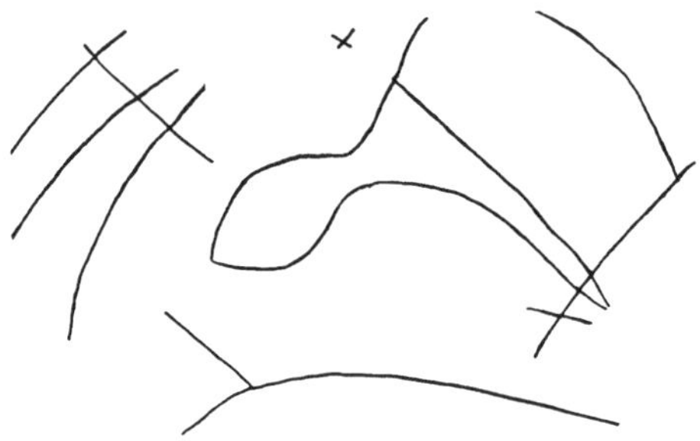

14. *UE III* : 81 (ms)	U 18 394	832 (?)	UM 33-35-264	SIS 4-5, Pit W

Catalogue: "Ur PG. Pit W, SIS IV–V. Found in storage 1989". Obverse: graven images, also the UR$_2$ sign. Reverse: broken and illegible. Most likely a jar stopper. Red-brown clay without visible admixtures.

Inscription:

UR$_2$ = see above, # 12. "Lap", "crotch", "sexual organs", "fecundation ritual".

IŠ = KUŠ$_7$ = ŠUŠ$_3$, *ZATU* No. 270 on p. 225, *MSVO 1* p. 115, as IŠ. This lexeme appears in Šuruppak texts (*Pomponio 1987*, 244–245) and in contemporary professional names (*Visicato 1997*, 125). A dub-sar-KUŠ$_7$ is attested to at Fara (*Visicato 2000*, 22). IŠ = *kizûm* = "equerry" (*Gelb-Steinkeller-Whiting 1991*, 184). *Mander 1986*, 112 (^{d}kuš$_7$-ba-ba$_6$, an Abu Salabikh deity). On this profession *Selz 1995*, 157 fn. 668 (KUŠ$_7$ = a shepherd), *Beal 1992* (ŠUŠ$_3$ or SUS/A/$_X$). SAHAR as professional name = šùš (*Cavigneaux 1992*). See also http://psd.museum.upenn.edu/epsd/nepsd-frame.html [accessed September 27, 2014], s. v. kuš$_7$. The earlier (Fara-age) reading seems to be rather kuš$_7$ "equerry, groom, chariot fighter" (*Visicato-Westenholz 2000*, 1112–1113). On KUŠ$_7$ = "groom, herdsman" see *Krebernik-Postgate 2009*, 19, register. Karin Rohn (*Rohn 2011*, 194) sees the sememe as obscure.

The above is a more likely alternative than GAR$_3$, *ZATU* No. 198 p. 209, missing in *MSVO 1*. Another possibility is *ZATU* No. 636, p. 314, also missing from *MSVO 1*, the reading of which is unknown.

Delivery of "fecundation fee", from Susa(??).

* * *

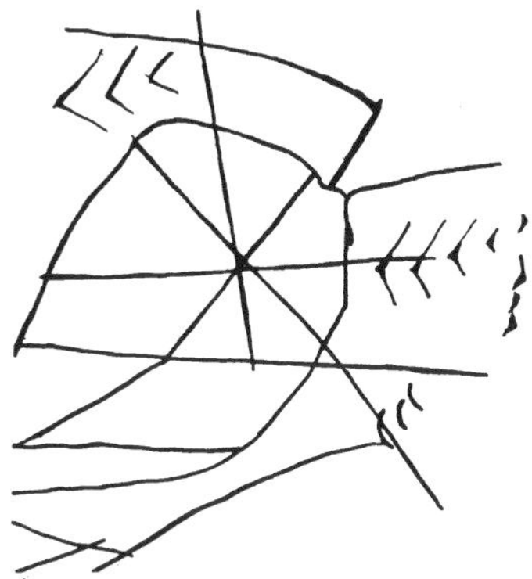

15. *UE III* : 83 (ms)	U 18 394	839	UM 33-35-276	Pit W, SIS 4-5

Catalogue: "Ur PG. PIT W SIS IV–V, found in storage 1989".Obverse: Inscised signs. ŠE ŠE ENGUR or NAMMU? Reverse heavily damaged, traces of a smoothed surface out of a which a peg, coiled around with cord, could protrude. No measurements can be taken off the peg traces, of the cord, only CT = 4.15 mm is legible. Red-brown clay without visible admixtures. The cord impressions show traces of fine fibres.

Inscription:

<u>AMA</u> = *ZATU* No. 28 p. 174, *MSVO 1* p. 88. Occurs in the personal names of Šuruppak texts (*Visicato 1997*, 11–12), see also *Attinger 2005*, 273–275. *Krecher 1987*, 10–11: AMA could be interpreted as eme_4, a general designation of the female gender or sex, also as an adult female individual of a given species who or which has delivered offspring (*Steinkeller-Postgate 1992*, 35, 82). A variant reading would be $ESIR_2$ = "bitumen"(?) (*Alberti-Pomponio 1986*, 57). The sign LAGAB × HAL may be read ésir = "bitumen" (*Stol 2012*, 48). $Esir_2$ (= *LAK* 173) is also interpreted as "sandals" (*Gelb-Steinkeller-Whiting 1991*, 296). Is there any connection to AMA.ERIM(-r), "Angehöriger einer bestimmter militärischen Einheit", known from Pre-Sargonic Lagaš (*Bauer 2001–2002*, 171, Exkurs)?

<u>ŠE + ŠE</u> = *ZATU* No. 511 p. 283, *MSVO 1* pp. 143–145.

<u>BAR</u> = *ZATU* No. 51 p. 180, *MSVO 1* p. 92. In Šuruppak, and in other third-millennium administrative texts, dub-bar-ra is "additional allocation to (those of) the tablet" (*Pomponio 1987*, 124). But BAR can also denote a textile product (*Gelb-Steinkeller-Whiting 1991*, 294). In Instructions of Šuruppak, bar-te gub = "to stand aside", "to stand apart", "to avoid", implying the sense "external", "outer" for bar (*Alster 1974*, 81–82). In ED proverbs, bar = "outer", "external" (*Alster 1991–1992*, 35, with antonym šà, also ibid. p. 11 ad line 28, translation on p. 20).

$\underline{UR_2}$ = see above, # 12: "lap", "crotch", "sexual organs", "fecundation ritual".

How is the inscription to be understood? Úr-še-še-ama-bar, "harvest of the maternal grain, external?" Or is it še-še-ama-bar úr, "(fodder) grain for female livestock, (in return for) the UR_2 fecundation ceremony"?

* * *

16. *UE III* : 84 (ms)	U 18 394	UM 33-35-274	Pit W, SIS 4-5

Catalogue: "UR PG.PIT W SIS IV–V, found in storage 1989". This bears an impression of the seal *UE III*: 238 (see below, # 35), of which four other impressions are known from this context. Obverse: signs GIR_2?, KID?, GA_2 × KISAL? SIKI? The SIKI? sign was engraved over the seal impression already in place. Reverse: extensive breakage areas difficult to interpret. Red-brown clay without visible admixtures.

Inscription:

PAP = see above, # 1. "She who fosters growth?" "Unfinished, open transaction"?.

$\underline{AB_2}$ = *ZATU* No. 12 p. 171, *MSVO 1* p. 87. AB_2 = *littum* = "cow" (*Gelb-Steinkeller-Whiting* 1991, 297). On AB_2 cf. *Attinger* 1997, 119–121, and *Krebernik-Postage* 2009, 18, register. There exists a $^{gal}du_6$-pa-ab_2-udu.

UDU = *ZATU* No. 575 p. 300, *MSVO 1* p. 158–159. Sheep.

ZATU 742 = this No. is on p. 330, reading unknown, consists of *ZATU* 737 + NIMGIR; missing from *MSVO 1*.

$\underline{E_2}$ = see above, # 1. "House", "agricultural district", "kin group"?.

A variant would actually be $\underline{SIG_2}$ = *ZATU* No. 452 p. 270, *MSVO 1* p. 139, but these latter variants do not closely resemble our sign. *Szarzyńska* 1996, 238: this sign denotes wool as a raw material, not as textile.

A cowherd and a shepherd, a storeroom (presumably) for wool(?).

* * *

17. *UE III* : 85 (ms)	U 18 394	837 (?)	UM 33-35-266	SIS 4-5, Pit W

Catalogue: "Ur PG. Pit W, SIS IV–V, found in storage 1989". Obverse: Incised signs, a star (DINGIR), a watercourse (?) and a razor or something of that kind, SI_4, SIG_4? Obverse: impression of a peg protruding from a coarse surface. The peg might have been coiled around with cord but the traces are unclear. Peg: d = approximately 50 mm. Of the cord, if it is one, only CT = 1.5 mm can be measured. Red-brown clay without visible admixtures.

Inscription:

AN (DINGIR) = *ZATU* No. 31 p. 175, *MSVO 1* p. 89. AN occurs in personal names of the Šuruppak texts (*Visicato 1997*, 16–18). *Moortgat-Correns 1994* identifies the rosette image as the DINGIR sign. On the rosette see most recently *Selz 2004b*, 201 (= Sumerian ul, "very powerful symbol of life"). A terra-cotta rosette on a pedestal(?), bearing the $EŠ_3$ sign on its shaft, turned up at Uruk (phase IV), in a debris stratum within square Qa XVI_2, northeast of the Red Temple (excavation # W 10220, Vorderasiatisches Museum Berlin # VA 14942; *Szarzyńska 2011*, 3).

LAL_2 = *ZATU* No. 325 p. 238, *MSVO 1* p. 122. Also LÁL = *MEA* No. 482 pp. 213–214 = *ṣamâdu* and *šaqālu*. *CAD* Š II pp. 1–13 = "to pay", "to weigh off" and the like.

ALAM(??) = *ZATU* No. 25 p. 173, missing in *MSVO 1*. In Sumerian proverbs ALAM = "statue?" (*Alster 1997*, 503), also *Attinger 2005*, 272. In ED Lagaš, a number of statues and one stele received regular offerings on festive occasions in the É-$šag_4$ shrine, of a square ground-plan with square side 3.715 metres long (*Rosengarten 1960*, 162).

Statues of divinities but also of worldly magnates constituted foci of special interest. A likeness of Šagšag, consort of Uruinimgina, made of rare substances, mainly from silver (according to text VAT 4853) received regular offerings even while the lady depicted was still alive. Statues were usually built of precious materials and solemnly introduced to their residences in temples. The initiation into their "cultic activity" took place with a ritual referred to as ka-du_8 = *pīt pî* = "mouth-opening", the statues received food and were clothed and attired. Conquerors frequently had statues taken off their pedestals and thrones, robbed and desecrated ("thrown into a well", for instance). A notable circumstance is the fact that the destruction of the statue brought about the death of the divinity (here, of Baba; *Selz 1992b*, cf. also *Selz 1995*, 384, in register). Most recently see *Dahl 2011*.

"Payment to the divine statue"?

* * *

18. *UE III* : 89 (ms)	U 18 394	894	UM 33-35-277	Pit W, SIS 4-5

Catalogue: "Ur PG. PIT W SIS IV–V. Found in Storage 1989". Obverse bears incised signs, an arc-shaped configuration, RU?, possibly divided in half. This is a jar stopper. Reverse smoothed. Diameter of the jar mouth = 87.6 mm, and thus it probably comes from a storage jar. Red-brown clay without visible admixtures, fingerprints.

Inscription:

<u>AL</u> (?) = *ZATU* No. 24 p. 173 = *MSVO 1* p. 88. AL = "hoe", "digging tool" (*Alster 1997*, 503), also *Attinger 2005*, 269–270 ("hoe"). *Selz 1995*, 256 fn. 1223: in Fara times, the reading of AL was mah_2, which may be connected with the goddess nin-mah (*Selz 1995*, 256 fn. 1223; *Steible-Yildiz 2008*, 186–187). Eventually, our sign could also be read MAH = *ZATU* No. 341 p. 241, but in *MSVO 1* there is only MAH+NA on p. 123, same as in *MSVO 4* (p. 63). In Fara texts the terms AL-DÙ and AL-AK mean "worked with the hoe", much as in Presargonic Girsu. Ur-III texts distinguish between al-du_3 and al-ak, and the al-du_3 procedure lasts three times shorter than al-ak (*Pomponio-Visicato 1994*, 222). In the "archaic kudurrus", áb = *littum* = "cow", counted in units (*Gelb-Steinkeller-Whiting 1991*, 297). In ED Lagaš, al___dù = "mit der Hacke anlegen" (*Selz 1995*, 244 fn. 1177). Associates with ŠE, SAL, SAG+MA, SAL+KUR, PAP+SAL. AL = hoe, *MEA* No. 298 p. 139. This is an extremely unsafe attribution.

Is this a designation of the origin of the goods once brought in this jar?

* * *

19. *UE III* : 90 (ms)	U 18 394	840	UM 33-35-269	SIS 4-5 Pit W

Catalogue: “Ur PG. Pit W SIS IV–V, [found in storage]”. Obverse: incised signs. Reverse: a peg coiled around with cord protrudes out of a smoothed surface. No measurements can be taken off the peg imprint, of the cord only CT = 3.7 mm can be measured. Red-brown clay without visible admixtures.

Inscription:

$\underline{\text{BULUG}_3 = \text{DIM}_4 = \text{MUNU}_4}$ = see above, # 1.”Malt”, “malster”?.

A contribution?

The rest can hardly be identified safely.

* * *

20. *UE III* : 91 (ms)	U 18 394	839	UM 33-35-268	SIS 4-5, Pit W

Catalogue: “Ur PG. Pit W. SIS IV–V, found in storage”. Obverse: incised signs. Reverse: broken and disturbed, impression of a peg. Peg: r = 12 mm, thus d = 24 mm. The peg protrudes perpendicularly from an even, much disturbed surface, in which an imprint of a rounded post(?), coiled around by a cord or organic fibre, may be surmised. Post: r = 7 mm, thus d = 14 mm. Of the tying material holding the construction together, only the CT = 2.3 mm may be measured. Red-brown clay without visible admixtures.

Inscription:

Most difficult to interpret. The sign on the edge could be

<u>MUŠEN</u> = *ZATU* No. 376 p. 249, *MSVO 1* p. 126.

<u>PAP</u> = see above, # 1. “She who fosters growth?” “Unfinished, open transaction”?.

<u>DIŠ</u> = *ZATU* No. 81 p. 187.

Remaining signs too fragmentary to be read safely.

“(A [quantity of] bird product of, going to) She who fosters growth?”

***

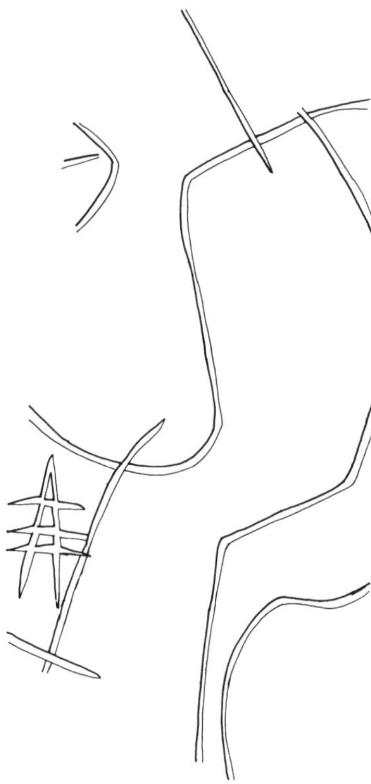

21. *UE III*: 102 = *Matthews 1993*, 70 = *Scott 2005*, 815	NUN, GIŠ$_3$+UR$_2$, SAL? *ZATU* 644 or -645 = SUMUN?	Door peg	No counter-mark

Inscription:

<u>NUN</u> = (= AGARGARA, ERIDU) = see above, # 1.”Noble”, “Noble (= Enki = Eridu)”? “The city of Eridu”?

<u>GIŠ$_3$</u> = see http://psd.museum.upenn.edu/epsd/nepsd-frame.html [accessed September 27, 2014] s. v. ĝeš$_3$ = penis, male, virile.

UR$_2$ = see above, # 12. "Lap", "crotch", "sexual organs", "fecundation ritual".

SAL = *ZATU* No. 443 p. 267, see also http://psd.museum.upenn.edu/epsd/nepsd-frame.html s. v. munus = woman, female.

An alternative reading of the NUN sign would be SUMUN = old, see http://psd.museum.upenn.edu/epsd/nepsd-frame.html [accessed September 27, 2014] s. v. sumun = old.

This is the most explicit statement in relation to the UR$_2$ procedure. Here we have a reference to sexual intercourse (GIŠ$_3$+UR$_2$, SAL?) bound to a geographical (or divine?) entity (NUN). The possibility to read the SAL sign as SUMUN does not fit in very well, unless it refers to "old" entities (arrears of due payments?). Here it seems that the carrying out of the UR$_2$ procedure is done by means of sexual intercourse, and on behalf of geographical communities. To me, this is suggestive of the traditional NA$_2$ fertility-triggering ceremony of the Uruk age (see above, # 13), and I suspect that this may be one of the early predecessors of what later evolved into the "sacred marriage"ceremony.

Or may this inscription contain a personal name? Ur$_2$-ni = "his lap" = "the deity's lap" is a scribe's name on an ED-IIIa-style highly prestigious cylinder seal: *Buchanan 1981*, No. 303 pp. 115 and 443–444.

* * *

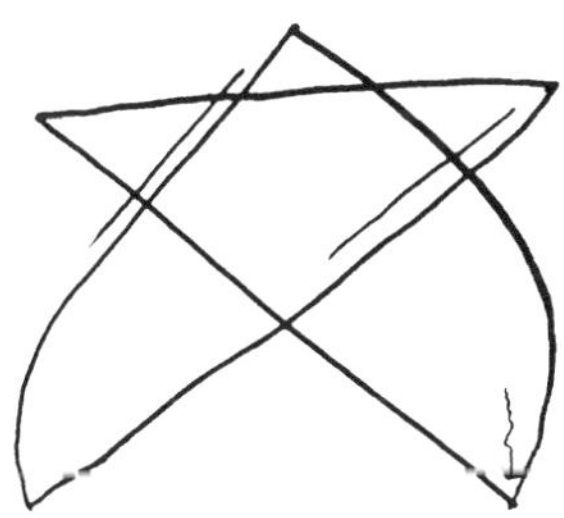

22. *UE III* : 105 (ms)	U 18 394	836 (?)	UM 33-35-265	SIS 4-5, Pit W

Catalogue: "Ur, PG. Pit W SIS IV–V, Found in storage 1989". Obverse: graven image of a five-pointed star (UB). Obverse: impression of a plaited-work wall and a peg coiled around with cord. Plaited work: widths of individual strands 8.7 mm, 9.4 mm, 8.75 mm and 9.4 mm. The strands run parallel to one another. Peg: d = 19.7 mm, thus r = 9.85 mm. Cord:

CT = 3.75 mm	ST = 2.35 mm	SI = 7.25 mm	S-spin

Red-brown clay without visible admixtures. The sealing was taken off when the clay was still wet and the peg impression was deformed by pressing the clay inwards.

Inscription:

UB = *ZATU* 572 p. 300, a city, also tribute, *MSVO 1* pp. 156–157, a city. The sign group UB ZI_a occurs in Uruk, Jemdet Nasr and possibly in Umma, in nine texts pertaining to barley, frequently with KU_{6a} $KISAL_{b1}$ (*Monaco 2007*, 8). *UET II* : 239 has a PN amar-UB. *MEA* No. 306 p. 139 – everything, all inclusive, the universum, *mimma šumšu*. But UB may be a reading for BAD_3 (*Carroué 1981*), which, according to *Owen 1995*, is to be sought in Syria. *Michalowski 1993*, 124, *Mander 1980*, 189 (UB, UB^{ki}), and *De Graef 2007*, 85, all consider this toponym unclear. On the six Mesopotamian BAD_3 see now *Frayne 2008a*, on BAD_3 in connection with the Muriq-Tidnim defence line *Lafont 2010*, 77–81. The UB sign is a hallmark of the UD.GAL.NUN scribal usance (Joachim Krecher, apud *Johnson 2014a*, 27).

A city name?

* * *

23. *UE III*: 114 (ms)	U 14 813	UM 31-16-652	SIS 4 (?)

Catalogue: "SIS place uncertain". Obverse: inscription, GIR_2, RU, HAL. Reverse: a conical peg coiled around by cord protrudes from an even surface. Peg: r = 17 mm, thus d = 34 mm. Only the CT = 5.75 mm may be measured. Inside surfaces smooth; organic fibre? Brownish to ochre clay without visible admixtures. Fingerprints.

Inscription:

RU = *ZATU* No. 435 p. 265 = *MSVO 1* p. 135 = *UET II*: 204 = *LAK* 281. A similar sign is the RU of Jemdet Nasr-aged NI + RU = *MSVO 1* pp. 128–137. *Gelb-Steinkeller-Whiting 1991*, 104: the sign group AN.RU may also be an abbreviated form of $^{d}Sud_3$ (SU.KUR.RU). This seems more likely to me. For ^{giš}RU = *tilpānu*, "(shooting) bow", see *Wilcke 1991*, and *Waetzold 2001a*, 110–111 (= giš-šub-ba "Los, das Los werfen"; ein Wurfholz, eine Art Bogen, Kurzspeer, Wurfspeer?).

Karin Rohn (*Rohn 2011*, 14, sub # 1), p. 106 fn. 874 translates "Wurfwaffe", Gebhard Selz (*Selz 2011b*, 229 sub # 3:1) refrains from a *verbatim* translation.

$\underline{GIR_2}$ = *ZATU* No. 218 p. 214, "knife", *MSVO 1* p. 110. GÍR = *patrum* = "dagger" (*Gelb-Steinkeller-Whiting 1991*, 296) = "Messer, Dolch" (*Edzard 1981*, 125) = "knife" (*Biggs 1974*, 69–70).

$\underline{HAL}$ = *ZATU* No. 250 p. 221, *MSVO 1* p. 113. Yıldız-Gomi 1993, text 1780, p. 79: HAL[zabar] = "auger of bronze". HAL = hal, usually "to divide", "to open" (*Steible-Yildiz 2008*, 196) or "to share" (*Civil 2013*, 24 ad 0.3). The lexemes hal and ús may refer to phases of threshing corn or rather grain: hal = *bêšu, petû*, or, alternatively, to certain quality of grain (*Steinkeller-Postgate 1992*, 42 *ad* hal). But HAL = min_5 = uru-min_5, "une ville étrangère" (*Durand 2003*).

Storage of metal products?

* * *

24. *UE III* : 117 (ms)	U 18 394	843	UM 33-35-271	Pit W, SIS 4-5

Catalogue: "Ur PG. PIT W SIS IV–V, found in storage 1989". Obverse: an inscription, GA_2 (*sensu lato*), UB. Reverse: a peg with a conical terminal, coiled around with cord, protrudes from a carefully smoothed surface. Peg: r = 22 mm, thus d = 44 mm. Cord: only CT = 2.0 mm can be measured. Organic fibre? Leather? Red-brown clay without visible admixtures, fingerprints.

Inscription:

ZATU $\underline{762 + NIM_2}$ = most obscure, perhaps *ZATU* No. 763 p. 333.

$\underline{MEN}$ = *ZATU* No. 360 p. 245, *MSVO 1* p. 125. Also a dignitary. *Steinkeller 1995*, p. 704 sub No. 360: EN is a phonetic indicator here. MEN = *agû* = "couronne, tiare", cf. *MEA* No. 270 p. 180, and also *Gelb-Steinkeller-Whiting 1991*, 296. The lexeme MEN occurs in Fara-age personal names (*Visicato 1997*, 63). In Abu Salabikh texts a [d]MEN turns up (*Mander 1986*, 115). MEN is the one and only ED notion for a divine crown, and thus it must refer to a horned crown. It is inherent to godhead and divinities such as Enlil, Enki or Inanna wear it. Constituting a frequent epithet of Nannar, it is most usually accompanied by the adjective kù = "holy". In a number of instances, ED horned crowns display ears of corn and leonine masks (*Asher-Greve 1995–1996*).

"Crown" storeroom for Elamite goods?

***

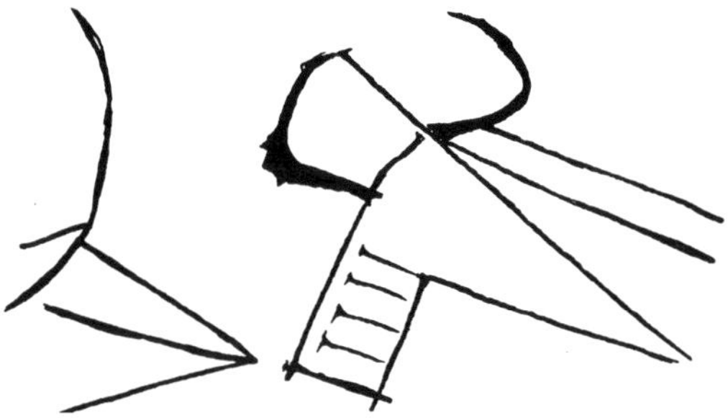

25. *UE III* : 119 (ms)	U 14 841	UM 31-16-642	SIS 4, perhaps 8

Catalogue: "Ur A (= SIS 4 or a lower stratum here?), or perhaps SIS 8". Obverse: sign of an animal head, a trident and a curved line. Reverse: a peg coiled around with cord protrudes from an even surface. The peg's end expands conically in a trumpet-like fashion. Peg: r = 17 mm, thus d = 34 mm. Cord:

CT = 3.0 mm	ST = 1.7 mm	SI '6.75 mm	Z-spin

Red-brown clay without visible admixtures, fingerprints.

Inscription: The animal-head sign could be:

GIR$_3$.gunu = *ZATU* No. 221 p. 215 (*Steinkeller 1995*, 702 sub No. 221: "analysis uncertain, possibly ALIM.gunu"), *MSVO 1* pp. 110–111; but rather

AZ = *ZATU* No. 38 p. 177 = *UET II* : 164, similar to our sign. AZ = *asu* B = bear (*CAD* A II p. 344). The phonetic complement NUNUZ (*Steinkeller 1995*, 698 sub No. 38) is missing here. Even more similar to our case is the sign *UET II* : 165. It turns up in text *UET II*: 143 : i : 5, a list of field plots with PN, summary: gana$_2$-EN-x-ša$_3$ (*UET II* 143 : iii : 4). *Visicato 1997*, 21 on the AZ lexeme in Fara-age PN (3 PN?). Of some relevance to this may be the gána-gibil, attested to in later ED Ur (*Alberti-Pomponio 1986*, 72, *ad* text 24). On the form of the sign see now *Mittermeyer 2005*, 10–16, on the AZ in general *Attinger 2006*, and now *Michalowski 2013*, 305–312.

Trident sign: *ZATU* Nos. 644 or 645 on p.315 = *MSVO 1* p.162, reading unknown, turns up in textile accounts. *Steinkeller 1995*, 711 sub No. 644 = an ancestor of TIL, SUMUN, UŠ$_2$. In later ED Ur, female weavers worked under the supervision of a female overseer (*Alberti-Pomponio 1986*, 85 ad text 33, personal name DI.NE, even a Hurrian personal name na-i-pe-la, where -e-la is a sister). SUMUN = old, see http://psd.museum.upenn.edu/epsd/nepsd-frame.html [accessed September 27, 2014] s. v. sumun = old. Or should this be read as SAL?

On this item see *Charvát 2014a*.
A personal textile account?

* * *

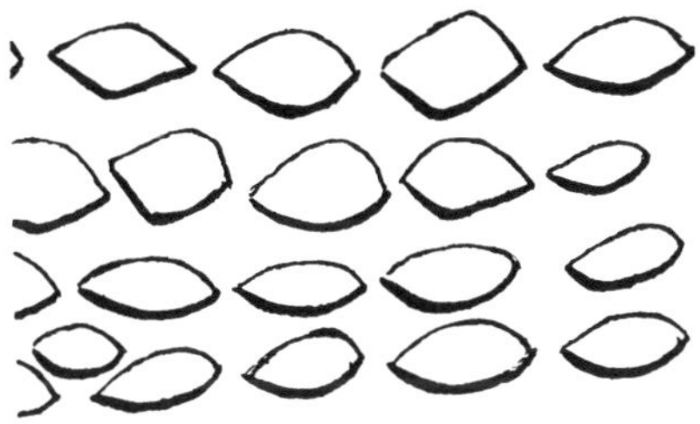

26. *UE III* : 134 (ms)	U 14 589	UM 31-16-646	SIS 4

Catalogue: "Ur (SIS 4), under A at -9.80". Obverse: Lines of double-pointed oval objects. Reverse: impression of a vessel rim. Diameter at least 113.9 mm. Orange- to ochre clay without visible admixtures.

Inscription:

A manually drawn sign $\underline{PA_4 = PAP}$ = see above, # 1. "She who fosters growth"? "Unfinished, open transaction"?.

* * *

27. *UE III*: 142 = *Scott 2005*, 45	GADA	Container (pot)	No counter-mark

Inscription:

GADA = *ZATU* No. 186 p. 207, usually in textile accounts; a sukkal-gada is attested to. *Bauer 1989–1990*, 90: gada = "Leinen(kleid)", gada = *kitûm* = "linen(-cloth)" (*Gelb-Steinkeller-Whiting 1991*, 294). In Ur-III texts "Leinen" (*Paoletti 2012*, 166). Establishments called na-gada + DIVINE NAME were probably cattle-breeding stations operated by particular temples (*Visicato 2000*, 37). NA.GADA = *nāqidum* = "shepherd" (*Gelb-Steinkeller-Whiting 1991*, 185). In later ED Ur, distribution of heads of cattle to temples and to secular recipients seems to have been done under royal supervision (*Alberti-Pomponio*

1986, 98–99 ad text 45). See also http://psd.museum.upenn.edu/epsd/nepsd-frame.html [accessed September 28, 2014], s. v. gada. GADA = "linen" (*Marchesi* 2011, 190–191).

Consignment of textile.

* * *

28. *UE III* : 155	U 18 399	881	UM 33-35-301	Pit W, SIS 4-5

Catalogue: "Ur PG. PIT W. SIS IV–V, Found in Storage 1989". Obverse: signs KI and GAN_2 disposed cross-wise. Obverse: broken off in large areas, impression of paralel linear features with fibrous matter (strips of reed?). One of the widths of such fibres(?) can be measured: 7.9 mm. Red-brown clay flaking off in stratum fashion, no visible admixtures.

Inscription:

$\underline{GAN_2}$ = *ZATU* No. 195 p. 209 = *MSVO 1* pp. 105–106. In Šuruppak, gána = "arable land" (*Pomponio* 1987, 217). GÁNA = gán = "Feld" (*Wilcke* 1996, 4 fn. 10). Gán = "field" (*Gelb-Steinkeller-Whiting* 1991, 213–214).

KI = *ZATU* No. 289 p. 230 = *MSVO 1* p. 118. ba-ki = tribute (*ZATU* No. 289 p. 230). The sign form is attested to at Abu Salabikh (*Biggs* 1966, table on p. 77)

"Revenue from the fields of the 'land'?"

* * *

29. *UE III*: 160 = *Scott* 2005, 328	ŠENNUR	??	No counter-mark

The large cross sign could be KIB = See http://psd.museum.upenn.edu/epsd/nepsd-frame.html [accessed September 28, 2014] s. v. šennur = plum or ULUL.

Inscription:

KIB or ŠENNUR = see above, # 10. "Fruit"? Defective writing for "Euphrates"? "Object"?

Consignment of fruit?

* * *

30. *UE III*: 172 = *Scott 2005*, 336	AB??	??	No counter-mark

Inscription:

AB = EŠ$_3$ = *ZATU* No. 7 p. 170 = *MSVO 1* pp. 86–88. A terra-cotta rosette on a pedestal(?), bearing the EŠ$_3$ sign on its shaft, turned up at Uruk (phase IV), in a debris stratum within square Qa XVI$_2$, northeast of the Red Temple (excavation # W 10220, Vorderasiatisches Museum Berlin # VA 14942; *Szarzyńska 2011*, 3). Cf. also *Edzard 1993*, 139 on reading of this sign, and *Steinkeller 1995*, 696 sub No. 7 (also a graph for UNUG). The Fara-age texts include one instance of DUMU.AB as a professional designation (*Visicato 1997*, 112). In texts from Fara this is interpreted as "household, centre of production, distribution", as well as a component of personal names pertaining to cultic, productional and organizational tasks (*Martin-Pomponio-Visicato-Westenholz 2001*, 25–26). In ED Lagaš AB = èš = "Heiligtum" (*Meyer-Laurin 2011*, 67).

* * *

31. *UE III*: 202	U 18 413	801	UM 33-35-399	Pit W, SIS 4-5

See *Scott 2005*, 185. Catalogue: "Ur PG. PIT W. SIS IV–V, Found in Storage 1989". Obverse: ibex in a jumping pose. Reverse: broken, impressions of a peg coiled around with cord (Scott: unknown). No measurements can be taken off the peg. Cord:

CT = 7.5 mm	ST = 3.2 mm	SI = 8.3 mm	Spin S

Red-brown clay without visible admixtures.

Inscription:

KAK = DU$_3$ = RU$_2$, = *ZATU* No. 280 p. 207 = *MSVO 1* pp. 116 and 163. *MEA* No. 230 pp. 125–126, gives a general sense of this sign as "to enact", "to make something", "to create". *Alster 1974*, 46–47, comments on the lines 207–208 of the Instructions of Šuruppak with the very famous Šuruppak proverb:

ša$_3$ ki-aga$_2$ nig$_2$-e$_2$ du$_3$-du$_3$-u$_3$-dam
ša$_3$ hul-gig nig$_2$-e$_2$ gul-gul-lu-dam,

that is, "a loving heart builds houses, and a heart full of hatred pulls them down".

Gelb-Steinkeller-Whiting 1991, 247: DU$_3$ = *kullum* = "to detain", "to hold". originally perhaps intransitive, with a meaning "to hold on" (to property). Could this refer to a delivery transferred to the property of the adressee? *Alster 1991–1992*, 28: DU$_3$ = "to build a house", in the sense of establishing a household. nig$_2$-du$_3$-a is a measure of fruit, possibly "what holds together" ("festhalten"), that is, a bundle. Nig$_2$-du$_3$(-a) = /šerku/ = "a string of dried fruit", replaced in Uruinimigina's inscriptions by the expression sag-keš$_2$ (*Selz 1995*, p. 33 fn. 106). In Fara nig$_2$-du$_3$ = "Maß-Behältnis für Feigen und Äpfel" (*Steible-Yildiz 2008*, 167). *Krebernik 1993–1994*, 90: du$_3$ = "aufpflanzen", *Bauer 1989–1990*, p. 83: sag-du$_3$ = "wörtlich: das Haupt aufrichtend", *Steinkeller 1989*, 52–54: du$_3$ = "to hold on". DU$_3$ = *kullum* = "to detain", "to hold". It might originally have been an intransitive verb, meaning something like "to hold on" (property). Does this mean that on seals, items transferred to the property of the adressee are so denoted (*Gelb-Steinkeller-Whiting 1991*, 247)?. Šuruppak: AL-DU$_3$ = "worked with the hoe", also in ED-IIIb Girsu. Ur III texts distinguish between al-du$_3$ and al-ak, with the former taking about three times less time than the latter (*Pomponio-Visicato 1994*, 222). Texts from Abu Salabikh know a person named DU$_3$.A.X, possibly from Umma (*Krebernik-Postgate 2009*, 16). In ED Lagaš, al___dù = "mit der Hacke anlegen" (*Selz 1995*, 244 fn. 1177). See http://psd.museum.upenn.edu/epsd/nepsd-frame.html [accessed September 28, 2014] s. v. du.

"(Contributed for) maintenance(?)".

* * *

See the drawing in *Matthews* 1993, 48, Fig. 18.

32. *UE III*: 209 = *Matthews* 1993, 48 = *Scott* 2005, 359	Edinnu, U4	Scott: pot with covering 1×, unknown 1×	No counter-mark

Inscription:

UNUG = *ZATU* No. 583 p. 303, *MSVO* 1 p. 160, the city of Uruk. *Steinkeller* 1995, 710 sub No. 583: Sumerian "city", iri or uru, originally written with the UNUG sign.The toponym occurs in Fara-age texts (*Visicato* 1997, 136).

U_4 = BABBAR = *ZATU* No. 566 p. 298, *MSVO* 1 pp. 153–154. *Steinkeller* 1995, 710 sub No. 566: has also a value HUD_2 = morning. *Szarzyńska* 1993, understands this sign as "day".

Edinnu = the inhabited world, *oecumene*? See above, # 62.

Mode of delivery, date?

* * *

33. *UE III*: 227 = *Scott* 2005, 363	UB	??	No counter-mark

Inscription:

UB = see above, # 22. "*Universum*"? "Fortified enclosure"?

* * *

34. *UE III*: 234	U 18 407	816	UM 33-35-374	Pit W, SIS 4-5

See *Matthews* 1993, 52 = *Scott* 2005,169, and http://www.cdli.ucla.edu/search/search_results.php?order=ObjectType&SealID=S006238 [accessed February 21, 2014]. Catalogue: "Ur PG. PIT W SIS IV–V, Found in Storage 1989". Obverse: lion attacking a quadruped, and a six-rayed star. Reverse: broken off in large flakes. Red-brown clay without visible admixtures.

Inscription:

UB = see above, # 22. "*Universum*"? "Fortified enclosure"?

An alternative reading could be

AN/DINGIR?? = see above, # 17. "Deity"? "Life"?

"(Contributed to/from) the Commonwealth (or one of its cities)"?

"(Contributed to) the deity"?

* * *

35. *UE III*: 238	U 18 407 = U 18 394 (2 fragments)	810	UM 33-35-358	Pit W, SIS 4-5

This find has no card on the catalogue but can be identified according to a photograph in *UE III*, Pl. 46. For an impression of this seal with a written gloss see above, # 16. Obverse: lions attacking a horned quadruped. Reverse: a thin and pointed peg coiled around with a cord. The peg has a diameter of

13.6 mm at the point where it protrudes from the flat surface. The peg issues out of a flat surface on which the fibrous end of the cord rests. The flat surface left impression of a double strand of plaited-work matter. Strand widths of these are 7.7 mm and 11.7 mm. Cord:

CT = 4.0 mm	ST = 3.0 mm	SI = 7.1 mm	Spin S

Red-brown clay without visible admixtures.

Inscription:

DUG = *ZATU* No. 88 p. 189, *MSVO 1* pp. 96–97. Probably identical with form DUG_a in MSVO in view of the spout depiction, albeit at a different angle. *Szarzyńska 1994*, 3: DUG = spouted jar may sometimes designate an individual person; DUG without a spout can also be a dairy product; DUG with handle = merchandise; spouted round jug = UKKIN. Dug-ŠID is "a type of pot" attested to in the Old Akkadian period (*Steinkeller-Postgate 1992*, 53). See also http://psd.museum.upenn.edu/epsd/nepsd-frame.html [accessed September 28, 2014] s. v. dug = ban, dug, ŠID.

UR_2 = see above, # 12. "Lap", "crotch", "sexual organs", "fecundation ritual".

The fish image is likely to refer to a fecundation ceremony performed as coitus, see below, my # 146, *Scott 2005*, 891 (no context).

The data of my # 16 may imply that the contribution was collected in animal products (AB_2, UDU).

"Personal (contributions for) fecundation"?

* * *

36. *UE III*: 239	U 18 404	742	UM 33-35-350	Pit W SIS 4-5

Catalogue: "Ur PG. PIT W SIS IV–V, Found in Storage 1989". Obverse: animals, an UB star, a square field with a chequerboard infilled with hourglass symbols, and a sign akin to a curved sickle. Obverse: broken, traces of a concave rectangular body, under which a rounded end of a protruding rod-like object is visible. A lock sealing? Red-brown clay without visible admixtures, flaking off in parallel straight folds.

Inscription:

UB = see above, # 22. "*Universum*"? "Fortified enclosure"?

The sickle-shaped sign could be either

UH_3 = UMMA = *ZATU* No. 579 p. 302, missing in *MSVO* 1. *Steinkeller* 1995, 710 s. No. 579: value UH_3 uncertain, a possible connection with $KUŠU_2$. Jeremiah Peterson now identifies $KUŠU_2$ as an aquatic animal other than turtle (*Peterson* 2007, 213–217). Might there be a connection with the site GIŠ.$KUŠU_2$.KI, of which a king named Aka dedicated a lapis-lazuli bead to Inanna, discussed by Gebhard Selz (2003, 506–511)?

Or, another explanation possibility, the now classic

UR_2 = see above, # 12. "Lap", "crotch", "sexual organs", "fecundation ritual".

"(A contribution of) Umma/Gišša (to) the Commonwealth (or one of its cities)"?

"(A contribution for) the fecundation of the Commonwealth (or one of its cities)"?

* * *

37. *UE III*: 239	U 18 407	782	UM 33-35-366	Pit W, SIS 4-5

Catalogue: "Ur PG. PIT W SIS IV–V, Found in Storage 1989". Obverse: animals, an UB star, a square field with a chequerboard infilled with hourglass symbols, and a sign akin to a curved sickle. Obverse: broken, illegible,possibly a peg impression. Peg: r = 12 mm, thus d = 24 mm. A lock sealing? Red-brown clay without visible admixtures.

For the inscription see the comments above by the preceding item (# 36).

* * *

38. *UE III*: 252	U 18 413	939	UM 33-35-430	Pit W. SIS 4-5

Catalogue: "Ur PG. PIT W SIS IV–V, Found in Storage 1989". Obverse: lion attacking an ibex and attacked by a male thrusting a spear into the lion's body. Reverse: impression of a peg protruding from a smoothed surface. The peg is either ribbed or coiled around by a cord with absolutely smooth surface. Peg: r = 10 mm, thus d = 20 mm. Cord(?): only the CT (cord thickness) can be measured: 3.4 mm. Or are these top parts of the peg ribs? Yellow-brown clay without visible admixtures.

Inscription:

$\underline{\text{UR}}_2$ = see above, # 12. "Lap", "crotch", "sexual organs", "fecundation ritual".

DIN = *ZATU* No. 79 p. 186 = *MSVO 1* p. 94 = *MSVO 4* p. 51. In the proto-cuneiform period, the signs U_{2b} DIN turn up at (probably) Jemdet Nasr and Umma (*Monaco 2007*, 5). *MEA* No. 465 p. 209: *balāṭu* = "to live", and *šikaru* = "beer", "beverage". *Gelb-Steinkeller-Whiting 1991*, 28–30 on the clause DUG.SILA$_3$ with a variant DIN.SILA$_3$, meaning probably something like "purchase", "alienation" or the like, which does not fit well here. See also http://psd.museum.upenn.edu/epsd/nepsd-frame.html, [accessed September 28, 2014] s. v. kurun = "a beer; blood; (to be) good; (to be) sweet".

DUG = see above, # 35. "Pot?" "Merchandise?" "Human individual?"

"(Contributed for) life-giving fecundation"?

"Beverage(s) (contributed for) fecundation"?

* * *

39. *UE III*: 254	U 18 407	815	UM 33-35-373	Pit W, SIS 4-5

Catalogue: "Ur PG. PIT W SIS IV–V, Found in Storage 1989". Obverse: lion attacking and ibex and attacked by a naked, spear-wielding warrior. Four-rayed rosette between lion and warrior. Counter-marked by a seal with a rosette. Rosette seal: d = 18.5 mm, thus r = 9.25 mm, making the perimeter of the cylinder 58.09 mm. Reverse: impression of a peg, coiled around with a cord, protruding from a smoothed surface. Peg: r = probably 17 mm, thus d = 34 mm. Cord:

CT = 3.9 mm	ST = 2.5 mm	SI = 10.9 mm	Spin S

Red-brown clay without visible admixtures.
Inscription (?):
AN/DINGIR?? = see above, # 17. "Deity"? "Life"?
"(Contributed to) the deity?"

***

40. *UE III*: 257	U 18 407	812	UM 33-35-370	Pit W, SIS 4-5

See *Scott* 2005, No. 167. Catalogue: "Ur PG. PIT W SIS IV–V, Found in Storage 1989". Obverse: lion attacking an ibex and attacked by a spear-wielding warrior. A large sign UR_2 between the lion and the warrior. Reverse: impression of a rim, neck and shoulder of a jar. The rim may show impressions of soft tissue, no traces of binding of any kind. Jar: neck radius = 62 mm, thus d = 124 mm. Probably a storage jar. Red-brown clay without visible admixtures.
Inscription:
UR_2 = see above, # 12. "Lap", "crotch", "sexual organs", "fecundation ritual".
AN/DINGIR?? = see above, # 17. "Deity"? "Life"?
"(Contributed to the) deity (for) fecundation"?

* * *

41. *UE III*: 275	U 18 402	754	UM 33-35-324	Pit W SIS 4-5

See *Scott 2005*, No. 30. Catalogue: "Ur PG. PIT W SIS IV–V. Found in Storage 1989". Obverse: animal heads, a geometrical composition and a sign read by Legrain as ag. Counter-marked by two impressions of a seal bearing a pattern which is a variation of the chequerboard. Legrain (*UE III* p. 29) points to a parallel to this in the Indus-culture script (Mohenjodaro). Diameter of the counter-marking seal: 19.4 mm, thus r = 9.7 mm. Perimeter length of the cylinder will thus amount to 60.92 mm, which makes the identity of the primary and counter-marking matrices possible. Reverse: impression of a construction from reed matting, of which the individual components are arranged in a herring-bone manner. Traces of this reed-matting surface are overlain by impression of a long and narrow cord-like object, the surface of which left imprints of plaited organic fibres. Is this an impression of a bale tied over by an organic-matter cord? Red-brown clay without visible admixtures.

Inscription:

AK = *ZATU* No. 23 p. 173 = *MSVO 1* p. 88. A personal name AK-^{d}Inanna is attested to in texts *UET II*: 70 (where he/she is a sanga), 212 and 360. In Šuruppak, AK frequently occurs in personal names (*Visicato 1997*, 8–11; *Visicato 2000*, 18; *Krebernik-Postgate 2009*, 16), in lexical lists of dignitaries and also cities. In one of the ED texts from Umma, Josef Bauer sees in ak "Kurzform für /aka/-^{d}NN = Geschöpf des Gottes NN", attested to at Umma, Uruk and Zabala (*Bauer 2012*, 70, # II: 9). The sign is *MEA* No. 97 p. 83 = "to perform", "to do", also "to cut", "to cut away", and "to plant". On this meaning see also *Alster 1991–1992*, 35 (register), and *Alster 1997*, 503 (register). *Selz 1995*, 113 fn. 415: AK = "Opfermaterie, sonst unbekannt" = a kind of cereal? It could also be an abbreviated rendering of kid_3-kid_3 = *kikkiṭṭû* = "Ritual"? Another possibility is M. Civil's (*1982*) reading AK = gug_x, "eine Art Opferkuchen"? On AK as referring to a creation act see *Andersson 2012*, 127–128 with fn. 695, 696 and 697.

"An offering"?

***

42. *UE III* : 281	U 14 825	UM 31-16-671	SIS 4

See *Mathews 1993*, 39 = *Scott 2005*, 3. Catalogue: "Ur, probably SIS 4 (or 5)". Obverse: a male holds two lizards; signs. Countermarked by a rosette seal, of an r = 9.6 mm, thus d = 19.2 mm. This would make an impression of the length of 60.29 mm; very difficult to form an opinion. Countermarking by rosette on all 5 surviving examples. Reverse: a peg coiled around by a cord protrudes from a smoothed surface. Peg: r = 19 mm, thus d = 38 mm. Only the CT = 3.05 mm can be measured on the cord. Cord surface is smooth: leather or other organic fibre? Ochre- to grey clay without visible admixtures.

Inscription :

<u>AN AN UB X X:</u> impressions illegible except <u>AN/DINGIR??</u> = see above, # 17. "Deity"? "Life"?

***

43. *UE III*: 296	U 18 413	910	UM 33-35-425	Pit W, SIS 4-5

Catalogue: "Ur PG.PIT W. SIS IV–V, Found in Storage 1989". Obverse: a naked human being (male?) holds an animal by the hind legs, carrying it to (or from?) a building superimposed by a spread-eagle emblem. Within the two compartments of this building, another naked human (male?) and an UR_2 sign may be seen. Reverse: impression of a smooth surface making up a curve in its upper part. Bundles of fine incisions may have been caused by the surface treatment. Also an impression of another, quite smooth and concave surface, running at an angle with the first. The rest of the reverse has been subject to a vigorous operation by a cutting tool. The sealing is robust and a considerable amount of force was required for its removal. A conceivable interpretation would be one of a sealing of an arched doorway in a clay-revetted building. Red-brown clay without visible admixtures.

Inscription:

$\underline{UR_2}$ = see above, # 12. "Lap", "crotch", "sexual organs", "fecundation ritual". "(Contributed for) fecundation"?

* * *

44. *UE III* : 304	U 14 163	UM 31-16-672	SIS 4

Catalogue: "SIS 4". Obverse: a naked male(?) drives an antelope(?). Reverse: impression of a rim, neck and shoulders of a vessel, with the neck tied around by a cord. Pot: rim r = 34 mm, thus d = 68 mm. Cord:

CT = 2.7 mm	ST = 1.6 mm	SI = 4.05 mm	S-spin

Cord possibly tied by a knot. Red-brown clay without visible admixtures.

Inscription: a single sign AN (DINGIR) = see above, # 17. "Deity"? "Life"?

The image includes (under the animal) a sign that can be read either as

DIN = see above, # 38. "Beverage?" "Life?"

Another possibility is

KAK = DU_3 = RU_2 = see also http://psd.museum.upenn.edu/epsd/nepsd-frame .html [accessed September 28, 2014] s. v. du.

$\underline{KAK = DU_3 = RU_2}$ = see above, # 31: "to enact", "to make something", "to create".

* * *

45. *UE III*: 311 = *Scott 2005*, 405	DUG? (in milking scene)	??	No counter-mark

Inscription:
<u>DUG</u> = see above, # 35. "Pot?" "Merchandise?" "Human individual?"

* * *

46. *UE III*: 315 = *Scott 2005*, 409	BAD AN BAD AN in what may well be a threshing scene	??	No counter-mark

Inscription:
<u>BAD</u> = see above, # 12. Threshing or husking grain? This would at least be implied by the seal image. On this item see *Charvát 2014b*.

* * *

47. *UE III*: 323 = *Scott 2005*, 413	$EŠ_2$ twice among sacrificial items?	Scott: door peg 1×, unknown 1×	No counter-mark

Inscription:

Inscription: See http://psd.museum.upenn.edu/epsd/nepsd-frame.html [accessed September 28, 2014] s. v. $eš_2$ = flour (signs under the spread eagle, right of the double-handled vessel). Also $EŠ_2$ = rope, cord (*Steinkeller 2013*, 136 ad I 5'). In ED Lagaš ŠÈ = šè = original éše = "Seil" (*Meyer-Laurin 2011*, 47).

* * *

48. *UE III*: 325 = *Scott 2005*, 414	BAD? DUG	??	No counter-mark

Inscription:
<u>BAD</u> = see above, # 12, and # 46. Threshing or husking grain?
<u>DUG</u> = see above, # 35. "Pot?" "Merchandise?" "Human individual?"

* * *

49. *UE III*: 329	U 18 409	855	UM 33-35-385	Pit W, SIS 4-5

Catalogue: "Ur PG. PIT W SIS IV–V, Found in Storage 1989". Obverse: a file of naked dancers with large DIN signs between them. Reverse: broken; impression of a peg. The peg had a square(?) section with convex sides. One measurable side of the peg: 16.6 mm. A moulded rib runs along the edges of the square. One of the sides displays what might have been a chip or paring of worked wood. Red-brown clay without visible admixtures.
Inscription:
<u>DIN</u> = see above, # 38. "Beverage?" "Life?"
"(Contribution of a life-giving) beverage (?)".

* * *

50. *UE III*: 330 = *Scott* 2005, 417	DUG DUG DUG	??	No counter-mark

Inscription:
DUG = see above, # 35. "Pot?" "Merchandise?" "Human individual?"
Potted commodities.

* * *

51. *UE III*: 349	U 18 404	724	UM 33-35-338	Pit W, SIS 4-5 (seven fragments)

See *Scott* 2005, 144. Catalogue: "Ur PG. PIT W SIS IV–V, Found in Storage 1989". Obverse: a hut with banners and emblem of a spread eagle, out of which comes a bull. A man sitting on a stool in front of the animal handles a storage jar, behind him stands a kind of huge bird (*contra UE III*). A sign UR_2 superimposed twice above the scene. Obverse: broken and illegible, possible impression of a peg off which no measurements can be taken. Red-brown clay without visible admixtures.

Inscription:
UR_2 (repeated twice here) = see above, # 12. "Lap", "crotch", "sexual organs", "fecundation ritual".
DIN = see above, # 38. "Beverage?" "Life?" Or is this
DUG = see above, # 35. "Pot?" "Merchandise?" "Human individual?"
"(Contributed for) fecundation"?

* * *

52. *UE III*: 349	U 18 404	730	UM 33-35-343	Pit W, SIS 4-5

Catalogue: "Ur PG. PIT W SIS IV–V, Found in Storage 1989". Obverse: same seal as # 51. Reverse: broken and illegible, flaking off in large fragments, possibly after cutting the sealing off. Trace of a smoothed surface bearing imprints of organic matter. Red-brown clay without visible admixtures. For the inscription see above, No. 51.

* * *

53. *UE III*: 370 = *Scott* 2005, 448	Coitus, a naked bearer of two hares, a woman with spread legs, two rosettes (= AN?)	??	No counter-mark

Inscription: Two rosettes, possibly <u>AN AN DINGIR DINGIR</u> = <u>AN/DINGIR??</u> = see above, # 17. "Deity"? "Life"?

* * *

54. *UE III*: 389 = *Matthews* 1993, 32 = *Scott* 2005, 86	GAR/NINDA (six times), EN?MEN?, KID or DUB (or UR_2?), X X X X ALAM?	"lock" (3×)	Rosette on 1 of 4 copies

Inscription:

GAR(NIG$_2$, NINDA)+GAR(NIG$_2$, NINDA) = *ZATU* No. 196 p. 209 = *MSVO 1* pp. 106–107 = *UET II*: 396. In texts presumably from Jemdet Nasr, GAR = "bread" (*Monaco 2007*, 165, *apud* CUSAS 1, 117, O0101). *Alberti-Pomponio 1986*, text 4, i: 1, read this sign as ninda. Gar = "to place" as submitting of a land-plot price does not seem to fit here (*Gelb-Steinkeller-Whiting 1991*, 229).

EN?MEN? = I do not dare to interpret this sign.

DUB = see http://psd.museum.upenn.edu/epsd/nepsd-frame.html [accessed September 28, 2014] s. v. dub = tablet, scribe, laborer?)?; UR$_2$? DUB = dab$_6$ = "to encircle, surround" (*Mirelman-Sallaberger 2010*, 183). On DUB = "tablet" see *Krebernik-Postage 2009*, 18, register.

ALAM? = see above, # 17. "Statue".

* * *

55. *UE III*: 390 = *Scott 2005*, 451	TU$_7$, DILMUN, TUN$_3$, UNUG, X, UDU, LUM? X X	??	No counter-mark

Inscription:

TU$_7$ = see above, # 3. "Soup".

DILMUN = see http://psd.museum.upenn.edu/epsd/nepsd-frame.html [accessed September 28, 2014] s. v. dilmun ="(to be) made manifest; (to be) heavy; (to be) important; ritually unclean, impure person; instruction". But I rather think that this is the toponym. On Dilmun see now *Marchesi 2011*.

TUN$_3$ = see http://psd.museum.upenn.edu/epsd/nepsd-frame.html [accessed September 28, 2014] s. v. tun$_3$, "ax, adze".

UNUG = see above, # 32. "The city of Uruk".

UDU = see above, # 16. "Sheep".

LUM = *ZATU* No. 335 p. 240, in lexical lists of trees, vessels, and plants, missing in *MSVO 1*. The sign is *MEA* No. 565 p. 283, signifying either "to shatter, crush" or "to destroy", and alternatively, "to fertilize", "to fructify". See also http://psd.museum.upenn.edu/epsd/nepsd-frame.html [accessed September 28, 2014] s. v. lum.

X (= TUN_3 ?)

X (= TU_7 ?)

Food?, Dilmun (or heavy?) axes, etc,, description of deposit?

* * *

56. *UE III*: 392 = *Scott 2005*, 453	GA_2+AŠ, X, URU?, [A]N, AN, X	??	No counter-mark

Inscription:

GA_2+AŠ = for a possible connection with the sign read later as MA see http://psd.museum.upenn.edu/epsd/nepsd-frame.html [accessed September 28, 2014] s. v. mada = "land", as well as http://psd.museum.upenn.edu/epsd/nepsd-frame.html [accessed September 28, 2014] s. v. ĝa = "house".

URU = *ZATU* No. 597 p. 306. In Šuruppak, URU is a "town" in the sense of an administrative centre of state economic enterprises (*Pomponio 1987*, 95–96).

AN AN = AN/DINGIR?? = see above, # 17. "Deity"? "Life"?

X

Storage structure?

* * *

57. *UE III* : 395	U 18 397	918	UM 33-35-290	Pit W, SIS 4-5 (3 fragments)

See also http://www.cdli.ucla.edu/search/search_results.php?order=ObjectType&SealID=S006221 [accessed February 22, 2014]. Catalogue: "Ur PG. PIT W. SIS IV–V, Found in Storage 1989". Obverse: a composition of leaves(?) and signs UR$_2$, probably KIN (on the other fragments) and a snail-like sign, possibly DA or GIŠ$_3$. A counter-mark seal with a rosette impressed into the surface. Counter-mark seal r = 18 mm, thus its diameter = 36 mm. The length of the seal's circumference would thus amount to 113.04 mm. Counter-marked once again in four other cases. Obverse: breakage lines and its surface are heavily damaged, with a dense pattern of small crackle fields. Red-brown clay without visible admixtures.

Inscription:

ALAM(??) = see above, # 17. "Statue".

UR$_2$ = see above, # 12. "Lap", "crotch", "sexual organs", "fecundation ritual".

KAB = *ZATU* No. 277 p. 227, *MSVO 1* p. 116 ("snail-like sign"). The profession NAM$_2$ KAB appears in the Archaic LU$_2$ A list (*Monaco 2007*, 8 fn. 49). *Steinkeller 1995*, 702 sub No. 277: this sign stands for both KAB and TUKU. *Englund 1990*, 147–149 fn. 467: KAB.IL = baskets in which fishermen carry fish, of an intake up to 120 sila; unaccompanied by the reeds determinative. In ED proverbs, Bent Alster reads this sign as NUMUN$_2$ (*Alster 1991–1992*, 37). The sign seems to alternate with TUKU and thus NUMUN$_2$ may not be the only reading possible. It refers to reed material used for mat-making and possibly also for the confection of a kind of clothing (túg-bar-dul$_5$) (*Alster 1991–1992*, 24 ad line 47). An ED proverb says that haš$_4$-sikil ur númun gu$_7$-è = "a girl's lap is a reed-eating dog", meaning that it is never saturated (*Alster 1991–1992*, 18, ad line 168, see also commentary on p. 30). In ED Lagaš, KAB = "Gehilfe" may be related to the lexeme GÁB (*Selz 1995*, 59 fn. 266, also in register on p. 399).

"Baskets (brought to the) statue (in reward for? For?) fecundation?"

* * *

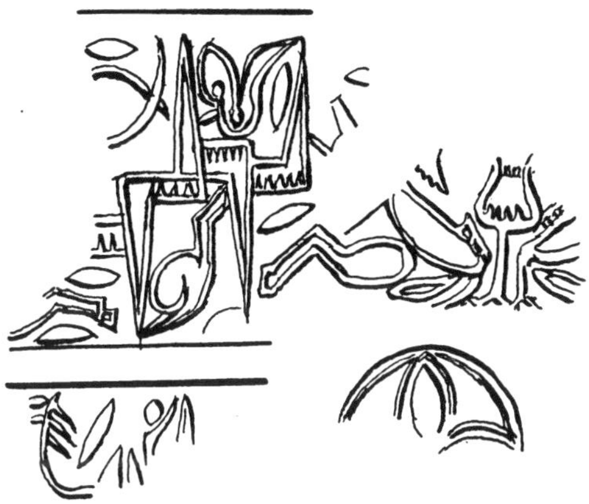

58. *UE III* : 395	U 18 397	918	UM 33-35-291	Pit W, SIS 4-5 (3 fragments)

See also http://www.cdli.ucla.edu/search/search_results.php?order=ObjectType&SealID=S006221 [accessed February 22, 2014]. Catalogue: "Ur PG. PIT W, SIS IV–V, Found in Storage 1989". Obverse: same as # 57. Reverse: broken, illegible. There seems to be a division point in which impressions of two cord bundles or strands, containing three and two parallel cord impressions each, diverge. Only the cord thicknesses = 3.9, and 3.9, as well as 2.8 mm, and 3.4 and 3.4 mm, can be measured. Red-brown clay without visible admixtures.

Inscription:

UR$_4$ = *ZATU* No. 592 p. 305, missing in *MSVO* 1. *Steinkeller* 1995, 710 sub No. 592: identification "not beyond doubt". Ur$_1$ = "to shear sheep" (*Visicato 2000*, 144) = *eṣēdu* = "einsammeln, zusammenraufen" (*Zgoll* 1997, 310). *MEA* No. 594 p. 243 = harvest, and also clip = wool shorn from sheep. *Bauer 1989–1990*, 85: ur$_4$ = "(Schafe) raufen".

KAB = see above, # 57. "Basket", "container".

"Wool clip etc. in baskets"?

* * *

59. *UE III* : 395	U 18 397	918	UM 33-35-292	Pit W, SIS 4-5

See also http://www.cdli.ucla.edu/search/search_results.php?order=ObjectType&SealID=S006221 [accessed February 22, 2014]. Catalogue: "Ur PG. PIT W. SIS IV–V". Obverse: same as No. 57. Reverse: broken. Impression of a "cornice" consisting of a torus, a hollow and another torus running parallel to one another. The respective widths amount to 8.4, 1.7 and 8.1 mm. Was this a structure of reed stalks? Red-brown clay without visible admixtures.

Inscription:

$\underline{UR_4}$ = see above, # 58. "To shear (sheep)".

<u>KAB</u> = see above, # 57. "Basket", "container".

$\underline{DU_8}$ = *ZATU* No. 85 p, 188, *MSVO 1* p. 95, *UET II* : No. 71, *LAK* No. 119. *MEA* No. 167 p. 107: also GABA, a confrontation; DU_8 = to open, to release, to liberate, to brim over, also bounty, plenty. Du_8 = "to free", "to manumit" (*Gelb-Steinkeller-Whiting 1991*, 102). du_8 = "to break", "to break into" (*Alster 1974*, 58 line 63 and p. 110). In ED Nippur, a month bore the name ^{giš}apin-du_8-a (*Cohen 1993*, 112); the evidence gathered by Mark Cohen suggests that šu du_8 = "to take in hand something", while du_8 = "to lay something down, aside". An ED proverb says ninda a-ta nam-du = "you will not bake bread of water" (*Alster 1991–1992*, 18, 21). In Abu Salabikh, šu-du_8 = "take, receive" (*Krebernik-Postgate 2009*, 20, register). In ED Lagaš, DU_8 = "ouvrir, libérer", where the baking of pastry takes place (*Rosengarten 1960*, 192–195). *Wilcke 1996*, 45: du_8 = "freikaufen". In later ED Ur, DU_8 may denote an age group, "weaned child" (*Alberti-Pomponio 1986*, 111–114 ad text 49). The occurrence together with the UR_2 sign within one single inscription may be meaningful.

"Wool clip in baskets, (brought to) the statue (in reward for activation of) fecundation, (in thankfulness for) bounty" ? .

* * *

60. *UE III* : 396	U 18 399	884	UM 33-35-304	Pit W, SIS 4-5

See *Matthews 1993*, 61 = *Scott 2005*, 34, and http://www.cdli.ucla.edu/search/search_results.php?order=ObjectType&SealID=S006247 [accessed February 22, 2014]. Catalogue: "Ur PG. PIT W.SIS IV–V, Found in Storage 1989". Obverse: a geometrical pattern and a six-pointed star. Reverse: a large, smooth, concave area with parallel fine incised lines. Impression of upper part of body of a big jar? Or was this a "lock", as assumed by Matthews and Scott? Red-brown clay without visible admixtures.

Inscription:

UB = see above, # 22. "*Universum*"? "Fortified enclosure"?

KAB? = see above, # 57. "Basket", "container".

"(Contribution of) a city So-and-so, (of) the Commonwealth"?

* * *

61. *UE III* : 397	U 18 397	936	UM 33-35-296	Pit W, SIS 4-5

See *Scott 2005*, 19. Catalogue: "Ur PG. PIT W SIS IV–V, Found in Storage 1989".Obverse: an inscription. Legrain reads, probably correctly, UB, and LARSA (AB + UD). Obverse broken and hardly legible, a smoothed plane with two shallow and wide grooves. Measurable widths: 10.9 mm. A package, or a container of plaited work or wickerwork (a basket)? Black clay without visible admixtures.

Inscription:

UB = see above, # 22. "*Universum*"? "Fortified enclosure"?

ARARMA$_2$ = *ZATU* No. 34 p. 176, a city, has bad$_3$; in archaic Ur texts PN 792 = *UET II* : 254 = ARARMA, Burrows reads KA-AŠ-BABBAR like *Deimel 1950*,

No. 1631, but such a sign (*UET II* : 254) does not exist in *ZATU*. *Steinkeller 1995*, 698 sub No. 34: in the Uruk IV period, this was a depiction of a divine standard, a crescent mounted on a shaft. The relation of this sign to U_4 + AB, documented since Uruk III, is "suspect". Denotes Larsa (*Visicato 1989*, UD.UNUG = Larsa).

To me, the signs look rather as E_2 + UD than AB + UD. *MSVO 1* pp. 153–154, has several instances of U_4 E_{2a}, which has either a $ŠITA_{a1}$ (who may consume, GU_7, something), or an UKKIN, and is situated at NUN or LAM (texts 84 – 2 instances, 112 – 2 instances, 213). *UET II* has only one single reference that could be related, a PN é-tin-nu-UD (p. 14, and PN 277 on p. 31). Could this refer to an unknown Ebabbar of Eridu?

$\underline{E_2}$ = see above, # 1. "House"? "Agricultural district"? "Kin group"?

A likely alternative is KID = *ZATU* No. 291 p. 230, *MSVO 1* p. 119 (on reading cf. *Steinkeller 1995*, 702–703 sub No. 291). See also http://psd.museum.upenn.edu/epsd/nepsd-frame.html [accessed September 28, 2014] s. v. KID = matting?.

$\underline{U_4}$ = see above, # 32. "Day"? "Time of the day"?

"City League".

* * *

62. *UE III* : 398	U 14 586	UM 31-16-602	SIS 4

See *Matthews 1993*, 11 = *Scott 2005*, 2, and http://www.cdli.ucla.edu/search/search_results.php?order=ObjectType&SealID=S006197 [accessed February 23, 2014]. Two other fragments of this seal image exist: U 14777 = SIS 4, U 17 883 = SIS 4-5. Catalogue: "Ur under A, at −9.80, SIS 4". Obverse: Animal and human swastika, cross with bladders. Signs: Uruk (UNUG), Eridu (NUN), Larsa (AB.UD). Reverse: a peg protrudes out of an irregular surface. Largest diameter 21.4 mm. Cord coiled around the peg:

CT = 4.1-4.5 mm	ST = 3.0 mm	SI = 7.9 mm	S-spin

Surface of cord covered with fine hair. One of the strands of the cord leaves the wound-around coils towards one side, running beneath a loop(?). The door or adjacent wall might have borne a peg and a cord-directing loop.

Matthews and Scott denote this sealing as borne by a lock" (3×) and as being counter-marked by a rosette (1× of 4).

Inscription: From right to left:

UNUG = see above, # 32. "The city of Uruk".

AB.UD (= U_4) = $ARARMA_2$ = see above, # 61. "The city of Larsa".

AG, close to the swastika: *ZATU* No. 23 p. 173 = AK = see above, # 41. "Creation"? "Sacrifice"? There exists a city ak-si[ki], ED ak-si-za[ki]. The AK sign does nonetheless never display the vertical division line through its middle part. That is shown by sign *ZATU* No. 624 p. 312, phase Uruk III, possibly GURUN. GURUN = Deimel *ŠL* No. 310 p. 536 = *inbu* = *CAD* I-J pp. 144–147: "fruit, offspring, sexual attractiveness and power". Antoine Cavigneaux (1987, 50–51) interprets níg-aka as a "machination", something finished, ended, craftily devised. See also (http://psd.museum.upenn.edu/epsd/nepsd-frame.html [accessed September 28, 2014] s. v. ak. Is this a city, or does the swastika possess magical power?

Pentagram by the swastika: UB = see above, # 22. "*Universum*"? "Fortified enclosure"? On pentagrams see also *Friberg 2011* (our item on p. 126, Fig. 4.2).

ŠU, = ?

NUN (= AGARGARA, ERIDU) = see above, # 1. "Noble", "Noble (= Enki = Eridu)"?"The city of Eridu"?

UNUG+U_4, = ? the "White temple" od Uruk?

UNUG+U_4, (U_4 upside down) = ?

Legcross = the inhabited world, *oecumene*? This interpretation has been proposed by Wiggermann and Johnson who refer to a drawing on the reverse of text SF 76 (*Johnson 2014b*, 54, Fig. 1 and fn. 28).

"City League"? Or cities and the four cardinal points?

* * *

63. *UE III*: 400 = *Matthews 1993*, 5 = *Scott 2005*, 454	U_4+NUN (Adab), UB, bird, Keš, URI_5, AN, *edinnu*	??	No counter-mark

Inscription:

ADAB = *ZATU* No. 19 p. 172. Cf. also *Steinkeller 1995*, 698 sub No. 19, and *Szarzyńska 1996*, 238, on UD.NUN = ADAB, and related issues, also *Michalowski 1993*. Occurs in Fara-age texts (*Visicato 1997*, 135).

UB = see above, # 22. "*Universum*"? "Fortified enclosure"?

KEŠ$_3$ = neither in *ZATU* nor in *MSVO 1* but cf. *MEA* No. 546 p. 227. *Cragg 1969*, 159–164: the hymn is Old Babylonian, the reading of the sign is ŠU$_2$ + AN DUG$_3$ + GADA = keš$_3$ (see now *Wilcke 2006*). The goddess Ninhursag was worshiped here. Earliest evidence from the Ur sealings where it turns up at least twice with Adab. It also appears in the Fara- and Abu Salabikh texts, as well as on Eannatum's Stele of the Vultures. Fara-age texts have a maškim kèš (*Visicato 1995*, 81 ad text 215, WF 103). Other references in the Agade period; Urnammu rebuilt the city for Ninhursag. Cf. also *Molina 1991*, 143 on Keš$_3$, as well as *Selz 1995*, 399 (register). *George 1993*, 108 No. 578 refers to é-kèš^{ki} = "temple of Ninhursag" at Keš, also temple of Nintu. Rebuilt by Urnammu, site of Rimsin II's elevation to kingship. In liturgical texts: é-gal kèš^{ki} –a, listed parallel to é-mah adab^{ki}". Other references: *Steinkeller-Postgate 1992*, 37; *Gelb-Steinkeller-Whiting 1991*, 102 (close to Adab, = Tell al-Wilaya?); *Mander 1986*, 75 and 107 (^{d}keš$_3$ in Abu Salabikh texts). Possibly Tell al-Wilaya itself (*Hussein-Altaweel-Rejeb 2009*).

URI$_5$ = *ZATU* No. 596 p. 306. *Steinkeller 1995*, 710 sub No. 596: the sign is ŠEŠ + AB. Also *Szarzyńska 1992*, 281 fn. 12: in archaic Uruk, ŠEŠ is Nannar, not Ur. Also *Michalowski 1993*, 120–121 (Ur is ŠEŠ.AB). *Pongratz-Leisten 1992*, 306, s. v. URI$_3$.GAL: the sign ŠEŠ is to be understood as URI$_3$ since Uruk III; depicts a standard that can be planted into earth, such standards may stand in pairs flanking doors.

AN (DINGIR) = see above, # 17. "Deity"? "Life"?

"City League".

* * *

64. *UE III*: 401	U 20 083 (U 13 943 in *UE III*)	421	UM 35-1-671	SIS 4

See *Matthews 1993*, 6 = *Scott 2005*, 455. Catalogue: "Ur PJ Stratum SIS 4-5, Found in Storage 1989, Accidentally burnt". Obverse: a legcross and signs of writing. Reverse: impressions of parallel flat strips tied over by a cord. One of these strips has a central "vein". Strip widths: 7.7 mm, 7.7 mm, 7.6 mm and probably also 7.6 mm. Cord:

CT = 1.9 mm	ST = 1.4 mm	SI = 4.0 mm	Spin S

Sealing of a bale in reed matting? Red-brown clay without visible admixtures.

Inscription:
URI$_5$ = see above, # 63."The city of Ur".
ADAB (UD+NUN) = see above, # 63. "The city of Adab".
KEŠ$_3$ = see above, # 63. "The city of Keš".
Legcross = the inhabited world, *oecumene*? See above, # 62.
"City League".

* * *

65. *UE III* : 402	U missing	UM 31-16-614	*UE III* : 402	SIS missing

See *Matthews* 1993, 7 = *Scott* 2005, 99, and http://www.cdli.ucla.edu/search/search_results.php?order=ObjectType&SealID=S006193 [accessed February 23, 2014]. No data in catalogue. Obverse: Keš, Adab, eagle(?), stars, scorpion. Reverse: a cord-coiled peg protrudes from a much weathered but probably originally even surface. Peg: r = 13 mm, thus d = 26 mm. Cord:

CT = 5.5 mm	ST = 4.2 mm	SI = 8.1 mm	S-spin

Fine fibre impressions visible on cord imprints. Red-brown clay without visible admixtures. The even surface (of a wall?) displays impressions of organic corpuscules. Fingerprints obliterated by the cylinder-seal impression.

Inscription: From left to right:
UB = see above, # 22. "*Universum*"? "Fortified enclosure"?
Twice sign AN (DINGIR = see above, # 17. "Deity"? "Life"?
UR$_2$ = see above, # 12. "Lap", "crotch", "sexual organs", "fecundation ritual".
KEŠ$_3$ = see above, # 63. "The city of Keš".

ADAB (UD+NUN) = see above, # 63. “The city of Adab”. “City League”.

* * *

66. *UE III*: 403 = *Matthews 1993*, 20	Toponyms – Adab, Ur?, Keš	Matthews: pot without covering	No counter-mark

Inscription: ADAB (UD+NUN) = see above, # 63. “The city of Adab”.; KEŠ3 = see above, # 63. “The city of Keš”.
“City League”.

* * *

67. *UE III* : 404	U 13 972	UM 31-16-674	SIS 4(?)

See *Matthews* 1993, 23 = *Scott* 2005, 34, and http://www.cdli.ucla.edu/search/search_results.php?order=ObjectType&SealID=S006209 [accessed February 23, 2014]. Catalogue: “Ur, SIS 4”. Obverse: a number of signs and symbols. A cross, E_2(?), KA_2(?), and AB between two sitting figures. Countermarked by a big rosette seal. Countermarking seal: d = 28.8 mm, thus r = 14.4 mm. Its circumference would amount to 90.43 mm. Reverse: broken and with traces of cutting. Possible peg impressions, imprint of a cord. Cord:

CT = 4.6 mm	ST = 2.8 mm	SI = 6.8 mm	S-spin

Red-brown clay without visible admixtures.
Inscription:
DIN = see above, # 38. "Beverage?" "Life"?
[UR]I$_3$ = see above, # 2. "Nannar"? "The city of Ur"?
UB = see above, # 22. "*Universum*"? "Fortified enclosure"?
U$_4$ = BABBAR = see above, # 32. "Day"? "Time of the day"?
IŠ = KUŠ$_7$ = ŠUŠ$_3$ = see above, # 14. "Equerry"? "Herdsman"? "The city of Susa"?
AN (DINGIR) = see above, # 17. "Deity"? "Life"?
Legcross = the inhabited world, *oecumene*? See above, # 62.
A[B + X], with bearer figure(s).
"City League"?

* * *

68. *UE III*: 405	U 18 413	907	UM 33-35-423	Pit W, SIS 4-5

See *Matthews* 1993, 69, and http://www.cdli.ucla.edu/search/search_results.php?order=ObjectType&SealID=S006255 [accessed February 23, 2014]. Catalogue: "Ur PG PIT W, SIS IV–V, Found in Storage 1989". Obverse: signs of writing. Obverse: heavily damaged, broken. Large areas of breakage and cutting. A possible cord impression in the upper part of the reverse. Cord:

CT = 4.8 mm	ST = 2.9 mm	SI cannot be measured	Spin Z (?)

Red-brown clay without visible admixtures.
Inscription:
X
IŠ = KUŠ$_7$ = ŠUŠ$_3$ = see above, # 14. "Equerry"? "Herdsman"? "The city of Susa"?
GAR(NIG$_2$, NINDA)+GAR(NIG$_2$, NINDA) = see above, # 54. "Location"? "Bread"?

KAŠ+AŠ(?) = *ZATU* No. 287 p. 230 (probably $KAŠ_B$ and $KAŠ_C$) = *MSVO 1* p. 117 = *UET II*: 344, 350 and 351. An alternative would be DUG = *ZATU* No. 88 p. 189 = *MSVO 1* pp. 96–97 = *UET II*: 348. *Attinger 1997*, 114: AŠ = "une catégorie de rationnaires?" Persons of minor age usually received lower rations. In Šuruppak, AŠ dub are small sundry tablets from which data were transferred into larger comprehensive texts (dub-gibil: *Pomponio-Visicato 1994*, 306), thus the AŠ sememe carries the idea of "individual", "minor", or the like. On the AŠ lexeme in Fara-age personal names cf. *Visicato 1997*, 21. In later ED Ur, a receptacle called HI × AŠ = sùr sometimes assumed gigantic proportions, as no less than 500 minas of copper were needed for its production; the lexeme also denoted a gigantic and cumbersome weapon there (*Alberti-Pomponio 1986*, 97 ad text 44). *Heeßel 2001–2002*, 43: AŠ = *eṭṭūtu* = spindle, in medicine texts.

X

"Bread and beer for shepherds"? "Bread and beer from/for Susa"?

***

69. *UE III*: 406 = *Matthews 1993*, 91 = *Scott 2005*, 814	DUB/KIŠIB??, GAR + GAR, GAN_2, LAGAB+ŠITA, KAK = DU_3 = RU_2, ŠEŠ?, X, KISAL, X	Door peg (2×)	No counter-mark

Inscription:

DUB/KIŠIB? = dub or kišib "to transcribe the (contents of the small) records (onto another document)" (*Maekawa 1997*, 118–120). SANGA.DUB is attested to under *ZATU* No. 444 p. 268. *MSVO 1* pp. 96 and 138. DUB = dab_6 = "to encircle, surround" (*Mirelman-Sallaberger 2010*, 183). On DUB = "tablet" see and *Krebernik-Postgate 2009*, 18, register. Or is this

GAN_2? = see above, # 28. "Field"? "Arable"?

X

LAGAB+ŠITA = ?

KAK = DU_3 = RU_2 = see above, # 31. "To enact"? "To make something"? "To create"? Here it is most difficult to interpret, insofar as it is not to be equalled to DU in the sense of *zaqāpu* = "ein- aufpflanzen" (in the sense of "what has been imposed on?" cf. *Steible* 1991, 176, as well as *Krebernik* 1993–1994, on du_3 = "Aufpflanzen").

URI_3? = see above, # 2. "Nannar"? "The city of Ur"? Due to the fact that the sign is depicted in a "supine" position, it may perhaps be

ŠEŠ? = *ZATU* No. 595 p. 306, *Steinkeller* 1995, 710 sub No. 595 (cf. see above, # 63). A profession šeš-ib is attested to in later ED Ur and in Ebla. These people were quite numerous and their social status was not high.They exercised cultic functions. "Brothers of a shrine"? (*Alberti-Pomponio* 1986, 63–64).

GAR(NIG_2, NINDA)+GAR(NIG_2, NINDA)? = see above, # 54. "Location"? "Bread"?

X

X

Second item:

X

KISAL = see above, # 5. "Forecourt"? "Gipar of Ur"?

Produce delivered to the forecourt (or to the Gipar) of Ur?

* * *

70. *UE III*: 407 = *Matthews* 1993, 16 = *Scott* 2005, 458	Toponyms: Nippur?, Larsa, X, Adab	Matthews: reed matting package	No counter-mark

Inscription:

E_2 = see above, # 1. "House"? "Agricultural district"? "Kin group"?

A likely alternative is KID = see above, # 61."Matting"?

EN?? = *ZATU* No. 134 p. 197, *MSVO* 1, 99–102, on the sign cf. also *Edzard* 1993, 139.

In the case of my # 91, Piotr Steinkeller (2010, 240, Fig. 1) reads these two signs EN.É (not EN.KID) and identifies them as the toponym of Nippur.

AB.UD = $ARARMA_2$ = see above, # 61. "The city of Larsa".

X

ADAB = see above, # 63. "The city of Adab".

"City League".

***

71. *UE III*: 408 = *Scott 2005*, 459	X, AB × X, X	??	No counter-mark

Inscription:

AB = $EŠ_3$ = see above, # 30. "Household, centre of production, distribution?"

"City League".

***

72. *UE III*: 409 = *Matthews 1993*, 21 = *Scott 2005*, 460	From right to left: AB × X, NIMGIR??, AB × Y; from right to left: AB × Z, NI = I_3, AB × AA	Door peg	0

Inscription:

NIMGIR = see above, # 5. "Herald".

UR_3 = see above, # 1. "Harrow"? "To seal off"? "To plaster"? "A temple"?

NI = I_3 = LID_2 = *ZATU* No. 393 p. 253 (both a city and an official) = *MSVO* 1 p. 128. See also http://psd.museum.upenn.edu/epsd/nepsd-frame.html [accessed September 29, 2014] s. v. NI = bur, gana, i_3, lidga, nunuz, zagin. On Sumerian oils see *Brunke-Sallaberger 2010*.

"City League"? Delivery of oil/comestibles?

* * *

73. *UE III*: 410 = *Matthews 1993*, 2 = *Scott 2005*, 461	Toponyms: Nippur?, NIMGIR, Larsa, X, Ur (URI_5), legcross, Keš	??	No counter-mark

Inscription:
$\underline{E_2}$ = see above, # 1. "House"? "Agricultural district"? "Kin group"?
A likely alternative is KID = see above, # 61. "Matting"?
EN?? = see above, # 70. "EN, arch-priest"?
NIMGIR = see above, # 5. "Herald".
$\underline{UR_3}$ = see above, # 1. "Harrow"? "To seal off"? "To plaster"? "A temple"?
AB.UD = $\underline{ARARMA_2}$ = see above, # 61. "The city of Larsa".
X
$\underline{URI_5}$ = see above, # 63. "The city of Ur".
Legcross = the inhabited world, *oecumene*? See above, # 62.
X
X
"City League".

* * *

74. *UE III* : 411	U missing	UM 31-16-613	SIS missing

See *Matthews* 1993, 31 = *Scott* 2005, 98, and http://www.cdli.ucla.edu/search/search_results.php?order=ObjectType&SealID=S006199 [accessed February 24, 2014]. No data in catalogue. Obverse: Ur (URI_5), a bull *couchant* and an eagle emblem. Reverse: a peg coiled around with cord protruding from a relatively even surface. No measurements can be taken from the peg. Cord:

CT = 4.5 mm	ST = 2.8 mm	SI = 9.0 mm	S-spin

Impressions of fine hair on the cord surface. Red-brown clay without admixtures, imprints of impurities on the even surface.

Inscription:

$\underline{URI_5}$ = see above, # 63."The city of Ur".

Legcross = the inhabited world, *oecumene*? See above, # 62.

"City League" – the city of Ur.

* * *

75. *UE III*: 412 = *Scott* 2005, 462	GU, Larsa, AB?, swastika, X, X	??	No counter-mark

Inscription:

<u>GU</u> = see http://psd.museum.upenn.edu/epsd/nepsd-frame.html [accessed September 29, 2014] s. v. gu = cord. In ED Lagaš GU = gu = "Flachs", "Faden"; syllabic gu-ul = "Groß machen", etc.; = lu_5-gu = "eine Abgabe" (*Meyer-Laurin* 2011, 54). In Ur-III texts gu = "Faden, Schnur, als Faden einer Halskette oder als Armband, meist ohne Materialangabe" (*Paoletti* 2012, 138). Or is this a simplified writing of UD.NUN, Adab?

ARARMA$_2$ = see above, # 61. "The city of Larsa".
"City League" – delivery of cords?

* * *

76. *UE III*: 413 = 415 = 459 = *Matthews 1993*, 3 = *Scott 2005*, 108	*Edinnu*, ŠU$_2$; SILA$_4$?, EŠDA or GU, ARARMA$_2$, X	"lock" (3×), unknown (2×)	Rosette, 1 of 5

Edinnu = the inhabited world, *oecumene*? See above, # 62.

Inscription:

ŠU$_2$ = *ZATU* No. 534 p. 289, in textile accounts. *MSVO 1* pp. 149–150. See also http://psd.museum.upenn.edu/epsd/nepsd-frame.html [accessed September 29, 2014] s. v. šu$_2$).

SILA$_4$ = *ZATU* No. 482 p. 275, also a dignitary? *Steinkeller 1995*, 708 sub No. 482, comments on the sign. In Abu Salabikh sila$_4$-nita = "male lamb" (*Krebernik-Postgate 2009*, 20, register). Sila$_4$-nim = *ḫurāpu* = spring lamb (*Steinkeller-Postgate 1992*, 35). Is it relevant to this place?

EŠDA? = see http://psd.museum.upenn.edu/epsd/nepsd-frame.html [accessed September 29, 2014] s. v. ešda "a metal cultic vessel", this is hardly likely, so better to interpret this sign as

GU: GU? = see above, # 75. "Cord".

AB.UD = ARARMA$_2$ = see above, # 61. "The city of Larsa".

Roger Matthews (*Matthews 1993*, 3) identifies this impression with *UE III*: 415 and 459.

City League, textile- and cord deliveries?

* * *

77. *UE III*: 414 = *Scott 2005*, 463	Toponyms: *edinnu*, X; AB+X, Adab, Larsa, AB?	??	No counter-mark

Inscription:
ADAB = see above, # 63. "The city of Adab".
ARARMA$_2$ = see above, # 61. "The city of Larsa".
Edinnu = the inhabited world, *oecumene*? See above, # 62.
"City League".

* * *

78. *UE III* : 416	U 11 680	UM 31-16-630	Royal Cemetery area

See *Matthews* 1993, 9 = *Scott* 2005, 93, and http://www.cdli.ucla.edu/search/search_results.php?order=ObjectType&SealID=S006195 [accessed February 25, 2014]. Catalogue: "Ur, Royal Cemetery area, PG, filling over PG 1236". Not from SIS. A tablet. Obverse: *Edinnu* in an oval, UD, Ur, unidentified sign and an eagle emblem. Reverse: AB, AŠ? Red-brown clay without visible admixtures.

Inscription:
Edinnu = the inhabited world, *oecumene*? See above, # 62.

UD = U_4 = see above, # 32. "Day"? "Time of the day"?

NU.gunu = *ZATU* No. 418 p. 259, 9 out of 10 items in textile accounts. *Biga 1978*, 94–95, on si-NU_X.U fish – could the NU.gunu sign refer to fish? *MSVO 1* p. 131: NU.gunu, occurs in text 116 there, which is a mixed account of foodstuffs returned (GI) by AB.NU.gunu and KAB?. LAGAB, both under the sovereignty of EN (on reverse).

BAD = see above, # 12, and # 46. Threshing or husking grain?

ŠEŠ = see above, # 69. "Brothers of a shrine"?

URI_5 = see above, # 63."The city of Ur".

DUG = see above, # 35. "Pot?" "Merchandise?" "Human individual?"

AB + AN: AB = *ZATU* No. 7 p. 170, *Steinkeller 1995*, 696 sub No. 7 (a graph for UNUG, cf. See above, # 32). An ED city is called [d]ab (ibid.). In Fara-age personal designations there is just one instance of DUMU.AB, a professional name (*Visicato 1997*, 112).

Spread-eagle emblem

X

X

"City League", and white(?) (or light?) commodities from *Edinnu*?

* * *

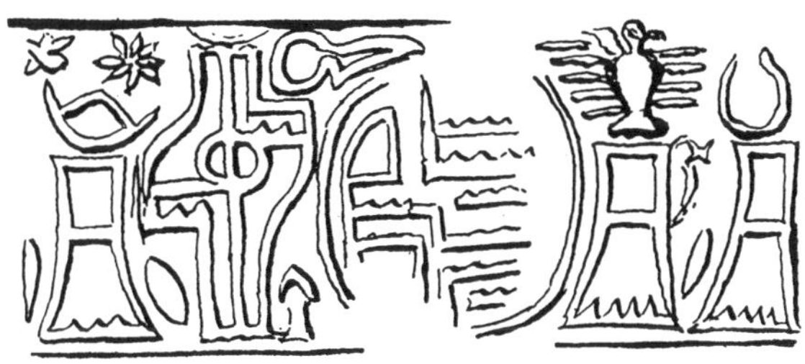

79. *UE III* : 417	U 14.594	UM 31-16-640	SIS 4

See *Matthews 1993*, 10 = *Scott 2005*, 94, and http://www.cdli.ucla.edu/search/search_results.php?order=ObjectType&SealID=S006196 [accessed February 25, 2014]. Catalogue: "Ur, Pit D, under PG 1332 (SE end), m. 9–10". Obverse: *Edinnu* and legcross in ovals, Larsa (UNUG.UD),, UNUG + eagle emblem, UNUG + coil emblem. Reverse: traces of folds of a pliable substance without any traces of its structure. Tied over by two strands of a cord, only the CT's (3.5 mm, upper, and 2.0 mm, lower) being measurable. A trace of a knot may be visible on the upper cord. Was this a leather sack tied over with an organic-fibre string? Matthews: a pot. Red-brown clay without visible admixtures.

Inscription:
ARARMA$_2$ = see above, # 61. "The city of Larsa".
AN (DINGIR) (twice?) = see above, # 17. "Deity"? "Life"?
Legcross = the inhabited world, *oecumene*? See above, # 62.
Edinnu
AB + bird emblem = IDIGNA? = *ZATU* No. 261 p. 223 (*Steinkeller 1995*, 702 sub No. 261: "very doubtful"); cf. *Mander 1986*, 75 and 107. See also *Amiet 1980*, 103: 1361, dated to ED-III. On IDIGNA and ^{id_3}idigna^{mušen} see *Attinger 2011*, 228.
AB + coil emblem = I do not understand this.
"City League".

* * *

80. *UE III* : 418	U 13 933	UM 31-16-645	*UE III* : 418	SIS 4

See *Matthews 1993*, 15 = *Scott 2005*, 85, and http://www.cdli.ucla.edu/search/search_results.php?order=ObjectType&SealID=S006201 [accessed March 2, 2014]. Catalogue: "SIS 4 [Larsa id.]". Obverse: *Edinnu*, legcross, a rosette, Larsa (UD.UNUG) and UNUG with an eagle emblem above (?). Reverse: markedly uneven and weathered. Three to four strands of cord converge together at a single spot. Cord:

CT = 3.1 mm	ST = 2.6 mm	SI = 6.65 mm	Z-spin

A container? Red-brown clay without visible admixtures.
Inscription:
X
ARARMA$_2$: see above, # 61. "The city of Larsa". Or is this
AB + NU?: for AB see above, # 30. "Household, centre of production, distribution".
NU = *ZATU* No. 417 p. 259, in metal accounts. *MSVO* 1 p. 131: NU.gunu, occurs in text 116 there, which is a mixed account of foodstuffs returned (GI) by AB.NU.gunu and KAB?.LAGAB, both under the sovereignty of EN (on reverse).

Legcross = the inhabited world, *oecumene*? See above, # 62.
Edinnu
"City League".

* * *

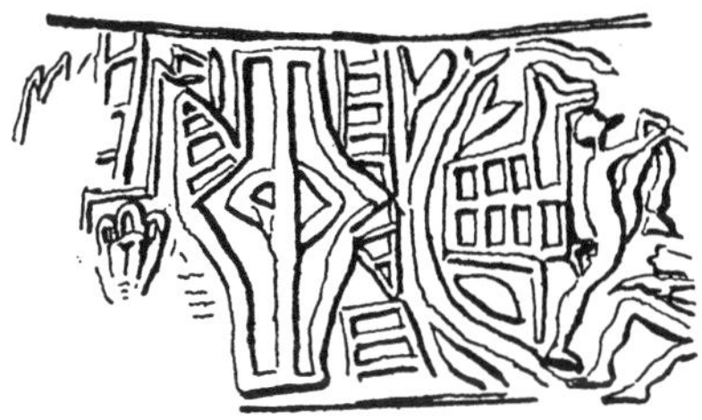

81. *UE III*: 419 = *Matthews 1993*, 25 = *Scott 2005*, 464	X, URI$_5$, legcross, GAN$_2$(?), X, *Edinnu*	Reed matting package	No counter-mark

Inscription:
URI$_5$ = see above, # 63."The city of Ur".
GAN$_2$ = see above, # 28. "Field"? "Arable"?
"City League"?

* * *

82. *UE III*: 420 = *Matthews 1993*, 22 = *Scott 2005*, 465	Legcross and AB with a superimposed bird (see above, No. 79, *UE III*: 417)	Probably leather-covered pot	No counter-mark

See http://www.cdli.ucla.edu/search/search_results.php?order=ObjectType&SealID=S006208 [accessed March 2, 2014].
Inscription:
AB + bird emblem = see above, # 79. IDIGNA?
"City League".

* * *

83. *UE III*: 421 = *Matthews 1993*, 8 = *Scott 2005*, 555; Scott: SIS 8, Matthews: probably SIS 4	AB+X, spread eagle, legcross, URI_5+AN, $ARARMA_2$	??	No counter-mark

See http://www.cdli.ucla.edu/search/search_results.php?order=ObjectType&SealID=S006194 [accessed March 2, 2014].

Inscription:

<u>URI_5</u> = see above, # 63."The city of Ur".

<u>AN (DINGIR)</u> = see above, # 17. "Deity"? "Life"?

<u>$ARARMA_2$</u> = see above, # 61. "The city of Larsa".

"City League".

* * *

84. *UE III*: 422 = *Scott 2005*, 466	Legcross	??	No counter-mark

Inscription:

Legcross = the inhabited world, *oecumene*? See above, # 62.

"City League" ?

* * *

85. *UE III*: 423 = *Matthews 1993*, 17 = *Scott 2005*, 467	X, ŠE, X, X, X; AB+X, DUG, UNUG, AB superimposed by a standard?	Door peg	No counter-mark

Inscription:
X
ŠE = see above, # 15. "Grain".
X
X
X
X
AN (DINGIR) = see above, # 17. "Deity"? "Life"?
DUG = see above, # 35. "Pot?" "Merchandise?" "Human individual?"
UNUG = see above, # 32. "The city of Uruk".
X
"City League", materials delivered.

* * *

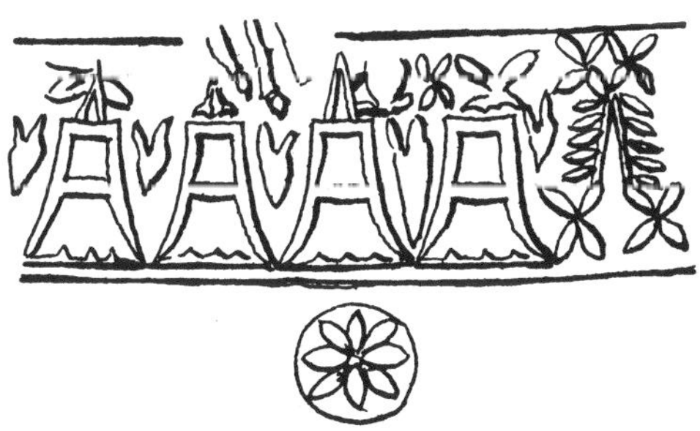

86. *UE III* : 424 = *Matthews 1993*, 4	U 13 912	UM 31-16-675	SIS 4

See http://www.cdli.ucla.edu/search/search_results.php?order=ObjectType&SealID=S006190 [accessed March 2, 2014]. Catalogue: "SIS 4". Obverse: alliance of variously denoted AB's interspersed with DUGs. Countermarked by a rosette seal, d = 17.2 mm, thus r = 8.6 mm. Its circumference would amount to 54 mm. Could be of the same cylinder seal (impression is incomplete). Obverse: a peg coiled around by cord protrudes from an even surface. Peg: r = 13 mm, thus d = 26 mm. The cord is smooth, only CT = 4.3 mm can be measured. Organic fibre? Leather? Ochre to yellowish clay without visible admixtures. Organic imprints on even surface.

Inscription:
DUG = see above, # 35. "Pot?" "Merchandise?" "Human individual?"
UNUG + AN; UNUG = see above, # 32. "The city of Uruk".
UNUG + X
UNUG + URI$_3$, *recte* ŠEŠ(?)
UNUG + AN
NUN + AN+AN.
"City League"?

* * *

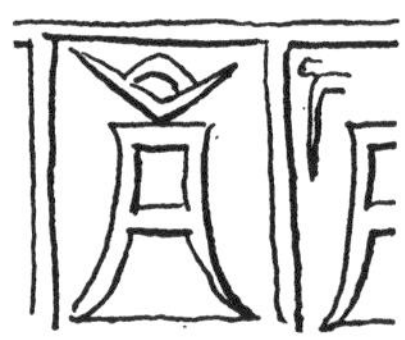

87. *UE III*: 425 = *Scott 2005*, 468	Toponyms: ARARMA$_2$, AB+X	??	No counter-mark

Inscription:
ARARMA$_2$ = see above, # 61. "The city of Larsa".
"City League".

* * *

88. *UE III*: 426 = *Scott 2005*, 469	Toponyms: KUR, URI$_5$?	??	Counter-mark: human face, d. 20

Inscription:

KUR = see http://psd.museum.upenn.edu/epsd/nepsd-frame.html [accessed March 2, 2014] s. v. kur = "underworld; land, country; mountain(s); east; easterner; east wind".

URI_5 = see above, # 63."The city of Ur".

Note the countermark other than rosette.

"City League"?

* * *

89. *UE III* : 427	U 15 045	UM 31-16-676	SIS 4

See *Matthews* 1993, 105 = *Scottt* 2005, 51, and http://www.cdli.ucla.edu/search/search_results.php?order=ObjectType&SealID=S006291 [accessed March 5, 2014]. Catalogue: "A = SIS 4". Obverse: a sign (UB?). Countemarked by an eight-pointed rosette seal. Seal diameter = 23.5 mm, thus r = 11.75 mm. Its circumference amounts to 73.8 mm. The conclusion that the butt of the same seal was used seems very unlikely but the impression can be a partial one. The cylinder-seal rolling is situated between two impressions of the countermarking seal, impressed close to time of the main sealing. Reverse: vestige of an even surface with imprints of organic particles. Bears traces of cutting. Red-brown clay without visible admixtures.

Inscription:

UB = big and elaborate form of sign. See above, # 22. "*Universum*"? "Fortified enclosure"?

"City League?

* * *

90. *UE III*: 428 = *Matthews 1993*, 19 = *Scott 2005*, 470	Toponyms: UNUG??; DUG, UNUG? AB+$AŠ_2$(?)	??	No counter-mark

Inscription:
X
DUG = see above, # 35. “Pot?” “Merchandise?” “Human individual?”
AB + AŠ$_2$(?) = see above, # 7. “City elder”? “Wittness”?
X
“City League”?

* * *

91. *UE III* : 429	U 18 397	919	UM 33-35-293	Pit W, SIS 4-5

See *Matthews* 1993, 1, = *Scott* 2005, 76, and http://www.cdli.ucla.edu/search/search_results.php?order=ObjectType&SealID=S006187 [accessed March 5, 2014]. Catalogue: “Ur PG. PIT W. SIS IV–V”. Obverse: Inscription. MES, UTU, EN(?), LÍL, UTUL(?), Larsa (AB.UTU), Keš, X, Ur (AB.ŠEŠ), Adab (UD.NUN). The length of the impression with city names can be measured: 34.2 mm, thus a radius of the relevant cylinder seal would amount to 5.45 mm. UTUL could also be read as ŠITA.NAM$_2$. Reverse: impression of two planes of chopped wood at right angles to each other. The bigger plane is pierced through by a hole through which a spherical object of a diameter at least = 37.8 mm is protruding. Red-brown clay without visible admixtures. “A kind of “lock” or package/box? (*Matthews* 1993, 61).

Inscription: From right to left:

Upper line:

ŠITA + GIŠ + NAM$_2$ = *ZATU* No. 387 p. 252, *MSVO 1* p. 127, *UET II* : 391, a ruler title (NAMEŠDA). Appears in the Archaic LU$_2$ A Profession List (*Monaco* 2007, 8 fn. 49). *Lambert* 1981, 94–97 on NAM$_2$ as the earliest Sumerian title for a ruler. P. 94: ED Lu list A (probably of Uruk III origin) has ŠITA + GIŠ + NAM$_2$, read possibly nám ^{giš}šita, “lord of the mace”, while ED Lu list E (Fara-age origin) has none. NAM$_2$ was dropped as early as the Fara texts, where the usual title is en$_5$-si. *Lambert* 1981, 95: NAM$_2$ occurs in divine epithets and also royal names in the ED age, for instance at Abu Salabikh, with “600 kings”, “600 maces”, and similar. The surviving ŠITA + GIŠ acquired the meaning “purification priest”. On the title also *Mander* 1986, 52 and 114 – a divine name ^{dingir}ŠITA + GIŠ + NAM$_2$. *Szarzyńska* 1996, 240: prefers reading NAM$_2$.ŠITA$_2$, as attested in later texts (a Sargonic personal name of Nam-šita). The same reading is proposed by *Steinkeller 1995*, 706 sub No. 387. The title is attested to at Abu Salabikh (*Biggs 1966*, table on p. 77). See also *Charvát 2012*.

$\underline{E_2}$ = see above, # 1. "House", "agricultural district", "kin group"?

A possible alternative is KID = see above, # 61."Matting"?

$\underline{EN}$ = see above, # 70. "Arch-priest"?

Piotr Steinkeller (*2010*, 240, Fig. 1) reads these two signs EN.É (not EN.KID) and identifies them as the toponym of Nippur.

$\underline{GAN_2}$ = see above, # 28. "Field"? "Arable"?

$\underline{U_4}$ = BABBAR = see above, # 32. "Day"? "Time of the day"?

Lower line:

$\underline{ARARMA_2}$ = see above, # 61. "The city of Larsa".

$\underline{KEŠ_3}$ = see above, # 63. "The city of Keš".

LAK 475 = a sign most probably close to *UET II* : 282, *hapax legomenon*.

$\underline{URI_5}$ = see above, # 63."The city of Ur".

$\underline{ADAB}$ = see above, # 63. "The city of Adab".

"ŠITA + GIŠ + NAM$_2$, Nippur, field of Utu? White field? City League."

There seem to have been two components of this seal – one of the "Sovereign" (ŠITA + GIŠ + NAM$_2$) and the other of the "city league".

***

92. *UE III*: 430 = *Matthews 1993*, 28 = *Scott 2005*, 471	Toponyms: NAGAR?? NUN, UB+KID (Nippur??); AB+X, E$_2$ or KID.U$_4$ (= shrine of Šamaš at Larsa or Sippar or Girsu?) GA$_2$ × AN, TAK$_4$, ŠA$_3$ IŠ(?) or KID	Reed matting package	No counter-mark

Inscription:

$\underline{NAGAR}$ = BULUG$_4$ = "boundary stele" (*Peterson 2009*, 238 fn. 13), with possible reading NAGAR = bulug$_4$; ibid. 238 fn. 13. In Ur-III texts, bulug$_4$ = "Pfriem"

(*Paoletti 2012*, 154). For NAGAR, see above, # 5 ad I 2. "Vegetation"? "Fertility"? "Carpenter"?

NAGAR = *ZATU* No. 382 p. 251, other reading $BULUG_4$ = *MSVO 1* p. 127. In *UET II* : 408, Eric Burrows cites this seal and reads nagar. BALA is supposed to be "term of office" (*Klein 1991*, 125 fn. 10). An unpublished text from Jemdet Nasr has BALA.NAGAR in an account of unclear contents (*MSVO 1* No. 234). In Instructions of Šuruppak bal, bala = "to turn around", "to change", the motion of a revolving spindle whorl (*Alster 1974*, 89–90). In Fara-age texts, bala+personal name = "term of office of PN" (*Steinkeller 1989*, 111, § 2.17.2). In ED Lagaš, BALA = "Pfründe, Pacht", literally "Übertragenes" (*Selz 1995*, 226 fn. 1091).

<u>NUN</u> (= AGARGARA, ERIDU) = see above, # 1. "Noble", "Noble (= Enki)"? = "The city of Eridu"?

<u>KID</u> = see above, # 61."Matting"?

May GA_2 × AN be interpreted as $ESIR_2$ or as defective writing for I_7? In such a case <u>$ESIR_2$</u> = "bitumen"(?) (*Alberti-Pomponio 1986*, 57). $Esir_2$ (= *LAK* 173) is also interpreted as "sandals" (*Gelb-Steinkeller-Whiting 1991*, 296). GA_2 = "un type d'enclos", "... où se tiennent souvent des bovins et des ovins" (= "Stall, Gehege" = *Attinger-Krebernik 2005*, 73 sub # 254'). GA_2 = "outbuilding, shed, barn" (*Andersson 2012*, 136 fn. 763).

<u>TAK_4</u>: = *ZATU* No. 548 p. 293, *MSVO 1* p. 151. *Steinkeller 1995*, 709 sub No. 548: save for vertical orientation, the sign is identical with *ZATU* 532 = ŠU. Ibid. sub No. 532: the occurrences of *ZATU* 532 and *ZATU* 548 in *Metal* 24–25 and 42–43 (*ATU 3* pp. 136–137) are consistently interpreted as ŠU in the corresponding ED mss. (MEE 3 pp.79-80 lines 24–25 and 42–43). In ED times the distinction between ŠU and TAK_4 thus does not appear to have been meaningful any more. Yet, Niek Veldhuis (1995, 436) observes that these are two different signs, confused in lexical lists, in which rotation (TAK_4 = ŠU rotated 90°) distinguishes different functions of the same sign. *Civil 1990*: "to send" = an errand boy? TAK_4 = "zurückhalten" (*Selz 1993*, 220–221). In Instructions of Šuruppak, TAK_4 (here TAG_4) means something like "to touch" (*Alster 1974*, 44–45 ad line 203).

The TAK_4.ALAN ceremony (*Charvát 1997*, 29, 61–63, 65, 69, 90) is attested to in Šuruppak texts, in ED LU_2, at Ebla (with a reading *la-a-núm*) and at Nippur. The Šuruppak texts mention a structure called é-TAK_4.ALAN. It may refer to a statue in a votive inscription (ABW 2 p. 342) (*Pomponio 1987*, 474). TAK_4.ALAN is likely to denote a statue and possibly also a sculptor (*Gelb-Steinkeller-Whiting 1991*, 69). In Abu Salabikh, TAK_4.ALAN = lan_x; UD-lan_x could mean an-lan_x = "scolpire il divino" = "to carve a deity" (*Mander 1986*, 52). In ED Lagaš, a number of statues and one stele received regular offerings on festive occasions in the É-$šag_4$ shrine, of a square ground-plan with square side 3.715 metres long (*Rosengarten 1960*, 162). The ceremony may be depicted on a cylinder seal found in the Jemdet-Nasr level at Ur (*Legrain 1951*, 11, No. 30 on Pl. 2 and possibly also on the seal UE III: 385).

In ED-IIIb inscriptions, SAHAR.DU$_6$.TAG$_4$ may mean "burial tell", with translation of TAG$_4$ as "leave behind" (*Richardson 2007*, 193–194; *Suriano 2012*, 218 fn. 36, in general 218–219). Is there any connection with burial ceremonies?

ŠA$_3$ = see above, # 4. "A field category"?

IŠ = KUŠ$_7$ = ŠUŠ$_3$, = see above, # 14. "Equerry"? "Herdsman"? "The city of Susa"?

"City League", delivery of products for a ceremony?

* * *

93. *UE III* : 431	U 14 896 A	UM 31-16-604	SIS 4

See *Matthews 1993*, 114 = *Scott 2005*, 62, and http://www.cdli.ucla.edu/search/search_results.php?order=ObjectType&SealID=S006300 [accessed March 5, 2014]. Another example of the same seal: U 18 398, Pit W, SIS 4-5. Catalogue: "SIS 4". Obverse: a cuneiform inscription. The cylinder was rolled eight times, first directed into the cardinal points and then again but turned by 45°. In between the individual rollings the sealing was countermarked by a rosette seal. Three of its impressions display a diameter 22.15 mm. The length of the impression should thus amount to 69 mm; this could be done with the same seal butt (the rollings are incomplete). Reverse: a peg protrudes from an uneven surface. Only the diameter, 15.55 mm, can be measured. Very crude and blurred impressions of a cord, of which only the CT = 3.7 mm can be measured.

The inscription occurs also on my ## 94, 95 and 96.

Inscription: reading according to *UE III* : No. 431, starting in the upper left corner and ending in the lower right corner:

Upper column:

(1') BAD$_3$, = *ZATU* No. 44 p. 179. The sign inscribed in the middle seems to be AŠ, not AN. It may thus refer to a site named Durum, as the AŠ = RUM phonetic complement might indicate (*Steinkeller 1995*, 698 s. No. 44). The sign is probably identical with *UET II* : 301 and 302, and with *LAK* Nos. 618 and 619. In ED Lagaš, BAD_3+divine name means "god XY is my protection" ("meine Mauer", *Selz 1995*, 23 fn. 41). According to *Carroué 1981*, BAD_3+AN may have been read UB in Pre-Sargonic Lagaš. The goddess Geštinanna was venerated at a site called sag-ub. In addition to that, BAD_3+ AN + KI may be Dēr, but essentially any fortified city (*Westenholz 1997*, 42–43 fn. 20). David Owen (1995) argues that BAD_3 is in Syria. *Michalowski 1993*, 124, *Mander 1980*, 189 (UB, UB^{ki}), and *De Graef 2007*, 85, all consider this toponym unclear. On the six Mesopotamian BAD_3 see now *Frayne 2008a*. BAD_3 as two sites named Der, a lowland- and one a highland one: *Michalowski 2013*, 303. BAD_3 in connection with the Muriq-Tidnim defence line *Lafont 2010*, 77–81. See above, # 22.

(2') BALA.NAGAR: BALA = *ZATU* No. 46 p. 179 = *LAK* 19 and 20. The formula nu-bala-bala = *nakārum* = "to change", "to violate", comes up as early as the Fara-age texts (*Gelb-Steinkeller-Whiting 1991*, 246).

For NAGAR see above, # 5 and # 92. "Vegetation"? "Fertility"? "Carpenter"?

An alternative explanation wil involve the reading bala-$bulug_4$, "contribution of the border regions"?

(3') UŠUMGAL = *ZATU* No. 607 p. 308, perhaps with components GAL + GAL + BUR_2 instead of the usual GAL + BUR_2. Attested to only in the Uruk III period. The ušumgal, of both male and female sex, assumed the form of a lion with back paws of an eagle and with wings, though they did not fly. These poison-spitting creatures, also connected to Nannar, were extirpators of evil and exuded fertility (*Westenholz 1987*, 42); Sumerian imagination portrayed them as strong, roaring (*grondant*) killers, with jaws wide open (*gueule béante*), but without independent authority (*Attinger 2012*, 370 # L.23). Is this a personal name?

(4') ŠE + NAM_2 = *ZATU* No. 513 p. 283, name of a dignitary and a toponym (see *Green 1980*, 8–10). Present in the Archaic LU_2 A Profession List (*Monaco 2007*, 8 fn. 49). At Ebla, this was read "su-šum". The last hitherto documented instances have turned up in Jemdet Nasr-period texts (*MSVO 1* p. 145). Was this a "feeder" (*Englund 1995b*, 29 fn. 26)?

(5') $ŠE_3$ + SUHUR + KI = an exceedingly difficult sign group. $ŠE_3$, $EŠ_2$, GI_7 = *ZATU* No. 516 p. 284 (also "Seil", *Meyer-Laurin 2011*, 47). The SUHUR sign (= *ZATU* No. 491 p. 278) is implied by the ED tribute form suhur-$še_3$. The GAL SUHUR functionary forms part of Archaic LU_2 A Profession List (*Monaco 2007*, 8 fn. 49). Sign *ZATU* No. 298 p. 232, KIŠIK, is hardly likely, as the tree name $^{giš\ u2}$$eš_3$-kišik shows. Neither is sign IDIGNA = *ZATU* No. 261 p. 223 probable. Other two possibilities extremely difficult to assess are *ZATU* No. 633 p. 313 (in tree names) and *ZATU* No. 667 p. 319 (U_4 + HI?), of which the readings are unknown. I believe that the most probable reading is that indicated above (a tribute in fish?). The A SUHUR channel of Lagaš was dug by Urnanše: *André-Salvini 2012*.

(6') $\underline{\text{GIZZAL}_X + \text{NUN} + \text{ŠE} + \text{ŠE} + \text{ŠE}_3 + \text{KI} = \text{SAMAN}_3\text{(??)}}$: The sign GIZZAL_X refers to a tree (= *ZATU* No. 231 p. 217). In Instructions of Šuruppak, gizzal kalam-ma = "the most intelligent one in Sumer" (*Alster 1974*, 42–43). But the divine name SAMAN_3 consists of signs NUN, ŠE, EŠ_2 and BU (*Gelb-Steinkeller-Whiting 1991*, 181). Our group displays the signs NUN, ŠE, ŠE, EŠ_2 (= ŠE_3), only instead of BU we have PI (if this is the reading of GEŠTU = *ZATU* No. 203 p. 211). In ED Lagaš, ^{d}samàn = šumannu = "Halteseil"; this divine name appears in Fara-age texts and the deity has a temple at Lagaš (*Selz 1995*, 274). Or should we see here the sign KAK = DU_3? This would be most difficult to interpret, insofar as it is not to be equalled to DU in the sense of *zaqāpu* = "ein- aufpflanzen" (in the sense of "what has been imposed on?" cf. *Steible 1991*, 176, as well as *Krebernik 1993–1994*, on du_3 = "Aufpflanzen"). Šuruppak: AL-DU_3 = "worked with the hoe", also in ED-IIIb Girsu. Ur III texts distinguish between al-du_3 and al-ak, with the former taking about three times less time than the latter (*Pomponio-Visicato 1994*, 222). Texts from Abu Salabikh know a person named DU_3.A.X, possibly from Umma (*Krebernik-Postgate 2009*, 16). In ED Lagaš, al___dù = "mit der Hacke anlegen" (*Selz 1995*, 244 fn. 1177). nig_2-du_3-a is a measure of fruit, possibly "what holds together" ("festhalten"), that is, a bundle. nig_2-du_3(-a) = /šerku/ = "a string of dried fruit", replaced in Uruinimigina's inscriptions by the expression sag-keš_2 (*Selz 1995*, p. 33 fn. 106). In Fara nig_2-du_3 = "Maß-Behältnis für Feigen und Äpfel" (*Steible-Yildiz 2008*, 167). DU_3 = *kullum* = "to detain", "to hold". It might originally have been an intransitive verb, meaning something like "to hold on" (property). Does this mean that on seals, items transferred to the property of the adressee are so denoted (*Gelb-Steinkeller-Whiting 1991*, 247)?. The KI sign might be a local determinative.

All in all, this line might mean something like "(what has been imposed on) the land of SAMAN_3".

Lower column:

(7') Several possibilities:

a) E_2+UR_3: E_2 = see above, # 1. "House"? "Agricultural district"? "Kin group"? UR_3 = see above, # 1. "Harrow"? "To seal off"? "To plaster"? "A temple"?

b) NIMGIR = + UR_3?; NIMGIR = see above, # 5. "Herald".

c) SANGA? = *ZATU* No. 444 p. 268. A group of archaic texts from Uruk(?), Jemdet Nasr and Umma(?) features the SANGA sign (*Monaco 2007*, 6–7), and the sign group NAGAR_a ZI_a SANGA_a (*Monaco 2007*, 4). In ED proverbs, SANGA is an organizer, and administrator (*Alster 1991–1992*, 19 ad line 206, comments on p. 31). It is difficult to decide what is the correct ED reading of this sign – šid or umbisag? The ŠID sign is a hallmark of the UD.GAL.NUN scribal usance (Joachim Krecher, apud *Johnson 2014a*, 27). He is definitely not "sanga-priest", but a special kind of scribe or registrar (of literary or lexical texts?); in Fara-age texts, sanga and dubsar are two different professions (Biggs 1967, 59 fn. 1).

Piotr Steinkeller (OA 20, 1981, 247, *apud Mander 1986*, 97) cites the following instance from the AN = *anum* lexical series:

$^{\text{d.al-mu}}$ŠID × A$^{\text{um-bi-sag-ga-ku}}$ = ^{d}al-mu

$^{\text{d.al-la-ma}}$ŠID × A = ^{d}al-la-mu

SANGA+DUB?, DUB = *ZATU* No. 86 p. 188. In Ur-III Lagaš, DUB = dub or kišib "to transcribe the (contents of the small) records (onto another document)" (*Maekawa 1997*, 118–120). DUB = dab$_6$ = "to encircle, surround" (*Mirelman-Sallaberger 2010*, 183). SANGA.DUB is attested to under *ZATU* No. 444 p. 268. *MSVO 1* pp. 96 and 138. On DUB = "tablet" see *Krebernik-Postage 2009*, 18, register. Also see above, # 69.

Most likely alternative seems to be SANGA + DUB.

(8') UZ + BULUG$_3$: UZ = *ZATU* No. 611 p. 309, also a kind of tribute. The lexeme occurs in Fara-age personal names, but only once (*Visicato 1997*, 104). For "uz- und u$_5$ am Anfang der Namen von Wasservögeln" see *Keetman 2012*, 33. On the later e$_2$-uz-ga see *Dahl 2006*, 83 and *Allred 2006*, 72–80. Jeremiah Peterson now translates "goose" (*Peterson 2007*, 49). In later ED Ur, sundry ducks were actually registered upon delivery (*Alberti-Pomponio 1986*, 86–88 ad text 35).

BULUG$_3$ = DIM$_4$ = MUNU$_4$ = see above, # 1. "Malt"? "Malster"?

"Tribute of She who fosters growth?"

(9') Is most difficult to decipher. The simplest solution would be AB = EŠ$_3$ + GAL. AB = *ZATU* No. 7 p. 170, GAL = *ZATU* No. 188 p. 207. In Ur-III texts, GAL = "Prunkbecher, Trinkgefäß", of metal, usually gold or silver, sometimes of copper or bronze, rarely of wood; weighed ⅓ to 1 mina of metal (= 166–500 g); assumed various forms including the "pine cone" (*Paoletti 2012*, 147). *Steinkeller 1995*, 696 sub No. 7: AB is also a graph for UNUG.

(10') NUN + TU + BU: NUN = see above, # 1. "Noble", "Noble (= Enki)"? = "The city of Eridu"?

TU = *ZATU* No. 554 p. 295 (city, tribute, fish). *Steinkeller 1995*, 700 sub No. 56: BU may have had a value of /muš/. *MSVO 1* pp. 93, 131 and 152. TU = Akk. *dû* = "platform in a cella" (*Scharlach 2000*, 135–136, sub text # 1621). In ED Lagaš TU = tu = tu^{mušen} = "Taube"; the sign may also be read dú, du$_8$ and durun, being a *hamtu*-root of the verb dú = "gebären" (*Meyer-Laurin 2011*, 53). ^{d}TU = "Muttergöttin", ED writing for a lexeme most probably equal to ša$_3$-tur$_3$ = *šassūru* = "uterus" (*Cavigneaux-Krebernik 1998–2001*, 507, see also *Steible-Yildiz 2008*, 158–159). TU = "mouton-TU" (*Lafont 2008*, 4, col. A: 10, 5 col. C: 6, Word List C, Ur-III period), as well as *Civil 2013*, 31 ad 10/38 (TU = "qualification of a kind of sheep").

BU = *ZATU* No. 56 p. 181. In ED proverbs BU = verb, of unclear meaning (*Alster 1991–1992*, 8–9). BU = "zerreisen" (*Alster 1992*, 190–191). Gebhard Selz (*Selz 2011b*, 233, sub # 1: 2 and 9:1) suggests bu/-r/ = *nasāḫu* = "herausziehen, herausreißen". In ED Lagaš BU = syllabic ^{geš}GUL-bu = "eine Baumart" = bu-bu-ra "Holzgegenstand" (*Meyer-Laurin 2011*, 55).

"Tribute of the exalted Inanna (muš)? City of the exalted Inanna? Tribute in fish from Eridu? (What has been) brought from Eridu and a City/Temple of Mother Goddess?"

(11') AB$_2$ + KU + KU = UDUL: AB$_2$ = *ZATU* No. 12 p. 171, *MSVO 1* p. 87. AB$_2$ = *littum* = "cow" (*Gelb-Steinkeller-Whiting* 1991, 297). On AB$_2$ cf. *Attinger* 1997, 119–121. On AB$_2$ = "cow" see now *Krebernik-Postage* 2009, 18, register.

KU = *ZATU* No. 300 p. 233, cf. also *Biggs* 1966, 77–78 fn. 37 (Abu Salabikh). In Instructions of Šuruppak, KU-bi-šè = "towards the place belonging to the relevant person", "there where he or she belongs", or simply "there" (*Alster* 1974, 105). In ED Lagaš KU in KU.KU = "die Verstorbenen", from ku = "sich zu Ruhe legen"? (*Meyer-Laurin* 2011, 54); in the same context KU = gu$_5$: gu$_5$-le = "Freund" (*Meyer-Laurin* 2011, 55). KU.KU = durun-durun = durun$_x$ (*Gelb-Steinkeller-Whiting* 1991, 55). KU.KU = DÚR.DÚR = TUŠ.TUŠ = "i residenti" (*Chiodi* 1997, 65–66). An ED proverb has DÚR(.DÚR) = érin as sedentary people subject to judiciary procedures (*Alster* 1991–1992, 17 l. 155, 19 l. 199, 29 and 31). *Ibid.* line 199: sikil ki-dúr-me nu-mu-da-gi$_4$-gi$_4$ = "a girl will not return into our house" (as she will marry an outsider), so again dúr = to reside permanently. UTUL = *ZATU* No. 610 p. 309. See also *Rosengarten* 1960, 90–91 fn. 4. AB$_2$.KU = unud$_x$ = "cowherd", also in Fara-age texts (*Steinkeller-Postgate* 1992, 21). AB$_2$.KU = /unud/= "Kühe hütend", AB$_2$.KU.KU is either a professional designation with reduplicated base or simply plural, reading of sign unknown (*Bauer* 2001–2002, 170, sub S. 172; *Bauer* 2004).

(12') *UET II* : 80, hapax legomenon. Among the possibilites:

RU = *ZATU* No. 435 p. 265, a site. Could this be a rudimentary NI + RU? Not attested to at Uruk, Jemdet Nasr only. See above, # 5.

Or is this

UH$_3$ = UMMA = see above, # 36. *ZATU* No. 579 p. 302? *Steinkeller* 1995, 710 sub No. 579: value UH$_3$ uncertain.

(13') Possibly NAGA = EREŠ$_2$ = NISABA$_2$ = UGA: *ZATU* No. 381 p. 250. *MSVO 1* p. 127. Appears in the Uruk-III City List (*Johnson* 2014a, 46, *Cities* 7, 46). *Visicato* 1989 subsumes the ED city list (Lista delle città): copies known from Abu Salabikh, Fara, Ur and Uruk, lists the cities of Ur, Nippur, Larsa, Uruk, Keš, Zabalam, Ereš. UD.UNUG = Larsa; ereš$_2^{ki}$ = ŠE.NAGA, identical with the Fara domain, possibly the ki-en-gi confederation (*Frayne* 2008b, 7–12). For NAGA as a kind of plant (myrtle?) see *Volk* 1990.

Cities, lands, dignitaries, institutions, personnel?

* * *

94. *UE III* : 431	U 14 896 B	UM 31-16-654	SIS 4

Catalogue: "Ur SIS 4 /later than 31-16-604 at A/". Obverse: the same inscription as in my No. 93, 95 and 96. Three impressions of a countermark seal with rosette. All diameters = 21.1 mm. Reverse: A peg coiled around by a cord protrudes from a coarse and uneven surface with organic imprints. Peg: r = 5 mm, thus d = 10 mm. Cord:

CT = 1,95 mm	ST = 1.3 mm	SI = 2.85 mm	Z-spin

Red-brown clay without visible admixtures. The peg impression shows traces of a tissue of fine paralel fibres, possibly wood. Imprints of fine hair on cord impressions.

For the inscription see above, # 93.

Cities, lands, dignitaries, institutions, personnel?

* * *

95. *UE III* : 431	U 18 392 or -8 (*recte* 18 398, see *UE III* p. 40)	UM 33-35-297	Pit W, SIS 4-5

Catalogue: "Ur PG. PIT W SIS IV–V, Found in Storage 1989". Obverse: an inscription identical to my Nos. 93, 94 and 96. Reverse heavily damaged and illegible. Red-brown clay without visible admixtures.

For the inscription see above, # 93.

Cities, lands, dignitaries, institutions, personnel?

* * *

96. *UE III* : 431	U 18 398	849	UM 33-35-298	Pit W. SIS 4-5

Catalogue: "Ur PG. PIT W. SIS IV–V, Found in Storage 1989". Obverse: inscription identical with that of my Nos. 93, 94 and 95. It may have been counter-marked by a rosette seal, of a d = 10 mm. The circumference of the relevant cylinder seal would thus be 31.4 mm, and so the possibility of counter-marking with the seal butt may be real. Reverse: imprint of a peg protruding from a smoothed surface and coiled around by cord. The base of the peg assumes a conical shape. The sealing was taken off the respective object while the clay was still wet, and pressed together so that a lobe of pliable clay adhering to the peg was pressed inside the hollow left by it. Peg: r = 8 mm, thus d = 16 mm. Cord: only the CT = 1.8 mm can be measured. Red-brown grainy clay, admixture of sand.

For the inscription see above, # 93.

Cities, lands, dignitaries, institutions, personnel?

* * *

A

97. *UE III* : 432	U 14 115	UM 31-16-651	SIS 4

See *Matthews 1993*, 115 = *Scott 2005*, 52, and http://www.cdli.ucla.edu/search/search_results.php?order=ObjectType&SealID=S006301 [accessed March 6, 2014]. Catalogue: "Ur SIS 4 (or 5), probably lower than SIS 4". Obverse: impressions of two cylinder seals with inscriptions. Impressions of fine parallel fibres, and also those crossing each other, in between both impressions. Wood or textile, or both? Texts: DIN, X, E_2, MU.X.X., MU.GIŠ.DU. The other: TI or BALA.GAR, TI or BALA.BA or IGI, TI + KU or LU GUR(?), X. Reverse: a peg coiled around with cord protrudes out of an even surface. Peg: r = 22 mm, thus d = 44 mm. Cord: CT = 2.4 mm, nothing else can be measured. Red-brown clay without visible admixtures. Fingerprints.

Inscription I: *UE III* : Pl. 24 upper left, from upper left to lower right:

Upper line:

(1') : missing

(2') : ŠILAM(?) = *ZATU* No. 648 p. 316. *Krecher 1983*, 187 : šilam = "Mutterkuh". The Late-Uruk sign ZATU No. 648 may refer to a "temple household" (*Englund 1995b*, 127). On cattle-keeping in early Mesopotamia see now *Pientka-Hinz 2011*.

(3') : BALA + DU_3 (= RU_2, KAK) + X + X: BALA = *ZATU* No. 46 p. 179, *MSVO 1* p. 91. BALA is supposed to be "term of office" (*Klein 1991*, 125 fn. 10). The formula nu-bala-bala = *nakārum* = "to change", "to violate" comes up as early as the Fara-age texts (*Gelb-Steinkeller-Whiting 1991*, 246). In Instructions of Šuruppak bal, bala = "to turn around", "to change", the motion of a revolving spindle whorl (*Alster 1974*, 89–90). In Fara-age texts, bala+personal name = "term of office of PN" (*Steinkeller 1989*, 111, § 2.17.2). In ED Lagaš, BALA = "Pfründe, Pacht", literally "Übertragenes" (*Selz 1995*, 226 fn. 1091). DU_3 (= RU_2, KAK): *ZATU* No. 280 p. 227, or *ZATU* No. 659 p. 317 (reading unknown), *MSVO 1* pp. 116 and 163. *Krebernik 1993–1994*, 90: du_3 = "aufpflanzen", *Bauer 1989–1990*, p. 83: sag-du_3 = "wörtlich: das Haupt aufrichtend", *Steinkeller 1989*, 52–54: du_3 = "to hold on". In ED proverbs, DU_3 = "to build a house" in the sense of "to establish a household" (*Alster 1991–1992*, 28). nig_2-du_3-a is a measure of fruit, possibly "what holds together" ("festhalten"), that is, a bundle. nig_2-du_3(-a) = /šer-ku/ = "a string of dried fruit", replaced in Uruinimigina's inscriptions by the expression sag-$keš_2$ (*Selz 1995*, p. 33 fn. 106). In Fara nig_2-du_3 = "Maß-Behältnis für Feigen und Äpfel" (*Steible-Yildiz 2008*, 167). DU_3 = *kullum* = "to detain", "to hold". It might originally have been an intransitive verb, meaning something like "to hold on" (property). Does this mean that on seals, items transferred to the property of the adressee are so denoted (*Gelb-Steinkeller-Whiting 1991*, 247)?. Šuruppak: AL-DU_3 = "worked with the hoe", also in ED-IIIb Girsu. Ur III texts distinguish between al-du_3 and al-ak, with the former taking about three times less time than the latter (*Pomponio-Visicato 1994*, 222). Texts from Abu Salabikh know a person named DU_3.A.X, possibly from Umma (*Krebernik-Postgate 2009*, 16). In ED Lagaš, al___dù = "mit der Hacke anlegen" (*Selz 1995*, 244 fn. 1177).

"Vegetation season (other than BALA.NAGAR)"?

Middle line:

(4') : missing.

(5') : LIBIR: not in *ZATU* but in *MEA* No. 231 p. 203 = "old" = *CAD* L p. 27 s. v. *labīru* = libir (*UET II* : 244). *Englund 1990*, 39 fn. 133: LIBIR = "alt" (fruit). *De Maaijer-Jagersma 1997–1998*, 287: libir = "backlog in an account, not age". As against this, cf. *Mallul 1989* for niĝir-libir-si, a paranymph seeking brides for prospective husbands, also a public dignitary who wears a weapon by his side and who pays for his office, first attested to in the "Instructions of Šuruppak". Also *Behrens 1998*, 129–130. In Šuruppak, libir = "old", also in the sense of a previous allocation (*Pomponio 1987*, 178), such as a "preceding" grain harvest (*Pomponio 1987*, 199).

"Arrears"?

(6') : GIŠ + MU + DU : GIŠ = *ZATU* No. 223 p. 215, MU = *ZATU* No. 363 p. 246, DU = *ZATU* No. 82 p. 187. GIŠ = tribute, MU.DU = a delivery, a disbursement, tax(?), cf. *Selz 1995*, 149 fn. 624 = "herrichten". On wood in early Sumer see now *Selz 2011b*. *Bauer 1989–1990*, 79: mu-DU "er hat hergebracht". In Šuruppak, mu-DU probably refers to the typology of the denoted text, being the only evidence item there, as all other texts have ba-DU (*Pomponio-Visicato 1994*, 196). But mu-DU may also mean "secured", "commanded to be carried out" there (*Visicato 2000*, 155 fn. 220, 160). Cf. *Englund 1988*, 145 fn. 18 on MU in archaic texts (quantities of foodstuffs, a type of grain or grain product; neither "year" nor "cook"). DU = *MSVO 1* p. 95, GIŠ = *MSVO 1* p. 111, MU = *MSVO 1* p. 125.In ED Lagaš DU = du, a *marû*-root of ĝen = "gehen", "stehen", "bringen", "geleiten", "eintreten", "mischen" (*Meyer-Laurin 2011*, 53, 212).

"A kind of delivery"?

(7') : GIŠIMMAR + UZ : GIŠIMMAR = *ZATU* No. 230 p. 217, *MSVO 1* p. 112. Appears in the Uruk-III City List (*Johnson 2014a*, 46, *Cities* 69).Gišimmar = "date palm" (*Gelb-Steinkeller-Whiting 1991*, 215). The prisoners-of-war of the newly published Kish plaque were set to work in date-palm orchards (*Steinkeller 2013*, 132). UZ = *ZATU* No. 611 p. 309, possibly a tribute. UZ = *ūsu* = duck, other than *paspasu*, Old Akkadian (*Steinkeller-Postgate 1992*, 57). For "uz- und u_5 am Anfang der Namen von Wasservögeln" see *Keetman 2012*, 33. Jeremiah Peterson now translates "goose" (*Peterson 2007*, 49). The lexeme occurs in Fara-age personal names, but only once (*Visicato 1997*, 104). In later ED Ur, sundry ducks were actually registered upon delivery (*Alberti-Pomponio 1986*, 86–88 ad text 35). On the later e_2-uz-ga see *Dahl 2006*, 83 and *Allred 2006*, 72–80. Other possibilities are $BULUG_3$ = *ZATU* No. 62 p. 183, or DANNA = *ZATU* No. 68 p. 184.

"Date palms of the demesne holding(s)"?

DA : *ZATU* No. 65 p. 183, also a tree. Could be also read SANGA = *ZATU* No. 444 p. 268, but in view of the sign form in *MSVO 1* p. 138 this does not seem likely. *MSVO 1*, text 154 quoted on p. 138 has EN PAP DU SANGA. A group of thirteen archaic texts from Umma(?) contains the sign group DA_a Pa_a, chiefly in connection with sheep (*Monaco 2007*, 4, 8). Da-bulug^{ninda} is a container wherein loaves of bread, but also arrows may be kept, or it might be a kind of pastry (*Visicato 2000*, 182 fn. 539). "Verbales da" = "to leave", "abfahren", "aufsteigen" (*Sallaberger 1993*, 181 fn. 851).

"A kind of container"?

(8') : DIN + SAL + E_2: DIN = *ZATU* No. 79 p. 186, a container. *MEA* No. 465 p. 209: *balāṭu* = "to live", and *šikaru* = "beer", "beverage". See also http://psd.museum.upenn.edu/epsd/nepsd-frame.html [accessed September 29, 2014] s. v. kurun = "a beer; blood; (to be) good; (to be) sweet". In ancient land-sale documents, the lexeme DUG.$SILA_3$, with a variant DIN.$SILA_3$, means something like "a purchase" or "alienation" (*Gelb-Steinkeller-Whiting 1991*, 28–30). This container sign could thus have a wider meaning, referring to a symbolical act in property transfers. SAL = *ZATU* No. 443 p. 267; E_2 = *ZATU* No. 129 p. 196. In Šuruppak, E_2 can also refer to a cluster of arable fields, "agricultural district" (*Pomponio 1987*, 298). In ED personal names, E_2 could stand for the god Ea (*Krebernik-Postgate 2009*, 15 s. v. E_2).

"(Produce in) containers of the Female House"?

Lower line:

Fragments only, of which only DU and GAR + GAR (= NINDA + NINDA?, see above, # 54) may be read. GAR = *ZATU* No. 196 p. 209.

Produce of trees, both in wood and in juices?

Inscription II: *UE III* Pl. 24 upper right:

Only two lines of the middle line can be read more clearly:

(10') : GAN_2 + URU + BA + TI: URU = *ZATU* No. 597 p. 306. In Šuruppak, URU is a "town" in the sense of an administrative centre of state economic enterprises (*Pomponio 1987*, 95–96). BA = *ZATU* No. 40 p. 178, also a tribute, ba-ki (*ZATU* No. 289 p. 230). GAN_2 = *ZATU* No. 195 p. 209. In Šuruppak, gána = "arable land" (*Pomponio 1987*, 217). GÁNA = gán = "Feld" (*Wilcke 1996*, 4 fn. 10). Gán = field (*Gelb-Steinkeller-Whiting 1991*, 213–214). TI = *ZATU* No. 551 p. 294. *Selz 1995*, 266 fn. 1289: TI = "leben, Leben" (to live). *Yoshikawa 1988*, 62 fn. 9: ti = to receive. In Šuruppak, ba-ti is exclusively a personal name (*Pomponio 1987*, 56, with ref.). The Abu Salabikh texts probably use TI in the /di/ value (*Meyer-Laurin 2011*, 210 fn. 289). In later ED Ur, we know of a personal name lugal-lú-ti-ti = "... gives life to men" (*Alberti-Pomponio 1986*, 39). In ED Lagaš, TI = "leben, Leben" (*Selz 1995*, 266 fn. 1289). In the same context, TI = ti = "sich annähern", but also ti = "Pfeil", and in syllabic use (*Meyer-Laurin 2011*, 48). Lexical lists from Ebla include the entry TI = *(w)ašābu* = *šubtu* = *mūšabu* (*Mayer 2005*, 163, ## 78–80).

"Delivered (tribute from the) fields of the city"? "Fields of those who live in the city"?

(11') : KI + UDU + DAB_5 + TI : DAB_5 = *ZATU* No. 300 p. 233, *Englund 1990*, 236–237: dab_5 = "(Fisch)fangen". TI = see above. *Rosengarten 1960*, 391–395 on díb = DAB_5 = "prendre en main, entreprendre, recevoir". UDU, LU = *ZATU* No. 575 p. 300. KI = *ZATU* No. 289 p. 230. In ED proverbs, the LU sign is interpreted as "to multiply" (*Alster 1991–1992*, 13 ad line 68, 15 ad line 68 and 15 ad line 99, 19 ad line 203, translations on pp. 20–21, comments on p. 31). In ED Lagaš, DAB_5 = "übernehmen" (*Selz 1995*, 81 fn. 336), also "packen" (*Zgoll 1997*, 405–406).

"Delivered and received (tribute from the) 'place of sheep' (= pastures?)"?

I do not dare to put forward any reasonable assumptions as to the reading of signs in lines 1 and 3.

Revenue from grain fields, orchards and from "land occupied by the sheep"?

The two seals may visualize storage of orchardry-, field- and livestock produce.

***

98. *UE III* : 433	U 14 883	UM 31-16-653	SIS 4

See *Matthews 1993*, 118 = *Scott 2005*, 90, and http://www.cdli.ucla.edu/search/search_results.php?order=ObjectType&SealID=S006304 [accessed March 6, 2014]. Catalogue: "SIS 4, A". Obverse: inscription. KI?, KI or NA?, U_3 + $EŠ_3$, NIM, DU.NIM, GAR?, X, DIM_2 or UR_2. Reverse: heavily weathered. A tapering wreath-like feature of conical form may be guessed to have protruded from a once even surface. Red-brown clay without visible admixtures.

Inscription:

Upper line:

(1') : X (destroyed)

(2') : X

(3') : KI? = *ZATU* No. 289 p. 230, *MSVO 1* p. 118.

Middle line:

(4') : GADA + DU : GADA: *ZATU* No. 186 p. 207, mostly in textile accounts. *Bauer 1989–1990*, 90: gada = "Leinen(kleid)". Gada = *kitûm* = "linen(cloth)" (*Gelb-Steinkeller-Whiting 1991*, 294). Establishments called na-gada + DIVINE NAME were probably cattle-breeding stations operated by particular temples (*Visicato 2000*, 37). NA.GADA = *nāqidum* = "shepherd" (*Gelb-Steinkeller-Whiting 1991*, 185). In later ED Ur, distribution of heads of cattle to temples and to secular recipients seems to have been done under royal supervision (*Alberti-Pomponio 1986*, 98–99 ad text 45). See below, # 106 (*UE III*: 442), upper column, line 1'. See also http://psd.museum.upenn.edu/epsd/nepsd-frame.html [accessed September 29, 2014] s. v. gada. GADA = "linen" (*Marchesi 2011*, 190–191).

"Delivery of linen"?

DU = *ZATU* No. 82 p. 187, *MSVO 1* p. 95. Cf. supra, text 1678 # 97 : I : 6'. In Šuruppak, ba-DU = "he has supplied", "has been supplied" (*Pomponio-Visicato 1994*, 293). In Šuruppak texts, we find also mu-DU, probably referring to the typology of the denoted text, being the only evidence item there, as all other texts have ba-DU (*Pomponio-Visicato 1994*, 196). But mu-DU may also mean "secured", "commanded to be carried out" there (*Visicato 2000*, 155 fn. 220, 160).

(5') : GADA : see above, # 27 (*UE III*: 142), upper line, 1', and below, # 106 (*UE III*: 442), upper column, line 1', and # 143. "Linen".

(6') : GAN_2 + LIBIR : GAN_2 = *ZATU* No. 195 p. 209, *MSVO 1* pp. 105–106. In Šuruppak, gána = arable land" (*Pomponio 1987*, 217). GÁNA = gán = "Feld" (*Wilcke 1996*, 4 fn. 10). Gán = field (*Gelb-Steinkeller-Whiting 1991*, 213–214). LIBIR = not in *ZATU* but in *MEA* No. 231 p. 203 = "old" = *CAD* L p. 27 s. v. *labīru* = libir (*UET II* : 244). *Englund 1990*, 39 fn. 133: LIBIR = "alt" (fruit). *De Maaijer-Jagersma 1997–1998*, 287: libir = "backlog in an account, not age". As against this, cf. *Mallul 1989* for niĝir-libir-si, a paranymph seeking out brides for prospective husbands, also a public dignitary who wears a weapon by his side and who pays for his office, first attested to in the "Instructions of Šuruppak". See also

Behrens 1998, 129–130. In Šuruppak, libir = "old", also in the sense of a previous allocation (*Pomponio* 1987, 178), such as a "preceding" grain harvest (*Pomponio* 1987, 199).

"Arrears from fields"? "Preceding (harvest) from fields"?

Lower line:

(7') : ŠIDIM = see above, # 1. "Architect"? "Builder"?

(8') : GIŠGAL : *UET II* : 337 (= *LAK* No. 597 p. 57), missing in *ZATU* but listed by *MEA* No. 19 p. 57: GIŠGAL = *manzāzu*, "a place", GAL$_3$ = "servant", and also "south, southern wind", as well as ULU$_3$ = "humankind". Component of Fara-age personal names (*Visicato* 1997, 43). Also in the same sense in ED Lagaš (*Selz* 1995, 285 fn. 1417).

"Southerners"?

Storage of textile products?

* * *

99. *UE III*: 434 = *Matthews* 1993, 121 = *Scott* 2005, 472	Toponyms: GAL??, X, GAN$_2$ or AK, URU?, GAN$_2$ or AK, X; spread eagle, SUR, LU$_2$, X	Door peg	*Edinnu*?, d. 2.0, a City League seal countermarked *edinnu*

Inscription:

GAN$_2$ = see above, # 28. "Field"? "Arable"?

AK = see above, # 41. "Ritual"? "Sacrifice"?

URU = see above, # 56. "Town"? "City"?

SUR = see http://psd.museum.upenn.edu/epsd/nepsd-frame.html [accessed September 29, 2014] s. v. kisura = border. Also, SUR = "half", but also "to press (e.g. oil from sesame)" (*Spada 2011*, 220, § 16, 1.iii.58; 226, § 23; 244). Moreover, sur = *ṭawû, ṭamû, ṭemû* = "to bind", e.g. whips or textiles (*al-Mutawalli 2010*, 54). In Ur-III texts sur = "(zusammen)drehen" in textile industry (*Paoletti 2012*, 162 s. v. sur-sur-ra).

LU_2(?) = see above, # 5. See also http://psd.museum.upenn.edu/epsd/nepsd-frame.html [accessed September 29, 2014] s. v. lu_2 = "who(m), which; man; (s)he who, that which; of; ruler; person".

Deliveries of produce from geographically distinct entities for a ritual?

* * *

100. *UE III* : 436	U 18 397	933	UM 33-35-294	Pit W, SIS 4-5

See *Matthews 1993*, 74 = *Scott 2005*, 27, and http://www.cdli.ucla.edu/search/search_results.php?order=ObjectType&SealID=S006260 [accessed March 6, 2014]. Catalogue: "Ur PG. PIT W. SIS IV–V ". Obverse: an inscription. Perhaps the prow of MAGUR, ÚR, KIN, UDU + X and a spouted storage jar. Legrain reads "ur ub kin en(?)". Reverse: impressions of wide and shallow folds of soft pliable tissue. Red-brown clay without visible admixtures.

Inscription:

X,

UR_4 = see above, # 58. "To shear (sheep)".

DUG ? = see above, # 35. "Pot?" "Merchandise?" "Human individual?"

UDU = *ZATU* No. 575 p. 300, *MSVO 1* pp. 158–159. Sheep.

X,

UR_2? = see above, # 12. "Lap", "crotch", "sexual organs", "fecundation ritual".

"Potted(?) clip of sheep wool for a fecundation ritual (?)".

* * *

101. *UE III*: 437 = *Matthews 1993*, 120 = *Scott 2005*, 474	Toponyms(?): DU_8??, AB + AN(?), X, $KUŠ_2$ or $ŠUR_2$	?Reed fastening	Rosette

Inscription:

DU_8 = see above, # 59. "Open"? "Finished"? "Bringing plenty"? "Age set"?

$KUŠ_2$ or $ŠUR_2$ = see http://psd.museum.upenn.edu/epsd/nepsd-frame html [accessed October 2, 2014] s. v. $kuš_2$ = tired, troubled, admittedly does not give much sense here, and http://psd.museum.upenn.edu/epsd/nepsd-frame .html [accessed October 2, 2014] s. v. $šur_2$ = furious, angry. Again, this does not give much sense, unless it is related to tumu $šur_2$ = "wind", see http://psd .museum.upenn.edu/epsd/nepsd-frame.html [accessed October 2, 2014] s. v. tumu, as a geographical indication of the origin of the goods deposited here ("quarter of the world", "cardinal point").

"Complete (deliveries to the City League) from the South"?

* * *

102. *UE III*: 438 = *Scott 2005*, 475	Toponyms(?): E_2+UR_2, NIN, PIRIG?, DU_6, GA_2 × AN or $ESIR_2$ or defective writing for I_7?	??	No counter-mark

Inscription:

E_2 = see above, # 1. "House", "agricultural district", "kin group"?.

UR_2 = see above, # 12. "Lap", "crotch", "sexual organs", "fecundation ritual".

NIN = see http://psd.museum.upenn.edu/epsd/nepsd-frame.html [accessed October 2, 2014] s. v. nin = "lady, mistress, owner, lord".

PIRIG = see http://psd.museum.upenn.edu/epsd/nepsd-frame.html [accessed October 2, 2014] s. v. pirig = "lion, bull, wild bull". The third-millennium Lagaš catchment area included a hill called DU_6 ANŠE/PIRIG $BABBAR_2$: *André-Salvini 2012*. Is PIRIG.KALAM in an archaic plaque from Kish (*Steinkeller 2013*, 138 ad v 2') a toponym?

DU_6 = see http://psd.museum.upenn.edu/epsd/nepsd-frame.html [accessed October 2, 2014] s. v. dud, du_6 = "mound", and *Cohen 1993*, 106–112 (*apud Mařík 2005*, 45–49). On DU_6 KU_3, a "sacred hill", the Anunnaki were born; it is a "place where destinies are determined" and "where heaven and earth embrace" (*Suriano 2012*, 220, 221 fn. 55). Possibly (also) a hill in a temple (*Suriano 2012*, 223), or a hill on which a temple is standing: see *Selz 2011b*, 244, "Skizze einer Idealflur". SAHAR.DU_6.TAG_4 is interpreted as "burial tell" (*Richardson 2007*, 193–194; *Suriano 2012*, 218–219). On DU_6 as a mythical locality linked with Sumerian cosmological and funerary ideas see most recently *Selz 2014a*, 207- 212. See also above s. v. PIRIG.

May GA_2xAN be interpreted as $ESIR_2$ or as defective writing for I_7? See above, # 92.

"NIN's penned animals of the Mound for the House of the Fecundation Ritual"?

* * *

103. *UE III*: 439 = *Matthews 1993*, 122 = *Scott 2005*, 476	X, X, X, X, GAN, X	Door peg	Rosette

Inscription:

GAN = see http://psd.museum.upenn.edu/epsd/nepsd-frame.html [accessed October 2, 2014]

s. v. šaĝan = flask, also *ibid*. s. v. ganum = "(vessel-)stand; a large vessel", OB ^{ĝeš}gan-nu-um, so possibly of wood.

* * *

104. *UE III*: 440 = *Matthews 1993*, 100 = *Scott 2005*, 477	DIM, DIŠ(?), MAGUR, $NINDA_2$ or NE, DIŠ(?), GAN, X	Matthews: ?, Scott: pot	Rosette

Inscription:

DIM = see http://psd.museum.upenn.edu/epsd/nepsd-frame.html [accessed October 2, 2014] s. v. dim = post, also knot, bond."Pole, band, knot" (*Selz 2011d*, 293 ad 3: 2).

DIŠ = *ZATU* No. 81 p. 187. Breadth? Or is this simply a column-division line?

MAGUR = see http://psd.museum.upenn.edu/epsd/nepsd-frame.html [accessed October 2, 2014] s. v. magur "barge".

$NINDA_2$ = see above, # 12. "Part of a plough"? "A kind of fish"?.

GAN = see above, # 103. "(Vessel-)stand; a large vessel"? "Container (possibly of wood)"?.

Delivery of seafood or fish???

* * *

105. *UE III*: 441 = *Matthews 1993*, 119 = Scott 2005, 478	SU_3, U_4, GIŠ, DU. BA, $GARA_2$, NUN, TI, X. DUB, animal head. X; SAL?, X, SAL+X?, X. ŠE+NAM_2 .	Test strip	No counter-mark

Inscription:

SU$_3$ = http://psd.museum.upenn.edu/epsd/nepsd-frame.html [accessed October 2, 2014] s. v. su$_3$ = "Empty, naked, strip". In ED Lagaš SUD = SU$_3$ = sù.ŕ = "lang sein", "entfernt sein", sù.g = "leer sein", "leer machen", "nackt sein", sù.g = "voll sein", sù = "erstatten" (*Meyer-Laurin 2011*, 56, 65).

U$_4$ = see above, # 32. "Day"? "Time of the day"?.

GARA$_2$ = see http://psd.museum.upenn.edu/epsd/nepsd-frame.html [accessed October 2, 2014] s. v. gara = "cream". In texts presumably from Jemdet Nasr, GARA$_2$ = "dairy products" (*Monaco 2007*, 251, *apud* CUSAS 1, 187). In the archaic Ur version of the LU$_2$ A list, GAL.GARA$_2$ corresponds to GAL.GA of Uruk, wherefore Camille Lecompte suggests an Ur reading GARA$_2$ for the Uruk GA (*Lecompte 2013*, 148).

NUN (= AGARGARA, ERIDU) = see above, # 1. "Noble", "Noble (= Enki)"? = "The city of Eridu"?

TI = see http://psd.museum.upenn.edu/epsd/nepsd-frame.html [accessed October 2, 2014] s. v. til = "to live, to sit (down), to dwell".

Does the sign group BA, GARA$_2$, NUN, TI indicate a personal name NUN-ba-gara$_2$-ti, "Enki gives life to Bagara?"

DUB = see above, ## 54 and 69. "Tablet, scribe, laborer?"?

SAL = see above, # 21. "Woman, female".

ŠE + NAM$_2$ = see above, # 93. A dignitary and a toponym. "Feeder"? Association of delivering agencies (personalities)?

* * *

106. *UE III* : 442	U 13 969	UM 31-16-644	SIS 4

See *Matthews 1993*, 117 = *Scott 2005*, 88, and http://www.cdli.ucla.edu/search/search_results.php?order=ObjectType&SealID=S006303 [accessed March 10, 2014]. Catalogue: "SIS 4". Obverse: an inscription. GAL.UNUG, ušu-búr, tur-dim... é-ki... lú-šu...? Reverse: impressions of cord coiled around a cylindrical object with smooth surface. Peg(?): r = 27 mm, thus d = 54 mm. Only the CT = 7.9 mm can be measured on the cord imprint. Traces of fine fibres on the cord impression. Orange- to ochre clay without visible admixtures, fingerprints.

Inscription: From left to right and from top to bottom:

Upper column:

(1') GADA = see above, # 27, # 98 and below, # 143. "Linen".

(2') LU_2.TAK_4: LU_2 = *ZATU* No. 332 p. 239, *MSVO 1* p. 122; TAK_4 = *ZATU* No. 548 p. 293, *MSVO 1* p. 151. *Steinkeller 1995*, 709 sub No. 548: save for vertical orientation, the sign is identical with *ZATU* 532 = ŠU. *Ibid*. sub No. 532: the occurrences of *ZATU* 532 and *ZATU* 548 in *Metal* 24–25 and 42–43 (*ATU 3* pp. 136–137) are consistently interpreted as ŠU in the corresponding ED mss. (MEE 3 pp. 79-80 lines 24–25 and 42–43). In ED times the distinction between ŠU and TAK_4 thus does not appear to have been meaningful any more. Yet, Niek Veldhuis (1995, 436) observes that these are two different signs, confused in lexical lists, in which rotation (TAK_4 = ŠU rotated 90°) distinguishes different functions of the same sign. *Civil 1990*: "to send" = an errand boy? TAK_4 = "zurückhalten" (*Selz 1993*, 220–221). In Instructions of Šuruppak, TAK_4 (here TAG_4) means something like "to touch" (*Alster 1974*, 44–45 ad line 203).

The TAK_4.ALAN ceremony is attested to in Šuruppak texts, in ED LU_2, at Ebla (with a reading *la-a-núm*) and at Nippur. The Šuruppak texts mention a structure called é-TAK_4.ALAN. It may refer to a statue in a votive inscription (ABW 2 p. 342) (*Pomponio 1987*, 474). TAK_4.ALAN is likely to denote a statue and possibly also a sculptor (*Gelb-Steinkeller-Whiting 1991*, 69). In Abu Salabikh, TAK_4.ALAN = lan_x; UD-lan_x could mean an-lan_x = "scolpire il divino" = "to carve a deity" (*Mander 1986*, 52). In ED Lagaš, a number of statues and one stele received regular offerings on festive occasions in the É-$šag_4$ shrine, of a square ground-plan with square side 3.715 metres long (*Rosengarten 1960*, 162). On statues see most recently *Dahl 2011*.

The ceremony may be depicted on a cylinder seal found in the Jemdet-Nasr level at Ur (*Legrain 1951*, 11, No. 30 on Pl. 2) and on the seal UE III: 385.

In ED-IIIb inscriptions, SAHAR.DU_6.TAG_4 may mean "burial tell", with translation of TAG_4 as "leave behind" (*Richardson 2007*, 193–194; *Suriano 2012*, 218 fn. 36, in general 218–219). Is there any connection with burial ceremonies?

(3') E_2.KI (just like Burrows): E_2 = *ZATU* No. 129 p. 196. An e_2 [ ] ki does exist. Also *MSVO 1* pp. 98–99. In Šuruppak, E_2 can also refer to a cluster of arable fields, "agricultural district" (*Pomponio 1987*, 298). In ED personal names, E_2 could stand for the god Ea (*Krebernik-Postgate 2009*, 15 s. v. E_2). KI = *ZATU* No. 289 p. 230, *MSVO 1* p. 118.

(4') ŠID[IM].SILA$_4$: ŠIDIM = *ZATU* No. 524 p. 286, *MSVO 1* p. 146. Food, and possibly also a dignitary. In Abu Salabikh, šitim = "architect" (*Krebernik-Postgate* 2009, 20, register). SILA$_4$ = *ZATU* No. 482 p. 275, also a dignitary? *Steinkeller* 1995, 708 sub No. 482, comments on the sign. In Abu Salabikh sila$_4$-nita = "male lamb" (*Krebernik-Postgate 2009*, 20, register). Sila$_4$-nim = *ḫurāpu* = spring lamb (*Steinkeller-Postgate* 1992, 35). Is it relevant to this place? In ED Lagaš, ŠIDIM = "Baumeister" (*Selz* 1995, 58).

(5') SU$_3$.ŠU$_2$: SU$_3$ = *ZATU* No. 487 p. 277. *Steinkeller* 1995, 708 sub No. 487: "insignificant variant of *ZATU* 56 = BU". ŠU$_2$ = *ZATU* No. 534 p. 289, in textile accounts. See *MSVO 1* pp. 149–150. A text from later ED Ur has a personal name en-bára-si GIŠ.TÚG ^{sù} sug$_x$, where sug$_x$ = PA.SIKIL. The SU$_3$ sign is likely to refer to a goddess named ^{d}kug-sù(g). A number of other references to this lexeme exist. Josef Bauer translates GEŠTUG sù sug as "ripe ear", or "part of an ear", with attestations in archaic Ur and in Fara. Is there any relation to cereals? Does this denote ripening of corn? (*Alberti-Pomponio* 1986, 30).

(6') NIMGIR.GAL: NIMGIR = *ZATU* No. 399 p. 255 = *MSVO 1* p. 130. In the Fara texts, the NIMGIR was in charge of uru-DU = foreign workers probably coming to the city (*Pomponio* 1987, 33) and of the nu-su personnel. He received 1 gur of barley monthly and must have been a rather high official, as only 24 of them are attested to in the Šuruppak texts (*Alberti-Pomponio* 1986, 108; *Pomponio* 1987, 33, 57). In Abu Salabikh, nigir = "herald" (*Krebernik-Postgate* 2009, 20, register). In Early Dynastic Lagaš, the NIMGIR (= nigir) publicly announced sales of houses. For the publication of field sales, another official, the dub-sar lú gán-gíd-da, was responsible. The NIMGIR also carried out the kag___dù and ì___ag ceremonies, consisting of driving a nail into the house wall and smearing its head with oil (*Gelb-Steinkeller-Whiting* 1991, 238 and 241). We know this official also from Early Dynastic Nippur (*Alberti-Pomponio* 1986, 109) and his title appears as component of a host of Early Dynastic, Akkadian and Ur-III personal names (*Alberti-Pomponio* 1986, 109–111). For the later ED Ur cf. *Alberti-Pomponio* 1986, 107–111 (ad text 48), and, in general, *Krispijn* 2008, 183, with ref.

Lower column:
(7'): X;
(8'): ŠIDIM, cf. supra line (4');
(9'): XX;
(10'): X E$_2$ (?);
(11'): X.

A list of institutions and dignitaries? A textile-storage complex?

* * *

107. *UE III*: 443 = *Matthews 1993*, 125 = *Scott 2005*, 479, SIS 2?	NIN TUR DU_3. ŠE TAB X X. $NINDA_2$ or SA_{10}, X. KAŠ+AŠ E_2, X;	??	No counter-mark

Inscription:

NIN = see above, # 102. "Lady, mistress, owner, lord".

TUR = see above, # 9. "(To be) small; to reduce, diminish; to subtract; (to be) young". Also "coral".

ŠE + TAB – any relation to the TAB+BA classification of arable in late ED texts (*Schrakamp 2012a*, 147 sub # 2 Vs. 1)?

NIN TUR – is this the Ninbanda of the "royal graves"?

KAK = DU_3 = RU_2, = see above, # 31: "to enact", "to make something", "to create".

ŠE = see above, # 15. "Grain".

TAB = see http://psd.museum.upenn.edu/epsd/nepsd-frame.html [accessed October 2, 2014] s. v. tab = "to double; to repeat; companion, partner". For še-zar-tab = "barley of a double sheaf" see http://psd.museum.upenn.edu/epsd/nepsd-frame.html [accessed October 2, 2014] s. v. še = "barley". The sign tab/táb = *ḫamātu*, *ṣarāpu* = "brûler"; níg-tab = *naṣraptu* = "crucible"; also "to burn" (leather, sealed document), and "to cause pain" (*Jaques 2006*, 116). In Ur-III texts ad-tab = "bridle, harness, part of the harness", usually from goat hair (ad-tab ur-ra = dog collar, *al-Mutawalli 2010*, 53).

$NINDA_2$ = see above, # 12. "Part of a plough"? "A kind of fish"?

E_2 = see above, # 1. "House"? "Agricultural district"? "Kin group"?

KAŠ + AŠ(?) = *ZATU* No. 287 p. 230 (probably $KAŠ_B$ and $KAŠ_C$) = *MSVO* 1 p. 117 = *UET II*: 344, 350 and 351. An alternative would be DUG = *ZATU* No. 88 p. 189 = *MSVO* 1 pp. 96–97 = *UET II*: 348. *Attinger 1997*, 114: AŠ = "une catégorie de rationnaires?" Persons of minor age usually received lower rations. In Šuruppak, AŠ dub are small sundry tablets from which data were transferred into larger comprehensive texts (dub-gibil: *Pomponio-Visicato 1994*, 306), thus the AŠ sememe carries the idea of "individual", "minor", or the like. On the AŠ lexeme in Fara-age personal names cf. *Visicato 1997*, 21. *Heeßel*

2001–2002, 43: AŠ = *eṭṭūtu* = spindle, in medicine texts. In later ED Ur, a receptacle called HI × AŠ = sùr sometimes assumed gigantic proportions, as no less than 500 minas of copper were needed for its production; the lexeme also denoted a gigantic and cumbersome weapon there (*Alberti-Pomponio 1986*, 97 ad text 44).

Delivery of agricultural products?

* * *

108. *UE III*: 446 = *Matthews 1993*, 36 = *Scott 2005*, 482	GAN_2+X, AB, *Edinnu*	Door peg	Rosette

Inscription:
<u>GAN_2</u> = see above, # 28. "Field"? "Arable"?
<u>AB</u> = see above, # 30. "Household, centre of production, distribution".

* * *

109. *UE III*: 447	U 18 409	853	UM 33-35-383	Pit W SIS 4-5

See *Matthews 1993*, 31 = *Scott 2005*, 63, and http://www.cdli.ucla.edu [accessed March 10, 2014]. SIS 4-6 or 8. Catalogue: "Ur PG. PIT W SIS IV–V, Found in Storage 1989". Obverse: part of Legrain's *Edinnu* sign, a cross resembling in shape a guitar (legcross), a house sign E_2 and what might represent montane tracts. Counter-marked with rosette. Reverse: a complete impression of a short peg, coiled around with a cord, of which the end tapers conically in an outward expansion. Peg: base r = 37 mm, thus d = 74 mm. In its middle part where it is coiled around with the cord, r = 26 mm, thus d = 52 mm. Tapering end: r = 28 mm, thus d = 56 mm. Two coils of cord:

CT = 4.7 mm	ST = 3.3 mm	SI = 11.0 mm	Spin S

Red-brown clay without visible admixtures. Matthews: "lock" (3×).
Inscription:
$\underline{E_2}$ = see above, # 1. "House"? "Agricultural district"? "Kin group"?
Or is this
KID = see above, # 61."Matting"?
UB = see above, # 22. "*Universum*"? "Fortified enclosure"?
Edinnu
Legcross = the inhabited world, *oecumene*? See above, # 62.
"City League".

* * *

110. *UE III*: 454	U 20 083 (U 14 618 in *UE III*)	UM 35-1-672	SIS 4

See *Matthews* 1993, 12 = *Scott* 2005, 239 (22 items on door pegs). Catalogue: "Ur PJ Stratum SIS 4-5, Found in Storage 1989, Accidentally burnt". Obverse: The *Edinnu* sign together with a fylfot (swastika) and four toponym signs. Reverse: heavily damaged, the sealing was probably pressed together by hand after removal from its original position. Impression of a peg coiled around by a cord. Peg: d = 46.7 mm, thus radius = 23.35 mm. Cord:

CT = 4.3 mm	ST = 3.1 mm	SI = 8.2 mm	Spin S

Yellow-brown clay without visible admixtures. Fingerprints.

Matthews and Scott – door peg (22×), unknown (6).

Inscription:

The *Edinnu* sign is surrounded by toponym signs, which, read from the upper left corner anti-clockwise, follow thus:

AB = EŠ$_3$ = see above, # 30. "Household, centre of production, distribution"; "Heiligtum"?

DUG DUG = see above, # 35. "Pot"? "Merchandise"? "Human individual?"

UB = see above, # 22. "*Universum*"? "Fortified enclosure"?

DUG = see above, # 35. "Pot"? "Merchandise"?

NIMGIR = see above, # 5. "Herald".

UNUG = see above, # 32. "The city of Uruk".

U$_4$ = BABBAR = see above, # 32. "Day"? "Time of the day"?

NI = I$_3$ = LID$_2$ = see above, # 72. "City"? "Official"? "Oil"?

An "alliance seal", joining in a union (swastika?) dignitaries of the sites AB = EŠ$_3$, UB, UNUG, and either U$_4$ or NI.

* * *

111. *UE III*: 455 = *Scott 2005*, 488	*Edinnu*, contains DU_3, AB+$AŠ_2$, AB+LAGAB?	??	No counter-mark

Inscription:
KAK = DU_3 = RU_2, = see above, # 31. "To enact", "To make something", "To create".
AB + $AŠ_2$ = see above, # 7. "City elder"? "Wittness"?
"City League"?

* * *

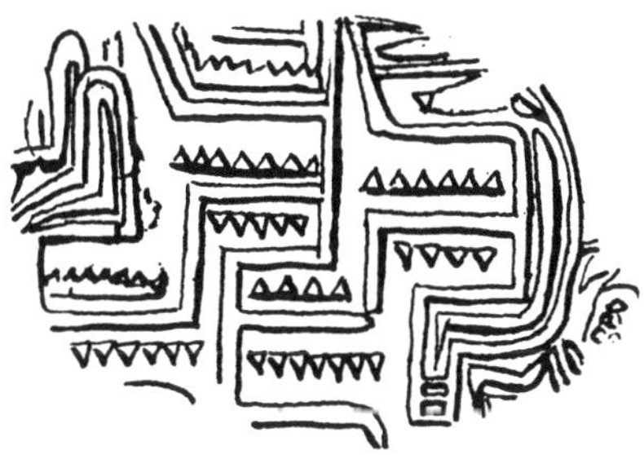

112. *UE III*: 458 = *Matthews 1993*, 66 = *Scott 2005*, 100	*Edinnu*, AN?	"lock"	No counter-mark

See also http://www.cdli.ucla.edu/search/search_results.php?order=ObjectType&SealID=S006252 [accessed March 12, 2014].

Inscription:
AN (DINGIR) – see above, # 17. "Deity"? "Life"?

"City League"?

* * *

113. *UE III* : 460	U 18 401	821	UM 33-35-314	Pit W, SIS 4-5

See *Matthews 1993*, 88 = *Scott 2005*, 24, and http://www.cdli.ucla.edu/search/search_results.php?SearchMode=Text&order=ObjectType&SealID=S006274& [accessed March 12, 2014]. Catalogue: ".Ur PG. PIT W SIS IV–V". Obverse: an oblong infilled by wavy lines, Legrain's reading LUM, and vestiges of an illegible sign, possibly a rosette- or eagle image. Reverse: smooth and quite plain. A tablet, or rather a jar handle. Red-brown clay without visible admixtures.

Inscription(?):

LUM = see above, # 55. "(To be) grown (tall)"? "To fruit"? "(To be) fructified"?

"(Contributed for) fecundation"?

* * *

114. *UE III*: 461 = *Matthews 1993*, 44 = *Scott 2005*, 77	*Edinnu*, swastika, $ŠU_2$	2 test strips, 1 pot without covering	No counter-mark

See also http://www.cdli.ucla.edu/search/search_results.php?order=ObjectType&SealID=S006230 [accessed March 12, 2014].

Inscription:

$\underline{ŠU_2}$ = see above, # 76. "Textile"? "Cover"?

"City League"? Textile delivery?

* * *

115. *UE III*: 463	U 18 409	851	UM 33-35-381	Pit W, SIS 4-5

See *Scott 2005*, 173. Catalogue: "Ur PG. PIT W SIS IV–V, Found in Storage 1989". Obverse: a cross-like feature possibly in relation to Legrain's *edinnu* sign. Reverse: impression of a smooth and plane concave surface, without any measurable parameters (*Scott 2005*, 173 = door peg). Red-brown clay without visible admixtures.

Inscription:

In addition to the *Edinnu* sign, the meaning of which is unclear, I see the sign

KAK = DU_3 = RU_2, = see above, # 31. "To enact"; "to make something"; "to create".

"(Contributed for) the maintenance of the Union(?)".

* * *

116. *UE III*: 464 = *Matthews 1993*, 42 = *Scott 2005*, 490	X, GA_2 or LAGAB?	Reed matting package	Rosette

Inscription:

GA_2 = PISAN = see above, # 5. "Outbuilding, shed, barn, pen".

LAGAB = see http://psd.museum.upenn.edu/epsd/nepsd-frame.html [accessed October 2, 2014] s. v. lagab = "block; stump (of tree)".

***

117. *UE III*: 471 = *Scott 2005*, 492	AB+AN, filled in with triangular incisions = mountains?	??	No counter-mark

Inscription:
AN (DINGIR) = see above, # 17. "Deity"? "Life"?
AB+AN = see also above, # 101, *UE III*: 437.

***

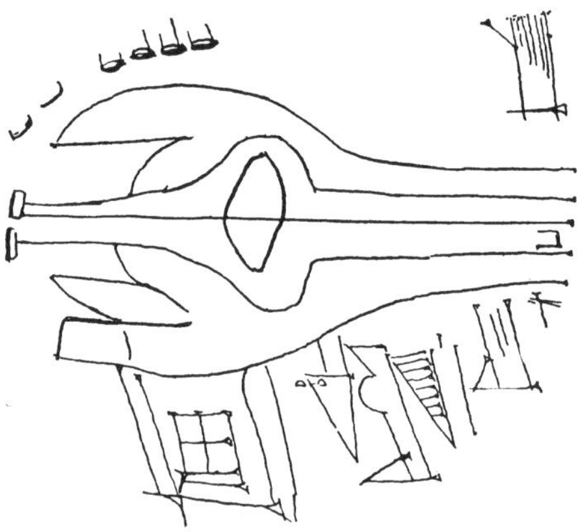

118. *UE III* : 474	U 18 394	841	UM 33-35-270	SIS 4-5, Pit W

Catalogue: "Ur PG. Pit W. SIS IV–V, found in storage". Obverse: a legcross and an inscription. Legrain: par maš par ir-da-bi udu, eight small oblongs. MAŠ, DA, AŠ, IR, DA, NI, RA or UDU? Reverse: smoothed. A tablet. Red-brown clay without visible admixtures. Fingerprints, a KISAL sign in the field.

Inscription:

PAP = PA_4 = see above, # 1. "She who fosters growth?" "Unfinished, open transaction"?

DA = see above, # 97. "Container"? "Pastry"? "To leave"?

IR = *ZATU* No. 267 p. 225, missing in MSVO. Frequently in lists of receptacles (vessels). In Šuruppak, this is a perfume (*Pomponio 1987*, 12), "perfume" = *MEA* No. 232 p. 127. *Gelb-Steinkeller-Whiting 1991*, 293: ir = *erīšu, erēšu* = smell, scent, fragrance. *Selz 1995*, 133 fn. 539: IR = "Wohlgeruch, Parfüm". In ED Lagaš IR = ir = "Geruch", "Duft" (*Meyer-Laurin 2011*, 61). The sign group A.IGI has a value /ir/ = "Träne" there (*Meyer-Laurin 2011*, 62 fn. 208). On aromatic substances in Sumer see now *Brunke-Sallaberger 2010*; *Schrakamp 2012*, 286–287.

DA = see above, # 97. "Container"? "Pastry"? "To leave"?

DUG = see above, # 35. "Pot"? "Merchandise"?

RA = *ZATU* No. 431 p. 264, missing in *MSVO 1*. *Wilcke 1988*, 20–21 n. 78–79 on kišib___ra = "to attach a seal". In Fara-age texts kišib PN ib-ra = "PN's seal was impressed by rolling" (*Visicato 2000*, 153 fn. 211). *Englund 1990*, 60 n. 202: še giš.ra = "Gerste dreschen".

KISAL = see above, # 5. "Forecourt"? "Gipar of Ur"?

Numerals on the perimeter of the legcross:

Two erect oblongs mean probably 60+60, usually written in pairs (*UET II* No. E Pl. 35). The rest of the oblongs lying prone are supposed to denote quantities of sixty (ibid. No. D). Why are they divided by the two erect ones is not clear to me. They could also be interpreted as N-57 and N-58 (*ZATU* p. 345, also *MSVO 1* pp. 217–220), not parts of a specific numerical system.

This seems to be a quantified delivery (DA) of the legcross entity (the inhabited world, *oecumene*? See above, # 62), disbursed at KISAL, in pots of malt and a fragrant substance(s) (PAP.DA IR.DA). These might have been sealed (RA).

* * *

119. *UE III* : 480	U 12 778	UM 31-17-352 B	Pit G, 7.60 to 8.00 m below plano-convex brick pavement

Two other fragments. Catalogue: "Ur, found 7 ½ to 8 m below brick pavement, dated ca. 3100 B.C. in the prehistoric settlement. Includes decorated pottery; clay animal; a number of seal impressions on clay jar stoppers; clay copies of shell bugle beads; bone tubular bead; copper needle, etc. Palmette enclosed (sealings)". Datable to the Jemdet Nasr period. Obverse: a palmette enclosed in a bottle (SA$_{10}$?). Reverse: a peg coiled around with cord(?) protrudes from a smoothed surface . Peg: r = 17 mm, thus d = 34 mm. Of the cord, only the CT = 3.3 mm can be measured. Red-brown clay without visible admixtures, fingerprints, especially where the sealing was pressed against the wall.

Inscription:

ŠAM$_2$(?) = *ZATU* No. 510 p. 282, *MSVO 1* p. 143. *Englund 1990*, p. 18 fns. 61, 62 and 63 proposes a translation of "tauschen". Fara-age texts have še šám kaš = "barley at the price of beer" (*Gelb-Steinkeller-Whiting 1991*, 292, see also ibid. 217). In Abu Salabikh šam$_x$ (NINDA$_2$ × ŠE) = "purchase" (*Krebernik-Postgate 2009*, 20, register). Other translations: "Entsprechendes ist es" (*Selz 1993*, 455–456), "Entgelt für den Kaufgegenstand" (*Wilcke 1996*, 10–12).

On the findspot and related matters see now *Charvát 2014c*.

Purchased (items) ?

* * *

120. *UE III* : 480	U 12 778	UM 31-17-352 R	Pit G, 7.60 to 8.00 m below plano-convex brick pavement

Two fragments. Catalogue: "Ur, found 7 ½ to 8 m below brick pavement, dated ca. 3100 B.C. in the prehistoric settlement. Includes decorated pottery; clay animal; a number of seal impressions on clay jar stoppers; clay copies of shell bugle beads; bone tubular bead; copper needle, etc. Palmette enclosed (sealings)". Datable to the Jemdet Nasr period. Obverse: a palmette enclosed in a bottle (SA$_{10}$?). Reverse: broken and illegible. Rims on two opposite sides could suggest a tag or tablet.Red-brown clay without visible admixtures. Large oval cavities, left by organic inclusions (e.g. fruit stones)? The item is bored through, and was thus brought for administrative treatment.

Inscription:
ŠAM$_2$(?) = see above, # 119. "Purchase".
Purchased (items)?

* * *

121. *UE III* : 518	U 13 607	UM 31-16-677	SIS 1

Catalogue: "Ur, pottery rubbish and ash filling against inner face of inner wall. S. E. end of Temenos, c. 50 cm below level of foundation". Obverse: Inscription, man-versus-lion fight, a swastika of naked bodies and a hero fighting a lion for a bull. Reverse: a peg coiled around with a cord, conically tapering, with an expanding terminus, protrudes from a smooth and even surface. Peg: r = 30 mm, thus d = 60 mm. Conical terminus: r = 23 mm, thus d = 46 mm. Cord:

CT = 6.2 mm	ST = 3.2 mm	SI = 7.3 mm	S-spin

Red-brown clay without visible admixtures, fingerprints.
Inscription:
(1) Mes-an-ne$_2$-pa$_3$-da
(2) lugal kiši^{ki}
dam nu-gig

Kiši = on archaic Kiš see now *Steinkeller 2013* (on p. 140 ad vi 6′for the sign KIŠ; pp. 145–151 for the early history of that city). The early carving from Kiš depicting two human figures in an interaction involving the touching of hair has been re-published recently: *Gubel 2012*.

Gig = missing from *ZATU* and from *MSVO 1* but exists in *UE III* : 175 = *LAK* 394. *MEA* No. 446 p. 201: gig = "grain" (froment), but also "taboo", and "illness". The name type X-an-né-pà-da is rare; attested examples relate only to rulers and to Enanepada, a priest in Ur, son of Urbaba of Lagaš (*Alberti-Pomponio 1986*, 33). On the KIŠ sign see now *Mittermeyer 2005*, 22–28, on the inscription on our seal *Zgoll 2006*, 113. See also *Nagel-Strommenger 1995*, esp. p. 461.

On Mesannepada and the "sacred marriage" see now *McCaffey 2013*, 228.

Impression of Mesannepada's royal seal.

* * *

122. *UE III*: 556	U 20 083h	828	UM 35-1-709	No context data given

See *Matthews 1993*, 46 = *Scott 2005*, 236. Catalogue: "Ur PJ Stratum SIS 4-5, Accidentally burnt, Found in Storage 1989". Obverse: a geometrical pattern of lozenges and oblongs and an emblem of a spread eagle over a scorpion. Reverse: impression of a structure of parallel flat stripes. A bale in reed matting? Stripe widths: 7.6 mm, 9.55 mm and 9.55 mm. Traces of cutting the sealing away. Red-brown clay without visible admixtures.

Inscription:

KAK = DU$_3$ = RU$_2$ = see above, # 31. "To enact"; "to make something"; "to create".

Is there any relation to the sign NAM$_2$, as visible on my # 6 = *UE III*: 26? I do not think so, though not enough of seal # 6 survives to confirm or refute this proposal.

The conjunction of a chequerboard (or the NAM$_2$ signs), scorpion, spread eagle and the KAK sign all point towards the symbolism of fertility and fecundity.

* * *

123. *UE III*: 559	U 20 083f	UM 35-1-707	No context given

See *Matthews 1993*, 51 = *Scott 2005*, 246. Catalogue: "Ur PJ, Stratum SIS 4-5, Accidentally burnt, Found in Storage 1989". Obverse: signs of writing. Reverse: impression of a flat surface with traces of fibrous matter of wood (a wooden board?). On this surface rests a thick strand of cord continuing into a knot. This may come from a wooden object (a box?) tied over with a cord. Cord:

CT = 9.9 mm	ST = 4.1 mm	SI = 14.2 mm	Spin S

Container (box?), Matthews: package/bale. Red-brown clay without visible admixtures.

Inscription:

Column I:

I: 1:

AL = see above, # 18. "Hoe", "field work with hoe".

Column II:

II: 1:

$\underline{\text{EN}_2\text{(?)}}$ = *ZATU* No. 138 p. 198 = *MSVO 1* p. 102. The problem is that the first component of the EN_2 sign is turned by 180°, and does thus represent rather LIŠ or DILIM_2 (= *ZATU* No. 331 p. 239, missing in *MSVO 1*, only as LIŠ+ŠIR in *MSVO* 4 p. 63) than ŠU_2 (*ZATU* No. 534 p. 289 = *MSVO 1* pp. 149–150).

$\underline{\text{AŠ}}$ = *ZATU* No. 37 p. 177 (in field surveying texts with meaning "length") = 1N_{57}, *MSVO 1* pp. 217–218. *Heeßel 2001–2002*, 43: AŠ = *eṭṭūtu* = spindle, in medicine texts.

$\underline{\text{DUG}}$ = see above, # 35. "Pot"? "Merchandise"?

Column III:

III: 1:

AŠ = *ZATU* No. 37 p. 177 (in field surveying texts with meaning "length") = 1N_{57}, *MSVO 1* pp. 217–218. *Heeßel 2001–2002*, 43: AŠ = *eṭṭūtu* = spindle, in medicine texts.

$ARARMA_2$ = see above, # 61. "The city of Larsa".

AB_2 × DIŠ(?) = *ZATU* No. 14 p. 171. Only AB_2 can be found in *MSVO 1* p. 87. On AB_2 = "cow" see *Krebernik-Postgate 2009*, 18, register.

ZATU No. 753, p. 332 = *MSVO 1* p. 165–166.

Column IV:

IV: 1:

X

AN (DINGIR) = see above, # 17. "Deity"? "Life"?

$UMUN_2$, DIM_6 = *ZATU* No. 582 p. 303 (with a variant simug) = *MSVO 1* p. 160.

This seal seems to document a unified entity reaping benefits from agriculture (AL), animal husbandry (AB_2+DIŠ and possibly *ZATU* 753) and craft activities ($UMUN_2$), collected (also?) from external territories ($ARARMA_2$).

* * *

124. *Matthews 1993*, 14 = *Scott 2005*, 14, probably SIS 4	$ARARMA_2$, AB+KI, IL_2, legcross	"lock"	Rosette, on 3 of 5

Inscription:

$ARARMA_2$ = see above, # 61. "The city of Larsa".

IL_2 = tax, see http://psd.museum.upenn.edu/epsd/nepsd-frame.html [accessed October 2, 2014] s. v. il_2. IL_2 in Fara texts: *Pomponio-Visicato 1994*,

193; in ED Lagaš evidence *Selz 1995*, 58 No. 111, 202–203 No. 70, 258 fn. 1240. Also in ED Lagaš ÍL = íl = "tragen" (*Meyer-Laurin 2011*, 57); other ED material: *Bauer 1989–1990*, 78; *Selz 1993*, 555–556; *Westenholz 1987*, 129 */íl tax levied on produce, not land, paid by higher officials to government after harvest/*; *Englund 1990*, 92 fn. 292 for Ur III material.

"City League".

* * *

125. *Matthews 1993*, 18 = *Scott 2005*, 570, no context	legcross, Keš, UNUG, DIŠ, UNUG	Door peg	No counter-mark

Inscription:

$\underline{\text{KEŠ}_3}$ = see above, # 63. "The city of Keš".

UNUG = see above, # 32. "The city of Uruk".

"City League".

* * *

126. *Matthews 1993*, 26 = *Scott 2005*, 568, probably SIS 4	X, X, U_4, UR_2, U_4+AŠ	Pot with leather and cord	No counter-mark

Inscription:

$\underline{U_4}$ = BABBAR = see above, # 32. "Day"? "Time of the day"?

$\underline{UR_2?}$ = see above, # 12. "Lap", "crotch", "sexual organs", "fecundation ritual".

$\underline{U_4\text{+AŠ}}$ = date? = one month? See *Englund 1988*.

Delivery for a (monthly) ceremony?

* * *

127. *Matthews 1993*, 27 = *Scott 2005*, 564, SIS 4-7	*Edinnu* containing UNUG?, [A]N, AN	??	No counter-mark

Inscription:
UNUG = see above, # 32. "The city of Uruk".
AN (DINGIR) = see above, # 17. "Deity"? "Life"?
"City League".

* * *

128. *Matthews 1993*, 29 = *Scott 2005*, 777, SIS 4	legcross, UNUG?	??	Rosette

Inscription:
UNUG = see above, # 32. "The city of Uruk".
"City League".

* * *

129. *Matthews 1993*, 33 = *Scott 2005*, 238, no context	$MUNU_4$ DU_3, $MUNU_4$, $MUNU_4$, X, AN, legcross	Scott: pot with covering, Matthews: pot with leather covering	No counter-mark

Inscription:
$BULUG_3$ = DIM_4 = $MUNU_4$ = see above, # 1."Malt", "malster"?
KAK = DU_3 = RU_2 = see above, # 31. "To enact"; "to make something"; "to create".
AN (DINGIR) = see above, # 17. "Deity"? "Life"?
Legcross = the inhabited world, *oecumene*? See above, # 62.
Delivery of malt in pots?

* * *

130. *Matthews 1993*, 40 = *Scott 2005*, 708, SIS 4-6	X, X, $ARARMA_2$, URI_5, *edinnu*?	Door peg	Rosette

Inscription:
$ARARMA_2$ = see above, # 61. "The city of Larsa".
URI_5 = see above, # 63."The city of Ur".
"City League".

* * *

131. *Matthews 1993*, 50 = *Scott 2005*, 672 (SIS 4)	URI$_3$, AB	??	No counter-mark

Inscription:

URI$_3$ = see above, # 2. “Nannar”? “The city of Ur”?

AB = EŠ$_3$ = see above, # 30. “Household, centre of production, distribution”.”Heiligtum”?

“City League”.

* * *

132. *Matthews 1993*, 53 = *Scott 2005*, 876 (PG1332 and area)	*Edinnu*, UB, X, X	Reed matting package 1x, unknown1x, door peg 1x	Counter-marked, illegible motif

Inscription:

UB = see above, # 22. *“Universum”*? “Fortified enclosure”?

“City League”.

* * *

133. *Matthews 1993*, 58 = *Scott 2005*, 577 (no context)	URI_3, *edinnu*?	Probable pot	Counter-marked, linear design

Inscription:
<u>URI_3</u> = see above, # 2. “Nannar”? “The city of Ur”?
“City League”.

* * *

134. *Matthews 1993*, 75 = *Scott 2005*, 657 (SIS 2)	ŠE?	Matthews: ?, Scott: pot with covering	No counter-mark

Inscription:
<u>ŠE</u> = see above, # 15. “Grain”.
“City League”.

* * *

135. *Matthews 1993*, 81 = *Scott 2005*, 816 (SIS 4)	??, KIB	??	No counter-mark

Inscription:

KIB or ŠENNUR = a kind of fruit (plum?), or defective writing for the Euphrates, see above, # 10.

Consignment of fruit?

* * *

136. *Matthews 1993*, 89 = *Scott 2005*, 812 (SIS 4, 5, 6 or 8)	GADA GADA GADA	Jar stopper	No counter-mark

Inscription:

GADA = see above, # 27, # 98, # 106, and # 143. "Linen".

Delivery of textile in a jar.

* * *

137. *Matthews 1993*, 90 = *Scott 2005*, 709 (SIS 4-6)	AB or Adab	Door peg, reed or palm frond midrib?	Counter-marked, rosette

Inscription:

AB = $EŠ_3$ = see above, # 30. "Household, centre of production, distribution". "Heiligtum"?

ADAB = see above, # 63. "The city of Adab".

"City League".

* * *

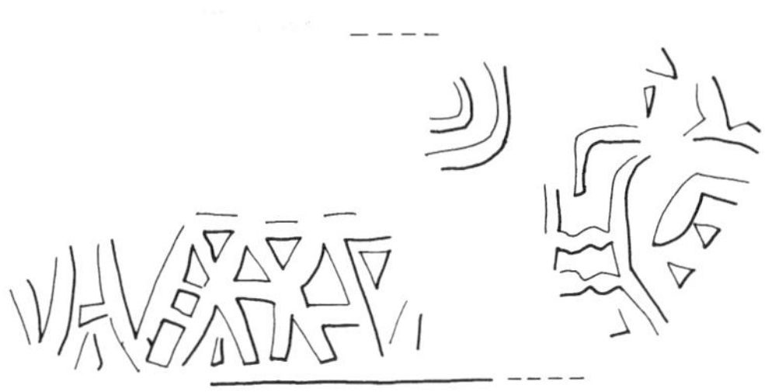

138. *Matthews 1993*, 93 = *Scott 2005*, 682 (SIS 4)	UNUG?, *Edinnu*?	Door peg, palm frond midrib?	No counter-mark

Inscription:
<u>UNUG</u> = see above, # 32. "The city of Uruk".
"City League".

* * *

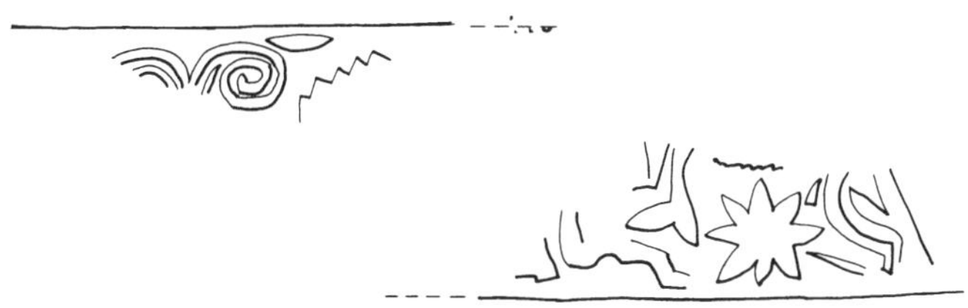

139. *Matthews 1993*, 98 = *Scott 2005*, 807 (SIS, place uncertain)	X, AN	Door peg	No counter-mark

Inscription:
<u>AN (DINGIR)</u> – see above, # 17. "Deity"? "Life"?

* * *

140. *Matthews 1993*, 102 = *Scott 2005*, 452 (SIS 4)	ARARMA$_2$, KIB = ŠENNUR, X	??	Counter-marked with butt of cylinder seal?

Inscription:

ARARMA$_2$ = see above, # 61. "The city of Larsa".

KIB or ŠENNUR = a kind of fruit (plum?), or defective writing for the Euphrates, see above, # 10.

Consignment of fruit?

* * *

141. *Matthews 1993*, 108 = *Scott 2005*, 576 (SIS, place uncertain)	Scorpion?, UNUG?	Door peg	No counter-mark

Inscription:

UNUG = see above, # 32. "The city of Uruk".

"City League".

* * *

142. *Matthews 1993*, 112 = *Scott 2005*, 668 (SIS 3)	X, URI$_3$	Door peg	No counter-mark

Inscription:

URI$_3$ = see above, # 2. "Nannar"? "The city of Ur"?

"City League".

* * *

143. *Scott 2005*, 770 (no context)	GADA	Package	No counter-mark

Inscription:
GADA = see above, # 27, # 98, and # 106. "Linen". Delivery of textile.

* * *

144. *Scott 2005*, 796 (no context)	UB	Door peg	No counter-mark

Inscription:
UB = see above, # 22. "*Universum*"? "Fortified enclosure"? "City League".

* * *

145. *Scott 2005*, 878 (no context)	URI_3	Door peg	No counter-mark

Inscription:
URI_3 = see above, # 2. "Nannar"? "The city of Ur"? "City League".

* * *

146. *Scott 2005*, 891 (no context)	Coitus scene accompanied by depictions of fish	Test strip	No counter-mark

This item does not, strictly speaking, belong here, as it bears no inscription. Yet, it is interesting from the viewpoint of iconography.

* * *

147. *Scott 2005*, 892, no context	URI_3	??	No counter-mark

Inscription:
URI_3 = see above, # 2. "Nannar"? "The city of Ur"? "City League".

* * *

148. *Scott 2005*, 958 (no context)	URI_3	basket	No counter-mark

Inscription:
URI_3 = see above, # 2. "Nannar"? "The city of Ur"? "City League".

* * *

III. THE CITY OF UR AT THE BEGINNING OF THE THIRD MILLENNIUM: IMAGES AND SIGNS, WORDS AND NOTIONS IN SEALS

Having examined the inscribed seals of archaic Ur, I now proceed to analyze the uninscribed ones. A long tradition of research characterizes the interpretations of the evidence given by the SIS seals and sealings by specialists in art history ever since the publication of the entire find group in 1935. The archaeological questions have been treated in the first chapter of this book.

It must be mentioned that the entire Ur corpus examined by Sarah Jarmer Scott, whose study is the most comprehensive one of the Ur material (*Scott* 2005), includes impressions of 764 seals. All of the sealings housed at the University Museum of Archaeology and Anthropology of the University of Pennsylvania at Philadelphia, and at the British Museum, were functionally analyzed by her, 5 more were analyzed by Matthews. This leaves 156 items from Baghdad that are not included in her functional analysis (*ibid.*, 219).

Let us now hear what the authors of the two most recent studies on the theme (*Scott* 2005; *Otto* 2010) have to say. The pertinent formulations of both experts carry so much relevance that it is worth quoting some of them in full.

The majority of the impressions discussed turned up in SIS 4-5; however, Charles Leonard Woolley describes some as coming from contexts that extend as far in time as SIS 8 (*Scott* 2005, 52).

If, however, the SIS 6-8 are archeologically assignable to the early part of Early Dynastic I, the sealings do not necessarily follow this date *stylistically* (italics by Sara Jarmer Scott). If any early Early Dynastic I and later Early Dynastic I seal chronology may be conceived, it is not present in the archaeological division between SIS 4-5 and 6-8 (*ibid.*).

"I believe this is the heart of the debate about dating the seals – the seals do not obey any stratigraphic correlation between the early and late Early Dynastic I layers, and so we must look at them stylistically rather than archaeologically" (*Scott* 2005, 52).

"My point here is that the impressions from Ur SIS 8-4 that are under debate, the imagery discussed here, is *clearly* part of an *early* Early Dynastic I tradition (italics SJS). There are very few images that depict stylistic traits of later Early Dynastic I imagery. These few images do show lither figures, with less deep modeling and more linear details, but they are not in the majority. The images discussed here all display basic traits of the early Early Dynastic I period ... Iconography includes scenes typical of this earlier phase, and certainly not limited to formulaic combats, as are corpuses from the later phase. Essentially, even if we were to still include Early Dynastic II as a period in this region, it would not matter with the Ur material because all of the stylistic and iconographic traits exhibited by the corpus (Levels 8–4) suggest it is Early Dynastic I" (*Scott 2005*, 63, for example).

"Overall, the Early Dynastic I material from Ur does carry iconographic varieties suggesting that some sealings might fall in the early portion of the Early Dynastic I phase (heraldic poses, horizontal combat scenes, processions), while others might be later (symposium, banquets)" (*Scott 2005*, 63–64).

For Adelheid Otto, though the sealings may be mixed in the layers of the pit, they do nonetheless constitute a fairly homogenous material group except some intrusive pieces (*Otto 2010*, 26). Most of the motifs stem from Late Uruk glyptic, and few relations to ED-II sealcutters' art manifest themselves.

"The SIS 8-4 art represents a local development of Late Uruk creations, and it may thus constitute a "missing link" between Late Uruk *oeuvres* and the fully fledged style of ED-I–II periods" (*Otto 2010*, 26), a major change being the ushering in of the man-in-the-kilt (sovereign?) figure who kills people and sits at banquets (*ibid.*).

"The majority of motifs turn up in several (up to ten) variants, which seems to correspond to administrative and/or economic units" (*Otto 2010*, 26).

Two conclusions follow out of this review of the latest opinions on the issue. First, the SIS seals and sealings constitute a stylistic unity, in spite of the stratigraphic distinction between the SIS 8-6 and SIS 5-4 groups. And second, this group of artistic creations possesses all the stylistic traits of the incipient, or, at any rate, early Early Dynastic I period, which confirms the archaeological conclusions put forward in the first chapter of this book.

If the SIS material displays the stylistic unity commented on above, then the conclusion that it represents an outcome of one single artistic centre, or a glyptic workshop, is possible. The anchoring of such an *atelier* within the social life of the Ur community appears then to have been firm enough to enable not only the emergence of a creative school distinct from that of the Late Uruk epoch at the dawn of the third pre-Christian millennium, but also the perpetuation of this creative tradition over a time period of some length.

And then, as the activities of this glyptic workshop apparently followed out of the designing, and building up, of the entire administrative apparatus of the nascent LUGAL-ship (?) of post-3000 Ur, we shall probably not miss the point too widely if we assume that the stylistic unity of the SIS sealings ensued out of a "*contrat social*", of a commission by one single organ of the central administration of Nannar's city from one single glyptic workshop. This gives us the chance to see in the SIS-seal imagery the manifestation of ideational strategy of one single governance centre, to the investigation of which I shall now proceed.

In order to make the presentation of material better structured, I shall resort to a procedure not quite usual in ancient Oriental studies. I classify the iconography of the Ur SIS material in four large groups, the designations of which I borrow from the allegorical description of the Four Ages of Man in early post-medieval European Humanism – AMOR (love), LABOR (labour), HONOR (honour), and DOLOR (woe, pain). This has nothing to do whatsoever with Sumerians at Ur – it is merely a device for an easier classification of our material. It seems to me that the inconography of the archaic Ur seals lends itself particularly well to such a presentation, giving us, in addition to a classificatory aid, a mental tool enabling to grasp our evidence better as a structured unit.

* * *

But before I begin with analysis of the main group of material, stemming from the SIS 5-4 strata, I prefer to give an account of the preceding phase of archaic Ur sealings, those of the SIS 86 layers. It has been noted above that these fall in with the rest of the early glyptic items as to art style. Yet, it might be interesting to look at them from the viewpoint of iconography and seal use.

ARCHAICA

Items: *UE III*: 1 (my # 1), 6, 8, 9 (my # 2), 10, 11, 14 (my # 3), 16, 17, 20, 24 (my # 4), 25 (my # 5), 27, 28, 29, 30, 34 (my # 7), 35 (my # 8), 37, 38, 39, 40, 42, 43 (my # 9), 44, 45, 46, 483, *Moorey 1979*, 561. Total 29 items.

As for the AMOR category, the "birthing" icon, depicting a female with spread legs, now enters our field of vision, in the company of two scorpions and what may be a bird (*UE III*: 42). A banquet(?) scene, featuring, in the lower register, a bull, a bird and possibly the UR_2 sign also belongs here (*UE III*: 46).

UE III: 42

UE III: 46

The LABOR category includes a human figure with a herd of goats or similar ungulates (*UE III*: 40, a similar theme in *Moorey 1979, 561*) or herds of goats without a shepherd (*UE III*: 39). A peculiar scene which might show a human being in a reed thicket displays a high degree of originality (*UE III*: 11). A human being(?), grasping two long sinuous objects (necks of mythical animals?, my # 9 = *UE III*: 43), may also belong here (on depictions of early mythical animals see now *Wengrow 2014*). The emblematic ungulates nibbling symmetrically at a tree turn up in seal *UE III*: 483[16], while a variant of this composition displaying a spread eagle on top of the tree occurs in *UE III*: 37. The labour theme of a human handling a storage jar(?) before a sacred hut is already present (*UE III*: 45, possibly also *UE III*: 16).

UE III: 40

16 Leon Legrain (in *UE III*, 43 sub # 483) gives the findspot of this sealing as "Pit G, 7.10 – 8.00 m below plano-convex brick pavement". A consultation of Leonard Woolley's stratigraphic summary (*Woolley 1955*, Pl. 83) shows that this spot must lie below layer H of Woolley's Pit F, and thus, according to Reinhard Dittmann (*Dittmann 2006*, 36, Tab. 1), fall into his "Jemdet Nasr" or even "Spät-Uruk" phase, thus confirming the early date of incipient sealings of archaic Ur. See below, at the beginning of the "Society" section.

UE III: 11

UE III: 483

UE III: 45

The HONOR category may be represented by a seal showing a human figure walking towards what might have been a sacred hut(?), again with the TU_7 sign (*UE III*: 10). That these early seals did homage to the "City League" is shown by the *edinnu* sign appearing on at least one of them (*UE III*: 29).

UE III: 10

UE III: 29

The later familiar spread-eagle symbol makes its appearance at this early age, accompanied by an antelope (*UE III*: 38). A remarkable set of emblems confronts us in *UE III:* 20: in the the central position it figures the spread-eagle icon, situated on a kind of tripod. This is flanked by two large scorpion images and depictions of an animal head and an animal protome. Is this a scene of sacrifice?

UE III: 20

Finally, the DOLOR rubric may be represented by a scene featuring two boats and a human figure raising his or her arms (in grief? *UE III*: 17). Or is this a dancing scene?

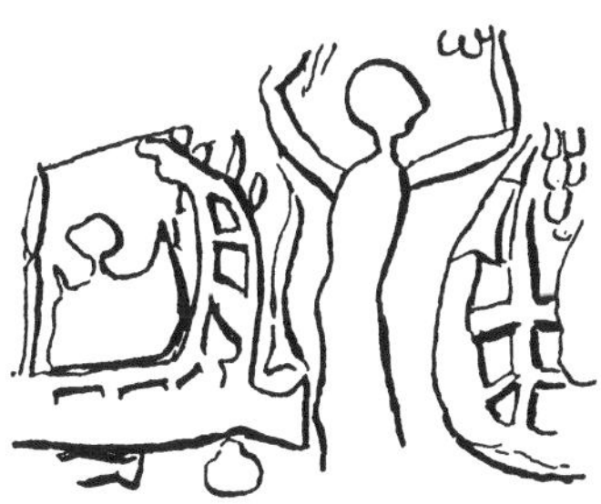

UE III: 17

Inscribed seals attest to a fairly complex degree of administrative practices of the earliest Ur management (the pisandubba sealing of *UE III*: 1 = my # 1). Others refer to URI_3, which is not surprising (my # 2 = *UE III*: 9), and to its "city elders" = AB + $AŠ_2$ (*UE III*: 34 = my # 7). They also tell us that one of the earliest Ur public buildings had a KISAL (or is this to be read $gipar_x$, *Selz 2011b*, 233 sub # 1: 3? not always: *Andersson 2012*, 158 fn. 912; on gipar see also *Lion 2009*, 179; *Westenholz 2013*, 254–256), and name other dignitaries such as NIMGIR and NAM_2 LA (*UE III*: 25 = my # 5, the latter also in *UE III*: 35 = my # 8).

Deliveries of comestibles include those of TU_7 (*UE III*: 14 = my # 3) and of what might have been a supply of seafood (*UE III*: 24 = my # 4).

Some of the Ur seals bear images alluding to common everyday tasks such as rows of storage jars (*UE III*: 6). A seal showing a net with fish did once close a pot (*UE III*: 44 = Scott 2005, # 222, p. 450). Geometrical compositions may, in fact, depict similar entities like, for instance, jars carried in nets (*UE III*: 8), though in some instances we may doubt whether a geometrical composition or an inscription was intended (*UE III*: 30). Lozenge-filled chequerboard fields do appear (*UE III*: 28), much as a row of rhomboids (*UE III*: 27).

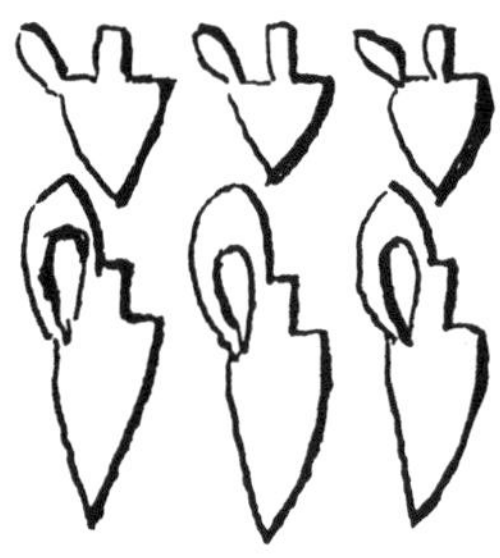

UE III: 6

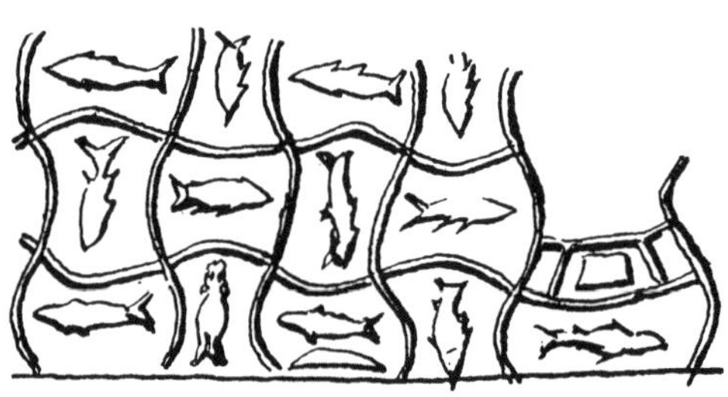

UE III: 44

UE III: 8

In conclusion, we may observe that the four essential categories of the images present on the "classical" impressions of the SIS 5-4 strata, which I have denoted as AMOR, LABOR, HONOR and DOLOR, have been present in the *répertoire* of the Ur sealcutters from the very beginning of the exercise of their craft in Nannnar's city onwards. At the same time, the early seals attest to the administrative complexity of the Ur polity from the Late Uruk – ED-I transition, as well as to the purely practical tasks which some of them played (denoting the contents of sealed containers such as baskets with tablets, but also storage facilities for comestibles including seafood).

Total count of sealings	Sealings of moveable items	Sealings of immovable structures	Same seal on both movables and immovables	Unidentified sealing carrier
29	12	9	3	5

***

Sealings from SIS 5-4

AMOR

BANQUET SCENES

Items: *UE III*: 169, 371, 373, 377, 381, 382, 383, 384. Total 8 items.

By common belief, the banquet scenes are considered to fall in with the general topic "procreation, fertility, sacred marriage" of ancient Sumerian system of beliefs. In addition to banquet scenes, this ideational complex includes themes of music, dance and *coitus* (see *Stauder 1970*, esp. pp. 174–175 and 223; *Selz 1995*, 104–105; recently *Marchetti 2006*, 184–190, *Rohn 2011*, 53–54, and *McCaffey 2013*, as well as *Selz 2012*, 66–70; on ED-III music *Cheng 2009*, esp. pp. 171ff.; on the interesting connection between music and payment to the Nether-World ferryman *Selz 2004a*, 54).

One of the first instances of commensality, *UE III*: 169, shows a seated personage holding a cup and serrved by a naked standing attendant, with depiction of a fish between the two. The scene also includes a harpist, and is supplemented by a zone of what may be called "chequerboard of hourglass configurations" above the banquet scene. One of the fragments of this sealing bears an impression of a second seal with a pattern of simple pointed-end ovals identical to that of *UE III*: 135, and of *UE III*: 134, which is my # 26 above, bearing the sign PAP = PA_4 ("Fertilisatrice"? see above, my # 1). The combination of a drinking bout with a harpist occurs also in *UE III*: 371. The next example, *UE III*: 373, associates a harpist figure and a seated personage with a storage-jar and spread-eagle icons. Two seated personages with cups and "filler motifs" of storage jars appear in *UE III*: 377, inexpertly cut of bone or wood(?). *UE III*: 381 and 383 feature what may be summary depictions of comestibles consumed in banquets – bread, fish and drink in jars – together with eating scenes. In *UE III*: 382, a commensality scene displays, among other "filler" motifs, also images of two scorpions and a horned ungulate, the whole seal being counter-marked with a rosette ensign.

UE III: 169

UE III: 373

UE III: 381

UE III: 382

Finally, *UE III*: 384 represents the oft-discussed scene of the animal banquet. I have suggested a connection with "totemic" symbolism above (*Charvát 2014a*) but I now have my doubts. In view of the fact that the banquet theme, and none other, associates with animal symbolism it may be legitimately asked whether the fertility- and fecundation symbolism, likely to have been involved in banquet images, does not apply in this case as well – the idea of activating fertility being extended not only to human but to animal worlds as well. After all, this image features real animals only, and not hybrid beings such as those depicted on objects from the later "royal graves" of Ur. The seal bears a counter-mark displaying a wild-boar icon, a scorpion and an "arrow-point" (*pace* Legrain: *UE III*: # 384 on p. 35).

UE III: 384

Catherine Breniquet (*Breniquet 2008*, 278–286) has recently published an ingenious interpretation according to which some of the "banquet" scenes do not represent drinking by means of straws, but pulling out a strip of wool to be spun from a vessel. This interesting suggestion is certainly worth pondering upon; in the archaic Ur scenes, I see a problem in the fact that this would be the only case of a craft motif except the livestock-keeping *répertoire*, for which see below, *sub* LABOR: Humans at work.

In conclusion, the banquet scenes involve seated personages frequently drinking from cups and served by naked attendants. Harpists figure in some of them, accompanying motifs including fish, comestibles (bread?, drink), "chequerboard of hourglass configurations", horned ungulate, spread eagle and scorpion. One of the banquet seals asociates with a seal showing pointed-end ovals and inscribed in one case with the PAP = PA_4 sign. The banquet may be impersonated by figures of real animals.

Total count of sealings	Sealings of moveable items	Sealings of immovable structures	Same seal on both movables and immovables	Unidentified sealing carrier
8	4	1	2 (*UE III*: 169, 384)	1

DANCE SCENES

Items: *UE III*: 258, 262, 263, 264, 266, 329 (my # 49), 364, 374. Total 8 items.

The *UE III*: 258 associates such a scene(?) with three scorpion images and a storage-jar likeness, but the lonely tiny naked figure in a dancing posture does not warrant a safe identification of the motif. The involvement of scorpion images in dance scenes appears also in *UE III*: 262 and 263 while a naked arm-lifting figure among trees(?) constitutes the motif of *UE III*: 264. *UE III*: 266 gives hardly any usable data beyond the figure of the naked dancer(?) and a cluster of "fillers" (comestibles??). A file of dancing figures interspersed with DIN signs (= beer), and with pointed-end ovals above their heads, fill in the space of my # 49 = *UE III*: 329 (and possibly also 328). The naked couple of a man and a woman with incomprehensible "filler" motifs and a storage jar hovering in between them of *UE III*: 364 may also represent a dance, much as *UE III*: 374 where three naked men(?) dance before a "sacred hut".

UE III: 258

UE III: 262

UE III: 264

UE III: 364

UE III: 374

It may thus be concluded that dance scenes feature scorpions, trees and storage jars as supplementary motifs, and involve a sign DIN (= beer, alcoholic beverage). The dance may take place before a "sacred hut".

Total count of sealings	Sealings of moveable items	Sealings of immovable structures	Same seal on both movables and immovables	Unidentified sealing carrier
8	2	0	0	6

BIRTHING SCENES

Sarah Jarmer Scott has given this name to a depiction of a naked figure shown en face as putting her legs apart so that in better preserved examples, the *vulva* is definitely there (on the icon see *Mazzoni 2002*). I now prefer this name to my former denomination of this icon as "wanton lady", admittedly not very elegant.

Items: *UE III*: 267(??), 268, 269, 270; *Moorey 1979*, 583 and 597; *Scott 2005*, 703. Total 7 items.

The fact that *UE III*: 267 shows a naked man hints at a possibility that the "birthing" scene may have had a male participant, since he is identified by two scorpions, much as the classical variants of the theme in *UE III*: 268, 269, in *Moorey 1979*, 597, and *Scott 2005*, 703. The better preserved example of *UE III*: 270 shows two interesting variations: first, the flowing and disheveled hair of the figure, and second, a scorpion and a lizard instead of the usual two scorpions. In *Moorey 1979*, 583 only the two scorpions are visible.

UE III: 267

UE III: 268

UE III: 270

Here we may conclude that the birthing scene invariably associates with scorpion- (and, in one instance, with lizard-) images.

Total count of sealings	Sealings of moveable items	Sealings of immovable structures	Same seal on both movables and immovables	Unidentified sealing carrier
7	2	3	0	2

COITUS SCENES

Items: *UE III*: 365, 366, 367, 368, 369, 370 (= my # 53), 385; *Scott 2005*, 891. Total 8 items.

These depictions bear witness to the intimate life of the elites of archaic Ur. Numbers *UE III*: 365 and 366 show the couples in sitting positions (with an accompanying scorpion in 366), and No. 367 prone-and-supine ("missionary") on top of an architectural structure. Fate has decreed the damage done to sealing *UE III*: 365 to an extent that will never allow us to check whether the attribution of the emblems accompanying the intimate partners – spread eagle for the male (left) and scorpion for the female (right) – corresponds to reality (so *Scott 2005*, 445 on p. 600). The *UE III*: 369 image integrates, to a certain extent, the themes of *coitus*, banquet and harp music. Again, the man and woman copulating *a tergo* are assisted by the attendant who touches the strands of the female's disheveled hair. In the upper register, another naked servant carries drinks while a harpist provides the music. The impression is counter-marked with a butt end of a cylinder seal. Item *UE III*: 370 features another scene of *coitus a tergo* together with a naked bearer of two hares and a birthing figure. The *UE III*: 385 ushers in a new version of the theme: the *coitus* is taking place on a roof of a presumably cultic building, in front of which a naked worshiper touches one of the standards set up there (in a TAK4.ALAN ceremony?). The AN sign (or is this the rosette, or the eight-pointed star of Inanna?) shows the celestial connotations of the scene. Finally, in *Scott 2005*, 891 the coitus scene is accompanied by a fish image.

UE III: 365

UE III: 367

UE III: 369

UE III: 370

UE III: 385

In *UE III*: 368 we see a *coitus a tergo*, with a female assistant touching the strands of the disheveled hair of the female partner, and a sitting personage holding a circular object in his or her hand. The impression bears a counter-signing imprint of a rosette seal. Here our interest focuses on the disc above the couple, filled in with a chequerboard of nine fields. My learned friend and colleague Jiří Prosecký has already noted that the ninefold division of this disc is likely to correspond to the ninefold division of the later "ark" of Uta-napištim of the Gilgamesh epic, built on the principle of likeness to the universe (*Prosecký 2008*, esp. p. 8). Moreover, the chequerboard motif implies again a symbolism of fertility and fecundity (*Charvát 2005a*, 44–48, 79–81, 101–102, 108, 162, 191–193). In this manner, the whole image can be "read" in the sense that what takes place in it should activate the fertility of the universe. This is a unique instance in which we may directly infer the significance of a scene depicted in an early Sumerian cylinder seal.

UE III: 368

The *coitus* scenes are thus likely to be interpreted not at face value[17], but as images and/or records of an activity of cosmic order, activating the fertility of the universe. The act may take place in connection with architecture, presumably of sacred character. Associated motifs include a scorpion (for the female partner?), possibly a spread eagle (for the male partner?), fish and the AN sign (in whatever sense the ancients understood it), and a whole "lump sum" of themes like banquet, harp music and "birthing".

Total count of sealings	Sealings of moveable items	Sealings of immovable structures	Same seal on both movables and immovables	Unidentified sealing carrier
8	2	2	0	4

AMOR: EMBLEMS

Due to the fact that some motifs appear frequently linked with scenes falling in with the AMOR sphere, it may be interesting to take a closer look at these devices.

Items: *UE III*: 102 (= my # 21), 259, 260, 271, 272, 363(?), 456, 487 (SIS 2), 488 (SIS 2), 556 (= my # 122), *Matthews 1993*, 24 (= *Scott 2005*, 779), *Moorey 1979*, 165, 578 (no context), 592 (no context), 594 (no context), *Scott 2005*, 621 (no context), 670 (no context), 680 (no context), 738 (no context), 742 (no context), 748 (no context), 793 (no context), 801 (no context), 820 (no context), 821 (no context), 882 (no context), 886 (no context), 945 (no context). Total 28 items.

The clearest case in connection with these designs relates to the sign UR_2, of which an interpretation provides the key opening the door towards the understanding of this symbolic sphere. As already hinted (see above,

17 Let me note *en passant* that during one of the *Rencontres Assyriologiques Internationaux*, somebody suggested that these sealings may come from the municipal brothel of Ur!

my # 12), the sign UR_2 = also URUM(?), is to be identified as *ZATU* No. 588 p. 304 = *MSVO 1* p. 160. The equation UR_2 = *sūnu* = "thigh" may be found in *MEA* No. 203 p. 117, similarly http://psd.museum.upenn.edu/epsd/nepsd-frame.html [accessed October 3, 2014] s. v. ur_2 = "root, base; limbs; loin, lap". *Sūnu* is identified in *CAD* S pp. 386–388 as "lap", "crotch", "sexual organs", and also, in general, "human body from the waist down", "lap", "foundation", but also "to sleep" and "to fecundate" (*rehû*).

The most explicit statement in relation to UR_2 and its meaning is that of my # 21 = *UE III*: 102, with signs NUN, $GIŠ_3$+UR_2, SAL? *ZATU* 644 or -645 = SUMUN?. Here we have a reference to sexual intercourse ($GIŠ_3$+UR_2, SAL?) bound to a geographical (or divine?) entity (NUN)[18]. Here it seems that the carrying out of the UR_2 procedure is done by means of sexual intercourse, and on behalf of geographical communities.

Within our ensign group, the UR_2 sign appears in three instances (*UE III*: 259, 271, 272). In 259, it associates with images of a tree, scorpion, "inverted tripod" URI_3 and with pointed-end ovals. It links up with a tree- and sign ibex image in 271 and with two "star" ensigns – one four-pointed and the other seven-pointed –, pointed-end ovals, a scorpion and a spread eagle in 272. This provides safer ground for the understanding of at least the most visible fertility devices – scorpion and spread eagle. Trees, pointed-end ovals and the rosette- or AN configurations apparently belong hither as well.

UE III: 259

UE III: 272

18 I confess that I do not understand the meaning of the SUMUN sign (were it to be read this way), unless it refers to "old" entities (arrears of due payments?).

The scorpion turns up in eleven other cases (*UE III*: 260, 363, 456, 556 = my # 122, *Moorey 1979*, 578, *Scott 2005*, 621, 680, 748?, 820, 821, and 886). An interesting combination is that of a snaketwist with scorpion in *Scott 2005*, 886. A snaketwist accompanies a triumphal scene in *UE III*: 286, and it may thus be asked whether the snaketwist represents a fertility- or a triumphal image. The association of the scorpion image with a human figure in a posture of a worshiper(?) with hands clasped before the chest in *UE III*: 363 may point to the sacrality of the symbol, but nothing certain can be deduced here.

UE III: 286

The spread eagle occurs in five compositions (*UE III*: 487, 488, 556 = my # 122, *Moorey 1979*, 594, *Scott 2005*, 621).The two latest examples of *UE III*: 487 and 488 (SIS 2) show well to what extent the spread-eagle composition became petrified in the form of a "canonical image" with advancing time (on Anzu as one of the possible interpretations of the spread eagle see *Andersson 2012*, 114–115; on the spread eagle as a cosmic bird *Lan 2012*, 78, 82, 85–86).

UE III: 488

As to other written signs, *UE III*: 556 (= my # 122) combines the scorpion- and spread-eagle icons with sign KAK. Here the meanings "to build" and "to plant; to fix upright, erect; to impregnate; to drive in, fix; a designation of grain" (see http://psd.museum.upenn.edu/epsd/nepsd-frame.html [accessed October 3, 2014] s. v. du_3) point towards the same (fertility-symbol) direction.

The peculiar position of the eight-pointed AN sign on tail tips of two scorpions in *UE III*: 260 may suggest that scorpion poison involves a divine substance, but hardly anything can be said on this subject.

UE III: 260

Let us notice that the *UE III*: 556 seal adds to the scorpion-, spread-eagle, and KAK motifs a peculiar form of chequerboard ornament. In addition to the eleven items listed below (see the "Hic sunt leones" section), the chequerboard occurs in nine other cases (*Moorey* 1979, 165, *Scott* 2005, 670, 738, 742, 779, 793, 801, 882 and 945). The *Scott* 2005, 793 sealing resembles rather the LUM(?) sign of *UE III*: 460 (my # 113), but the meaning of the sign points nonetheless the same way (see above).

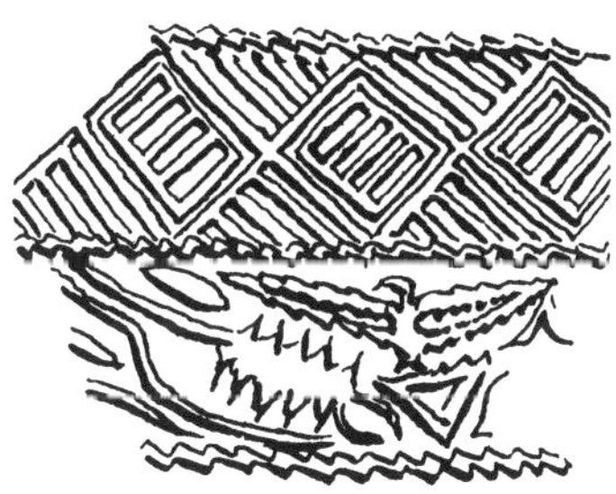

UE III: 556

The fish may fall in with this sphere in view of images like *Moorey 1979*, 592, with ibexes and ungulates symmetrically disposed around a tree, or with a *coitus* scene in *Scott* 2005, 891.

It may thus be concluded that in view of their associations with the UR_2, KAK = DU_3 = RU_2, and possibly also LUM cuneiform signs, the devices that I have termed AMOR emblems can be actually demonstrated to allude to the sphere of fertility and fecundity. This pertains first and foremost to the scorpion- and spread-eagle icons, and possibly also to those of chequerboard, rosette- and related, tree, tripod, pointed-end oval, ibex, fish, snaketwist and that of two ungulates disposed symmetrically around a tree. The presence of the URI_3 sign in UE III: 259 provides a link of such emblems with the Nannar shrine at Ur.

Total count of sealings	Sealings of moveable items	Sealings of immovable structures	Same seal on both movables and immovables	Unidentified sealing carrier
28	10	8	0	10

***

LABOR

HERDING

Items: *UE III*: 167, 168, 188, 189, 190, 191, 192, 193, 194, 195, 197, 198, 199, 200, 201, 202 (= my # 31), 203, 204, 205, 207, 210, 211, 212, 213, 214, 219, 222, 223, 280, 287, 288, 291, 304, 305, 306, 307, 308, 309, 310, 311 (= my # 45), 312, 313, 314, 316, 317, 318, 319, 320, 321, 324, 345, 346, 349, 362, 380, *Moorey 1979*, 279, 566 (no context), 576 (no context), 580 (no context), 582 (no context), 585 (no context), 586 (no context), 587 (no context), 588 (no context), 589 (no context), 590 (no context), 598 (no context), 609 (no context), *Scott 2005*, 91, 262, 291, 673 (no context), 675 (no context), 691 (no context), 697 (no context), 702 (no context), 715 (no context), 725 (no context), 731 (no context), 745 (no context), 747 (no context), 806 (no context), 808 (no context), 811 (no context), 911 (no context), 940 (no context). Total 86 items.

In seals of archaic Ur the herds were composed mostly of quandrupeds such as bulls, goats, ibexes or oryx antelopes, possibly even of horse (*Moorey 1979*, 279). Being not an expert based on biology, I rely on identifications current in specialized literature on the subject. The theme must have been popular, as shown by the sheer number of examples displaying related images. The animals depicted freely roam over the grazing grounds, or line up in rows, frequently looking in one single direction (= files).

In some instances the seal-carvers clearly wished to show parts of animal bodies, especially their heads. What did they mean by this is most difficult to guess; this might have been a device for symbolizing whole animals in the tiny space of the seal surface, but also a depiction of real heads presented, for instance, as sacrifices in temples. In combat themes, such gruesome details might add the flavour of true "wildlife scenery" (see below).

Of the accompanying motifs we have already seen not a few. Let us refer to trees (*UE III*: 191, 204, 222, *Moorey 1979*, 580, *Scott 2005*, 91), rosettes in four- or eight-rayed variants (*UE III*: 191, four-rayed; *Moorey 1979*, 580, with tree and an eight-rayed rosette; *Moorey 1979*, 590, five-rayed), tripods or trilobes

(*UE III*: 193), storage jars (*UE III*: 188, 189, 211, 280) or to pointed-end ovals (*Moorey 1979*, 585). In some instances, an association with architecture seems to be referred to (*UE III*: 313). How does the swirl ornament(?), associated with an ibex image (*UE III*: 203), fit in?

UE III: 204

UE III: 193

UE III: 280

UE III: 203

As to the emblems cited in the previous chapter, the ubiquitous spread eagle (*UE III*: 202, 211, 212, 219, 222, 280) and scorpion (*UE III*: 280, with lizard) occur in the animal world fairly frequently. Chequerboard ornaments of various kinds (*UE III*: 168) complete the picture.

UE III: 168

Proto-cuneiform signs, already known to us, turn up here as well: UR_2 (*UE III*: 199), or KAK (*UE III*: 202).

UE III: 199

UE III: 202

A particular kind of composition is represented by the pairs of beings symmetrically arranged around the central axial object. This may be a tree

(*UE III*: 197, 198, *Scott 2005*, 675, 731, 811, 911), a spread eagle (*UE III*: 207, with four-rayed rosettes, pointed-end ovals and a storage jar, *Scott 2005*, 940) or a combination of the two (*UE III*: 213, 214), some other object like an ibex head (*UE III*: 102), but also an imaginary axial line (*UE III*: 167, 312). In some instances both the animals look in the same direction and the device thus lacks a strict symmetry (*UE III*: 190).

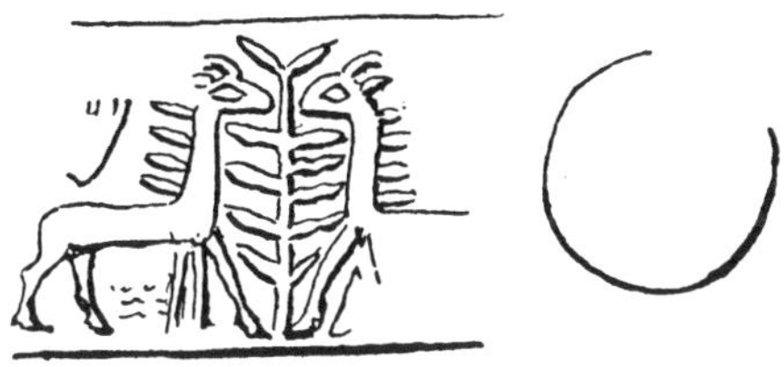

UE III: 198

UE III: 207

UE III: 195

UE III: 312

UE III: 190

Another peculiarity with which we have to cope here is a representation of a presumably insubstantial architectural creation with plaited-work walls and a round roof, provided sometimes with "ear-shaped" eaves and referred to by Sarah Jarmer Scott as "birthing hut". I prefer the designation "hut with protrusions", as this structure stands in evident relation with similar creations known from the art of the preceding, Late-Uruk development phase of ancient Mesopotamian civilization (on the possibility of identification of this structure with sign TUR_5 see *Szarzyńska 1996*, 241 sub # ZATU-416). Text W 20044, 59 from Uruk, listing probably "rations" over a period of time ($1N_{34}$ [ ] $3N_{14}$; U_4 ZATU-759; BA), bears an impression of a seal depicting light-material shelters out of which calves are seen to issue (*Boehmer 2001*, 11, Taf. 96, text on Taf. 36, transcription on p. 44). Various animals freely associate with this architecture which may be designated by diverse emblems – a spread eagle (*UE III*: 223, 349) or the ŠEŠ = URI_3 sign (*UE III*: 349) insofar as it is not an emblemic component of the structure. The omnipresent UR_2 sign occurs here as well (*UE III*: 349). In repeated instances the quadrupeds are shown as emerging out of the "hut with protrusions" (*UE III*: 345, 346, 349). Or was this a temple kitchen (*Charvát 2014b*)?

UE III: 349

The area before the "hut with protrusions" may serve for unspecified work activities like a possible instance of milking an animal (*UE III*: 362). Accompanying motifs include storage jars: *UE III*: 205; 223, with bull; *UE III*: 349, with two animals issuing out of the hut designated by the ŠEŠ signs, spread eagle and a sitting figure holding a storage jar, just as rosettes (*UE III*: 346) and possibly trees (*UE III*: 205).

The herding-sphere images include a fair amount of scenes involving a human-animal interaction.

UE III: 205

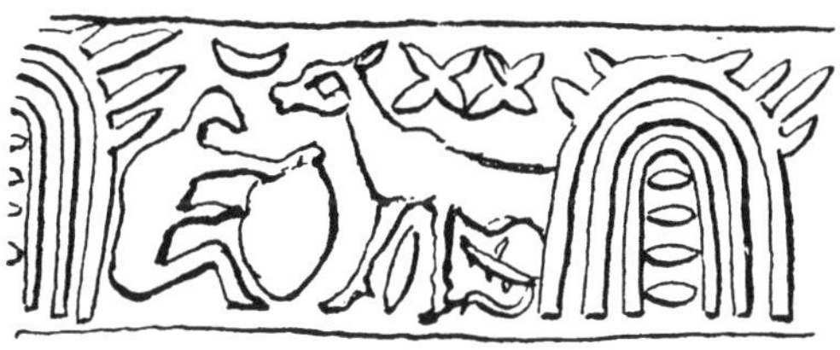

UE III: 346

The most comprehensible ones feature contact of an animal with a human wielding a stick or staff, who seems to drive the quadruped in the desired direction (*UE III*: 304, 305, 308, 314, 316, 317, 319, 320, 321). It is difficult to guess whether this pertain also to scenes where humans with sticks only show up; these could, in fact, refer also to combat themes (*UE III*: 306, 380). Accompanying motifs include rosettes (*UE III*: 304, eight-rayed, 308, four-rayed, 317, four-rayed, 380, eight-rayed,), the spread eagle (*UE III*: 305, 316, 380), scorpions (*UE III*: 316), trees (*UE III*: 304, 305, 317, 319, 320, 321), and storage jars (*UE III*: 305, 314, 317). Hither belong also coercion scenes in which a human leads a bull by a nose-rope (*UE III*: 324), or holds the bull's tail (*UE III*: 309).

Proto-cuneiform signs cropping up here are represented by the KAK sign (*UE III*: 304).

UE III: 308

UE III: 316

UE III: 380

UE III: 317

UE III: 324

Another action, involving an archer figure with bow and arrow, and a hind(?) with spread eagle above, may find a simple explanation in an assumption of (an outcome of?) hunting activities (*UE III*: 288).

UE III: 288

In other cases the explanation of the action presents certain difficulties. Scenes where humans lift their arms above the backs of bulls or ibexes (*UE III*: 307, 310, 311) or touch the horns of ibexes (*UE III*: 318) represent a mystery. Some of the accompanying motifs like trees (*UE III*: 307, 310, 318) we have already met, others, like architecture (*UE III*: 311) or the DUG cuneiform sign (*UE III*: 311), not yet. Do we have before our eyes the conferment of fertility by humans on animals here?

UE III: 310

UE III: 318

UE III: 311

Something of this order could be hinted at by other, possibly related scenes. In one instance, two humans, disposed symmetrically along the central axis, extend their arms to a tree and an animal each, the composition complemented by a storage jar in between them and by a chequerboard of "hourglass motifs" in lower register (*UE III*: 167). A closely related image features two men symmetrically disposed bowing down, one above a tree, the other above an ungulate, supplemented by a pointed-end oval and by a spread eagle in the middle above them (*UE III*: 312). A relation to these of another rather enigmatic device, in which two human figures assume positions symmetrically opposed along the horizontal axis in upper and lower register, one thus standing and the other upside down, with participation of an ibex standing on hind legs in the manner of the well-known "ram caught in a thicket" of the "royal graves", and of the UR$_2$ sign (?, *UE III*: 291) can be only guessed at. Similarly, we stand hapless in a case where a composition of ibexes running, enriched by pointed-end ovals and by the cuneiform sign ŠEŠ (= URI$_3$)(?), features a human holding a W-shaped object, perhaps to be interpreted as the cuneiform sign UR$_2$(?) (*UE III*: 287). It is, however, a question how far the interpretation of such icons in the sense of conferment of fertility and fecundity on natural beings, possibly alluded to by the cuneiform sign UR$_2$, would involve a *petitio principii.*

UE III: 167

UE III: 291

UE III: 287

In conclusion, the herding scenes probably represent a wide range of subsistence-to-cultic activities, reaching from the common everyday chores of both livestock-keeping and possibly also hunting, as far as possible ritual activities undertaken with the intention to ensure fertility and fecundity of the natural entities surrounding the life of early inhabitants of Ur. Here also, a range of emblems that we have already met and cuneiform signs enhance the concern with assuring plentiful food supplies by means of evoking the procreation capacities of beings of living nature.

Total count of sealings	Sealings of moveable items	Sealings of immovable structures	Same seal on both movables and immovables	Unidentified sealing carrier
86	20	31	4	31

COMBAT

Items: *UE III*: 215, 216, 217, 218, 224, 226, 227, 228, 229, 230, 231, 232, 233, 234 (= *Matthews* 1993, 52 = my # 34), 235, 236, 237, 238, 241, 242, 243, 244, 245, 246, 247, 248, 249, 250, 251, 252, 253, 254, 256, 257 (my # 40), 261, 322, 558, *Moorey* 1979, 289, 581 (no context), 584 (no context), 595 (no context), 612 (no context), *Matthews* 1993, 96, *Scott* 2005, 695 (no context), 730 (no context), 790 (no context), 809 (no context), 913 (no context). Total 48 items.

The combat scenes may be generally divided in two types – those involving animals only and those displaying animals and humans (on these see also *Marchetti* 2006, 188–190).

As to the animals engaged in conflict, this pertains mostly to ungulates being attacked and sometimes torn apart by lions or large felines. In *UE III*: 243, the beast of prey seems to have acted so vigorously that it tore off the ungulate's head lying on the ground severed from the animal's body. Scenes displaying other animals together with that attacked by a beast of prey may imply that the artist has depicted happenings that he or she truly observed in nature, where lions frequently run into animal herds in order to identify the handicapped ones slow to take flight (*UE III*: 232, 233, 234, 236, 237, 238). Lions can take action in pairs (*UE III*: 215, 235, 247, 558) or even in groups of three (*UE III*: 238). In some instances the seal-cutter has produced a truly heraldic composition of symmetrical character, featuring two ungulates and two lions, which may even be crowned with the central image of a spread eagle (*UE III*: 215). Our *répertoire* does include scenes involving symbolic devices, as those in which the predators attack pairs of ungulates disposed symmetrically around trees (*UE III*: 215, 217, 226, 227?, 230, 244?, 252?, 322?). Such compositions can be doubled in two registers on the same seal (*UE III*: 226).

UE III: 243

UE III: 237

UE III: 238

UE III: 215

UE III: 226

The participation of humans usually takes the form of a naked hero attacking the lion who has jumped on his prey. In two instances the animal predator dares to engage a human being directly (*Moorey 1979*, 289). In one case only the human champion wears a kilt (*UE III:* 255, *UE III*: 243). The human hero usually wields a spear but he may use bow and arrow as well (*UE III*: 247).

UE III: 255

UE III: 243

UE III: 247

The combat scenes again include "fillers" and symbols of which some may seem surprising in scenes featuring aggressive and presumably dangerous behaviour. So appear the pointed-end ovals (*UE III*: 215, 216, 228, 243, 249, 250, 257), playing company to a device so close to the sickle shape of a new moon that we might even see in them the likeness of stars (*UE III*: 243, 250). The spread-eagle icon we now know from a host of depictions (*UE III*: 215, 216, 217, 218, 236, 242, 243, 244, 246, 257, 558). Other symbolic devices(?) include a tree (*UE III*: 218, 232, 322, 558), and, surprisingly, a harp and what appears to be a chequerboard composed of ovals (*UE III*: 224). Storage jars accompany a number of these compositions (*UE III*: 235, 251, *Scott 2005*, 730). Birds may sometimes turn up as well (*UE III*: 231, 246, 254) and, especially unexpected here, scorpion images (*UE III*: 233, 261) and fish depictions (*UE III*: 237, 238). The sole animal head sticking out between the legs of the participants in *UE III*: 254 implies again that scenes from nature may be referred to.

UE III: 250

UE III: 558

UE III: 224

UE III: 235

UE III: 231

UE III: 233

UE III: 237

UE III: 254

Again some signs of writing do figure in our compositions. This is first and foremost the ubiquitous UR_2 sign (*UE III*: 218, 238, 247, 252, 253, 257?), UB (*UE III*: 227, 234) and DUG, if the storage-jar image may be rendered so (*UE III*: 238). The DIN sign (see http://psd.museum.upenn.edu/epsd/nepsd-frame.html [accessed October 3, 2014] s. v. kurun = "a beer; blood; (to be) good; (to be) sweet"; *UE III*: 241, 252) accompanies the sprinkling of AN devices, of eight (*UE III*: 241, 558, *Scott 2005*, 809, *Scott 2005*, 913), six (*UE III*: 244) or four rays (*UE III*: 241, 253, 254, 256, 257); sometimes the number of rays does not show up clearly (*UE III*: 247, 254). The KAK sign, which we have already met, re-surfaces here (*UE III*: 249, *Matthews 1993*, 96).

UE III: 238

UE III: 234

UE III: 252

UE III: 249

In conclusion, the combat scenes are likely to refer both to real-life situations observed in the wildlife around Ur, and to symbolic actions taken by the society's paragons to protect human life and property. Rather unexpectedly, here also a range of emblems that we have already met, and proto-cuneiform signs, seem to evoke the concepts of fecundity of (plants?), animals and humans. In what manner the motifs of conflict pertain to the sphere of fertility is not clear, but the scorpion- and spread-eagle images, as well as the UR_2, DIN, KAK and AN signs, hardly carry a message other than that of fruitfulness of organic life.

Total count of sealings	Sealings of moveable items	Sealings of immovable structures	Same seal on both movables and immovables	Unidentified sealing carrier
48	9	17	2	20

HUMANS AT WORK

Items: *UE III*: 293, 315 (= my # 46), 325 (= my # 48), 330 (= my # 50), 331, 332, 336, 337, 338, 339, 340, 341, 342, 343, 344, 347, 348, 349 (= my Nos. 51 and 52), 353, 354, 355, 356, 357, 358, 359, 360, 361, 376, 484, *Moorey 1979*, 596 (no context), *Matthews 1993*, 75 (= my # 134), 89 (= my # 136), *Scott 2005*, 698 (no context), 700 (no context), 704 (no context), 707 (no context), 724 (no context), 769, 770 (= my # 143), 946. Total 40 items.

This motif takes us into a sphere where the sacred and the profane blend so imperceptibly that we are at a loss how to interpret each particular case. Nevertheless, an attempt at this is well worth undertaking.

Much as before, here also the scenes concerned fall into two broad categories: work themes as such, and compositions involving in one way or another the particular architectural creation which Sara Scott terms "birthing hut", and for which I prefer the designation "hut with protrusions", as in a number of cases it displays two conical configurations protruding from its walls below the top. In addition to the suggestion of reading TUR5 mentioned above, an eventual relation of this structure to an edifice named in Sumerian texts E_2.NUN, with possible reading agrun ("reed sanctuary"), must be investigated in the future (*Andersson 2012*, 158 fn. 914). Or could this be enun, "the innermost room" (see http://psd.museum.upenn.edu/epsd/nepsd-frame.html [accessed October 3, 2014] s. v. enun)? For the possibility of interpretation as a temple kitchen see *Charvát 2014b*.

Signs included in the work scenes help, in a number of cases, in their identification, referring, for instance, to threshing of grain (BAD, *UE III*: 315 = my # 46, 325 = my # 48). In fact, the lexeme may not refer literally to threshing, but to a procedure described by a 19th-century author in relation to maize and perfectly applicable to cereals, as I believe: "Sometimes the women stamp it in a wooden mortar with one, or sometimes two, long pestles to get off the outer husk" (*Buckland 1893*, 40; see *Charvát 2014b*). The *UE III*: 325 icon, involving, together with a naked human figure and the BAD sign, likenesses of a storage jar and a horned quadruped, heralds the components of a number of related scenes. This seems to point to the (possible) conclusion that the threshed or otherwise processed grain, stored in jars, could be fed to animals, as implied by the occurrence of the BAD sign in a "pastoral" scene of *UE III*: 340. Human figures, handling storage jars and appearing together with horned quadrupeds, figure in seals *UE III*: 330, 331 and 332.

UE III: 340

UE III: 331

In a few instances the sealings mention directly the goods conveyed: grain (ŠE, Matthews 1993, 75) and textiles (GADA, *Matthews 1993*, 89, *Scott 2005*, 770).

The "hut with protrusion" scenes figure invariably a naked human figure carrying out his or her task in front of the structure (*UE III*: 336). Most frequently, he or she handles a storage jar and the respective activity is witnessed by a horned quadruped which may emerge from the same, or a second, "hut with protrusions" (*UE III*: 337, 338, 339, 340, 341, 344, 347, 348, *Moorey 1979*, 596). The scene may involve two human figures (*UE III*: 339). In some instances the humans may actually be feeding the animals concerned (*UE III*: 342, 484), but sometimes the animals are absent (*UE III*: 355, 356, 357). This may simply result from the state of preservation of the sealings in question (e.g. *Scott 2005*, 698, 700, 704, 707, 724, 769, 770, 946).

UE III: 337

UE III: 342

In a variant of this scene, the naked human touches (or just lifts hand in front of) the wall of a structure either identical with, or perhaps akin to, the "hut with protrusions"; storage jars may figure here also (*UE III*: 353, 354, 358). In one instance the human both handles a jar and touches hut (*UE III*: 359).

Two compositions involving the "hut with protrusions" motif stand out by their apparently religious context, and merit particular attention. In *UE III*: 349, a sitting naked human, handling a storage jar, sits between two horned quadrupeds emerging from two huts with pairs of ŠEŠ standards, superimposed by spread-eagle emblems. The scene is complemented by signs UR_2, UR_2, DIN, and by what appears to show a fish image, and is thus likely to fall within the sphere of fertility symbolism. The *UE III*: 361 seal displays the image of a rectangular hut, on one side of which a naked human handles storage jar, while on the other side a naked human, and a horned quadruped standing on hind legs, lift hands and forehooves (in reverence?) before a spread-eagle symbol. Here we may witness a scene where denizens of the earth implore their deities to convey fecundity to the material world from which they derive their sustenance. The ŠEŠ = URI_3 standard and spread-eagle emblem appear also in a related scene in *UE III*: 360.

UE III: 359

UE III: 349

UE III: 360

UE III: 361

"Filler" motifs include again images of a tree (*UE III*: 332, 355, 356, 357, 358, 359, *Scott 2005*, 707), of a curious animal, perhaps a feline, and a scorpion (*UE III*: 348), of fish (*UE III*: 349?), as well as bird likenesses (*UE III*: 484).

UE III: 348

UE III: 484

As to signs of proto-cuneiform writing, the AN appears again in many instances (*UE III*: 315). It may consist of eight (*UE III*: 315), six (*UE III*: 343) or four rays (*UE III*: 338). In *UE III*: 343, the four-rayed AN sign turns up between the mouth of a storage jar placed on the earth level and the mouth of a quadruped standing above it. Does this convey the message of the nourishing substance (of divine origin) partaken by the animal as fodder? The BAD sign, referring to grain processing and already commented upon, may have denoted the kind of commodity delivered under the respective seal or seals (my # 46 = *UE III*: 315; my # 48 = *UE III*: 325), but it seems to have referred also to animal fodder (*UE III*: 340). The occurrence of the DIN sign presents now no surprise (*UE III*: 332, my ## 51 and 52 = *UE III*: 349, *Moorey 1979*, 596). An image of a naked human handling storage jars conveys the semantic message of the DUG sign (my # 50 = *UE III*: 330). In a few instances of this theme the Ur-, or rather Nannar-temple toponym, occurs directly (ŠEŠ = URI_3, my ## 51 and 52 = *UE III*: 349; *UE III*: 360). Of course, the UR_2 sign shows up here as well (my ## 51 and 52 = *UE III*: 349).

UE III: 343

A third category of images, of rather loose connection with this general theme, represents two "master of animals" icons (*UE III*: 293 and 294). This is a motif on which much has been written, but the sense of which still eludes us (see also *Charvát 2006*).

UE III: 294

We may finally state that the "humans at work" category of the Ur images presents no simple task for unravelling its message. We start with straightforward designations of the character, or state of treatment, of the goods conveyed under the respective seals (BAD, GADA, ŠE), or containers in which they were delivered (DUG). For the most part, however, the rather sophisticated icons linking the "hut with protrusions" with human and animal figures taking various actions might have referred to a wide range of ideas, beginning with the fairly simple tasks of livestock-keeping, and ending in highly complex notions involving rituals of activation of fertility through veneration of supernatural forces symbolized by sacred emblems. Unlike the other iconic themes, the "humans at work"compositions display a clear connection with the temple of Nannar at Ur (the ŠEŠ = URI_3 toponym).

Total count of sealings	Sealings of moveable items	Sealings of immovable structures	Same seal on both movables and immovables	Unidentified sealing carrier
40	5	8	1	26

The high number of unidentified items is probably caused by the fact that a number of seals with this motif are deposited in the Iraq Museum at Baghdad, and thus unavailable for examination at present.

* * *

HONOR

HONOUR TO GODS

Items: *UE III*: 158, 187, 220, 273, 275 (= my # 41), 276, 277, 296 (= my # 43), 302, 303, 323 (= my # 47), 326, 333, 334, 335, 350, 351, 352, 372, 375, 378, 379, 383, 386, 387, 395 (= my # 58, 59), 460, 468, 547, *Moorey 1979*, 491, *Scott 2005*, 261, 457, 649, 713, 719, 767, 925, 956. Total 38 items.

With this theme, the sacred world of the inhabitants of early Ur, present *in nuce* in other iconic compositions that have been treated already, stands out clearly in front of our eyes.

In general, compositions belonging to this sphere may be divided into three broad circles: cultic architecture and its appurtenances; provisioning the cult and ritual; and depiction of – or reference to – the acts of devotion.

Architecture of presumably religious character we may have already met, for instance, in the case of the "humans at work" sceneries. Here some items feature structures either standing alone (*UE III*: 220, 333, 334, 335, 386, 468), also because of the state of preservation of the particular sealings, or within their landscape settings (*UE III*: 158). Likenesses of naked humans kneeling in front of some of them and lifting hands imply the religious character of such structures (*UE III*: 350, 351), although in some instances the mortals are merely sitting beside them (*UE III*: 352). Sometimes our edifices welcomed groups of offering-bearers, or even dancers (*UE III*: 375, not very clear).

UE III: 335

UE III: 386

UE III: 158

UE III: 351

UE III: 352

UE III: 375

Some compositions also show objects which we have identified earlier as emblems involving presumably the religious sphere. These are, for instance, the spread eagle and the scorpion (*UE III*: 273). The icon *UE III*: 296 (= my # 43) seems to show a complete sequence. Here the architecture possesses two "inner compartments", in one of which a naked attendant stands ready for service, while the other is occupied by a large UR_2 sign. This incidentally proves that the value of the UR_2 sign definitely goes beyond a simple "filler motif". The edifice displays a spread-eagle emblem above, and an offering-bearer(?) is approaching it. A similar case is represented by *UE III*: 387, where a human figure in a pleated skirt naked to the waist, standing under a porch(?) of a temple superimposed by the spread-eagle emblem, seems to greet a group of visitors coming to his or her abode with plentiful gifts. An actual offering scene may be shown in *UE III*: 547.

UE III: 273

UE III: 387

UE III: 547

The temple *devotionalia* saw not only offerings brought to them, but also witnessed tactile contact with humans (*UE III*: 372 – architecture, or an idol?).

The provisioning of the cult and ritual involves, first and foremost, the procession scenes, though these could also depict acts of devotion. Sumerian temples of the early third millennium B.C. were approached by processions of humans (*UE III*: 302, 378, 379, 383, *Scott 2005*, 457, 649, 413, 719, 767, 925 and 926), files of animals (*UE III*: 187), or by mixed groups (*UE III*: 303, *Moorey 1979*, 491). The rather naturalistic severed animal heads, turning up in a group of compositions (*UE III*: 275, 276, 277, *Scott 2005*, 261), may symbolize offerings, as is indicated by the AK sign of *UE III*: 275 (= my # 41). Here i opt rather for the opinions of Gebhard Selz[19] and Miguel Civil[20] than for that of Jakob

19 *Selz 1995*, 113 fn. 415: AK = "Opfermaterie, sonst unbekannt" = a kind of cereal? It could also be an abbreviated rendering of kid$_3$-kid$_3$ = *kikkiṭṭû* = "Ritual"?.

20 *Civil 1982*, reading AK = gug$_x$, "eine Art Opferkuchen"?

Andersson, however justified that is as well[21]. In other cases, comestibles, but also works of art, made up the gifts brought by worshipers to the temples of their gods (UE III: 323 = my # 47).

UE III: 372

UE III: 378

UE III: 187

UE III: 303

21 On AK as referring to a creation act see *Andersson 2012*, 127–128 with fn. 695, 696 and 697.

UE III: 276

The acts of devotion show worshipers doing homage in temples by ritual gestures, such as lifting the hand between two ring standards (*UE III*: 326). They do nonetheless include also scenes the sense of which eludes us today (*UE III*: 187, gesture of the naked human).

UE III: 326

Signs of proto-cuneiform writing complement our scenes. The AN sign in its eight- (*UE III*: 273, 303) and four-rayed versions (*UE III*: 273, 277) leads the way. Sign $EŠ_2$ (= flour; or cord, rope?) figures in a scene of offering sacrifice to (divine?) emblems (*UE III*: 323 = my # 47). We get the fullest description of a ritual available from the sealings of archaic Ur in composition *UE III*: 395 (my ## 57–59). Here the sign group UR_4 KAB ALAM UR_2 DU_8 may be rendered as "wool clip in baskets, statue, fertility ritual performed (or, alternatively, fertility released)". The existence of the works of sculptor's art in early Sumerian temples, and their role in ritual proceedings taking place therein, find confirmation in this elegant proof of the ancient seal-cutter's skill. A vestige of an actual temple offering may be represented by the item *UE III*: 460 (= my # 113). This pot handle bears the proto-cuneiform sign LUM, commented upon above, the fertility connotations of which stand out clearly.

A management- and logistics detail may be culled from the fact that one of our sealings (*Scott* 2005, 767) displays two holes bored through its substance. This shows that much as other sealings, this also went to the central (royal?) registry to be checked against the records after having been taken off its original position (a covered pot).

The conclusion of this section re-creates before our eyes the world of early Sumerian places of worship. We perceive the architectures, both of permanent construction and of lighter materials, take their positions within the structured landscapes of the Mesopotamian world. We look into their "holies of holies" where the idols worshiped, sometimes statues, were addressed by the cult attendants in order to convey the messages of mortals to the world of the gods. We realize how much the ritual performances were imbued with concern for fertility and activation of the fecundity of all living beings. We accompany the worshipers entering respectfully the temples and expressing their awe and dedication by the ritual gestures. Ultimately, we have before our eyes hosts of citizens streamed in from far and wide, bringing the temples offerings to their deities.

Total count of sealings	Sealings of moveable items	Sealings of immovable structures	Same seal on both movables and immovables	Unidentified sealing carrier
38	12	13	2	11

HONOUR TO COMMUNITIES

Items: *UE III*: 142 (= my # 27), 155 (= my # 28), 160 (= my # 29), 209 (= my # 32), 281 (= my # 42), 389 (= my # 54), 390 (= my # 55), 391 (= my # 140), 392 (= my # 56), 396 (= my # 60), 397 (= my # 61), 398 (= my # 62), 400 (= my # 63), 401 (= my # 64), 402 (= my # 65), 403 (= my # 66), 404 (= my # 67), 405 (= my # 68), 406 (= my # 69), 407 (= my # 70), 408 (= my # 71), 409 (= my # 72), 410 (= my # 73), 411 (= my # 74), 413 (= *UE III*: 415 = *UE III*: 459 = my # 76), 414 (= my # 77), 416 (= my # 78), 417 (= my # 79), 418 (= my # 80), 419 (= my # 81), 420 (= my # 82), 421 (= my # 83), 422 (= my # 84), 423 (= my # 85), 424 (= my # 86), 425 (= my # 87), 426 (= my # 88), 427 (= my # 89), 428 (= my # 90), 429 (my # 91), 430 (= my # 92), 431 (my ## 93–96), 432 (= my # 97), 433 (= my # 98), 434 (= my # 99), 437 (= my # 101), 438 (= my # 102), 439 (= my # 103), 440 (= my # 104), 441 (= my # 105), 442 (= my # 106), 443 (= my # 107, SIS 2), 446 (= my # 108), 447 (my # 109), 448, 449, 450, 452, 453, 454 (= my # 110), 455 (= my # 111), 458 (= my # 112), 461 (= my # 114), 462, 463 (= my # 115), 464 (= my # 116), 465, 469, 471 (= my # 117), 472, 473, 554, 559 (= my # 123), *Moorey 1979*, 454, 564, 567, 568, 569, 571 (= my # 126), 572, 573, 577 (no context), 578 (no context), 579 (no context), *Matthews 1993*, 14 (= my # 124), 29, 33 (my # 129), 34 (no context), 40, 41, 43, 45, 50, 53 (= my # 132), 56, 59, 62, 67, 68, 71, 72, 74 (= my # 100), 81 (= my # 135), 84 (no context), 90, 93, 98 (= my # 139), 99 (bored through), 101, 103 (no context),109, 112 (SIS 3), *Scott 2005*, 416, 611 (no context), 614 (no context), 726 (no context), 791 (no context), 796 (= my # 144, no context), 878 (= my # 145, no context), 892 (= my # 147, no context), 958 (= my # 148, no context). Total 121 items.

The results of this part of my analysis, focusing first nad foremost on the "City League" seals, are given in detail below, in Chapter IV under the "City League" heading.

I have included in this category of sealings also those containing signs the meaning of which remains unknown at present, namely those of the *legcross* and *edinnu*, as used in current specialized literature (*Matthews* 1993; *Scott* 2005; on the "city league" list see *Visicato* 1989). They may have represented symbols of the inhabited world, *oecumene*, see above, # 62 (*Johnson 2014b*, 54, Fig. 1 with fn. 28). After some hesitation, I decided not to omit the various forms of the AN sign, chiefly because they turn up frequently with toponyms of the "city league".

In some instances, it will be observed that the seal inscriptions do not contain any toponyms, but refer to various concrete and particular tasks, or entities, instead. It may be legitimately asked how far such creations belong to the sphere of communal undertakings. I believe that they actually did, as the fact that goods, services, elements of societal order or those of religious and spiritual life entered the area of socially engineered exchange of material and/or immaterial commodities, operated and symbolized by means of seals, does imply that these things happened within the wider, communal context.

At the end of their "turn of duty", our sealings, taken off their respective carriers, probably travelled to the central management agency of Ur to be checked against the "taxpayers" "records (and ultimately discarded in the municipal waste-disposal area). This is indicated by the seal *Matthews 1993*, 99, which is bored through (presumably for suspension, to be carried). I have tried to describe this administrative *chaîne opératoire* elsewhere (*Charvát 2013*, 635–636) For this reason, I assume that all these sealings went through the same administrative routine, and thus were handled by the same management centre – possibly that of the LUGAL of Ur. I therefore suggest that the inscribed seals not referring to the "City League" visualize procedures initiated and carried through by the agency of the LUGAL of Ur.

The "City League" stands out before our eyes like a huge social mechanism, built for the purpose of maintenance of the unity of the Sumerian world even after the demise of the Uruk-age corporate polity. Its managers collected taxes and contributions of every kind in produce of the fields, gardens and pastureland, and in profits from trade. Its wheelings and dealings united, in a common effort, the forces and energy of inhabitants of the cities of Sumer, from their foremost elite representatives to simple servant girls. A part of the surplus collected ended up in temples, to reward the gods for the favours which they had showered on the corporate community, operated and directed from the abode of Nannar.

Total count of sealings	Sealings of moveable items	Sealings of immovable structures	Same seal on both movables and immovables	Unidentified sealing carrier
121	29	45	1	46

HONOUR TO PRINCES

Items: *UE III*: 131 (= UM 33-35-354), 206, 255, 274, 286, 292, 297, 394, 399, 412 (= my # 75), 466, *Scott 2005*, 694. Total 12 items.

In this particular instance, the evidence does show some specific traits. In fact, we dispose of one single scene in which an elite personage, sitting in heroic nakedness on a throne and sporting long hair, beard and possibly a horn on his head, grasps a long curved object, possibly a sceptre of some kind (*UE III*: 292). Yet, the hornless quadruped standing on hind legs before him does rather point towards the sphere of fertility symbolism. This may accord well with some of the LUGAL names known from Early Dynastic sources: the sceptre as LUGAL's insignia (*Andersson 2012*, 90), and the LUGAL as a source of plenty (*Andersson 2012*, 134–137). Nonetheless, in view of the scenes described below we shall do well to reconsider this interpretation, and to inquire whether the seal-cutter did not intend to show us a divine personage. This would be strange, as, for instance, only half-moon standards represent the iconography of the god Nannar until the advent of the Akkadian dynasty (*Braun-Holzinger 1993*, 120), but let us not jump to premature conclusions.

UE III: 292

Alternatively, however, the Ur sealings show a personage who is either bald-headed, or wears his hair cropped close to the head. Dressed in a freely flowing robe, and/or trousers, he hits with a long weapon, held in his right hand, a swastika made up by two humans whom he holds with his left hand (*UE III*: 286). In the other scene in which we see him, he grasps the hair of another personage, kneeling before him, with his left hand, while he either takes something from the kneeling person, or grasps the latter, by his right hand (*UE III*: 297 and, upon collation, also *UE III*: 131). The image of the lion attacking a quadruped in the same scene does indicate that a scene of military triumph is likely to be meant. The same idea seems to follow out of the first-named icon (*UE III*: 286), in which the victor subdues the two-man swastika.

The link between the human swastika and the idea of a military victory directs our attention to the device of a swastika of human, or animal (cattle) heads, present in the archaic seals of Ur. Being made up by either two or four participants, such swastika compositions can well stand for the idea of two, or alternatively four "corners of the world", and thus represent (also) those parts of the ancient *oecumene* subjected to the power of the commissioner of the work of art bearing this scenic motif (on the fourfold division of the world in Mesopotamia see *Glassner 1984*; on the swastika of human bodies as a symbol of this fourfold division see *Marchesi 2004*, 182, fn. 168, with ref.). Such a rendering comes to full swing with the fourfold swastika of naked humans shown on the seal of king Mesannepada of Ur and Kish (my # 121 = *UE III*: 518), likely to stand for the populations subdued by him (on a possible incarnation of this idea in burial practices of al-Ubaid see below). The combination of human and cattle heads may then refer to the booty taken during such a military operation (*UE III*: 206, 255, 274, 394, 399, 412, 466, and *Scott 2005*, 694).

UE III: 286

UE III: 297

UE III: 206

UE III: 274

A remarkable icon (UE III: 412 = my # 75) links a "City League" seal referring to GU (cords) with an image of a highly stylized swastika. Is this a record of a victory achieved by some "city league" military operation?

As to the minor motifs, we have already commented the lion-attacking-quadruped composition of *UE III*: 131 and 297. The same item contains an AN sign (6-rayed), another AN sign (7-rayed), a DIN(?) sign, and the spread-eagle icon. The horned quadruped by tree, and another image of a horned quadruped, show up in *UE III*: 255. Severed animal heads, included repeatedly (*UE III*: 274, 394), provide an interesting insight into the military-victory idea. Do these recall the brutal power of the vanquisher, or are they supposed to stand for the offering of (a part of) the booty from such a conflict to the gods, as witnessed above, in the temple scenes? The guilloche pattern and the knot of snakes, complementing these scenes (*UE III*: 286, 399), hardly offer any satisfactory conclusions. The apparently later, Fara-style sealing *UE III*: 298 with a combat scene displays what may be the first ever depiction of military dogs in action (*Tsouparopoulou 2012*, 10).

UE III: 286

UE III: 298

The scenes of triumph may thus commemorate victories of the rulers of Sumer, possibly even of a confederate army, in military actions, bringing home, among others, prisoners of war and herds of cattle as booty.

Total count of sealings	Sealings of moveable items	Sealings of immovable structures	Same seal on both movables and immovables	Unidentified sealing carrier
12	3	5	1	3

DOLOR

WATERS OF DEATH?

Items: *UE III*: 17 (SIS 8), 300, 301 ("Royal Cemetery area"), 492 (SIS 2), 521 ("Royal cemetery" area, "2 m down"), 522 (SIS 1), 523 (SIS 1), 524 (SIS 1). Total 8 items.

The boating scenes, admittedly the least represented ones among the seal iconography of archaic Ur, do nevertheless carry a high measure of interest, as they may shed light on a hitherto not illuminated aspect of the ideas of suzerainty in the incipient third pre-Christian millennium (see most recently *Breniquet 2008*, 364–367, and *Ławecka 2009*, 131–143 on the "boat god").

We shall obviously open our investigation with inspecting the earliest images, those of *UE III*: 17, 300 and 301. The first of these, *UE III*: 17 of SIS 8, boasts two boats, one of which carries a cloaked(?) and bald-headed figure. Another cloaked and bald-headed figure with hands lifted above head is shown between the two boats, likely to be standing on one of the watercourse banks. *UE III*: 300 depicts a boat with foliate prow and stern, with two personages sitting in it. The first of them, a bald-headed and kilt-clad male(?), holds a curvilinear scepter. The other, also kilt-clad, wields a long stick or a pole with which he may be propelling the boat, and/or directing its course. Two personages standing on the riverside accompany this scene. One of these, who is naked and bald-headed, holds a short stick(?), from which tassels seem to be suspended, with his both hands. The other is shown with his or her hands above the head. Outlines of riverside trees may be guessed behind both persons, and fish below boat confirm that it is actually sailing on water.

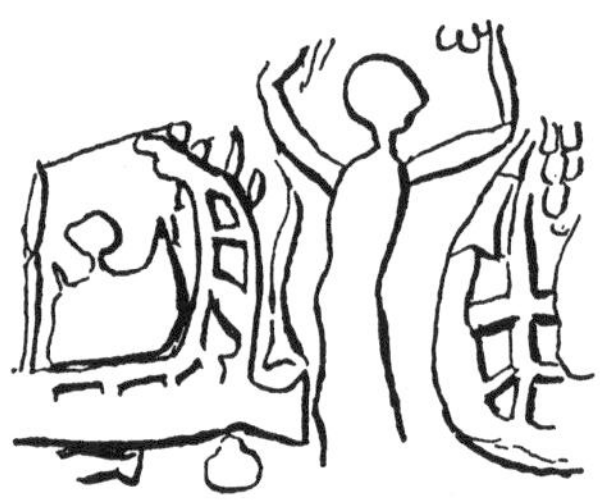

UE III: 17

UE III: 300

UE III: 301 shows some variation. The fish below boat are still there, but the half-figure within it is apparently naked and bald-headed, carries with him or her provisions in a storage jar. Something that may either be the boat's stern, or a riverside tree, shows up behind the figure's back.

UE III: 301

The rest of the boat scenes come from markedly later contexts, namely from SIS 2-1, insofar as the find contexts are known. The simplest of these is undoubtedly *UE III*: 521, in which two naked(?) and bald-headed persons drink from cups, with a faint outline of a storage jar standing between them. Other scenes seem to include a more elaborate cargo. The lower register of *UE III*: 492, with cattle images in the upper register, shows a ship occupied by three passengers. The central one wears a horned crown and a kilt and lifts his or her hand. The two remaining ones, kilted and bald-headed, hold oars. Trees grow on both banks of the watercourse through which the boat passes. A series of objects represented by pointed-end ovals, possibly a piece of textile(?) and a storage jar represent the boat cargo of *UE III*: 522, occupied possibly by a sitting kilted person of which a tiny vestige may be still seen, with a riverside tree in sight. *UE III*: 523 and 524 alike display boats in which pairs of kilt-clad bald-headed figures, drinking a beverage from storage jars by means of straws, are sitting. In both cases riverside trees complete the scenery.

UE III: 521

UE III: 492

UE III: 522

UE III: 524

The elements on which we shall be leaning in further reasoning, are

- the gesture of hands above head in the attendant personages of *UE III*: 17 and 300,
- the sceptre of *UE III*: 300;
- the horned crown of *UE III*: 492;
- the repeatedly depicted act of drinking, and
- the riverside trees, complemented with the foliate prow and stern of the *UE III*: 300 boat.

The gesture "both hands above head" shows up several times in the iconography of archaic Ur. The *UE III*: 262 scene, for instance, shows naked bald-headed personages lifting both hands above head, disposed *tête-bêche* on the seal's surface, with scorpion images inserted between them. *UE III*: 375 and 377 seem to depict naked dancers while *UE III*: 388, one of the most dramatic scenes of the entire archaic Ur *thesaurus*, may make us privy to a moment of conquest of a city, the inhabitants of which lift their hands in despair or capitulation. Here we shall notice a small naked(?) personage tearing at his or her flowing hair with both hands in a gesture well known even from later historical contexts. It would thus seem that the "both hands above head" gesture carries the meaning of a strong emotional display of the person showing it, be it in joy (dance) or grief (destruction). As for the sceptre and the horned crown, a well-known ensign of divine status (*Romano 2008*), a naked personage seated on a throne(?) and boasting long hair and beard(?) wields both these attributes.

UE III: 262

UE III: 375

UE III: 388

The act of drinking probably falls within the abovementioned AMOR sphere of fertility symbolism. The same possibly goes for the tree image, also accompanying icons related to this general theme.

Such scenes do have antecedents in the art of the Late Uruk-age seals. Two recently published impressions from Uruk display the boat motif. One of them shows a boat approaching a "temple", with naked rowers and a naked helmsman(?) (*Boehmer 2001*, 11, Taf. 95: 1). The other depicts also a boat approaching a "temple". In this case, clothed figures in the ship lift their hands in a clasping gesture while another large clothed figure holds something hanging down (a waistbelt?) close to a "temple" building, all of these being also located within the ship. The edifice on the bank features the distinctive protrusions and a clothed human (female?) figure standing by it holds a staff(?) with both hands (*Boehmer 2001*, 11, Taf. 95: 2). This is the only instance when the "hands above head" gesture associates with a boat motif.

A most interesting body of information has been presented by Herbert Sauren (1980). According to his observations, the goddess Inanna possesses a heavenly bark, functioning also as the bark of the dead, which may be used to reach the Nether world (most recently see *Selz 2014b*, 63–65). In addition to this, the goddess of the realm of the dead is also a moon goddess. Inanna's role in liminal situations has also been commented upon by Caitlín Barrett (2007). Here we have a direct link between the spheres of fertility and death. Our version of the "boat of the deceased" may thus point, with the symbolism of travel upon the fateful waters, to the realm of moon deities, reigning supreme at Ur.

Catherine Breniquet (*Breniquet 2008*, 364–367) has recently put forward a most interesting proposition according to which boating scenes, chiefly of the Akkad age, may symbolically refer to re-birth of the boat passenger(s). A link with our imagery, which may also refer to re-incarnation of the journey's chief protagonist(s), seems to be quite in place.

It remains only to be added that a number of specialists associate boat-travel scenes with the Nether-World voyage of the solar deity, possibly Šamaš, and even with the moon god Sin (as reviewed in *Ławecka 2009*, 134–136). A link between the *dieu-bateau*, Sin's moon sickle, and the horned tiara as a divine ensign has been established recently (*Romano 2008*, esp. pp. 47–49). Gebhard Selz (*2004a*, 45–46, fn. 127) has commented upon the boat models, known from slightly later Ur burials (e.g. *Woolley 1934*, 71, in PG 789), as vehicles for the journey into the kingdom of the dead.

As to the connection between boats and a LUGAL, we may point to a personal name lugal-ma$_2$-tab-ba = "LUGAL … a two-pronged boat(?)" (*Andersson 2012*, 180, fn. 1091).

In conclusion, the boat scenes may depict voyages of personages of perhaps divine, or at any rate elevated social status, refreshing themselves by drinking, sometimes supplied by provisions, and served by attendants who direct the course of the boat. The foliate prow and stern of one of the boats (*UE III*: 300) finds counterparts in trees growing along the watercourse banks. In two cases, persons watching the scene from dry land display a state of high emotional excitement. The equivalence of death with crossing of a body of water (the Hubur river) has also been pointed out as one of the independent Mesopotamian traditions of passing away by both Jean Bottéro (1980, 31, 32) and Wilfred Lambert (1980, 59).

On the other hand, crossing a body of water does also symbolize birth, as noted by Manfred Krebernik (apud *Andersson 2012*, 69, fn. 345 and 346, and 152). The link between boat imagery and childbirth has recently been illuminated by Therese Rodin (*Rodin 2014*, 145–148).In second-millennium incantations, even the moon god assists human birth (*Andersson 2012*, 135).

Things being as they are, we cannot get rid of the assumption that what we have before our eyes are scenes of departure of important personages – deities, kings, deified kings? – from this life, or, alternatively, of their arrival to those who eagerly await their returns. The high status of the boats' occupants, the emotion shown by their attendants, and the fertility symbolism of the trees, drinking scenes, and possibly by other provisions contained within the vessels, all induce me to suppose that these scenes depict the departure of (deified?) elite individuals, of a status equal to one of the dying and reviving deities (Dumuzi, for instance), from this life, or, alternatively, their return to our world and to its denizens.

If this is so, then the provisions carried within the boats would symbolize the actual grave goods deposited within the burials, and the oarsmen could stand for persons who accompanied the principal occupants of the "royal graves" in the nether world. That, however, would mean stretching the available evidence too far.

Total count of sealings	Sealings of moveable items	Sealings of immovable structures	Same seal on both movables and immovables	Unidentified sealing carrier
8	0	1	0	7

HIC SUNT LEONES

Under this heading I include all motifs from the archaic Ur seals which I am at a loss to understand.

Items: *UE III*: 134 (= my # 26), 136, 145, 146, 147, 149, 154, 157, 163, 164, 166, 170, 171, 172 (= my # 30), 173, 174, 176, 177, 178, 179, 182, 183, 208, 221, 265, 278, 435, 451, 457, 467, 470, 553, *Moorey 1979*, 184, 563 (no context), 565, 570, 575 (no context), 591 (no context), *Matthews 1993*, 30, 86, 94, 95, 97, 106, *Scott 2005*, 163, 171, 199, 212, 251, 252, 255, 265, 290, 296, 371, 480, 502, 613, 617, 626, 654, 660, 662, 663, 674, 677, 684, 690, 705, 706, 710, 712, 714, 717, 723, 735, 736, 737, 739, 741, 743, 757, 763, 768, 775, 776, 780, 781, 786, 787, 788, 789, 792, 794, 795, 797, 800, 802, 803, 804, 810, 817, 819, 842, 877, 879, 880, 908, 912, 926, 949, 974, 982, 992, 1026. Total 115 items.

Two categories of seal impressions may be found herewith: those which, though more or less complete, do not fit into any of the abovementioned categories, and those which have sustained damage to such an extent that they fall short of providing any more extensive contextual information on the pictorial contexts conveyed.

Sealings *UE III*: 18 and 170 convey, by means of their double swirl, information relevant from the viewpoint of a wider historical context. They find their counterparts in motifs of wall paintings from the Banesh phase of the site of Tall-i Malyan (Anshan, late fourth to early third pre-Christian millenium, see *Sumner 2003*, Fig. 19).

UE III: 170

An example of the former category is constituted by seals *UE III*: 145, 146 and 147, carrying an ornament of a row of rhomboids filled in by oblique lines. A relation to *UE III*: 26 (= my # 6) may be presumed, but I see no way of confirming it, or, for that matter, of using it for any reliable and dependable argument.

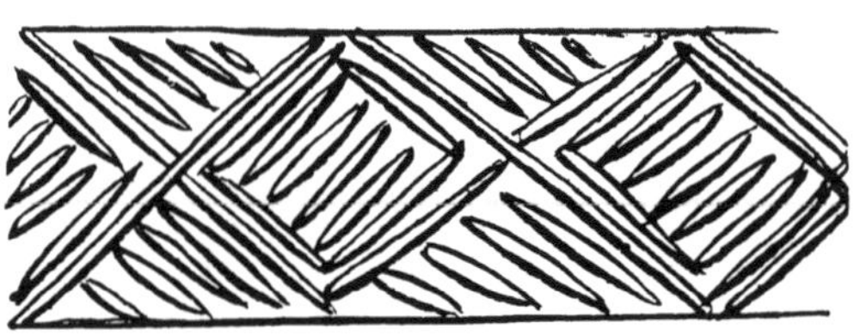

UE III: 146

Here an interesting detour may take us towards the chequerboard patterns, once so prolific on the painted potteries of prehistoric Susa, for instance (*Charvát 2005a*, 44–48, 79–81, 101–102, 108, 162, 191–193). The motif is early (*UE III*: 28, SIS 6-7) and surprisingly, it turns up at archaic Ur composed of the biconical ornament elements which may be termed "hourglass" or "butterfly" (*UE III*: 165, 167, 168 and 169). The pastoral motifs in *UE III*: 167 and 168, and even more the banquet scene of *UE III*: 169, may imply fertility symbolism, as is also suggested by the composition of UE III: 209 (= my # 32), linking the chequerboard with images of a spread eagle laying its claws on the hind parts of two symmetrically disposed hornless quadrupeds, an *edinnu* image and the U_4 sign. The geometrical composition involving a bovid(?), a group of symmetrically disposed horned animals (antelopes?), a chequerboard pattern and an UB sign in *UE III*: 239 (= my # 36) belongs to the most elegant creations of the seal-cutters of archaic Ur. Finally, a definite case of the association of chequerboard with fertility is provided by the *coitus* scene of *UE III*: 368 which I have already mentioned (see above, the "AMOR – emblems" section).

UE III: 28

UE III: 169

The latter group of examples suffers, of course, from the fortunes of object preservation, which sometimes inflicted considerable damage on the information value of the sealings in question. This is particularly painful in case of proto-cuneiform script signs which are thereby deprived of the chances they would have had if the respective compositions survived in their entirety. The cases in point include *UE III:* 134 (= my # 26), in which the handwritten gloss denotes the adressee of the delivery(?), but gives no clue as to its content. The same goes for *UE III*: 154 with its 7-rayed AN sign, for UE III: 278 with its images of a tree, a bird and an 8-rayed AN sign, or for *UE III*: 172 (= my # 30) with swirls and the AB sign.

UE III: 278

The item *Scott 2005*, 199, does probably not represent a sealing. This may be a fragment of an envelope of a cuneiform tablet bearing sings of writing. At first sight, signs like numeral denotations, SAR, MUNUS or DU_8, may be distinguished.

Total count of sealings	Sealings of moveable items	Sealings of immovable structures	Same seal on both movables and immovables	Unidentified sealing carrier
115	18	46	0	51

* * *

VOICES AND IMAGES OF THE PAST: SIGNS OF PROTO-CUNEIFORM WRITING WITHIN SEAL ICONOGRAPHY OF ARCHAIC UR

UR_2

Let us now see in what way the pictorial evidence supplied by the seals of archaic Ur may be rendered more transparent by taking into consideration the signs of proto-cuneiform writing included in individual iconic schemes.

With the UR_2 sign, the first sphere proposed, that of AMOR, displays it only with other symbols that I have termed emblems. However, at least the first of these, my # 21 (*UE III*: 102), speaks with unusual clarity, identifying the event with sexual intercourse of man and woman and adding a community name (see above). Three other instances – those of *UE III*: 259, 271 and 272 – include the sign among images of a URI_3 standard, scorpion, "inverted tripod" and with pointed-end ovals (*UE III*: 259), depictions of a tree and an ibex (*UE III*: 271), and two "star" ensigns – one four-pointed and the other seven-pointed –, pointed-end ovals, a scorpion and a spread eagle (*UE III*: 272). Thus all these emblems presumably fall within the same sphere of fertility and procreation force.

UE III: 259

UE III: 272

In view of LABOR, only once does the UR_2 sign link up with an image of a herd of animals (UE III: 199).

UE III: 199

Surprisingly enough, six items may be assigned to the combat sphere. No more than two cases involve an animal conflict: lion-versus-quadruped, with a spread eagle (*UE III*: 218), and three lions against horned quadruped, with another quadruped fleeing (*UE III*: 238). In four cases, the UR_2 sign makes up a component of a scene showing a quadruped attacked by a lion who, in his turn, is attacked by a human hero (*UE III*: 247, 252, 253 and possibly also 257). Once the sign crops up in a labour image: in *UE III*: 349, a human personage touches a jar in front of a hut with two animals issuing out of it (the sign appearing twice).

UE III: 218

UE III: 238

UE III: 257

We get most interesting information from the HONOR sphere. Two scenes of divine cults merit particular attention. The UR_2 may represent a symbol situated in the temple cella, or may simply stand for what was being worshiped there (my # 43 = *UE III*: 296). Alternatively, the UR_2 might have possessed its own house (*UE III*: 438 = my # 102: E_2+UR_2, NIN, PIRIG?, DU_6, GA_2 × AN or $ESIR_2$ = house of UR_2 ritual?, NIN, animals?, sacred hill, bitumen?). Also, various commodities were brought to (cultic?) statues under the UR_2 title (my ## 57–59 = *UE III*: 395, with the sign group UR_4 KAB ALAM UR_2 DU_8 = "wool clip in baskets, sttatue, fertility ritual performed (or, alternatively, fertility released)". The supplying of a clip of sheep wool, noted down in *Matthews* 1993, 74 (= my # 100, UDU UR_4 DUG UR_2) probably belongs hither as well. This kind of service might have been undertaken (also?) by communities. Once a "City League" seal features the UR_2 sign (my # 65 = *UE III*: 402). Such deliveries might have even been taking place with a certain periodicity: the seal *Moorey* 1979, 571 (= my # 126), displays signs U_4, UR_2, U_4+AŠ, and may thus hint at a monthly repeated event.

No references to UR_2 turn up in the "honour to princes" sphere, nor are they to be found in the DOLOR-sphere images. This might hint that the entity was supposed to be activated for the benefit of a common good, to enhance life and fertility, not having anything in common with the Nether world.

In this particular instance we may be confronted with a polyvalent sign used in actual practice. The core sememe probably alluded to a fertility-triggering ceremony, as mentioned in *UE III*: 102. In actual practice, however, the sign could also refer to a symbol worshiped in a temple, to deliveries supplied either in reward for carrying out the ceremony, or to fulfil a duty towards the abovementioned idol, or even to venerate (other) temple statues. The other images of the herding-, combat- and labour spheres might then represent further supplies intended for the ceremony. Or do they simply refer to contributions (= tributes, taxes), accruing to the central administration from these economic pursuits – from herding, and expoitation of uncultivated landscape?

UR_2 – table of occurrences of the sign in the imagery of the archaic Ur seals

AMOR	Banquet	Nil
	Dance	Nil
	Birthing	Nil
	Coitus	Nil
	Emblems	4
LABOR	Herding	1
	Combat	6
	Humans at work	1

HONOR	Gods	2
	Communities	4
	princes	Nil
DOLOR	Waters of eternal return	Nil

DIN

The sign DIN (see http://psd.museum.upenn.edu/epsd/nepsd-frame.html [accessed October 4, 2014] kas or $kaš_2$, "alcoholic drink") constitutes a less transparent example of utilization of proto-cuneiform signs in image composition of the archaic Ur seals. Within the AMOR sphere, one clear attestation relates to dance (my # 49 = *UE III*: 329), which might be expected. The LABOR sphere contributes five examples in all. Two examples find accommodation within the combat sub-sphere: *UE III*: 241 and *UE III*: 252, both featuring a classical group of quadruped attacked by lion attacked, in its turn, by a naked hero. Was the sign truly used as a filler motif to avoid empty spaces in the composition here? Three other examples supply an additional aspect to the labour scenes joining together human figures touching large jars, quadrupeds, and "huts with protrusions":*UE III*: 332, *UE III*: 349 and *Moorey* 1979, 596. The "touching of the jar" could thus have something in common with brewing, but then what are the animals doing there? Finally, let us note the one single instance in which the DIN sign falls to the HONOR sphere, turning up with "City League" toponyms (*UE III:* 404 = my # 67).

UE III: 241

UE III: 332

In this case the DIN sign appears well and nigh where we would expect it to be, denoting seemingly a companion to merrymaking. The only exception, constituted by its appearance in the combat sub-sphere, is difficult to explain.

DIN – table of occurrences of the sign in the imagery of the archaic Ur seals

AMOR	Banquet	Nil
	Dance	1
	Birthing	Nil
	Coitus	Nil
	Emblems	Nil
LABOR	Herding	Nil
	Combat	2
	Humans at work	3
HONOR	Gods	Nil
	Communities	1
	Princes	Nil
DOLOR	Waters of eternal return	Nil

KAK

This sign, with other readings DU_3 and RU_2 (*ZATU* No. 280 p. 207 = *MSVO* 1 pp. 116 and 163) has a general sense "to enact", "to make something", "to create". See now the PSD, http://psd.museum.upenn.edu/epsd/nepsd-frame.html [accessed October 4, 2014] s. v. du (= Akkadian *banû* "to create; build; engender"). As such it may be expected to line up with the same fertility-symbolism sphere as the UR_2 sign.

In the AMOR: emblems subsphere, it does indeed occur with chequerboard, spread eagle, and scorpion icons, all pointing to the abovementioned symbolism (my # 122 = *UE III*: 556). Two cases of appearance of this sign link up with the LABOR: herding sub-sphere, accompanying images of a quadruped with curved horns and a spread eagle (*UE III*: 202) and of a tree, a quadruped and a naked human propelling another quadruped with stick (*UE III*: 304). Other two instances fall within the LABOR: combat sub-sphere. One shows the classical quadruped-lion-human schema (*UE III*: 249), the other a human-lion conflict (*Matthews 1993*, 96). Finally, the HONOR: communities sphere shows one single instance where this sign accompanies an *edinnu* device (my # 115 = *UE III*: 463).

UE III: 304

UE III: 249

Here it seems that the sign "behaves itself" and occurs in contexts rather similar to the UR_2 grapheme, but the low number of examples warns against putting forward any more general conclusions. In fact, however, this could as well be taken at its face value, and be interpreted as a reference to a contribution (tribute, tax) for building, since the ED-I city of Ur saw a great deal of building activities, and the community could have been called upon to help bear the material costs of erection of the new communal edifices. Who will ever discern the truth?

KAK – table of occurrences of the sign in the imagery of the archaic Ur seals

<table>
<tr><td rowspan="5">AMOR</td><td>Banquet</td><td>Nil</td></tr>
<tr><td>Dance</td><td>Nil</td></tr>
<tr><td>Birthing</td><td>Nil</td></tr>
<tr><td>Coitus</td><td>Nil</td></tr>
<tr><td>Emblems</td><td>1</td></tr>
<tr><td rowspan="3">LABOR</td><td>Herding</td><td>2</td></tr>
<tr><td>Combat</td><td>2</td></tr>
<tr><td>Humans at work</td><td>Nil</td></tr>
<tr><td rowspan="3">HONOR</td><td>Gods</td><td>Nil</td></tr>
<tr><td>Communities</td><td>1</td></tr>
<tr><td>Princes</td><td>Nil</td></tr>
<tr><td>DOLOR</td><td>Waters of eternal return</td><td>Nil</td></tr>
</table>

* * *

AS TIME GOES BY: ARCHAIC UR SEAL IMAGERY WITHIN THE DEVELOPMENT OF SUMERIAN GLYPTIC, C. 3500–2200 B.C.

The time has now come to situate the seal images of archaic Ur within the historical context of nascent statehood of ancient Mesopotamia. Let us see how numerous the particular categories of the Ur sealings are. At first, let us inspect the earliest SIS 8-6.

Representation of motifs, Ur SIS 8-6

AMOR	Banquet	1
	Dance	Nil
	Birthing	1
	Coitus	Nil
	Emblems	2
AMOR total		4 (= 13.8%)
LABOR	Herding	4
	Combat	1
	Humans at work	5
LABOR total		10 (= 34.4%)
HONOR	Gods	1
	Communities	8
	Princes	Nil
HONOR total		9 (= 31.0%)
DOLOR	Waters of eternal return	1 (= 3.4%)
HIC SUNT LEONES		5 (= 17.2%)
GRAND TOTAL		29

Now let us survey the situation of SIS 5-4 from which most of the sealings were retrieved.

Representation of motifs, Ur SIS 5-4

AMOR	Banquet	8
	Dance	8
	Birthing	7
	Coitus	8
	Emblems	28
AMOR total		59 (= 11.2%)
LABOR	Herding	86
	Combat	48
	Humans at work	40
LABOR total		174 (= 33.0%)

HONOR	Gods	38
	Communities	121
	Princes	12
HONOR total		171 (= 32.5%)
DOLOR	Waters of eternal return	8 (= 1.5%)
HIC SUNT LEONES		115 (= 21.0%)
GRAND TOTAL		527

These two tables will constitute our departure point for a comparative study of the archaic Ur seal imagery with iconographic *thesauri* of the epochs that preceded the early ED-I (Late Uruk – Jemdet Nasr) and that followed it (ED-II–III and Akkad). I proceed to classify the seal imagery of the adjacent historical periods by means of the same concept and categories, so that the similarities and differences will stand out clearly.

***

THE ANCESTRAL EXPERIENCE: LATE URUK – JEMDET NASR GLYPTIC

At first the Late Uruk to Jemdet Nasr seal depictions shall be studied on the base of a sizable sample of the period's glyptic assembled Elena Rova (*Rova* 1994). The results are subsumed in the following table.

Seal imagery of the Late Uruk to Jemdet Nasr periods (comprehensive)

AMOR	Banquet	1
	Dance (here music)	2
	Birthing	5
	Coitus	Nil
	Emblems	1
AMOR total		9 (= 0.9%)
LABOR	Herding	28
	Combat	38
	Humans at work	119
	Animal files	300
	Human files	84
	Human and animal files	34
	Provisions	82
LABOR total		685 (= 71.1%)
HONOR	Gods	38
	Communities	2
	Princes	9
	Buildings only	21
	War scenes (incl. POW)	8
HONOR total		78 (= 8.1%)

DOLOR	Waters of eternal return	7 (= 0.7%)
SIMULACRA	Artificial compositions	82 (= 8.5%)
HIC SUNT LEONES		103 (= 10.7%)
GRAND TOTAL		964

The differences between the then ancient Late Uruk and archaic Ur strike the eye. In both its chronological segments, the archaic Ur material shows proportions amounting to slightly above ten per cent (AMOR), roughly one-third (LABOR), roughly one-third (HONOR), up to ten per cent (DOLOR) and around twenty per cent for the LEONES sections. As against this, the Late Uruk – Jemdet Nasr figures show a definite prevalence of the LABOR sphere with its amazing 71 per cent, with HONOR, SIMULACRA, AMOR and DOLOR reaching less than ten per cent each, and the LEONES value slightly surpassing ten per cent. The Proto-literate LABOR and HONOR spheres also display a more complex articulation, and the SIMULACRA section, accounting for the artificial and fantastic devices seen on Late Uruk – Jemdet Nasr seals such as the "heraldically disposed lions" or the mythical birds enclosed in guilloche-framed compartments, does not exist at Ur at all.

Here the shift towards the social and representational aspects of the seal imagery of archaic Ur from purely economic and production-oriented icons of the Late Uruk – Jemdet Nasr age makes itself manifest, though it must, of course, be acknowledged that the sphere of earlier seals did not include "City League" matrices – but, after all, this is one of the innovations which we are keen to discern.

In order to achieve a more informative insight into the Late Uruk – Jemdet Nasr glyptic, let us now investigate it by an "anatomical dissection" showing transformations of the iconographic *thesaurus* over the Late Uruk period. This will be done with recourse to the chronology of the earliest Late Uruk seal impressions submitted by Rainer Michael Boehmer (1999).

Seal imagery of the Uruk V sub-phase (*Boehmer 1999*, 3–33)

LABOR	Combat	3
	Animal files	4
	Provisions	5
LABOR total		12
HONOR	Gods	3
	Princes	2
	Buildings only	1
	War scenes (incl. POW)	5
HONOR total		11
SIMULACRA	Artificial compositions	2
GRAND TOTAL		25

This review shows a rather more nuanced vision of the Late Uruk glyptic. The LABOR sphere is more or less on a par with that of the HONOR, emphasizing, aside of economic aspects, the warrior ethos of the initial Late Uruk endeavour.

Seal imagery of the Uruk IV-b sub-phase (*Boehmer* 1999, 34–48)

LABOR	Combat	1
	Animal files	9
	Human files	1
	Provisions	1
LABOR total		12
SIMULACRA	Artificial compositions	5
GRAND TOTAL		17

Things have moved visibly by now. No more war exploits, just the procurement of bare necessities of everyday provisioning commands the day.

Seal imagery of the Uruk IV-a sub-phase (*Boehmer* 1999, 49–80)

AMOR	Birthing	2
AMOR total		2
LABOR	Combat	3
	Animal files	10
	Human files	2
	Human and animal files	1
LABOR total		16
HONOR	Gods	1
	Princes	1
	War scenes (incl. POW)	3
HONOR total		5
SIMULACRA	Artificial compositions	10
GRAND TOTAL		33

Here the economy still prevails, but due honour is being rendered both to deities and to princes. We begin, however, to discern the winds of change.

The first representative of the archaic-Ur AMOR sphere turns up with the "birthing" icon. However, only in one case does the "wanton lady", as I have denoted the naked human (female?) figure sitting *en face* with legs spread apart, appear in a context in which she could symbolize the procreative forces of nature (*Boehmer* 1999, Abb. 66, p. 54, with animals). The other case (*Boehmer* 1999, Abb. 65, p. 54) features the figure, accompanied by horned quadrupeds, in an upper register of a seal, the lower register of which displays rows of prisoners of war detained by guardians. Here we are tempted to interpret the "wanton lady" image as an ensign of troops of the Late-Uruk polity, bringing in human booty after a victorious military campaign.

This image also points to the fact that war is back on the glyptic scene.

Seal imagery of the Anu-ziggurat at Uruk (by and large, Uruk IV-a sub-phase, *Boehmer 1999*, 81–104)

LABOR	Animal files	4 on stamp seals, 4 on cylinder-seal impressions
	Human files	1
	Human and animal files	2
	Provisions	2
LABOR total		4 stamp seals, 9 cylinder-seal impressions
HONOR	Gods	2
HONOR total		2
SIMULACRA	Artificial compositions	4
HIC SUNT LEONES		2 on stamp seals, 5 on cylinder-seal impressions
GRAND TOTAL		6 stamp seals, 20 cylinder-seal impressions

The character of the Anu seals accords, by and large, with the last phase of the Late Uruk seal imagery, though the composition of the group with its stamp seals does betray a certain traditionalism of this find set.

Seal imagery of the clay *bullae* of Late Uruk culture of Uruk (by and large, "frühe Späturukzeit" = Uruk IV-b sub-phase, *Boehmer 1999*, 105–111)

LABOR	Combat	1
	Animal files	13
	Human files	1, 1 on counter-marking stamp seal
	Human and animal files	1
LABOR total		16, 1 on stamp seal
HONOR	Princes	1
	Buildings only	2 on counter-marking stamp seals
HONOR total		1, 2 on stamp seals
SIMULACRA	Artificial compositions	7
HIC SUNT LEONES		3
GRAND TOTAL		27, 3 on counter-marking stamp eseals

Though Rainer M. Boehmer notes the Elamite character of the seals used on clay bullae (*Boehmer 1999*, 105–108), the iconography falls in with the middle stage of the Late Uruk cultural phase. Here the interesting feature may be seen in the first instances of counter-marking the *bullae* closed by cylinder-seal impressions, by the use of stamp seals (*Boehmer 1999*, p. 111, ## 54 and 55).

These observations outline the extent of the archaic Ur innovations with sufficient clarity. In the Late Uruk – Jemdet Nasr glyptic phase, the AMOR sphere was next to non-existent and the heavily prevailing LABOR images dominated the field, with an exception of the initial Late Uruk sub-phase charaterized by a more balanced relation between the LABOR and HONOR complexes. With respect to this feature the archaic Ur seal-cutters might be said to have reverted to age-old patterns of their craft, though, of course, this must not be taken literally, as some five to three hundred years lied between them and their initial Late Uruk ancestors.

It should also be observed that the particular iconic themes underwent a thorough re-working in the archaic Ur vision. The Uruk version of the AMOR birthing image differs, in its ensign function, considerably from that of Ur. The LABOR icons feature many more actual scenes of humans at work in Uruk than in Ur. Moreover, the specific categories of human-, animal- and human-cum-animal files figure much more prominently at Uruk than at Ur. Archaic Ur seal-cutters did not use the theme denoted here as Provisions, chiefly Boehmer's "Ölgefäße mit Fransentücher", which he (probably correctly) interprets as referring to textile deliveries in pottery (storage-) jars. The Ur craftsmen who carved seals belonging to the LABOR: combat subsphere knew nothing about the "caged lion" icon of Tell Brak, though they put forward their own version of the "king spearing a lion" motif (*McMahon 2009*). At Uruk, the HONOR sphere shows many brutally realistic war depictions, including treatment of captives, than we may register from archaic Ur. The Uruk SIMULACRA category ushers in compositions of decorative or even ornamental character either completely invented, or such using real entities in a fancy manner, such as "heraldically disposed lions", for instance.

Elaborating on the heritage of their predecessors, the artists of archaic Ur nevertheless chose to pose their accents as they themselves deemed expedient. It is, however, a question whether the archaic Ur ideas already fixed some of the Uruk images into *morphómata*, canonized art devices carrying fixed semantic contents pertinent to the *Herrschaft* sphere (here perhaps best translated as "suzerainty"), in the sense proposed by Dietrich Boschung and Günther Blamberger (*Boschung-Blamberger 2011*). At least in some cases this seems to apply. The *coitus* scenes from Ur find a parallel in a "cylinder-seal" impression from Khirbet ez-Zeraqon in Palestine (*de Miroschedji 2011a*, 115–116, Fig. 4: 1 on p. 116; on the overall context see *de Miroschedji 2011b*). A number of parallels for the "birthing" icon have been collected by Stefania Mazzoni (2002).

THE INHERITORS OF ARCHAIC UR: LATER THIRD-MILLENIUM SUMERIAN GLYPTIC

In enquiring how the iconographic *thesaurus* created by the authors of the archaic Ur seals, I shall take up the evidence from Fara, ancient Shuruppak, as a pilot site. The excavations at Fara have yielded a sizeable group of glyptic finds, reaching from the Jemdet Nasr- down to the earlier ED-III time periods (around, say, 2500 B.C.). Therefore, the evidence it offers gives us a unique advantage of surveying a development of glyptic throughout the period of our interest at a single archaeological site.

Fara (Shuruppak): ED-I seals (*Martin 1988*, 69–70, # 111–228)

AMOR	Banquet	1
	Emblems	9
AMOR total		10
LABOR	Herding	7
	Combat	24
	Humans at work	4
	Animal files	17
	Human files	9
	Human and animal files	10
LABOR total		71
HONOR	Gods	5
	Princes	1
HONOR total		6
GEOMETRICA	Geometrical compositions	9
SCRIPTURA	Writing	1
HIC SUNT LEONES		22
GRAND TOTAL		109

This result shows that considerable variety still reigned during the ED-I age in Mesopotamia. The preponderance of the LABOR category stands out, though this might be caused by the fact that some of the less well-preserved "files" scenes could have originally belonged to the veneration themes (rows of animals and/or humans approaching temples or princes = HONOR). It seemed opportune to me to single out geometrical-ornament seals under a separate category GEOMETRICA, with a single SCRIPTURA occurrence of an inscribed seal (Martin 1988, 238, Cat. No. 131). Of course, the low count of the HONOR category follows out of the fact that no "City League" seals or sealings turned up at ED-I Fara.

Fara (Shuruppak): ED-II seals of the Elegant style (*Martin 1988*, 73, # 227–361)

AMOR	Emblems	3
LABOR	Herding	2
	Combat	83
	Combat, spread-eagle emblem	7
	Human files	2
	Animal files	11
	Human and animal files	7
LABOR total		112
SIMULACRA		4
HIC SUNT LEONES		15
GRAND TOTAL		134

Here the trend towards preponderance of the combat scene, especially the "Master of animals" variety, comes to the fore for the first time.

Fara (Shuruppak): ED-II seals of the Crossed style (*Martin 1988*, 74, # 362–416)

LABOR	Combat	46
	Combat, spread-egale emblem	3
	Animal files	1
LABOR total		50
HIC SUNT LEONES		5
GRAND TOTAL		55

The combat themes dominate by now the glyptic iconography of Fara.

Fara (Shuruppak): ED-IIIa seals (*Martin 1988*, 78–79, # 421–500)

LABOR	Combat	55
	Combat, spread-eagle emblem	2
	Human files	3
	Animal files	14
	Human and animals files	2
	Animal protomes and masks	1
LABOR total		77
HIC SUNT LEONES		3
GRAND TOTAL		80

Here also, the combat themes constitute a major feature of the glyptic iconography of Fara.

The ED-II–IIIa imagery of Fara (Shuruppak) seals did nonetheless include other themes as well. These include the banquet scenes, which, unfortunately, cannot be more closely dated (*Martin 1988*, 79, # 506–544). These supply 39 examples, including one example of a spread-eagle icon, 2 scorpion images and 4 depictions of music-making.

Another example of a traditional scene may be seen in boating scenes of Fara (*Martin 1988*, 79–80, # 545–560). In two instances the boat crews seem to hunt animals with spears (*Martin 1988*, # 545, 546, probably ED-I). Two other instances do, however, show the boats accompanied by a plow and a (human-headed) lion, both of which accompanied the water-craft *(dieu-bateau)* of the solar deity, Šamaš, on later, Akkadian seals (*Martin 1988*, 80, # 558–559). Is this a testimony of the character of these scenes in which the boats carried their passengers into other worlds?

It is now clear that with the progress of the third pre-Christian millennium, the iconic *répertoire* of archaic Ur underwent a substantial truncation. Instead of the original richness and variety of the glyptic themes, later Early Dynastic seal imagery displays no more than three main motifs:

- the heavily predominant combat scenes,
- with banquet-, and
- boating devices leading a not very close second and third position.

Nevertheless, in these three seal-image categories the posterity of archaic Ur lived visibly on.

Let us now see how far the compositions carved by the seal-cutters of archaic Ur into their products consolidated into *morphómata*, canonized art devices carrying definite semantic contents, pertaining, in our case, to the *Herrschaft* sphere (here perhaps best translated as “suzerainty” or “governance”), in the sense proposed by Dietrich Boschung and Günther Blamberger (*Boschung-Blamberger 2011*). For this purpose I shall consult another sizeable sample of third-millennium cylinder seals of the Early Dynastic to Akkadian ages (c. 2700–2200 B.C.): those bearing inscriptions, and treated presently by Karin Rohn (*2011*).

It follows out of the investigations of this author that by far the most frequent device borne by seals of that age is the *Tierkampfszene* motif, my combat theme, which the authors of the archaic Ur seals, taking up the heritage of their ancestors, certainly launched into a very high orbit (*Rohn 2011*, Kap. 2, 14–51). In the scene of the “king versus lion” combat this design lived for more than two thousand years (*McMahon 2009*, 121–123). The second place goes to the clearly less frequent banquet seals (*Rohn 2011*, Kap. 3, 52–59). The fact that two seals combine the *Tierkampf* and banquet themes merits attention, but neither of these items does have an archaeological context, both having been acquired by purchase (*Rohn 2011*, 16, # 24 and 25). From among the “Other scenes” (*Rohn 2011*, Kap. 6, 86–98), we may also notice

- hunting motifs, and
- those showing defence of domestic animals against beasts of prey (*Rohn* *2011*, 90). Next in line are the
- human-file compositions (*Rohn 2011*, 92),
- one single *coitus* depiction (see also the abovementioned Khirbet ez-Zeraqon “seal impression” from Palestine), and
- the device of two quadrupeds arranged symmetrically with a tree in between them (*Rohn 2011*, 96).

All of these ensigns last down to the Akkadian period.

To this should now also be added the “birthing” icon, first occurring in Late Uruk seal imagery but definitely passed on by the artists of archaic Ur and subsisting until the early second millennium (*Mazzoni 2002*).

These icons can thus be said to approach the *morphómata* category, though we do not know their precise meaning, or rather, it remains hidden from us whether such images carried a definite and fixed semantic content. The latter seems to apply to the *Tierkampfszene* motif, clearly a status marker of Mesopotamian elite personages of the second and third Early Dynastic periods and the Akkadian era (c. 2600 – c. 2200 B.C.), unlike the earlier times, when these heroic exploits represented but a part of the entire iconographic *répertoire*. Neither was the occurrence of this icon limited to Mesopotamia only: some 80% of the ED glyptic from Tell Brak, Syria, bear contest scenes (*Matthews 1997*, 132). It may be asked how far king Mesannepada of Kiš and Ur (2563–2524 B.C.) who had used this device on his official seal (my # 121 = *UE III*: 518), introduced this motif as a sort of a “coat-of-arms” of Sumerian and Akkadian ruling-class individuals; Adelheid Otto (*Otto 2013*) does not hesitate to mark the man-versus-animal combat scenes as prerogatives of kings.

* * *

IV. THE CITY OF UR AT THE BEGINNING OF THE THIRD MILLENNIUM: SUMMARY OF WRITTEN AND ARCHAEOLOGICAL EVIDENCE

Contemporary authors dwelling on post-Uruk developments within ancient Mesopotamian polities draw a gloomy picture of collapse of the once unified Late-Uruk commonwealth and its decomposition into a host of city states gradually entering the arena of public competition. These polities, vying for a domination of the Sumerian political sphere, are held responsible for he internecine wars characterizing the later part of the Early Dynastic period of Mesopotamian history (roughly 3000–2334 B.C.). Such stormy events are then deemed to have taken an abrupt end with the sweeping conquest of the brilliant strategist and commander who entered history under the name which he appropriated upon his conquest – Sargon (Šarrukin, the "legitimate king"), builder of a unified Akkadian empire and restorer of imperial peace (for the last comprehensive presentation of this concept see *Edzard 2009*; for an excellent introduction to recent developments within Near Eastern archaeology see *Lehmann 1999*).

Various reasons have been proposed for what has just been described. For the time being, the greatest influence is exercised by a treatise seeking the explanation in economic and political superiority of southeastern Mesopotamia, historical Sumer, over what it terms the "periphery" of the Near Eastern world at the beginning of its ancient history (*Algaze 1993*). This hypothesis, inspired by modern economic theories, has received an illumination from a work published three years after its printing, that of Alan Lupton (1996). The latter author took an in-depth view of the historical development of communities outside Sumer before, during, and after what he termed the contact phase, namely the era during which these communities, situated mostly within the region known as the Fertile Crescent, found themselves facing the economic, political and spiritual challenge presented by the core area of accelerated historical development, that of Sumer. Lupton's most important contribution to our knowledge lies in his observation that the only change apparent during this historical epoch is the fact that in the post-contact period, communities outside Sumer felt the need to provide for their own defense, and thus took care to protect their members by means of military facilities, especially by fortifications (recently the same observation in *Erarslan 2009*; on Algaze's theories now also *Mazzoni 2008*, 39; *Frangipane 2010b*, esp. p. 301; *Selz 2011c*, 24; *Rothman 2013*).

Whatever the original state of things may have been, any questions linked to the demise of the Late-Uruk commonwealth must be clearly answered with reference to original sources, either historical (written texts), archaeological (artifacts and their contexts) or pictorial (iconographical materials). Let us now review all that we know from the city of Ur at the onset of the Early Dynastic period. The city of Nannar has been blessed both by an abundance of sources of this kind dating to the period under scrutiny, and by the systematic, assiduous and inspired approach of the leader of 20th-century excavations at the site, Leonard Woolley (later Sir Leonard Woolley), whose contribution to our knowledge of early history of ancient Mesopotamia cannot be overestimated.

It will be necessary that I usher in this study by a few words concerning the use of seal impressions, or sealings, as I will henceforth call them for the sake of brevity, as a major source material for historical studies, especially those of this monograph (on the interpretation of their reverses supplying the information necessary for interpretations of this kind see *Martin-Matthews 1993*, esp. p. 37; *Matthews 1993*, 44–46).

Let me begin with the essentials. In general, when we speak about sealing, that is, impressing seal matrices into soft carrier materials, we define it, implicitly or explicitly, as a physical manifestation of a relationship between an animate subject and an inanimate object. However, to apply notions like "commerce", "property", "commodity exchange" or "control", let alone "individual" or "proprietor", indiscriminately, without any attempt at closer specification of these terms with recourse to the particular spatiotemporal context in which we are moving, may lead the interpretation effort astray as we hazard to operate with ideas borrowed from modern times applicable to ancient evidence only after a rigorous source critique has been performed. Therefore, we must first ask how can we substantiate the commonly held assumption that seals constituted personal and individual emblems from time immemorial (see *Charvát 1988*; *Charvát 1992; Charvát 2005b*).

First things first: how, in fact, did the seals of the ancient Near East work? At the beginning of their history, movable-container sealing prevailed, with "lock"-sealings, those of storeroom doors, clearly in the minority, if any (see *Charvát 1992*). As far as we now know, first storeroom sealings appeared at Susa (*Amiet 1997*, 15 Fig. 2), followed by Uruk (see, for instance, *Collon 1981/1982*) and by the new evidence from Tell Brak-Majnuna (*McMahon-Oates 2007*, 164–165). In this particular instance such packages – let us adduce examples of the "mobile containers" like pots, sacks, bales, packages in various kind of wrapping and the like – visualize a unilineal interaction, and are thus apt to fall under the heading of **reciprocity** (on this see *Racine 1986*). Let me explain what I mean by an example. A delivery of goods is sealed in point A, and travels to point B, where the despatched goods are unpacked and go their way (while something else presumably goes back to the original supplier agency in compensation). Procedure of this kind may be imagined for most of the prehistoric seals and sealings of Mesopotamia. That, of course, does not authomatically exclude the existence of any other form of socially engineered exchange. In consideration of the transitory nature of a great majority of materials handled by the bearers of the prehistoric cultures of the Near East, we should better not hazard unwarranted opinions. All that can be legitimately inferred from such sealings themselves, however, is the idea of this unilateral journey of the seal-bearing commodities.

As against this, door sealings on storerooms represents a new, and historically very relevant change. Controlling access to storage facilities stands for a higher form of socially engineered exchange of goods, namely **redistribution**. First you put something **in**, and then you check how it goes **out** – goods' movement in two steps, not only one, must be presumed. In fact, this implies the presence of an administered form of social organization, chiefdom or state (see especially *Dalton* 1969, 74, Fig. 1).

On the sealed "test strips", which might also represent vouchers exchangeable for different goods or services, see now *Bretschneider-Jans* 2012, esp. pp. 16–17.

THE CITY OF UR IN THE INCIPIENT THIRD MILLENNIUM

According to the estimates of Henry T. Wright, the city of Ur occupied at that time an area of some twenty hectares, and offered home to about four thousand inhabitants, living perhaps in 600 residence units. Near Ur, a borough some eight hectares in extent housed roughly 1,600 people. In addition to this, the Ur *oecumene* comprised a few rural settlements, a rural centre with a shrine, and some (at least two) cemeteries. Approximately 6,000 hectares of arable were lying within working distance of these settlements (*Wright* 1969, 117; see also *Wilkinson* 2003, 77, Fig. 5: 3). In comparison to catchment areas of coeval Mesopotamian cities, the agricultural hinterland of the city of Ur belonged to those which were big but not biggest in extent (see the maps in *Richardson* 2012, 13, Map 2, and 15, Map 3).

SUBSISTENCE

Let us now see how did the suppliers of the bare necessities of human life fare at archaic Ur.

A branch canal of the Euphrates coming from northeast and curving around the southwest side of the Ur mound was perhaps the main source of water for the area during the early 3rd millennium (Benati 2015, 13).

Unfortunately, a limited number of palaeobotanical samples were collected during the Ur excavations, a fact which causes our blindness towards one of the most important sources for human subsistence activities. Peasants residing at the ED-I village of Sakheri Sughir by Ur left behind two grains of hulled six-row barley, and other two grains of barley not identifiable as to variety (*Wright 1969*, 90; on Late Uruk agriculture, albeit from a different geographical setting, see now *MacMahon-Oates 2007*, 166–167). Impressions of cereal grains on pottery from Ur allowed the identification of barley, followed by emmer wheat and flax, in the Ubaid period; barley only appeared on ED pottery (*Helbaek 1960*, 194–195).

We can, however, observe in this aspect is the first instance in the history of Mesopotamia when fields of Ur display the threefold administrative division into the "demesne domain" (later ni_2-en-na), "remuneration land" (šuku) and "rented-out arable" (apin-la_2), know from the later history of Sumer (*Wright 1969*, 109–111; *Pettinato 2005*, 59; on šuku in Abu Salabikh see now *Krebernik-Postgate 2009*, 20, register; most recently *Schrakamp 2014*, 696–697, fn. 11, 12). Henry T. Wright (*Wright 1969*, 111) observes that gán uru_4 (= apin-la_2) comprised large blocks of 300–400 iku and were allotted to cultivators in plots of various sizes. Gán šuku formed large blocks of 450–1100 iku, and could either be further subdivided into smaller plots, or worked by a large group. Finally, gán en occurred in large blocks of about 500 iku and might be suballotted to cultivators. The field acreages of archaic Ur were demonstrably smaller than those attested to in Late Uruk – Jemdet Nasr texts (*Pomponio 2008*, 17–19).

On the other hand, accountants responsible for field management used at least some of the traditional terms usual in earlier proto-cuneiform texts. A case in point is the še mú = "(Feld) mit Gerste bestanden", turning up in text *UET II* No. 160 line 1, and *UET II*: 359 l. 1, with a parallel in an earlier text VAT 17785+119 (*Bauer 2001–2002*, 173).

The system of capacity measures for grain utilized at archaic Ur found a widespread diffusion throughout Sumer, including Susa and also Mari. As against this, Fara, Abu Salabikh and Nippur subscribed to a different value of one gur-sag-gál = 8 bariga (*Visicato 1991*, 54; *Visicato 1994*, 88; also *Krebernik-Postgate 2009*, 12 sub # IAS 550, and 19, in register sub gur).

The distinction between arable and pasture land seems to be reflected in the GAN_2 URU and KI UDU of my # 97 = *UE III*: 432. How are the GAN_2 KI of sealing *UE III*: 155 (= my # 28) to be interpreted is not clear to me at present.

Among the commodities deposited in the storage facilities of the Ur administration, we find agricultural produce: grain, probably including threshed (or otherwise processed) cereals, flour, malt, fruit, beverages, wool or sheep fleece, orchardry- and livestock products. Archaic Ur texts record barley (še), various wheats (zíz, gig, gíg), flax (gu), and malt ($munu_4$) (*Wright* 1969, 113).

Deliveries simply denoted as ŠE give evidence on the basics of agricultural production (my # 85 = *UE III*: 423; my # 134 = *Mathews* 1993, 75). Did the Ur peasants know "barley of a double sheaf" (ŠE TAB, my # 107 = *UE III*: 443)?

Scenes displaying the BAD sign show that this probably referred to processing of grain, possibly in a mortar-like device (my # 12 = *UE III*: 79, my # 46 = *UE III*: 315, my # 48 = *UE III*: 325, my # 78 = *UE III*: 416). In fact, the lexeme may not refer literally to threshing, but to husking, a procedure described by a 19th-century author in the case of maize, but prefectly applicable to cereals, as I believe: "Sometimes the women stamp it in a wooden mortar with one, or sometimes two, long pestles to get off the outer husk" (*Buckland* 1893, 40; *Charvát* 2014b).

Flour (or cords?) appears among sacrificial offerings put in front of the spread-eagle emblem in my # 47 = *UE III*: 323.

Agricultural products ultimately acquired the form of comestibles such as bread (my # 68 = *UE III*: 405; my # 69 = *UE III*: 406?).

Beer might have been found on the premises of archaic Ur frequently (my # 68 = *UE III*: 405, and my # 107 = *UE III*: 443 – beer rations?). We read of malt (my # 93 = *UE III*: 431; my # 129 = *Matthews* 1993, 33), and an entire storeroom might have been reserved for it (my # 19 = *UE III*: 90).

The DIN sign, referring to a beverage (beer?) figures rather prominently in the Ur sealings (my # 38 = *UE III*: 252; perhaps my # 44 = *UE III:* 304; my # 49 = *UE III:* 329; my # 67 = *UE III*: 404; my # 97 = *UE III*: 432).

Comestibles containing fat in various forms, alluded to probably by the sign NI (= I_3 = LID), supplemented the diet of inhabitants of archaic Ur (my # 72 = *UE III*: 409; my # 110 = *UE III*: 454).

Palm groves offered shade and protection within the cultivated landscape around Ur (my # 97 = *UE III*: 432). Fruit orchards may have served the Ur population if the KIB/ŠENNUR sign refers to fruit (plums?) (my ## 10 = *UE III*: 77; 11 = *UE III*: 78; 29 = *UE III*: 160; 135 = *Matthews* 1993, 81; 140 = *Matthews* 1993, 102).

As to livestock-raising, evidence for domestic sheep, goat, cattle and possibly domestic pig has been gathered at the ED-I village of Sakheri Sughir by Ur (*Wright* 1969, 91; in general on this see *Englund* 1995a; Late-Uruk data, albeit from a different geographical setting, *MacMahon-Oates* 2007, 167–168). Harvests from fields of archaic Ur also supplied fodder for livestock (*Pomponio* 1991).

We may, however, surmise with a degree of probability that, continuing the practice of their predecessors, the Ur breeders tended herds of shorthorn cattle, introduced during the Late Uruk times, probably in view of their economic importance and higher productivity in terms of milk (*Kawami* 2001, for a depiction on a stone bowl from Ur see *Woolley* 1955, Pl. 35 No. U.18118, as well as *Sürenhagen* 1999, 240, Taf. 71: 1 and 3; in general see also *Pientka-Hinz* 2011).

Cows have entered the wold of the archaic Ur seal inscriptions (my # 97 = *UE III*: 432) together with their keepers (my # 93 = *UE III*: 431), as well as sheep (my # 16 = *UE III*: 84) and their wool (my ## 57–59 = *UE III*: 395; my # 100 = *UE III*: 436). The PIRIG were apparently also kept (my # 102 = *UE III*: 438). According to the archaic Ur texts, sheep and goat made up large herds there (from 100 up to more than 280 animals, *Wright* 1969, 121), and were probably distributed by some central agency for shearing, as well as meat consumption (*Wright* 1969, 105–106).

Treatment of milk products, including butter-making, finds a welcome illustration in the well-known al-Ubaid "milking-frieze", albeit from a slightly later time period (most recently *Charpin* 2011, 419–420).

We dispose of some information on sheep keeping, both from written texts and sealings (*Charvát* 2011a). Comparing the Ur evidence with that of Late-Uruk sources, we cannot fail to observe that the entire *chaîne opératoire* of wool treatment finds its reflection in Late-Uruk texts. After shearing, the clippings were at first stored in special facilities and then they travelled to treatment plants. From there, the finished textile products found their way into still other storage facilities, from which the notables of the Late-Uruk commonwealth directed their disbursement to particular consumers. In addition to increased demands on transport time, the whole process required additional energy inputs, as the managers of that era employed large jars for transport of textiles. The sheep had to be shorn in winter- or summer pastures, as the case might have been (for data from later texts of ED Lagaš see *Hruška* 1995, 81–82), but the peregrinations of bales of wool through the Late-Uruk landscapes definitely consumed time and energy.

In comparison with the Late Uruk situation, three differences in administrative practices stand out:

1) In Late Uruk times, scribes preparing documents set down in writing actually wrote their texts in the field, outside the municipal centres. Opposed to this, the agents of the archaic Ur administration operated by means of seal impressions, not by writing.

2) Late Uruk seal-bearing officials did not use inscribed seals. Opposed to this, the Ur officials carried "standardized" seals with impressions enabling them (also) to identify the products raised for the central administration (for the first time ever). Such office holders did not employ writing but they were obviously literate.

3) In Late Uruk times the wool clippings had gone through four (to five) spatially distinct treatment stages before it ended up in the Uruk storerooms.

Opposed to this, the Ur taxpayers(?) delivered the harvest shares due to the paramount administration directly to the centre, presumably, to "suburban" storage facilities, possibly on the outskirts of Ur[22]. From there the wool travelled to the weaving shops, and the sealings, as accounts, to the central registry, from the administrative discards of which the disused sealings were retrieved after nearly five thousand years.

What comes out of these observations is an image of a large organized cluster of Late-Uruk age communities, transformed into smaller, but more efficient and more 'rational' paramount administration of Early Dynastic polities. The central administration at Ur obviously cut the "carrying charges" of goods travelling throughout its realms, and entrusted the qualified treatment of raw materials – sheep wool, in our instance – to workshops situated presumably somewhere in the vicinity of its seat. It must also be seen that the Ur administration continued to employ literate officials, just as their Late-Uruk predecessors.

Here the takeover (evolution?) of the Late-Uruk commonwealth by particular Early Dynastic polities resulted in a rationalization of their procedures as well. *Si duo faciunt idem, non est idem.*

At Ur, sheep wool went sometimes to the gods, or to their statues, as sacrifice (my ## 57–59 = *UE III*: 395).

Keeping poultry may be attested to by inscriptions including the MUŠEN sign like my # 20 = *UE III*: 91.

Inscriptions on sealings from Ur also mention the output of the uncultivated landscape such as fish and other sea creatures (e.g. $KUŠU_2$, my # 4 = *UE III*: 24, or SUHUR in my # 93 = *UE III*: 431; possibly also my # 104 = *UE III*: 440).

Management of uncultivated landscape found reflection in written evidence of archaic Ur. Five documents mention reeds and reed products such as mats and baskets (*Wright* 1969, 104). The archaic Ur texts furnish information on fishing and possibly catching of wildfowl (ducks; *Wright* 1969, 104). A recently published Early Dynastic statuette of dugong ivory points to the exploitation of a whole range of maritime resources (*Caubet-Poplin* 2003).

Rings of pottery, found at Sakheri Sughir, an ED-I village by Ur, have been singled out as net sinkers and may thus attest to fishing, much as a bitumen fragment of coating of a small water craft, or *quffa*, found at the same site (*Wright* 1969, 58, 60 Fig. 14: d, 61). The inhabitants of this village supplemented

22 That is, if the reverses of sealings ## 20 (*UE III*: 91), 22 (*UE III*: 105), and 59 (*UE III*: 395) actually copy surfaces of shelters built of wickerwork (Woolley's "improptu shelters"?, see above). On the other hand, ## 65 = *UE III*: 402; 86 = *UE III*: 424; 89 = *UE III*: 427; 96 = *UE III*: 431; and 119 = UE III: 480 come from smooth even walls, possibly more permanent storage facilities; the first three bear imprints of organic matter, showing that agricultural pursuits might have taken place nearby.

their diet with three kinds of fish (carp, drum and catfish), and probably ate freshwater mussels. They hunted wild pig, equids of ass size and perhaps gazelle, and brought down two categories of birds, of the duck- and dove sizes (*Wright* 1969, 90).

TECHNOLOGY

We shall also do well to inquire into the technologies and productional know-how accessible to the craftsmen and craftswomen of archaic Ur.

Let us at first point to the occurrence of **artificial materials** in strata belonging to the epoch which we consider here. A small cup excavated from the archaic layers displays a regular white-colour frit as material, attesting thus to the knowledge of this technology here (*Sürenhagen* 1999, 200, Taf. 57: 1). Other finds from this material have turned up here as well (pot: *Sürenhagen* 1999, Liste 5, pp. 281–290, 282 item 23; beads: *ibid.* 287 item 95; *ibid.* 288–289 items 120–121).

In view of work with **clay**, the most visible feature on our archaeological horizon is definitely the "Great Sherd Dump", documented especially by Woolley's Pit F. This might be characterized as a pottery-production area with a sequence of layers of vessel fragments, pottery-production wasters, kiln facilities and tools of various kind, several metres thick and beginning in (at the end of ?) the Ubaid culture. The dump went out of use sometime in the Jemdet Nasr period, that is, around 3000 B.C. (*Sürenhagen* 1999, esp. pp. 188–208; *Dittmann* 2006, *passim*, esp. Tab. 1 on p. 36). This, of course, tells us little about the actual state of the potter's art of archaic Ur. The removal of this production facility, which must have been a nuisance due to the dirt and fumes ensuing out of its operation, and a danger in view of the use of fire threatening the adjacent public and private structures, from the proximity to what now became a supra-regional administrative centre and a site of considerable prestige, represents a step in no way unusual. In fact, the ground of the disused dump was soon built over (*Sürenhagen* 1999, 201). One of the rooms excavated in the layer H of Pit F (ED-I) even yielded the find of a potter's wheel, so that the production could have continued on the spot but in different conditions (*Sürenhagen* 1999, 203–204 fn. 171).

Of course, this measure gives evidence on spatial changes within the landscape of production of archaic Ur, indicating a re-organization of both public and private space in connection with the changing status of the city around 3000 B.C.

Under the fingers of the skilled workers, clay assumed most diverse shapes of small utility objects such as necklace beads, rattles (*Sürenhagen* 1999, 184 = *Woolley* 1955, 77 Fig. 16; *Sürenhagen* 1999, 187), clay figurines (*Sürenhagen* 1999, 185) or even wagon- and chariot models (*ibid.*, for all categories see also Liste 5, pp. 281–290; a reconstruction of a chariot in *Woolley 1955*, 37, Pl. 24 below centre).

It goes without saying that clay served as a ubiquitous material for the building industry, first and foremost, for fashioning bricks.

The scribes of the texts of archaic Ur did, for the first time in Sumerian history, distinguish between copper (URUDU) and bronze (zabar = UD+KA+BAR) (*UET II*: 373; *Moorey 1985*, 127–128; on URUDU now *Marchesi 2011*, 191 sub # 5). This information links up with what we know about the very first occurrences of tin bronze in ancient Mesopotamia, datable to this very period of time (ED-I: *Müller-Karpe 1990*, 164; *Müller-Karpe 1991*, 111; see also *Müller-Karpe – Pászthory – Pernicka 1993*; for the presence of tin at ED-I Mari see *Fenollós-Ruiz 2004*). This indicates that the **metalworkers** of archaic Ur knew, and applied, the latest production methods current in their trade, insofar as they did not invent the new technology themselves. In fact, the *kabalum* lexeme, denoting a kind of bronze and possibly borrowed from Sumerian into Eblaite, and then into Hurrian, could imply something of this kind (*Zaccagnini 1988*). A metal-processing workshop may be mentioned in my # 123 = *UE III*: 559.

Of actual proofs of the Ur metalworkers' skill we may point to the hooves of a bull statue, mounted perhaps originally on a pedestal, which turned up probably in one of the SIS levels (4-5? *Sürenhagen 1999*, 186 No. 8 = *Woolley 1955*, 38, Pl. 29, U.14462). This statue represented a superior-quality product, implying external procurement of rare raw materials, skilled craftsmen, and complex casting activities in this phase at Ur (*Benati 2015*, 20). Not only that; the relevant masters delivered to their customers tools and weapons for practical use such as fishhooks, pins, chisels, small spoons or spear points (*Sürenhagen 1999*, 200–201; *ibid.*, Liste 5, pp. 281–290). One of the storerooms of archaic Ur contained "Dilmun axes" (my # 55 = *UE III*: 390)

The lead tumblers, frequent in the earlier phase of Woolley's "Jamdat Nasr cemetery", did not live on until later times and thus we do not know what became of treatment of lead after 3000 B.C. (*Sürenhagen 1999*, 221, see also *Quenet 2008*, 126). The "Jamdat Nasr" items gave evidence of cold-working, but also of soldering or sweating-on techniques (*Woolley 1955*, 31). One of the "Jamdat Nasr" graves contained earrings and beads of silver (JNG 219: *Sürenhagen 1999*, 235), but this was the only case within the whole cemetery (*Woolley 1955*, 30). Other finds from here included two copper mirrors (*ibid.*).

Copper axes, copper daggers, and a number of copper vessels went to the graves of persons laid to rest at the Ubaid cemetery near Ur (*Wright 1969*, 81).

Unfortunately, products of **organic materials** are outside our view almost completely. We have seen above that the sealings of archaic Ur yield abundant information on work with perishable matters such as sacks, bales, reed products, textiles, leather(?) and cords of all kinds. This evidence, albeit valuable, just adds to our picture the realization that such products undoubtedly belonged to common everyday features of the life of archaic Ur, but we can hardly dare anything else than observe their presence, without any chance at quantification of the information, or measuring the technical progress that might have happened within this sphere.

Spindle whorls of clay and stone bear wittnes to textile production (*Sürenhagen 1999*, Liste 5, pp. 281–290; *Woolley 1955* Pl. 16; on Sumerian textiles see now *Garcia-Ventura 2012*, esp. pp. 243–248).

In some instances, inhabitants of archaic Ur helped themselves to artifacts of bone such as pins (*Sürenhagen 1999*, 241).

The sea, not very distant from the walls of Ur, delivered materials shaped by the Ur artists into objects of both decorative and practical uses. Here belong the beads and necklace elements cut out of seashells (*Sürenhagen 1999*, 185–186; *Quenet 2008*, 139–140), as well as "conch shells" made into lamps (*Sürenhagen 1999*, 220 fn. 179).

The later "royal graves" of Ur have yielded evidence for the use of boxwood and pistachio wood, most probably imported from elsewhere (*de Schauensee 1998*, 22, 25). How far such products of faraway regions were available to artisans of archaic Ur remains unknown. Excavations at Sakheri Sughir brought to light remains of tamarisk and poplar wood used as fuel (*Wright 1969*, 89). Archaic texts from Ur refer to loads of wood, as well as to poles and logs; in one instance, poplar wood appears (*Wright 1969*, 104).

Textiles are repeatedly mentioned in the seal inscriptions (on Sumerian textiles see now also *Ventura 2008*, esp. pp. 250f.; *Wasserman 2013*). A certain regard for economy may be discerned from the fact that old textiles(?) filled in a whole storeroom (my # 25 = *UE III*: 119).

The cylinder seal found in Pit F, level 7.80 cm (*Dittmann 2006*, 29 = "ausgehende Späturuk-Zeit"; see *Legrain 1951*, 11 # 31 = *Sürenhagen 1999*, 200, 286 sub # 79, Taf. 57: 7) may, in fact, depict women weavers. In such a case its retrieval from a pottery-production plant (*kiln stratum* 4) offers an interesting hint at the spatial proximity of various craft workshops of pre-archaic Ur (on weaving in Bronze-Age Mesopotamia see *Breniquet 2008*; *Breniquet 2010*).

Cords or ropes might have been delivered through the channels of the "City League" (possibly my # 75 = *UE III*: 412; my # 76 = *UE III*: 413). Were such products needed for transport of heavy loads by means of storage jars carried in nets, as depicted by my # 50 = *UE III*: 330?

We also read about fragrant substances, the presence of which would be most difficult to prove by archaeology (my # 118 = *UE III*: 474).

The archaic Ur sealings may mention bitumen (my # 92 = *UE III*: 430; my # 102 = *UE III*: 438). Bitumen figured rather prominently among finds from an ED-I village by Ur, Sakheri Sughir. Its consumers availed themselves both of bitumen cakes, presumably imported from elsewhere, and of the liquid form of this material, obviously heated in pottery vessels (*Wright 1969*, 58–59). As to its particular use, it seems that bitumen served as a mastic for both light architectural features and waterproofed small water craft serving the village inhabitants (*Wright* 1969, 59).

Traces of reed mats appeared at Sakheri Sughir (*Wright* 1969, 59).

The Ur specialists used various kinds of **stone** – diorite and limestone, for instance – to fashion small utensils such as necklace beads or vessels (*Sürenhagen* 1999, 184–186; *Sürenhagen* 1999, Liste 5, pp. 281–290; *Woolley* 1955, Pl. 31–34, from his "Jamdat Nasr graves"; ibid. Pl. 65–67, also "Jamdat Nasr"), some of which are likely to have served as cosmetic containers (*Sürenhagen* 1999, 216).

Stone submitted to being employed as a building material for house foundations (*Woolley* 1955, 31, see also *Tunca* 1984).

Ground-stone industry items include hoes and axes (*Sürenhagen* 1999, Liste 5, pp. 281–290; *Woolley* 1955 Pl. 14) as well as a macehead (*ibid.*, 290 item 148). The inhabitants of an ED-I village close to Ur, Sakheri Sughir, used grinding slabs and stone bowls (*Wright* 1969, 58).

The very traditional chipped-stone industry supplied sickle blades fixed into handles with bitumen (*Sürenhagen* 1999, Liste 5, pp. 281–290, 298, item 93; *Woolley* 1955 Pl. 13) but even arrowheads (*ibid.*, 289 item 124; *Woolley* 1955 Pl. 12: a, b). A number of denticulated sickle blades with sickle sheen turned up at Sakheri Sughir, the ED-I village close to Ur (*Wright* 1969, 56–57).

Stone offered a medium for artistic expression; a statuette of a wild boar might have once decorated a standard or a piece of furniture (*Woolley* 1955, 31, 67, Pl. 37: U.14459; *Sürenhagen* 1999, 200, Taf. 57: 5). A bowl of stone bore depictions of cattle with ears of corn (*Woolley* 1955, Pl. 35 No. U.18118, for other such finds see *Sürenhagen* 1999, Taf. 71: 1–3). The "Jamdat Nasr cemetery" lamp with many wicks in the form of a flying bat represents a charming little work of art (*Woolley* 1955, 31, Pl. 32 No. U.19745).

TRADE, CHANGE, INNOVATION

Some important studies of ancient Mesopotamian trade and exchange appeared recently (*Schmidt* 2005, and especially *Quenet* 2008), and a treatise on precious stones in Mesopotamian texts has been submitted some time ago (*André-Salvini* 1995). The Ur sealings supply evidence for purchasing items of interest of unusually early date, from at least the JN-ED-I transition (my # 119 = *UE III*: 480; my # 120 = *UE III*: 480). The fact that our second item is bored through seems to confirm that it travelled to the central storerooms of Ur as a tag attached to a delivery of goods. One of the seal impressions accompanying these finds has been shown to display a connection with the Iranian art (*Ishida* 2006, esp. p. 14 fig. 3; on this see below; see also *Charvát* 2014c).

A specific fate awaited the deliveries of the beautiful blue semiprecious stone, lapis lazuli, which the artisans of Late Uruk age had learnt to appreciate (see also *Casanova* 1995). During ED-I, supplies of this stone to Mesopotamia from the source regions of present-day Afghanistan and Pakistan ceased, and were renewed only during ED-III, perhaps in the 27th–26th centuries B.C. (*Schmidt* 2005, 56–60; on the deposits *Quenet* 2008, 87–91). The families of those deceased buried in the "Jamdat Nasr cemetery" at Ur had nonetheless no dearth of lapis lazuli, as the graves yielded a quantity of products of this stone (see *Sürenhagen* 1999, esp. p. 237, Tab. 52).

A marked presence likely to have been caused by trade activities is that of chalcedony and chalcedony-related minerals, as well as carnelian, at Ur. Out of the 370 interments of the "Jamdat Nasr cemetery", 93 contained chalcedon artifacts, and all in all, they yielded more than 400 carnelian items. In this, archaic Ur does not differ from the situation in Upper Mesopotamia, and it may thus be supposed that unlike the seashell material tending to remain home (see below), these commodities streamed northwards through the agency of Ur (*Quenet* 2008, 97). These stones might have come in from the Gulf (*Quenet* 2008, 132–137, esp. p. 135; see also *Inizan* 1995, esp. pp. 21–23). Tiny carnelian beads turned up at the site of an ED-I village by Ur, Sakheri Sughir (*Wright* 1969, 58).

The early, Jemdet Nasr-age layers of archaic Ur yielded a chip, or chips, of obsidian and a fragment of an obsidian vase, which had to come from the mountains in the north or east (*Quenet* 2008, 159–162; see below).

How far the changing fashions of stone use apparent in the "Jamdat Nasr cemetery" can give evidence on trade currents remains to be seen. Philippe Quenet observes a trend from the earlier limestone and diorite towards the later alabaster and calcite, and towards the advent of chlorite. It is nonetheless perfectly possible that limestone, calcite, alabaster and diorite came from local sources in southeastern Iraq (*Quenet* 2008, 128–129, 143; for chlorite vessels see *Woolley* 1955, 32, Pl. 35: U.19 085; perhaps also Pl. 35: U.7145 and *ibid.* Pl. 36: U.210 and U.211).

However, not only decorative stones were imported into Ur. The fine to medium grain, homogenous or mottled light grey-brown flint, used for the production of chipped industry of Sakheri Sughir, an ED-I village close to Ur, cannot be traced to any local source and must thus have been introduced from elsewhere (*Wright* 1969, 56).

The production of tin bronze, introduced at the beginning of 3rd millennium (see above), necessitated deliveries of copper and tin. Sumerian smiths might have obtained these from Anatolia (*Vandiver et al.* 1993, esp. p. 298; *Schmidt* 2005, pp. 93–94). A likely alternative for copper is offered both by the Oman deposits and by those of the Iranian site of Anarak (*Woolley* 1934, 287; *Quenet* 2008, 147–152) while tin might have been procured from Anatolia

(*Quenet 2008*, 164–175; for the presence of tin at ED-I Mari see *Fenollós-Ruiz 2004*). One of the seal inscriptions of archaic Ur, listing, among others, "Dilmun axes", bears out the Gulf connection (my # 55 = *UE III*: 390).

For gold and silver, so plentiful in the later graves of the Ur cemetery sunk into the strata containing the SIS, Sumerian consumers had to wait for some two to three hundred years; or is it simply that these materials did not enter the archaeological record? Both metals might also have come from Anatolia (on their occurrence at the Syrian Ebla see *Pomponio 1998*, espl. pp. 131–132, and *Archi 1990*, esp. pp. 102–104; a silver bead in Halaf-culture Domuztepe: *Campbell-Carter-Gauld 2003*, 127, 128 Fig. 14).

That the interconnection sphere of Ur covered mainly the Gulf area seems to be implied by finds of seashells (*Quenet 2008*, 139–140), of which the more visible artifacts include the beads carved out of the spiraliform shell cores and their clay imitations (*Quenet 2008*, 125).

In Jemdet Nasr-age Ur, a connection with the north has manifested itself in the presence of an obsidian vase (*Quenet 2008*, 159–162). Nevertheless, this link seems to have been rather weak, as seashells of every kind, fairly common at archaic Ur, found their way into Upper Mesopotamia only from Early Bronze Age II (*Quenet 2008*, 141).Though some Ur links with the North come out in the glyptic (Tell Brak), they constitute rather an exception, not a rule (*Matthews 1997*, 131).

The question of perfumes or fragrant substances, definitely present at Ur (my # 118 = *UE III*: 474) presents a dilemma. These are more likely to have been imported than home-produced, but no evidence on this is currently disponible (see *Brunke-Sallaberger 2010*, esp. p. 48). The same goes for possible exports of Sumerian textiles abroad, which have recently been hypothetically sought at Shahr-i Sokhta in southeastern Iran (*Good 2006*, 202).

Interesting informations on the inclusion of Nannar's abode into the large-scale circuits of international connections of its epoch have become available in connection with studies of the Glazed-Steatite Glyptic. The city of Ur came only into an ephemeral contact with it (*Quenet 2008*, 119), and stylistically, the SIS glyptic displays next to no contact with this sphere (*Quenet 2008*, 189).

Selective orientation of the Ur long-distance trade and exchange sphere might be further confirmed by the fact that no evidence known to date has reached us concerning the more visible, and, before all, surviving "foreign" imports of the age of archaic Ur, namely the so-called Canaanean blades. The deposits of raw materials for these distinctive tools of striped stone had been discovered previously, in the Late Uruk period, and a special facility managing their exploitation and manufacturing emerged on the upper Euphrates River (Hassek Höyük: *Otte and Behm-Blancke 1992*, esp. p. 173; *Matney-Algaze 1995*, pp. 45–46; see also *Quenet 2008*, 162–164, a map on p. 183 Pl. 22/2). The export of these tools survived the demise of the Late-Uruk commonwealth and continued well into the third millennium BC.

SOCIETY

We have gone through the material appurtenances of life at archaic Ur. Now we shall dedicate our attention to the conditions of community life in the city of Nannar.

At first, let us look at the very beginnings of higher forms of social life attested to at Ur. The materials of relevance here come from one of the deepest soundings into the history of the Ur excavations. Their provenance is given as "Pit G, 7 to 7½ m (alt. 7,10–8m) below brick pavement dated c. 3100 B.C. in the prehistoric settlement" (see the UM catalogue entries above, and *UE III*, pp. 42–43, *apud* my ## 480, 481 and 483; for the situation of Pit G in the southern corner of the Ur *temenos* see *Woolley 1955*, Pl. 1, and *Sürenhagen 1999*, 178). Consulting of Leonard Woolley's stratigraphic summary (*Woolley 1955*, Pl. 83) shows that this spot must lie below the level of layer H of Woolley's Pit F, and thus, according to Reinhard Dittmann (*Dittmann 2006*, 36, Tab. 1), fall below the "Älteres Frühdynastikum" phase, probably into somewhere within the Jemdet Nasr age.

In other words, these sphragistic items give evidence of the beginnings of sealing practices at Ur before, and around, 3000 B.C. I know of no earlier instances of seal impressions from Ur.

The finds in question are UM 31-17-351A (from package), UM 31-17-351P (from storage jar), UM 31-17-351S (from door peg), UM 31-17-351T (from door peg), UM 31-17-352B (= my # 119, from door peg), and UM 31-17-352R (= my # 120, a clay tag = "test strip").

Two catalogue entries of the University Museum of Archaeology and Anthropology (University of Pennsylvania, Philadelphia) inventory give evidence on the find context of these seal impressions. The first one (*apud* UM 31-17-351A) runs thus: ""Ur, found 7 to 7½ m below brick pavement dated c. 3100 B.C. in the prehistoric settlement. Includes painted pottery; obsidian chips; and obsidian vase; 3 clay copies of shell bugle beads; 5 seal impressions on clay jar sealings; animal figures; handles; sickle".

The other, *apud* UM 31-17-351B, gives the following data: "Ur, found 7½ to 8 m below brick pavement dated c. 3100 B.C. in the prehistoric settlement. Includes decorated pottery; clay animal; a number of seal impressions on clay jar stoppers; clay copies of shell bugle beads; bone tubular bead; copper needle, etc.".

As to the dating of the whole find group or groups, all the clues that we can hope for follow out of Leon Legrain's meagre data in *UE III*, supplemented by those furnished by the UM catalogue and obviously drawn from the

Woolley-expedition field records. Fortunately, the summary inventories of the cultural layer(?) characterizing the "prehistoric settlement" do include an artifact category with a rather short circulation period. These are the "clay copies of shell bugle beads". Roger Matthews (*Matthews 2002*, 31, fig. 54: 8–31, pl. 43) refers to them as to "baked clay beads with distinctive spiral grooving along the length", and notes that they appear to be restricted to the Jemdet Nasr period. This confirms the early dating suggested by stratigraphy, and indeed shows that we move somewhere at the turn of the fourth and third millennia BC.

The artistic character of the seals does merit some consideration. Their iconography includes two instances of landscape compositions – two caprids arrayed symmetrically around a tree, and a particular rendering of a tract of woodland (UM 31-17-351A, UM 31-17-351S) –, a group of caprids or ibexes combined with ears of corn (UM 31-17-351T) and a most impressive rendering of a rampant beast of prey about to attack (UM 31-17-351P).

Iranian affiliations have been remarked for the woodland-tract seal (UM 31-17-351S: *Ishida 2006*, esp. p. 14 fig. 3).

As to the rest, the caprids-cum-tree composition does not lend itself to a particularly fine chronological analysis, as the motif occurs both earlier and later. The seal discussed here does nonetheless show some differences in comparison with the later renderings within the ED-I glyptic of the Ur SIS strata: the animal bodies display more massivity, but the rendering emphasizes the linear features and outlines of the entities, and it would be somewhat out of place to apply the label "gouged style", by which Holly Pittman and Sarah Jarmer Scott have fittingly described the ED-I glyptic idiom of the SIS sealings, to our particular case (UM 31-17-351A). Here a citation of a similar Uruk seal (of Uruk IVa date) may be relevant (*Boehmer 1999*, 53, Abb. 55; also p. 72, Abb. 55, 56).

The other composition, linking caprid- or ibex images with ears of corn, also follows rather early Uruk V–IVb models (*Amiet 1980*, No. 171 on Pl. 9, but see also ibid. No. 213 pl. 12 for an Uruk-III example; *Boehmer 1999*, 46–48, Abb. 34–39). Parallels may be adduced from Amiet's *époque prédynastique* from Uruk and a complete cylinder seal from Ur itself, repeating this scene *tête-bêche* (*Amiet 1980*, Nos. 362 and 363 on pl. 22).

The same goes for the rampant beast of prey, recalling parallels among the Uruk IVa creations (*Boehmer 1999*, esp. pp. 57–59, Abb. 41–59; Taf. 47–49, 51). The beast-of-prey image finds convincing parallels in earlier Uruk glyptic as well (*Amiet 1980*, No. 196C pl. 11).

It may thus be concluded here that from the viewpoint of their execution, these "deep-well" sealings reflect an earlier tradition.

An even more interesting piece of information can be culled from the protocuneiform sign which two of these sealings bear (UM 31-17-352B and UM

31-17-352R). The ŠAM$_2$ sign (= *ZATU* No. 510 p. 282, *MSVO 1* p. 143), conventionally interpreted as "to pay for, buy; to be paid for, sell" (see http://psd.museum.upenn.edu/epsd/nepsd-frame.html [accessed October 4, 2014] s. v. sa), has also been translated as "tauschen" (*Englund 1990*, p. 18 fns. 61, 62 and 63). Fara-age texts include an expression še šám kaš = "barley at the price of beer" (*Gelb-Steinkeller-Whiting 1991*, 292, see also ibid. 217). Other translations which have appeared in specialized literature are "Entsprechendes ist es" (*Selz 1993*, 455–456), or "Entgelt für den Kaufgegenstand" (*Wilcke 1996*, 10–12).

In addition to the written testimony for selling and buying at Ur around 3000 B.C., these objects carry an additional measure of interest by what medium they were applied to. One of them seems to have originally closed a storage facility. while the other, displaying two rim vestiges at opposite sides of the clay plaque and a hole bored through, might have once, as a clay tag or label attached to a material delivery, denoted goods purchased directly at the marketplace. One and the same seal thus "went out" to the market place and designed items purchased for its bearer, and then "returned home" and closed a storage facility of the initiator of the transaction (see now *Charvát 2014c* on this issue).

This evidence offered by the earliest attestations of the use of writing at archaic Ur finds an echo in archaeological materials retrieved from early Ur. Most significantly, "obsidian chips" (or a single chip) and an "obsidian vase"-came from the same settlement layer as the sealings at the bottom of Pit G (see above, UM 31-17-351A, P, S and T; *Woolley 1955*, 71; *Quenet 2008*, 161).

In the Jemdet Nasr epoch, the abode of Nannar felt no shortage of imported luxury materials, as we have already heard. The graves of the "Jamdat Nasr cemetery" at Ur yielded a quanitity of products of lapis lazuli (*Sürenhagen 1999*, esp. p. 237, Tab. 52). The "Iranian connection" by which the blue stone is likely to have been supplied to southern Mesopotamia finds a fitting expression in one of our sealings inspired by Iranian art (see above, UM 31-17-351S, *Ishida 2006*).

On the occurrence of chalcedony and carnelian at archaic Ur see above under the heading 'Trade, Change, Innovation.' These stones might have came in from the Gulf (*Quenet 2008*, 135, 132–137), or the southern Caucasus or Iran. Even the subsequently abundant chlorite has made its first appearance at this early date (*Quenet 2008*, 143).

That the Ur commerce focused chiefly on sea trade seems to be indicated by the absence of Glazed Steatite Glyptic items below the walls of Nannar's sacred precinct. Contacts with this sphere may be characterized as ephemeral at best (*Quenet 2008*, 119), and stylistically, the SIS glyptic displays next to no contact with southernmost Mesopotamia (*Quenet 2008*, 189). Finds of seashells, presumably from the Gulf area, point in the same direction (*Quenet 2008*, 139–140).

Thus, the beginnings of higher forms of organized social life of the city of Ur may obviously be derived from its *metropolis* at Uruk, to which the Jemdet Nasr-age Ur seems to have served as a trade entrepot.

* * *

The Ur seals have brought forth one of the rare pieces of evidence datable after 3000 B.C.E., shedding light on a little known but apparently important office of early historic Sumer, denoted by the title commonly read as **NAMEŠ-DA** (my # 91 = *UE III*: 429 = *Matthews 1993*, 1 = *Scott 2005*, n. 76). The designation has already caught the eye of scholars (see *Selz 1998a*, 295–301 and 326; *Selz 2000*, 187–188; *Selz 2010*, 8; *Charvát 2012*).

This office turned up in the lexical lists of the preceding, Late Uruk epoch, in which it figured at the very first position opening the Professions List (see *ATU 3* and *ATU 5* on p. 14, fn. 20 in the Introduction, as well as *Selz 1998a*, 294–309; *Glassner 2000*, p. 130 fn. 14, and pp. 251–256; *Glassner 2003*, p. 98 fn. 14, and pp. 193–197; *Veldhuis 2006*). Unfortunately, this agency clearly failed to produce written materials on non-perishable vehicles. We are therefore entirely in the dark as to the agenda and significance of the dignitary bearing this title. Modern students tend to perceive the heroic figure of Late-Uruk art, usually referred to as *Mann im Netzrock* (on which see now *Boese 2010*), as EN, but this could as well represent an image of the NAMEŠDA.

The title does make an appearance, albeit of low profile, in Late-Uruk economic texts (see Charvát 2012).

The Ur sealing naming NAMEŠDA supplies rather important information (a photo in *Selz 2010*, 25, Ill. 1). First and foremost, the seal inscription names this title in connection with Nippur, and also with "fields of Utu" the sun-god, if my reading is correct (GAN$_2$ U$_4$). However, the greatest interest lies in the fact that the impression comes from a "corporate seal", linking the NAMEŠ-DA, the Nippur fields of Utu(?), and a truncated form of the "City League" (see below). In addition to the rather significant connection of NAMEŠDA with the city of Nippur, this shows that this office still carried enough social weight to be a partner to a (con)federation of Sumerian cities.

This, however, is one of the last instances when the NAMEŠDA office played any significant social role. Texts of the subsequent historical period, that in which the documents found at Fara (Shuruppak) were written, know this lexeme only as a designation of one of the lesser deities of the Sumerian pantheon (see *Glassner 2000*, p. 269 fn. 18, a *Glassner 2003*, p. 207 fn. 18).

* * *

Among the inscribed sealings of archaic Ur (SIS 4-8), the most visible political body seems to have been the confederation of municipal communities referred to in specialized literature as the **City League** (see *Matthews*

1993, *Selz 1998a*, 309–312, and also *Steinkeller 2002a* and *2002b*, more recently *Sallaberger 2006–2008*, 35). This political(?) body emerged at the turn of the 4th and 3rd millennium B.C.E. (see text *MSVO 4* No. 15 on p. 116, No. 28, pp. 23 and 37, and Pl. 16–17, from the site of Tell Uqair); a colleague has recently proposed a re-dating into the Late-Uruk age (*Hookman 2008*).

The earlier, Jemdet-Nasr version of this corporate body comprised eleven toponyms and probably included Ur, Larsa, Zabalam, UR_2 HA RAD (is this a toponym?), BU.BU.NA_2 (= $arina_x$?) and Keš, and perhaps omitted Nippur, Uruk and Cutha (*Steinkeller 2002a*, 254). The bearer(s) of the "City League" seal visited the member communities, collected contributions in kind and confirmed their receipt by sealed documents (*Steinkeller 2002a*, 256). Such contributions consisted of usually standardized quantities of figs, apples, wine (grapes, raisins?) and GA_2 + GEŠTUG = /adaku'a/, which seems to have been a fish product (*Steinkeller 2002a*, 252).

A large group of Ur sealings bearing the names of "City League" member communities attests to their activites, obviously important in communal, and hence political, life of the land of Sumer in the early third millenium B.C. The "City League" consisted of the major municipalities of early historic Sumer, and, taking into account its image in the inscribed sealings of the SIS 4-8 strata, we may imagine it as a self-governing body with its own

- identity and coherence,
- fund of material goods of which it freely disposed,
- administrative apparatus (seals and seal-bearers), and procedures resulting especially in a circulation of goods sealed in its name, and probably also
- religious unity, maintained by means of contributions to a fund(?), established for the purpose of carrying out a specific ritual which might have functioned as a cementig agent of the "City League" unity (see below).

This entity may be considered a political unit, albeit of a loose and nebulous nature. The reasons for this follow here.

First and foremost, it displayed a proper seal which its managers used to designate goods dispatched to other member communities of the "City League".

Second, some of the deliveries circulating within the "City League" circuits travelled to the consumers under the designation of IL_2, "tax", linked to a group of toponyms in text of my # 124 (= *Matthews 1993*, 14 = *Scott 2005*, 14; IL_2 in Fara texts: *Pomponio-Visicato 1994*, 193; in ED Lagaš evidence *Selz 1995*, 58 No. 111, 202–203 No. 70, 258 fn. 1240; other ED material: *Bauer 1989–1990*, 78; *Selz 1993*, 555–556; *Westenholz 1987*, 129 */íl tax levied on produce, not land, paid by higher officials to government after harvest/*; *Englund 1990*, 92 fn. 292 for Ur III material).

As to the geographical extent of the "City League", Roger Matthews and Giacomo Benati have provided a map of it (*Matthews 1993*, Fig. 26; *Benati 2015*, 21, Fig. 6). The solution for the question of its northern frontier will depend on whether the KIB sign meant fruit (plums?), or whether it referred to a locality in the Euphrates region, possibly Sippar (see above, *apud* my # 10 = *UE III*: 77). Also, the pictorial evidence from the Ur sealings, especially that of my ## 46 and 48, implies that sign BAD, for which I suggested a possible reference to a "lord of the North" (*Charvát 2010b*, 47), be better interpreted as BAD = "to thresh grain (or to process it in some similar way)" (in my # 12 = *UE III*: 79, # 46 = *UE III*: 315, # 48 = *UE III*: 325, # 78 = *UE III*: 416).

The "City League" collected its membership fees from a variety of taxpayers, and under what may have been a multitude of modes. In this connection, we may point to two signs of the SIS 4-8 sealings which we do not understand at present. These are the enigmatic *edinnu* sign, as Leon Legrain once baptized it, and to a figure that Roger Matthews and Sarah Jarmer Scott define as *legcross*. Once only the relevant seal patterns included a bare *edinnu* (my # 32 = *UE III*: 209), and once the bare *legcross* signs (my # 84 = *UE III*: 422). Also, one single instance shows a "City League" sealing countermarked with a stamp seal featuring the *edinnu* sign (my # 99 = *UE III*: 434).

Of the *edinnu* we can hardly say anything, save for a rather unexpected parallel in decoration motifs of the Ninevite-V pottery of northern Mesopotamia (*Matthews-Matthews- McDonald 1994*, 180–182, 188, with a pattern on Fig. 4: 7, p. 182, alluding possibly to the *edinnu* sign of archaic Ur sealings). This entity might have represented a notion close to a designation of the inhabited world, *oecumene*. The *edinnu* had been present amog the Ur sealings at least since SIS 7-6 times (*UE III*: 29 = *Matthews 1993*, 77 = *Scott 2005*, 216). At least in one case, the *edinnu* entity received revenue by means of redistribution from a "City League" fund, when a "City League" sealing was counter-marked by a seal bearing the *edinnu* sign (my # 99 = *UE III*: 434 = *Matthews 1993*, 121 = *Scott 2005*, 472).

In some cases the seal texts supply additional information. So, in *UE III*: 461 the *edinnu* turns up together with the ŠU$_2$ sign, impying that the delivery in question came in in textiles (ŠU$_2$ = *ZATU* No. 534 p. 289, in textile accounts, also in *MSVO 1* pp. 149–150, See also http://psd.museum.upenn.edu/epsd/nepsd-frame.html [accessed October 4, 2014] s. v. šu$_2$). The *edinnu* directs its own house in my # 109 = *UE III*: 447.

The *legcross* seems to represent a particular fashion, or perhaps a legal title, under which the contributions to the "City League" funds came in. F. Wiggermann and J. Cale Johnson suggest that it might have stood for the inhabited world, *oecumene* (see above, # 62: *Johnson 2014b*, 54, Fig. 1 with fn. 28). At least one of the documents shows that the *legcross* referred to quantifiable entitites collected in vessels (my # 118 = *UE III*: 474). If the *edinnu* represented the entire *oecumene*, then the quadrilateral *legcross* could have stood for the (contributions of the) sedentary population living in settlements established in accordance with the rules of the universal order (four corners of the world), but this is pure speculation.

At the collection points in Ur, the "City League" deliveries were frequently deposited in storage spaces (see, for instance, my # 110 = *UE III*: 454, attested to with 22 impressions of door pegs: *Matthews 1993*, # 12, 63–64).

Once deposited in the storage spaces of Ur, the "City League" deliveries might possibly undergone redistribution to different consumers. I imagine that this was visualized by counter-marks or counter-signs pressed into the still damp clay of the sealings by stamp seals (on this see most recently *Zettler 2007*). This custom had precedents: the first instances of counter-marking turn up with Late Uruk *bullae* from Uruk, closed by cylinder-seal impressions, by the use of stamp seals (*Boehmer 1999*, p. 111, ## 54 and 55). One of the texts from Jemdet Nasr (*MSVO 1* # 221 Pl. 82) bore an impression of a cylinder seal counter-signed by a seal bearing a rosette design (*Steinkeller 2002b*).

In some cases of archaic Ur, the "City League" sealings of storage spaces received no further supplement in the form of impressions of counter-marking seals, including such instances as seal of my # 110 = *UE III*: 454, surviving in 27 examples which are entirely free of counter-marks. Counter-marks in the form of the rosette (on this icon see most recently *Selz 2004*, 201) were also observed; instances, in which in repeated sealings by one single carrier seal these were available, showed such frequencies as one counter-marked against four non-countermarked (my # 76 = *UE III*: 413), three counter-marked against two bare (my # 124 = *Matthews 1993*, 14 = *Scott 2005*, 14) and one counter-marked with two bare (my # 129 = *Matthews 1993*, 31 = *Scott 2005*, 63).

Of course, the rosette-design seals did not supplement "City League" sealings only. We see them present on seals without inscriptions, and it seems that at least in one instance, two rollings of one and the same seal received impressions of two different counter-marks, one bearing a rosette and one a boar icon. This pertains to seal No. *UE III*: 297, displaying probably a triumph scene. In one case this seal bears a counter-mark with a rosette seal (*UE III*: 131, upon collation of the bearer seal); in another, a seal bearing a boar icon (*UE III*: 297). Thus, a particular storage space (or the contents thereof), closed by one single bearer seal, could have been counter-marked with different secondary seals.

The Ur archaic text *UET II*: 51, a ration list, bears on its obverse a depiction of a rosette and, in addition to other marks representing possibly the grand total, the toponym URI$_5$. This may indicate that the rosette stood for the city of Ur, and counter-marking seals bearing this emblem denoted that share in the "City League" (or other) consignments which fell to the abode of Nannar. However, this assumption cannot be substantiated from any other source.

This phenomenon makes me think of the counter-marking seals as indicators of redistribution of the goods collected by the original agency towards various sub-consumers who received consent to share the original agency's revenues.

In four instances the "City League" sealings bore counter-marks other than the rosette:

Publication No.	Motif of counter-marking seal
My # 88 = *UE III*: 426	Human face
My # 99 = *UE III*: 434	*Edinnu*
My # 133 = *Matthews 1993*, 53 = *Scott 2005*, 876	Illegible
My # 134 = *Matthews 1993*, 58 = *Scott 2005*, 577	Linear composition

As to the overall importance of counter-marking of seal impressions, some numbers may be of interest. Of the 437 uninscribed seals published in *UE III*, 22 (= 5,03%) bore counter-marks. As against this, of the 148 inscribed items of both the *UE III* and this monograph, 25 (= 16,90%) received counter-signs. This obviously bears out the higher incidence of counter-marks on inscribed seals.

Let us now see to what extent the inscribed seals of archaic Ur open the way towards better understanding of the "City League".

Agricultural pursuits in fields find reference with inscriptions like *UE III*: 155 (= my # 28: GAN_2 KI, though its precise meaning remins unknown). Another category of land or immovables find mention in seal *UE III*: 392 (= my # 56): GA_2+AŠ URU (municipal land or house?). Arrears in field deliveries may be suspected in *UE III*: 433 (= my # 98, GAN_2+LIBIR?). Simple reference to a field or fields show up in *UE III*: 419 (= my # 81), in *UE III*: 434 (= my # 99), and in *UE III*: 446 (= my # 108) as GAN_2.

Of course, harvests of grain kept the Ur society going: *UE III*: 443 (= my # 107) = NIN TUR DU_3, ŠE TAB X X. $NINDA_2$ or SA_{10}, X. E_2 KAŠ+AŠ, X (Nintur, KAK, ŠE+TAB grain in containers, house of ration-takers?, of SIS 2). Malt also finds reference in a single case: *Matthews 1993*, 33 (= my # 129). However, a number of references do not specify the kind of comestibles delivered: so *UE III*: 406 (= my # 69), featuring DUB/KIŠIB??, GAR + GAR, GAN_2, LAGAB+ŠITA, KAK = DU_3 = RU_2, ŠEŠ?, X, KISAL, X, which may be rendered as "registered comestible produce from fields, in containers, KAK, forecourt of Ur?" Is the KISAL sign to be read $gipar_x$ (*Selz 2011b*, 233 sub # 1: 3; on gipar see also *Lion 2009*, 179; *Westenholz 2013*, 254–256)? This may not always be so: *Andersson 2012*, 158 fn. 912. Another similar case is seal *UE III*: 416 (= my # 78), linking "city league" toponyms with NU.gunu, BAD, and DUG = comestibles in containers? (same in *UE III*: 418 = my # 80, NU).

The produce of an agricultural estate may be surmised in seal *UE III*: 432 (= my # 97). This probably includes such items as livestock (ŠILAM), wood

(GIŠ+MU+DU), date palm (GIŠIMMAR+UZ), beer (DIN+SAL+E_2), and some commodities in DA containers. The prisoners-of-war of the newly published Kish plaque were set to work in date-palm orchards (*Steinkeller 2013*, 132). A distinction between various types of landed property may possibly be perceived in the same seal's references to GAN_2 URU and KI UDU. Another, possibly similar case concerns the seal *UE III*: 559 (= my # 123), with its signs AL, AŠ, DUG, AB_2 × DIŠ, $UMUN_2$. Was this an entity reaping benefits from agriculture (AL), animal husbandry (AB_2+DIŠ and possibly *ZATU* 753), and craft activities ($UMUN_2$), collected (also?) from external territories ($ARARMA_2$)?

Some items mention deliveries of fruit (*UE III*: 160 = my # 29; *UE III*: 391 = my # 140, *Matthews 1993*, 81 = my # 135), of course, unless the KIB sign refers to a geographical entity linked with the Euphrates river. Comestibles and heads of livestock were registered: *UE III*: 390 (= my # 55) – TU_7, TUN_3 DILMUN, UDU, UNUG, LUM, or "soup", Dilmun axes, sheep, Uruk, fecundation ceremony(?). Wool clipped from sheep shows up as well (my ## 57–59 = *UE III*: 395; *Matthews 1993*, 74 = my # 100, UDU UR_4 DUG UR_2).

Of the various art- and craft products exchanged, textiles may be mentioned (*UE III*: 142 = my # 27, = GADA, *UE III*: 461 = my # 114, $ŠU_2$). Seal *UE III*: 433 (= my # 98) may even register taxpayers rendering their dues in textiles (GADA+DU, GADA). A similar case may be supposed in seal *UE III*: 442 (= my # 106), with its signs GADA, LU_2+ TAK_4, E_2+ KI, ŠIDIM+$SILA_4$ (architect?), SU_3+$ŠU_2$ (tributary of textiles?), NIMGIR+GAL, featuring personages, dignitaries, institutions, and professions, as well as taxpayers. Supplies of textiles and cords appear also (*UE III*: 413 = *UE III*: 415 = *UE III*: 459 = my # 76, ŠU, GU = textile, cord).

Trade activities obviously linked Ur with Gulf sites, as indicated by seal *UE III*: 390 (my # 55): TU_7, TUN_3 DILMUN, UDU, UNUG, LUM – "soup", Dilmun axes, sheep, Uruk-Warka, fecundation ceremony?

Inscriptions on archaic Ur seals shed light on the social contexts of the "City League" communities. Most remarkably, LUGAL is virtually missing from them, but we do find his *consors thori*, NIN: *UE III*: 438 (= my # 102) = E_2+UR_2, NIN, PIRIG?, DU_6, GA_2 × AN or $ESIR_2$ (house of ritual, NIN, animals?, sacred hill, bitumen?). In seal *UE III*: 443 (= my # 107), with its signs NIN TUR DU_3, ŠE TAB X X. $NINDA_2$ or SA_{10}, X. E_2 KAŠ+AŠ, X (Nintur, KAK, grain in containers, house of ration-takers?, of SIS 2), even the NIN.TUR of one of the "Royal-graves" seals may graciously receive us, at least *in effigie*.

Various dignitaries or professionals frequently appear in the seal inscriptions, such as NIMGIR (*UE III*: 409 = my # 72, NIMGIR, NI; *UE III*: 410 = my # 73, NIMGIR?, *UE III*: 454 = my # 110) or others (*UE III*: 433 = my # 98 includes ŠIDIM and GIŠGAL/?/). Seal *UE III*: 441 (= my # 105), displaying signs SU_3, U_4, GIŠ, DU, BA, $GARA_2$, NUN, TI. DUB, animal head, X. SAL?. SAL+X?. ŠE+NAM_2, may contain a personal name (NUN-ba-gará-ti, = "Enki gives life to Bagara?"), as well as allusions to other dignitaries or functions (ŠE+NAM$_2$) and to servile personnel (SAL?, SAL+X?). Here we may also recall seal *UE III*: 442 (= my # 106), with its signs GADA, LU$_2$+TAK$_4$, E$_2$+ KI, ŠIDIM+SILA$_4$ (architect?), SU$_3$+ŠU$_2$ (tributary of textiles?), NIMGIR+GAL, featuring personages, dignitaries, institutions, and professions. Personnel receiving rations may also come before our eyes in seal *UE III*: 443 (= my # 107), with signs NIN TUR DU$_3$, ŠE TAB X X. NINDA$_2$ or SA$_{10}$, X. E$_2$ KAŠ+AŠ, X (Nintur, KAK, grain in containers, house of ration-takers?, of SIS 2).

The city elders of Sumerian cities may for the first time enter our field of vision with the early Ur seals like *UE III*: 34 (my # 7), *UE III*: 428 (= my # 90), as AB+AŠ$_2$(?), or *UE III*: 455 (= my # 111), again AB+AŠ$_2$.

A faint outline of the structure of public institutions of early Sumer appears in seal *UE III*: 429 (= my # 91). Here, the NAMEŠDA title links up with GAN$_2$ U$_4$ of the city of Nippur, the same seal matrix combining this reference with a version of the "City League". Thus, the NAMEŠDA, who apparently disposed of immovable property in various cities of Sumer, carried the same political weight as the "city league". Who are the "men of the city border" or "men of the border city" (*UE III*: 434 = my # 99: GAN$_2$, AK, URU, SUR, LU$_2$ – fields, men, city, border, offering?)?

A true panoply of political agents of all kinds is spread before our eyes by seal *UE III*: 431 (= my ## 93–96). The respective signs may be read as BAD$_3$, BALA.NAGAR, UŠUMGAL, ŠE+NAM$_2$, ŠE$_3$+SUHUR+KI, SAMAN$_3$, AB, NUN+TU+BU, UDUL, SANGA+DUB, UZ+BULUG$_3$ and EREŠ$_2$. Of these, the highest interest lies with the EREŠ$_2$ entity, denoting possibly the ki-en-gi confederation (*Visicato 1989*: ereš$_2$^{ki} = ŠE.NAGA, identical with the Fara domain, on ki-en-gi *Cooper 1999–2002*, 78–82; *Frayne 2008b*, 7–12). The rest probably represents communities, dignitaries (or personalities or professionals?), maybe even temporal data (BALA.NAGAR)?, tribute-payers (in fish?), lands, and institutions.

That the "City League" deliveries streamed in as a kind of tax is demonstrated by the seal *Matthews 1993*, 14 (= my # 124), with its sign IL$_2$.

A number of management tasks find reflection in the early seals of Ur. So, we have references to the containers in which the goods came in: *UE III*: 396 (= my # 60), mentioning KAB (= receptacle/s/?), and *UE III*: 404 (= my # 67) with DIN and U$_4$ (the meaning of U$_4$ is not clear to me here). Transport in DUG containers takes place in seals *UE III*: 423 (= my # 85), *UE III*: 424 (= my # 86, DUG or DIN), *UE III*: 454 (= my # 110, DUG AB?), and in *Matthews 1993*, 74 (= my # 100). Our inscriptions do not make it particularly clear whether the GAN was a container of some sort or, eventually, a storage structure of wood (*UE III*: 439 = my # 103, also *UE III*: 440). The manner of commodity transport finds revelation in seal *UE III*: 440 (= my # 104), with signs DIM, DIŠ, MAGUR, NINDA$_2$, GAN (boat, container/s/, bundle, storage?).

We may even find registering of journey provisions, if the sign IŠ (=ŠUŠ$_3$ or SUS/A/$_x$.) in *UE III*: 405 (= my # 68) really means the city of Susa (GAR+GAR, KAŠ+AŠ = bread and beer?, but see the cautious stance of *Rohn 2011*, 194). A newly published archaic-Ur text lists individuals (certainly more than 200 and possibly up to 400 men) sent from Ur to an institution (e$_2$-nun-gal) located at Uruk, offering evidence of strong interaction between these two cities (Benati 2015, 11).

A most interesting category of information supplied by the ancient Ur seals pertains to the religious and spiritual life of the community or communities concerned. Here we must take into particular consideration the combination of the "City League" toponyms with various motifs already encountered: *UE III*: 209 (= my # 32) displays, in additon to geographical names, images of a hornless quadruped, a spread eagle and chequerboard. Seal *UE III*: 281 (= my # 42) features an icon of a man with a large lizard. A scorpion accompanies the "City League" toponyms in seal *Moorey 1979*, 578.

Some of the rituals known to us re-appear in connection with the "City League": *UE III*: 402 (= my # 65) features the sign UR$_2$. The UR$_2$ organizers disposed of a house for the ceremony: *UE III*: 438 (= my # 102) = E$_2$+UR$_2$, NIN, PIRIG?, DU$_6$, GA$_2$ × AN or ESIR$_2$ (house of ritual, NIN, animals?, sacred hill, bitumen?). Clip of sheep wool represented one of the forms of offerings sent in for this occasion (*Matthews 1993*, 74 = my # 100, UDU UR$_4$ DUG UR$_2$). Deliveries for this event came in with a certain (monthly?) periodicity, as shown by the seal *Moorey 1979*, 571 (= my # 126), featuring signs U$_4$, UR$_2$, U$_4$+AŠ. The TAK$_4$ ceremony(?) turns up in seal *UE III*: 430 (= my # 92), joining "city league" toponyms to the signs NAGAR, GA$_2$ × AN, TAK$_4$, ŠA$_3$ (vegetation season, bitumen??, ceremony, field plot?). Is the LU$_2$ TAK$_4$ of seal *UE III*: 442 (= my # 106), with its signs GADA, LU$_2$+TAK$_4$, E$_2$+ KI, ŠIDIM+SILA$_4$ (architect?), SU$_3$+ŠU$_2$ (tributary of textiles?), NIMGIR+GAL, featuring personages, dignitaries, institutions, and professionals, a cultic attendant or a sculptor (*Michalowski 2003*, 4–5)? The "sacred hill" (DU$_6$) constituted an object of worship in one of the Ur shrines: *UE III*: 438 (= my # 102) = E$_2$+UR$_2$, NIN, PIRIG?, DU$_6$, GA$_2$ × AN or ESIR$_2$ (house of ritual, NIN, animals?, sacred hill, bitumen?). Gebhard Selz (*Selz 2014a*, 207–212) has most recently described DU$_6$ as a mythical locality linked with Sumerian cosmological and funerary ideas. We may see in it also a hill on which a temple is standing (*Selz 2011b*, 244, "Skizze einer Idealflur"; see *Cohen 1993*, 106–112, *apud Mařík 2005*, 45–49). But in ED-IIIb inscriptions, SAHAR.DU$_6$.TAG$_4$ may mean "burial tell", with translation of TAG$_4$ as "leave behind" (*Richardson 2007*, 193–194; *Suriano 2012*, 218 fn. 36, in general 218–219). Is there any connection with burial ceremonies?

What does the sign KAK (e.g. *UE III*: 463 = my # 115) refer to in our context?

Various aspects of cultic procedures find illumination with seals like *UE III*: 389 (= my # 54), with the inscription GAR+GAR EN?? DUB ALAM, possibly alluding to a delivery of registered comestibles for a (ritual involving?) a statue. Material appurtenances for the LUM ceremony(?) were delivered under seal *UE III*: 390 (= my # 55): TU_7, TUN_3 DILMUN, UDU, UNUG, LUM, tentatively: "soup", Dilmun axes, sheep, Uruk-Warka, fecundation ceremony?. If AK really means "Opfermaterie", then seal *UE III*: 434 (= my # 99), mentioning GAN_2, AK, URU, SUR, LU_2 (fields, men, city, border, offering?) carries some relevance here.

The question how far the "City League" constitutes a forerunner of the subsequent political groupings such as the ki-en-gi, a later denotation of the geographical entity "Sumer", constitutes a topic for debate (e.g. *Visicato 1989*, s. v. $ereš_2$; *Pomponio-Visicato 1994*, p. 11; on ki-en-gi *Cooper 1999–2002*, 78–82; *Frayne 2008b*, 7–12).

Our evidence does nonetheless show that the "City League" was not the only actor at the political scene of early dynastic Sumer. Regardless of the fact that there might have been more "City Leagues" at one single moment, we do possess at least one document sealed with a matrix bearing both "City League" emblems and reference to a dignitary the title of which I have interpreted as the enigmatic NAMEŠDA of the early lexical lists. The fact that the seal inscription links this dignitary with the city of Nippur, and with what are probably the fields of the sun-god Utu, shows that the significance of this agency definitely surpassed both local and regional *milieu*.

On the corporate seal of the NAMEŠDA and the "City League" I have already commented above.

* * *

The third component of the political structures visible in the texts and sealings of archaic Ur is the **city ruler himself, LUGAL**, and his administrative apparatus. Let us now dedicate our attention to this topic (see now *Sallaberger 2010*, 33–35 and *Andersson 2012*, 37–38), doing so by analysis of a set of key terms used by the written texts of archaic Ur, and referring to the socially most prominent entities of Nannar's abode, AB, $ENSI_2$, LUGAL and SANGA (see also *Charvát 1997*, 77–81). What has Walter Sallaberger to say on this?

Is the AB, so prominent in the texts of archaic Ur, a temple or a palace? The AB is usually equated with èš, "sanctuary" or "temenos". Best known of these is, of course, Enlil's èš of Nippur. But what was the situation at archaic Ur? The occurrence of the sanga title seemingly confirms the religious character of the institution. However, sanga is also known as a profane manager or administrator of the é-gal in Lagaš. We may also translate AB as a great complex, or even precinct. The lexeme appears in many city names, and may well have meant something like "place", in a quite general sense. One of the ED lexical lists cites the equation AB.UNUG = ki = "place".

The second sign, ŠID, is normally read sanga (saŋŋa) and interpreted as a "priest" or "administrator", "manager", etc. The sign may also be read as umbisag (though we do not know much about this reading), with a meaning "scribe", "author", "the responsible one". In addition to this we may cite the reading of this sign as *šed* = "calculate", "count". SANGA appears in archaic Ur sealins (my # 93 = *UE III*: 431) and in the coeval texts, this title usually links up with large quantities of grain (*Wright* 1969, 107 sub # 5).

Now let us try to discern whether SANGA $EŠ_3$ is really a "priest of the sanctuary". Unfortunately, as late as the Fara times both signs display a high degree of fluidity and polyvalence. How does the situation look like in some particular documents from Ur? Text *UET II*: 162 displays a subscript lugal ŠID še, while *UET II*: 182 shows ŠE ŠID AB. Both subscripts can easily derived from a common model formula of še lugal ŠID ("accounts of grain of the king settled") and še AB ŠID ("accounts of grain of the precinct settled"). Text 162 also includes a clause of še lugal sanga, "grain of king and administrator".

Text *UET II*: 95 then has a subscript of še gu_7 AB, "grain consumed in the AB (building or institution)". Note that this text refers both to AB and to URI_5 (= ŠEŠ.AB). Lines 1–3 of the same text say: 73 (gur?) $šam_2$ ($NINDA_2$×ŠE) $NINDA_2$×ŠIM, AB, $urim_5$ ="73 (Kor? of grain) as price for sourdough (for the production of beer) for AB (and) Ur."

Another text, *UET II*: 93, shows the following formula: ii 3–4: 10 KAL $inda_3$, 1 dug AB. Then follows: ii 5–7: 10 KAL $inda_3$, 1 dug $urim_5$, AN E_2. Is AN É a (personal or topographical) name? May it be read thus: é dingir "house of god(s)"? We may then understand the whole as: Expenditure for: "Temples of the gods in the AB and in Ur".

Is, then, the AB a temple? Any evidence of offering to deities being brought or made there is missing. The "fields of Nanna" may link up with the high priestess of this god, bearing the title zirru (on them see *Wright* 1969, 112). This title has now been interpreted as an original epither of Ningal, consort of Nannar (*Glassner* 2009, 221–222). Usually, land was transferred to temples by the palace, which managed it. AB and Urim may thus be comprehended as "palace and city", much as in Ebla with its formula sa za_x *wa* Ibla, "Palace and Ebla".

It may, then, be suggested that the AB does not stand for the temple of Nanna, but for a precinct within the city of Ur. References to institutional consumption in Ur texts may thus relate to that of the AB. This, in fact, may follow out of other documents. Text 348, for instance, shows the following subscript: /x\ AB e_2 lugal, MUNUS.MAŠ? NANNA.ZI (= zirru, see *Glassner* 2009, 221–222). This may be rendered as: × "precinct, house of the king, the high priestess (of Nanna)". Text *UET II*: 112 gives, in a list of persons, a dignity of nu-bànda é-gal, "lieutenant of the palace".

The PA.SI, or PA.SI $urim_5$ (= énsi), referred to in a group of texts (*UET II*: 83 i 2; *UET II*: 86 i 2; *UET II*: 88 i 3), may then have been somebody like "mayor" or "burgomaster", as the lexeme appears with toponyms known to have designated fields. The archaic Ur texts describe the connection of this title with harvests, quantities of bread, seed and transport of large quantities of grain (*Wright 1969*, 107 sub # 7). In the carrying out of his tasks, PA.SI might have been assisted by the "city elders" (my # 7 = *UE III*: 34; possibly also my # 90 = *UE III*: 428; my # 111 = *UE III*: 455). Sealing of my # 97 = *UE III*: 432 contrasts GAN_2 URU ("city fields"?) with KI UDU (pasture land?). These dignitaries of the city might have congregated in the already institutionalized **assembly**, **UKKIN** (see *UET II*: 108, rev. ii: A.$ŠA_3$ GAN_2 GAL UKKIN; personal name UKKIN GAL, *UET II*: 340: 4).

Free citizenry of Ur may be referred to by the term $\mathbf{LU_2}$ (my # 99 = *UE III*: 434). Among the population of archaic Ur, the texts help to distinguish groups of "minor" and "important" people. Minor farmers worked land parcels of six to twenty-four iku of land; eleven of these may be found in the texts (*Wright 1969*, 118). Major figures managed land plots amounting to thirty to four hundred and twenty-nine iku of land (*Wright 1969*, 106); twenty-six of these figure in the texts (*Wright 1969*, 118).

The personal name contained in text *UET II*: 281 ii 5, read by Gianni Marchesi (2004, 195–197) as $pabilga_x$-mes-utu-pà-da = "Gilgameš is the one whom Utu has selected", shows that the bilateral and "telescoped" kinship system known from later Mesopotamian texts, with $pabilga_x$ as father's father or father's brother (*Götzelt 1995*, esp. pp. 179–180), is likely to have structured (at least some of) the broad strata of Ur society as early as this time. I have attempted to distinguish achieved- versus ascribed status (that is, "naturally attained" as against "socially assigned" social position) in personal names of archaic Ur (*Charvát 1997*, 32–35, 72–74).

The Ur sealings do not refer to **slaves and slave girls**. On the contrary, these turned up in the archaic texts of Ur, (also) as recipients of victuals (e.g. *UET II*: 50; *UET II*: 93; *UET II*: 259). In some instances it is not clear how far the "slave" lexeme constitutes a personal-name component (*UET II*: 128: iv: 5, IR_3 LUGAL).

Let us now go for an overview of how the whole Ur arrangement might have looked like. Within the AB, "royal precinct", the palace, which included the actual residence or seat of the king, was managed by the sanga. The government of the city of Ur belonged to the énsi, "mayor". The texts of archaic Ur show the regional perspective, while the "City League" seals visualize interactions of Ur within southern Mesopotamia. Piotr Steinkeller has proposed that in the time of archaic Ur, the deliveries of goods marked by the rosette still went to Uruk (*Steinkeller 2002b*), but as most of the "City League" seals come from doors, it is difficult to see how such shipments could be leaving Ur.

It may, then, be proposed that the king (LUGAL), dwelling in the inner quarters of the Precinct, took over the responsibility for political decisions. The City, and its rural hinterland area, fell under the sway of the énsi, and behaved like self-directing political entities, but their agricultural activities were managed by the royal quarter.

So much Walter Sallaberger (*2010*, 33–35).

Surprisingly enough, the LUGAL, an office that we would assume almost authomatically to turn up in the SIS 8-4 sealed materials, is nearly completely absent from among them (*Visicato-Westenholz 2005*, 55). We will, however, do well to notice that exclusion from inscriptions on seal matrices points to the conclusion that the LUGAL office did not constitute an original part of the SIS seal world.

Both sealing references to this office at our current disposal merit attention. This is the sealing *UE III:* 118, a handwritten gloss bearing signs I_3, AB_2, $BARA_2$ and LUGAL (re-published as *UET II*: 312, see also http://cdli.ucla.edu/search/archival_view.php?ObjectID=P005899 [accessed September 8, 2014]). The sign I_3 (*ZATU* No. 393 p. 253, both a city and an official = *MSVO 1* p. 128, see also http://psd.museum.upenn.edu/epsd/nepsd-frame.html [accessed September 8, 2014] s. v. NI = bur, gana, i_3, lidga, nunuz, zagin) appeared in the archaic sealings (my ## 72 and 110 = *UE III*: 409 and 454). Together with the AB_2 sign, it may probably be taken at its face value as "cow butter" or "cow fat" = i_3 ab_2 (of any kind; see the PSD entries for i and ab, and *Englund 1995b*, 128 fn. 17). The signs $BARA_2$ and LUGAL may refer either to the "throne-dais of the LUGAL", or they simply represent a personal name (lugal-bára, bára-lugal, see *Andersson 2012*, 90). The "cow butter" apeared as an offering in a text accounting for offerings for the deities and deceased rulers of Lagaš including Gudea, possibly by the consort of Nammahni (*Perlov 1980*). Recently, the lexeme has been rendered as "butterfat" (Eric Cripps, apud *Schrakamp 2012a*, 160, sub # 42 Rs. 6). Does the Ur case also refer to offering matter? The second instance (*UET II*: 290), another handwritten gloss, seems even to be referring to "kingship", or at least to the "king's domain" (NAM.LUGAL.BAR – *Charvát 1997*, 78, fn. 861, on the concept *Andersson 2012*, 97–98). This would indicate a rather high position of the prince of Ur.

With LUGAL virtually absent, we acknowledge at least the presence of his partner, NIN (my # 102 = *UE III*: 438; my # 107 = *UE III*: 443).

The LUGAL of the city of Ur figures prominently in the texts written there and discovered mostly in the SIS 4-5 strata. These texts, at least partly contemporary with our sealings, give evidence on the LUGAL office especially in the form of personal names. They show beyond all doubt that the role of the pristine LUGAL of Ur was not only secular, but sacerdotal and ritual as well (see below; *Charvát 1997*, 78–80; *Andersson 2012*). This evidence makes the LUGAL first and foremost a provider of plenty, a guarantee of activation of forces of fertility and fecundity of the nature and its living components including people. The name of the later king Meskalamdu/Mesugedu of Kiš and Ur translates as "hero who provides well-being for the land" (*Frayne 2008b*, E1.13.3, p. 385). The activation of fertility always played a major role in the "professional qualification" of early Mesopotamian elites (see, i.a., *Hurowitz 1992*, 45–61 on Gudea, *Tinney 1999*, and *Jones 2003*, most recently *Nissinen-Uro 2008*)[23]. Thus, the Ur LUGAL of the ED-I–II times is hardly the "king" of later ages. We shall do more justice to him, and to NIN, his partner and consort, by translating the LUGAL and NIN (on NIN in archaic Ur see *Charvát 1997*, 85–87) titles as "lord" and "lady", in accordance with the Old English versions of these titles, *hlāford* (http://en.wiktionary.org/wiki/lord#Etymology, accessed July 20th, 2010) and *hlāfdiga* (http://en.wiktionary.org/wiki/hl%C3%A6fdige, accessed July 20th, 2010), meaning "bread-keeper", "bread-kneader", "bread-provider" or the like (see also *Marchesi 2004*, 163–164 and 174–175, but ultimately loyal to the traditional kingly interpretation: *ibid*. 186). For more information see Chapter V, Conclusions.

In this book I have also used a rendering "prince of Ur" for the LUGAL (from Latin *princeps*).

The tasks for which the Ur LUGAL was held responsible did doubtlessly included defense of the community against external enemies. This might be reflected not only in the seal scenes if military triumph (*UE III*: 131 and *UE III*: 297) and references to fortified (?) cities (my # 93 = *UE III*: 431), but also in the inscription of sealing of my # 23 = *UE III*: 114, which may refer to an "arsenal" (bows or "Wurfwaffen", as Karin Rohn translates, and daggers/swords) either delivered by the HAL entity, or for use in expeditions abroad.

Among the "courtiers" of the Ur LUGAL (?), the NIMGIR figures prominently (my # 5 = *UE III*: 25; my # 72 = *UE III*: 409; my # 73 = *UE III*: 410; my # 110 = *UE III*: 454). We even hear of a NIMGIR.GAL (my # 106 = *UE III*: 442).

A few words on the most important office of the preceding Late Uruk times, the EN. As early as the Late Uruk times, we know of a personal name (?) En-Nanna (*Cohen 1996*, 9; *Charvát 1997*, 57, fn. 646). In opposition to Uruk where the male EN served the goddess Inanna, the EN of Ur was female, an arch-priestess of Nannar, the gender of whom has been determined by opposition to the gender of the municipal deity. The EN of Ur took refuge in the city temple, serving the moon god as faithful consort and servant (see *Weadock 1975*; *Lion 2009*; *Westenholz 2013*).

23 Though the following citation pertains to early medieval Ireland, I find it fitting to the Mesopotamian situation to such an extent that it is well worth quoting in full: *The metaphor of the sacred marriage of king and goddess and the notion of the king's righteousness that made the world fruitful were elaborately articulated in the vernacular literature and skilfully integrated with Christian concepts of kingship by a learned clergy* (*Ó Corráin 1995*, 46).

The political changes in the public role of Ur resulted in transformations perceptible archaeologically. Before 3000 B.C.E., Ur and al-Ubaid represented a pair of "shrines", probably more or less of the same consequence. After 3000, when Ur assumed the role of a hegemon of the power situation within Sumer, the sacred functions of al-Ubaid died out and for the most the ancient part of ED, the latter site served as a rural borough. In was only with Aanepada, son of Mesannepada and king of Ur (2523–2484), that a temple edicated to the goddess Ninhursag grew up at el-Obeid (see *Wright* 1969, 32–42, 77–87, and *Tunca* 1984, 95–96, and Figs. 142–144).

* * *

Having paid due attention to Ur's relations within Sumer proper, we will do well to inquire about possible testimonies of "**international relations**" of this early age. The *ZATU* 762+NIM$_2$ MEN of our sealing # 24 = *UE III*: 117 implies connections with Elam, only natural in southeastern Mesopotamia. The same might be borne out by the use of the IŠ lexeme, if the reading suggested by *Beal* 1992 (ŠUŠ$_3$ or SUS/A/$_x$) really relates to the Elamite capital (= my # 14 = *UE III*: 81, # 67 = *UE III*: 404, # 68 = *UE III*: 405, # 92 = *UE III*: 430; a reserved stance is taken by *Rohn* 2011, 194).

A topic raising many questions is hinted at by the sealing of my # 25 = *UE III*: 119, bearing an inscription which can be read as AZ SUMUN. Whatever the reading of the SUMUN sign, the AZ, denoting a bear, cannot fail to evoke in our minds the sealing *UE III*: 384 with its famous animal fable showing an enthroned bear served by his animal courtiers. Beyond the "animal-fable" metaphor (on animal myths in Mesopotamia see *Haul* 2004, 248ff.; on the occurrence of the AZ sign, read PIRIG × A, in text *UET II*: 164 see *Mittermayer* 2005, 10–16), this scene has defied interpretation for a long time, and thus we may attempt one or two here. The animal icons of early Ur include, in addition to the abovementioned bear, also the depiction of wild boar which has already figured among the finds referred to (*Woolley* 1955, 31, 67, Pl. 37: U.14459; *Sürenhagen* 1999, 200, Taf. 57: 5). In fact, this boar finds a parallel in the motif carried by the seal that counter-signed the above cited sealing *UE III*: 297 (but also that which counter-marked our impression, *UE III*: 384, the boar image accompanied by those of a scorpion and an "arrow-point"). The other impression of the same cylinder seal as *UE III*: 297, *UE III*: 131, received an imprint of a counter-marking device bearing the rosette motif. Now the rosette, having been recognized as a "very powerful symbol of life" (*Moortgat-Correns* 1994; *Selz* 2004b, 201), could well allude to some kind of social embodiment of this idea (= receiver of the goods consigned by the counter-marking seal), like, for instance, to a temple – or to the city of Ur, as we have seen. In such a case, the boar icon may also be interpreted as an emblem of a wider social grouping – and the bear insignia also (see *Charvát 1994; Charvát 2007; Charvát 2014a*).

Yet, as the "animal banquet scene" represents the only indication that animal fables or "totemic symbolism" (expressing social structures by means of metaphors from nature) may apply here, it seems legitimate to ask a question whether we should not turn for interpretation to the banquet symbolism, clearly alluding to ideas of fertility and fecundity. Does the "animal banquet" scene hint that the fertility-activation function of banquets does apply not only to human but to the animal world as well, as might be intended by the scorpion image on the counter-signing seal?

In a possibly related case, sealing of my # 88 = *UE III*: 426 bears a counter-mark in the shape of a human face. In the light of images like my # 62 = *UE III*: 398, with its cross-shaped device composed of human faces, and evoking very likely the idea of the four cardinal points of the civilized world, the human face may also stand for a whole population of a particular circumscribed area.

All this is admittedly pure speculation. The "enthroned bear" of *UE III*: 384 does, however, loom large on our horizon as the only representative of a literary genre attested to among the Ur sealing. Why is this scene so unique? It might be worthwhile at least to attempt an interpretation taking into account a wider context of iconography of the Ur sealings.

However that issue may turn out in the future, it does seem probable that in addition to occasional belligerent action beyond the borders of their realms (see the GIŠ GIGIR$_2$ NUN, possibly a war chariot, in *UET II*: 182 B), the sovereigns of Ur strived to maintain friendly, or at least peaceful, relations with foreign powers (wider kinship units? ethnic groups?) and might have exchanged gifts with them as a token of good will.

MANAGEMENT

In this section, I am trying to investigate the essential mechanism behind the traffic of sealed goods within the (economic only?) circuits of archaic Ur.

The earliest sealings

As may be seen, the second earliest stage of the Ur sealings, dating to the very beginning of the third millennium (SIS 8-6), does already show a rather high degree of sophistication of the administrative machinery of this early Sumerian state (for a list see also *Charvát 2010b*, 40–43).

First, we have the very simplest form of goods' movement – comestibles sealed and delivered in movable containers, presumably for direct consumption (my # 3 = *UE III*: 14, my # 4 = *UE III*: 24).

Next, there are commodities in mobile containers bearing seals which denote sets of institutions, offices and communities (my # 1 = *UE III*: 1, my # 2 = *UE III*: 9, my # 5 = *UE III*: 25).

Finally, the evidence of sealing of storage spaces under the names of various dignitaries bearing traditional (Late Uruk-age) titles hints at redistribution of goods on behalf of the Ur polity (my # 6 = *UE III*: 26, my # 7 = *UE III*: 34, my # 8 = *UE III*: 35, my # 9 = *UE III*: 43?).

At least in the case of my # 1 = *UE III*: 1, originally a basket sealing, I suggest that this is an early example of a pisandubba, container tag referring to written materials contained within the receptacle thus closed. The same assertion would be difficult in cases of my # 5 = *UE III*: 25 and my # 7 = *UE III*: 34, because Roger Matthews believes that these come from door pegs. Nevertheless, the first case attests to a respectable age of the archival practice current in the classical age of the cuneiform documents of ancient Mesopotamia.

A particular situation is represented by sealings of my ## 119 and 120 = *UE III*: 480, denoting the manner of acquisition of the goods marked ($ŠAM_2$ = "purchased"), which have already been commented upon. They come from a "lock" sealing and a moveable "tag" with a hole bored through it. This may again point to the use of a travelling seal, belonging to an official who traveled and applied his seal at the production site. Subsequently, having deposited them in a special storage facility, he or she closed its entrace with the very same seal with which the goods had been signed.

* * *

The entire body of evidence given by the seals and sealings of archaic Ur leads me to the following reconstruction of the administrative routine for the SIS 5-4 material:

1) material deliveries were carried to Ur under whatever title this might have taken place, and deposited in storage spaces;
2) the storage spaces were sealed by the suppliers of the goods, or alternatively, by "royal" officials charged with supervision of the correctness of such material deliveries;
3) (some of) the sealed storerooms were then counter-signed, or counter-marked, by (other?) officials of the administrative centre, presumably to show secondary branches of the redistribution process, and the flow of goods collected for the centre towards those consumers privileged to share revenues collected by the centre;
4) the storerooms were opened and the goods stored went their various ways;
5) the sealings were collected by officials of the administrative centre, and the correctness of all deliveries was checked by the central registry office (on this in Ebla see *Micale-Nadali 2010*, 21);

6) finally, when all the controls showed the completeness and correctness of the whole process, all the administrative materials were audited and then discarded (see also *Charvát 2013*).

It seems that at least some of these activities could be outlined by following the procedures connected with deposition of grain in the granaries in connection with the guru$_7$-a im-ùr-ra clause (*Huber 2000*). The interpretation "to plaster the guru$_7$ with clay, to close, seal the guru$_7$", proposed by the author (*Huber 2000*, 491) logically seems to involve closing (also) with seal impressions, and thus the whole operation, illuminated by written sources, could well shed light on the practicalities of sealing storage spaces. Huber (2000, 468) notes a) that the process referred to as guru$_7$-a im-ùr-ra represents an end-point of a chain of transport-related activities, b) that it might have taken place still in the fields, at the threshing floor, or c) after shipping, at the quay, in cities or at a specified guru$_7$. He also lists the following activities as taking place before (and never after) the guru$_7$-a im-ùr-ra (*Huber 2000*, 468–469):

- še bal-a = filling grain into containers,
- še ga$_6$-gá = transport of grain,
- še du$_3$-a = "erection" of grain in heaps(?, any connection with our KAK sign?),
- še KIN-a = obscure, does not refer to harvest,
- še guru$_7$-a e$_3$-da = ?, possibly from verb e$_{11}$,
- še zi-ga, še má-a zi-ga = transport of grain, shipping of grain,
- má-gíd-da = rowing on boat (with grain),
- má bal-ak = ?
- má bal-zíd ak-a = ?

The ùr operation took place at regular intervals, during a certain month, which, in Pre-Sargonic Lagaš, was referred to as itid guru$_7$ im du$_8$-a = "month when granaries are closed with clay" (*Huber 2000*, 482–484).

All this indicates the complexity of procedures linked with the deposition of commodities in storage, and leaves plenty of room both for the use of "travelling seals" closing harvest shares in containers for transport, and for the application of seals on the clay closures of storage facilities.

Some examples show that the counter-marking seals left their imprints in a moment definitely not much longer after the matrix seal had been used, and, indeed, there are instances when the matrix- and the counter-signing seal(s) make up a harmonious whole, having been clearly apposited at the same time (e.g. my # 89 = *UE III*: 427; my # 93 = *UE III*: 431).

Other finds bear out the conclusion that the sealings were taken off the media to which they were applied when the clay was still wet (my

43 = *UE III*: 296, with traces of cutting; my # 67 = *UE III*: 404, with traces of cutting; my # 68 = UE *III*: 405, with traces of cutting; my # 96 = *UE III*: 431; my # 110 = *UE III*: 454).

In conjunction with information provided by their reverses, the seal inscriptions may attest to forms of delivery of the goods which they mark. This is the case of the produce of GAN_2 KI, delivered in a container (bale?) in the case of my # 28 = *UE III*: 155. The GAN_2 also furnished commodities in connection with the "City League" in my # 81 = *UE III*: 419. Elsewhere, the central administration received processed goods, like the threshed (or otherwise treated) grain mentioned probably in the cases of four items of which two (my ## 46 and 48) carry images showing the the BAD sign refers to threshing (or other treatment) of grain there (my # 12 = *UE III*: 79, my # 46 = *UE III*: 315, my # 48 = *UE III*: 325, my # 78 = *UE III*: 416).

The geographical origin of the supplies sealed in the storage facilities may be given in the case of a reference to "south" (GIŠGAL: my # 98 = *UE III*: 433). A similar notion may be operative in the case of the lexeme $ŠUR_2$ = tumu = "wind" in the sense of "(one of the) cardinal point(s)" (my # 101 = *UE III*: 437). The archaic texts of Ur include a personal name Šubur which Piotr Steinkeller relates to Assyria (*Steinkeller 2013*, 138–139 ad v 4').

With respect to terminology, in addition to the already mentioned IL_2 "tax" (my # 124 = *Matthews 1993*, 14 = *Scott 2005*, 14), sealing of my # 97 = *UE III*: 432 has MU.DU, also a possible reference to tax obligations.

The Ur seal inscriptions sometimes referred to the manner in which the goods came in. The scribes and/or seal-cutters might have noted the kind of delivery receptacles: DUG, GAN, KAB, $NINDA_2$, DIN(?), and some of them might even have left impressions of their surfaces on the sealing reverses (see *Zettler 1989*). These sometimes left archaeologically visible traces: the age-old practice of transporting textiles in pottery vessels as containers is borne out by the Ur material (my # 27 = *UE III*: 142; my # 114 = *UE III*: 461; my # 136 = *Matthews 1993*, 89).

KISAL (is this to be read $gipar_x$, *Selz 2011b*, 233 sub # 1: 3? not always: *Andersson 2012*, 158 fn. 912) is named in a position likely to have been the place where the goods were disbursed (my # 69 = *UE III*: 406; my # 118 = *UE III*: 474; on gipar see also *Lion 2009*, 179; *Westenholz 2013*, 254–256). In other instances, particular storerooms obviously received the disbursements (GA_2+AŠ, my # 56 = *UE III*, 392; LAGAB+ŠITA, my # 69 = *UE III*: 406; GA_2 or LAGAB?, my # 116 = *UE III*: 464). Of course, GA_2 itself may, in certain contexts, mean "un type d'enclos", "... où se tiennent souvent des bovins et des ovins" (= "Stall, Gehege" = *Attinger-Krebernik 2005*, 73 sub # 254') or be interpreted as GA_2 = "outbuilding, shed, barn" (*Andersson 2012*, 136 fn. 763).

As to the periodicity of the deliveries, sealing of my # 126 (= *Matthews 1993*, 26) includes the sign U_4+AŠ, probably interpreted as "one month"

(*UET II*: # 199). What does the reference to U_4, "day", (in my # 32 = *UE III*: 209, and No.110 = *UE III*: 454) mean? It seems reasonable to assume that some kind of periodicity (office? tax-payment obligation?) hides behind the lexeme BALA (my # 93 = *UE III*: 431; my # 97 = *UE III*: 432), but no precise data are available.

The registrars and accountants of archaic Ur kept track of the deliveries due to the central administration and noted arrears, possibly by the term LIBIR (my # 97 = *UE III*: 432; my # 98 = *UE III*: 433).

Among the institutions charged with the collection of revenue, the facility known later as e_2-uz-ga may be present at this early date (my # 5 = *UE III*: 25; my # 93 = *UE III*: 431; my # 97 = *UE III*: 432; on the institution see *Dahl* 2006, 83; *Allred* 2006, 72–80).

Giacomo Benati (*Benati* 2015, 8) observes that the metrology of the archaic Ur texts follows Late-Uruk textual usage. This goes for the domain of inscribed seals as well.

METAPHYSICS

Let us now turn to the sphere of things beyond the perception of human senses, or to metaphysical or cultural-cognition concerns of the archaic Ur society. In this aspect, a major change attesting to a "revivalist" atmosphere of this epoch of time is the return to burying the dead by inhumation, a custom highly unusual in the preceding, Late Uruk times (a review in *Pollock* 2007b, 211–212). The Late Uruk age left us but a sprinkling of graves, in which the deceased were usually laid to rest in positions obviously not fixed by any prescribed burial rite, but with fairly rich burial equipment (e.g. *Su Kyung Huh* 2008, esp. pp. 270–271). It must nevertheless be conceded that the largest Uruk-age cemetery, that of the Telloh hill of Lagaš, comprised but twenty-three burials (*de Genouillac* 1934, 66–68). This is highly unusual, given the large settlement agglomerations of the Middle- and Late-Uruk period, and we can legitimately ask what became of the thousands of bodies which must have been left behind, for instance, by the inhabitants of the city excavated at the site of Habuba Kabira in Syria.

As against this, the "Jamdat Nasr cemetery" of Ur (see *Sürenhagen* 1999, 209–243; *Dittmann* 2006), as well as the cemetery of al-Ubaid (*Wright* 1969, 77–87; *Martin* 1982) not only contain the expected numbers of bodies (c. 370 dead in the "Jamdat Nasr cemetery", but 16 [*Martin* 1982, 165], or 28 coeval burials at Ubaid), but they do convey important information of economic and social order. The personages entombed in the Ur burial ground do show a differentiation between male and female bodies (*Forest* 1983, 117–132), and this must reflect a specific perception of social status vis-à-vis the mortuary situation of indvidual society members. The equality in post-mortem treatment of the deceased in the Late Uruk era gave way to a new "social persona" of Ur citizens, differentiated – at least in the funerary sphere – according to gender. This shows well the dynamics of historical development in this transitory age: the custom of burying deceased community members in specific areas singled out for that purpose, presumably with respect to ancestor worship, returned, but the ancient liberality in choosing the position of the dead body and its equipment gave way before the new structuration of society into gender categories.

Nevertheless, things were not so plain and simple. A deeper look at the Tell Ubaid cemetery (*Wright* 1969, 77–87, and *Martin* 1982) reveals some most interesting patterns shedding light on a number of questions concerning life and death at early Ur. As the physical-anthropology analyses show, people who found their final resting place at Ubaid had long narrow heads and prominent noses, and displayed heavy muscular relief, at least in the neck area. With eight of the fifteen investigated individuals having died at an age of sixty and more years, life expectancy seems to have been unusually high, though the sample of human remains might be biased (*Wright* 1969, 78). As against the Ur "Jamdat Nasr cemetery", females buried at Ubaid received no funerary equipment (*Wright* 1969, 79).

A most interesting characteristic, however, is displayed by the position of the bodies in graves. Their heads tend to heed northwest or southwest, while the faces frequently turn northeast or northwest (*Wright* 1969, 81–83, Fig. 24 on p. 82). This means that the Ubaid dead were laid to rest in orientations making up two arms of a cross (the NW and SW one) turned by 45° from the cardinal-point directions, while their faces, looking in a clockwise direction, made thus the whole arrangement similar to half of a swastika turning right (clockwise). This device parallels depictions of humans making up a two arm- or four-arm swastika compositions in seals of archaic Ur, called by Sarah Jarmer Scott "pinwheel" (*UE III*: 286 or *UE III*: 518). These "swastikas of human beings" appeared in triumph scenes, and are thus likely to convey the meaning of a sum of population of a certain region or regions, doing homage to the winsome hero who had subdued them (on the fourfold division of the world in Mesopotamia see *Glassner* 1984; on the swastika of human bodies as a symbols of this fourfold division see *Marchesi* 2004, 182, fn. 168, with ref.). Subscribing to such an interpretation, we could see in the manner of deposition of the Ubaid dead a reflection of the construction of the nether world like unto the four corners of the world of the living, and an attempt to bury (all) the deceased in accordance with the highest order of the universe, not according to such earthly characteristics as the gender. However, more evidence is needed to substantiate this hypothesis.

A certain universalism may also be seen in the burial equipment of the Tell Ubaid dead. The most ubiquitous items – jars and cups – show that for the nether world, the socially relevant category of feast-giving, not personal wealth, played the most prominent role (*Wright 1969*, 83–86). "There is evidence for only one social class..., there is no evidence for kin groups" (*Wright 1969*, 87). Are these the LU_2, as attested to in texts of archaic Ur?

The question of end of the "Jamdat Nasr cemetery" of Ur and the location of the city's ED-I burial ground offers much food for thought but positive evidence is lacking. At any rate, even the subsequent ED cemetery of Ur entombed far less bodies than the actual number of the deceased must have been (*Pollock 2007a*, 99). We may, for instance, ponder upon the possibility of burial of the dead in swamps, attested to later (*Beaulieu 1988*), but the sources are silent on this.

* * *

The focus of religious life of the Ur community was no doubt constituted by the temple of the municipal god, the moon deity Nannar (*Wright 1969*, 32–42; *Weadock 1975*; *Tunca 1984*, 85–90, 172–179, 239, 244, as well as Figs. 124–130 on pp. 95–99; *Cohen 1996*; *Marchesi 2004*, passim; *Benati 2013*). Of the temple buildings, or rather what was left of them, likely to have been erected around and/or after 3000 B.C.E., we better give the word to the personage best qualified for their description, Leonard, later Sir Leonard, Woolley:

"*Below the Ziggurat terrace and terrace buildings of Ur-Nammu there survives a Ziggurat terrace, complete in its ground-plan, of the time of the First Dynasty of Ur, and below this again and serving in the main as a foundation for the later construction is a third Ziggurat terrace with its attendant shrines built just as the Jamdat Nasr period came to an end*" (*Woolley 1955*, 35–36; for a recent review of evidence of early Mesopotamian ziggurats see *Pfälzner-Schmid 2008*).

In fact, at least some of the architectural fragments documented included both flat and plano-convex bricks (*Woolley 1955* Pl. 10: c).

Insofar as the lamentable state of the architectural vestiges surviving from the time close to that of the SIS 8-4 sealings permits, it seems that it first assumed the form of an oblong enclosure, the corners of which were oriented towards the cardinal points. The central cult feature, Nannar's shrine buried under the successive ziggurat phases, received additions in (at least) two courtyard-centered architectural complexes situated in the northern (N) and southeastern (SE) corners of the enclosure. To what original purpose(s) these might have served remains hidden from us (*Tunca 1984*, plans in Figs. 127 and 128; *Benati 2013*, 198 Fig. 2).

Various possibilities exist as to the interpretation of the architectural traces unearthed. A platform built of three course of baked bricks with bitumen-coated surface displaying two cavities, situated in the central court (angle E. locus FF, *Tunca 1984*, Fig. 127) of the SE complex could, for instance, refer to a twin cultic object (two standards?), reserved to a cult of two deities, for instance, Nannar and Ningal. The series of narrow parallel spaces with massive, bitumen-coated floor constructions, abutting the northwestern wall of the SE complex (*Tunca 1984*, 166, 229–230), strongly recall storage spaces[24]. The westernmost of these, Locus A, opened towards the south-lying court (locus BB) by means of what Woolley called "raised causeway", but what, according to Tunca (*1984*, 166–167), could have served as water-evacuation conduit line (canalization), conveying undesirable water out of the court area by means of channels passing the entrance passage to the BB court and draining outside the edifice (*Tunca 1984*, 166–167). Thus this entire unit, consisting of the storage spaces(?) A, B, C, D and F and the court BB, separated from the west-lying courtyard-centered unit and provided with its own entrance (passage AA), could have served for supplying and storage of the material appurtenances of the cult[25]. Rooms DD and EE of the SE complex, as well as 6 and 7 of the N complex, contained remains of both circular and apparently rectangular brick platforms bearing traces of intense, and long-term, exposure to fire, interpreted as cooking installations (*Tunca 1984*, 172–175).

But all this is clearly too nebulous to warrant any certain conclusions.

An interesting discovery awaited Woolley's workmen in the courtyard of the temple precinct close to its southwestern corner, between the ziggurat and the N complex (*Tunca 1984*, 266). A hoard of possibly disused cultic inventory went into the earth here, encapsulated in a pottery vase. Among the objects found, including stamp seals in the traditional style, animal and human statuettes and beads, our attention immediately focuses on the object resembling an "eye idol", omitted by Tunca but mentioned (though not depicted) by Leonard Woolley (1955, 43, U.17836). If this find really represents a discard of cultic inventory, it may well indicate the character of temple furnishings no more of relevance to the incipient third-millennium society. But again, our data are too meagre to allow any better-founded conclusions.

The highest and most important dignitary who resided, and carried out her office, within the sacred precinct was the EN, priestess of Nannar, the moon god (see *Lion 2009*, esp. p. 166, fn. 4 with ref., and 170–171; *Westenholz 2013*, 248–258). The EN was of a gender opposite to that of the municipal deity, and occupied the position of his or her spouse (*Westenholz 2013*, 248). It seems that the deity himself gave a disposition as to who should occupy this office by means of an oracle (*Westenholz 2013*, 253). The EN went through a rather elaborate "ordination" in the Ekišnugal temple of Nannar, where she was purified and received her name. Then, having been raised to the status of Nannar's spouse, she took her residence in the Gipar (*Westenholz 2013*, 254–256). In later

24 Might some of the SIS 8-4 seal impressions, especially those with reverses copying smooth walls, have come from here?

25 Could this possibly have been the KISAL?

times royal princesses frequently filled this post. The EN had to pray for the life of the king (LUGAL), cater to the needs of Ningal, Nannar's divine consort, and to manage the estate making up the appurtenances of her office. She also carried out purification rites, took care of Nannar's daily provisions, and accompanied his statue on solemn voyages, especially during the akitu festival, celebrated twice at Ur – in the first and seventh month (*Westenholz 2013*, 257–259). The EN's marital duties included lying down in Nannar's bedroom E_2.NUN = agrun (*Westenholz 2013*, 259). Deceased EN's found their last resting place in a particular cemetery within the area of their Ur residence, Gipar (*Weadock 1975*, 101–104, 109–110, and 119; *Lion 2009*, 179).

In addition to the EN, another minister of Nannar entered our sources under the name of zirru (= MUNUS.NUNUZ.ZI). She may have participated in festivals, and received "rations" (*Westenholz 2013*, 249–251).The zirru title has now been interpreted as an original epither of Ningal, consort of Nannar (*Glassner 2009*, 221–222).

Unlike the preceding two offices, the position of the Ur ereš-dingir remains unclear. In Lagaš, she served the goddess Baba. The ereš-dingir obviously disposed of a considerable property and visited festivals (*Westenholz 2013*, 260–261).

It is unfortunate that only standards with half-moon represent the iconography of Nannar prior to the onset of the Akkadian dynasty (*Braun-Holzinger 1993*, 120).

What was going on the the temple(s) of Nannar's city? In this connection, let us focus our attention on the sign UR_2, occurring fairly frequently in seal insciptions of archaic Ur. Against the assumption that UR_2 denotes a toponym, I present the following arguments, as I have done before (see above, my # 12). I do believe, however, that the repetition will bring out things more clearly.

UR_2 = also URUM(?), is to be identified as *ZATU* No. 588 p. 304 = *MSVO 1* p. 160. The equation UR_2 = *sūnu* = "thigh" may be found in *MEA* No. 203 p. 117, similarly http://psd.museum.upenn.edu/epsd/nepsd-frame.html [accessed October 5, 2014] s. v. ur_2 = "root, base; limbs; loin, lap". *Sūnu* is identified in *CAD* S pp. 386–388 as "lap", "crotch", "sexual organs", and also, in general, "human body from the waist down", "lap", "foundation", but also "to sleep" and "to fecundate" (*rehû*).

The lexeme occurs in Fara-age personal names (*Visicato 1997*, 101). In Instructions of Šuruppak, ÚR.AŠ may be a honorific epithet of Šuruppak (*Alster 1974*, 25). *Westenholz 1987*, 43, refers to a binary lexeme A_2+UR_2, attested to in Agade-period texts, probably a_2-ur_2 = *mešrêtu* = limbs, described as "right" and "left". This seems to allude to limbs of the human body above, and below, the waist, most probably to arms and legs of statuettes produced separately from the bodies. On the lexeme see also *Alster 1991–1992*, 19 and

21, ad ll. 192–193 (ur_2-sikil = "a girl's lap"), and *Mander 1986*, 96 ($^{d}ur_2$ = "il dio delle fondamenta"?). Recently this lexeme has been commented by Jeremiah Peterson (2007, 567–571). *Selz 1995*, 285 ($^{d}ur_2$-nun-ta-e_3-a = "Die aus dem Schosse des Fürsten hervorgegangene"), interprets this name (= rain cloud, a fertility symbol) as that of one of the septuplet daughters of the goddess Baba, lukur priestesses, venerated in the Gudea-period in the ^{d}lama-$ša_6$-ga temple of Lagaš. Seven lukur priestesses are known as early as ED Lagaš, where they were nin $ensi_2$-ka. We may also notice Ur_2-ni = "his lap" = "the deity's lap", a scribe's name on an ED-IIIa-style highly prestigious cylinder seal: *Buchanan 1981*, No. 303 pp. 115 and 443–444. In Ur-III texts DUR_2 = "Standfläche, Standring (von Gefäßen)", and, in general, base of any object; the texts distinguish between UR_2 = "Schoß" and DUR_2 = "buttocks"; in descriptions of vessels, UR_2 = those with figural decorations inside, DUR_2 = only if the lower part of vessel is of a different material (*Paoletti 2012*, 147).

The *gunnû*-form of the UR_2 sign (UR_2 × TAG_4), probably linking up with sign LAK 289, later evolved into the UMBIN sign, denoting a kind of vessel or receptacle. One UMBIN may equal 2 $SILA_3$. A similar case is UR_2 × GAR, attested to in the Old Babylonian period (*Gelb-Steinkeller-Whiting 1991*, 54). Was the UR_2 delivery a reward for the holding of the TAG_4 ceremony, supplied in hollow measures?

All this leads me to believe that in the sealings of archaic Ur, the sign UR_2 referred to a particular event linked with fertility and procreative force. This seems to me to suggest a ceremony triggering off these powers of nature, and crucial for the fecundation of the land and its denizens. I assume that such a ceremony had been taking place in Sumer at least since the late Uruk period (*Charvát 2005a*, 168–170), and that its presence at archaic Ur may be hinted at by seal iconography displaying overtly sexual connotations, as indicated by the intercourse scenes (in *UE III*: 364–370). I therefore propose to interpret the UR_2 ceremony as the equivalent of the NA_2 procedure of the Late Uruk times, ritual release of procreative forces of nature and living beings (see also *Charvát 1997*, 10–12, 27, 57–59), which later evolved into the "sacred marriage" rite, celebrated by kings of the Third dynasty of Ur and of Isin (see *Selz 2012*, 66–70 for ED Lagaš, *Hurowitz 1992*, 45–61 on Gudea, *Selz 1995*, 175 sub # 12, *Tinney 1999*, and *Jones 2003*, most recently *Nissinen-Uro 2008; Selz 2008*, 20–22; *Keetman 2010*, esp. pp. 45–46; *McCaffey 2013*).

The most explicit statement concerning this event is that of my # 21 = *UE III*: 102 (NUN, $GIŠ_3$+UR_2, SAL? *ZATU* 644 or -645 = SUMUN?). Here we have a reference to sexual intercourse ($GIŠ_3$+UR_2, SAL?) bound to a geographical (or divine?) entity (NUN)[26]. Thus the performance of the UR_2 procedure

26 I confess that I do not understand the meaning of the SUMUN sign (were it to be read this way), unless it refers to "old" entities (arrears of due payments?).

involves sexual intercourse, and is done on behalf of localized communities. To me, this is suggestive of the traditional NA_2 fertility-triggering ceremony of the Uruk age, and I suspect that this may be one of the early predecessors of what later evolved into the "sacred marriage" ceremony.

An iconographic testimony of the character and whereabouts of the UR_2 event follows out of the depiction on sealing of my # 43 = *UE III*: 296. The sign UR_2 occupies one of the "rooms" of a two-compartment building here. A naked male figure stands in the other while a spread eagle hovers above the building. Another male carries an animal (game?) towards the building. We can hardly escape the conclusion of being privy to a scene of bringing sacrifices into a temple in reward for what takes place within its premises

We get some hints at information on the UR_2 from the sealings of my ## 57–59 (= *UE III*: 395). The seal which left them bore an inscription consisting of signs UR_4 KAB ALAM UR_2 DU_8, which may be perhaps rendered as "wool clip in containers (brought to) the statue for the completed UR_2". If this interpretation fits, then we have at least one testimony on what the UR_2 ceremony involved, and what did it require (on divine statues see most recently *Dahl 2011*). The UR_2 event might have taken place in its own house (*UE III*: 438 = my # 102).

The UR_2 links up with geographical entities and commodities delivered for its purpose are named either in kind (ŠE, DIN?) or with reference to containers in which they came ($NINDA_2$, DUG, DIN?). Statues (ALAM) obviously played a role in the proceedings linked with this event, as I have already observed. The building in which this ceremony took place frequently bore the emblem of the spread eagle (see above, my # 43 = *UE III*: 296).

Another cultic proceeding likely to have taken place below the roof of the Ur temple might be referred to by the sign TAK_4 (my # 92 = *UE III*: 430; my # 106 = *UE III*: 442). The TAK_4.ALAN ceremony(?) is attested to in Šuruppak texts, in ED LU_2, at Ebla (with a reading *la-a-núm*) and at Nippur. The Šuruppak texts mention a structure called é-TAK_4.ALAN. The term may refer to a statue in a votive inscription (ABW 2 p. 342) (*Pomponio 1987*, 474). TAK_4.ALAN is likely to denote a statue and possibly also a sculptor (*Gelb-Steinkeller-Whiting 1991*, 69). In Abu Salabikh, TAK_4.ALAN = lan_x; UD-lan_x could mean an-lan_x = "scolpire il divino" = "to carve a deity" (*Mander 1986*, 52). In ED Lagaš, a number of statues and one stele received regular offerings on festive occasions in the É-$šag_4$ shrine, of a square ground plan with square side 3.715 metres long (*Rosengarten 1960*, 162; on divine statues most recently *Dahl 2011*). The ceremony may be depicted on a cylinder seal found in the Jemdet-Nasr level at Ur (*Legrain 1951*, 11, # 30 on Pl. 2 = *Sürenhagen 1999* sub # 47, Taf. 55: 10, found in *kiln stratum* 4 of Pit F, dating to the "ausgehende Späturuk-Zeit": *Dittmann 2006*, 28–29 and possibly also on seal UE III: 385).

In ED-IIIb inscriptions, SAHAR.DU_6.TAG_4 may mean "burial tell", with translation of TAG_4 as "leave behind" (*Richardson 2007*, 193–194; *Suriano 2012*, 218 fn. 36, in general 218–219). Is there any connection with burial ceremonies?

I have suggested that the TAK_4 event, "touching a statue", possibly a bearer of procreative force, may have been done for the purpose of charging oneself with fertility (see *Charvát 1997*, 11–12, 57–58), as indicated by the involvement of statues in the UR_2 ceremony as noted above. Do we have an illustration of this act (also) in *UE III*: 385, where a naked long-haired figure touches a standard standing before the temple with his or her hands while a coitus takes place on the temple's roof?

One single reference to a DU_6, "sacred hill" (*Cohen 1993*, 106–112, *apud Mařík 2005*, 45–49; *Suriano 2012*, 217–223), turns up in the archaic Ur sources (my # 102 = *UE III*: 438). The DU_6, a place with cosmogonical and funerary connotations (*Selz 2014a*, 207–212), may also denote the hill on which a temple is standing (*Selz 2011b*, 244, "Skizze einer Idealflur").

Cultic appurtenances referred to in the Ur sealings include statues, turning up not infrequently (my # 54 = *UE III*: 389; my ## 57, 58 and 59 = *UE III*: 395). Some of the sealings mention "offering", "offering matter" or the like (AK, my # 41 = *UE III*: 275; my # 99 = *UE III*: 434; see http://psd.museum.upenn.edu/epsd/nepsd-frame.html [accessed October 5, 2014] s. v. ak, "offering, offering matter?"). The counter-marking of the matrix seal with the elegant lattice-pattern sign (my # 41 = *UE III*: 275) may refer to a (religious?) establishment or community other than that designated by the rosette. Flour (or cord?) has been deposited as sacrifice in front of the spread-eagle emblem in my # 47 = *UE III*: 323. Substances of this kind may be guessed behind references to deities with designations of containers and/or commodities (my # 44 = *UE III*: 304, AN KAK = DU_3 = RU_2) or goods delivered (my # 46 = *UE III*: 315, BAD AN BAD AN?).

The worshipers of archaic Ur did obviously take part in still other religious ceremonies. The UR_2 event links up with an action designated as DU_8, which may perhaps occur independently in some sealings (my # 101 = *UE III*: 437???). Another case concerns the "boating ritual" (?), MAGUR, referred to in one case, possibly in connection with a "knot, bond" (my # 104 = *UE III*: 440, with, i.a., sign DIM). A handled pot with designation LUM (my # 113 = *UE III*: 460) may point to still another cultic proceeding, but I know nothing else about this.

The lexeme NAGAR represents a somewhat mysterious entity which may also belong to the world of the mind. I must confess that the exact interpretation eludes me for the moment, and I cannot think of anything else than a link with symbolism of the vegetation cycle, perhaps quite simply "vegetation (season)" (my # 92 = *UE III*: 430; my # 93 = *UE III*: 431).

The concern with fertility finds reflection even in such "everyday magic" finds as a phallus-shaped amulet (*Sürenhagen 1999*, Taf. 57: 19, Liste 5, pp. 281–290 on p. 287 item 96). Among other religious(?) symbols found here we must mention a (probably disused) "eye idol" found in layers of archaic Ur (see above; *Woolley 1955*, 187, item U.17836, Pl. 15).

A question of potentially great interest concerns the possible existence of a temple of Inanna at Ur. Text *UET II*: 72 records distribution of bread linked with Inanna's name. Thirty loaves are divided among the goddess, who receives eight of them, and a group of consumers who get the rest (*Wright 1969*, 42). The goddess Inanna also appeared in personal names of archaic Ur (INANNA AMA GAL, *UET II*: 259: iv: 1, 288: iv: 2). If there really was an Inanna temple at Ur, then the parallel with Late Uruk may go still farther, with an initial attempt to imitate the twin structure of Uruk shrines: the Uruk couple of An – Inanna might have originally been proposed as Nannar – Inanna at Ur (for the list of ED Inanna shrines see *Selz 1992a*, 195–196; see also *Rodin 2014*). However, our evidence is too limited to warrant any certain conclusions. The goddess Inanna did not enjoy particularly high popularity at Fara (*Steible-Yilidiz 2008*, 189).

At what point in the Early Dynastic period may we expect the establishment of the Ur shrine of the god Ninazu cannot be said at present (*Drewniowska 2012*, 43 fn. 74).

* * *

A major innovation for which Assyriologists will never cease to render words of thanksgiving is represented by the establishment of a school (on the earliest schools of Mesopotamia see *Veldhuis 1997*, esp. pp. 13, 83) and scribal centre (*scriptorium*) at Ur in the years close to 3000 B.C.E. (see recently *Lafont 1999–2002*, 143, and *Visicato 2000*, 14–18). This intellectual focus then introduced one total novelty that was to dominate Sumerian (and not only Sumerian) written word from now on: the texts of archaic Ur constitute the very first instance of cuneiform documents that can actually be read, and that in the Sumerian language. It seems likely that by taking over the tradition of the written word, the elite of archaic Ur wished to assert the cultural continuity of the intellectual heritage of the Late Uruk era, demonstrating thus their social aspirations at the role once played by the universally respected Uruk polity in general (*Trigger 1998*, 57, 59). Cuneiform texts written on clay tablets cropped up both in SIS strata and in some unstratified test trenches. The scribal ductus shows a marked degree of unity, and it seems the the local *scriptorium* could boast considerable stability and permanence of writing tradition. The archaic Ur documentary fund includes

- 30 school tablets, and 40 others bearing only seal impressions,
- 290 records of administrative character including those tracing transfers of cereals (11%), transactions in land (23%), rations of bread, flour and beer to temple(?) employees (27%, see on this the image of my # 47 = *UE III*: 323 where, i.a., flour is sacrificed before the spread-eagle emblem), personnel matters (6%), sheep-rearing texts (6%) and registrations of movement of such materials as wood, metal, leather, and reeds (3%), and
- 23% of texts of undetermined character.

The texts seem to have been written over a relatively short period of time. Prosopographical analysis of 25 personal names shows that three and more of them appear together in eighty texts. For more detailed information see below, in the "Conclusions" section.

* * *

V. CONCLUSIONS

Let us now pass in review the three centuries or so between, say, 3100 and 2700 B.C., when the city of Ur led the public life of Sumerian communities into what we call today the third millennium BC.

The city of Ur started its historical existence as modest settlement with production facilities of the Late Uruk period (c. 3500–3200 BC). In the Jemdet Nasr age (around 3,000 B.C.), Ur was already a busy place. Together with the adjacent site of Tell al-Ubaid, it assumed the form of a twin agglomeration, of which both settlement segments hosted "public buildings" decorated by mosaics done in terra-cotta cones (on which now see *Van Ess* 2012). What has been happening in these we do not know for certain, but life teemed outside their walls. The Ur craftsmen and craftswomen operated a huge pottery-production plant not far from the local high-status edifice, possibly also a textile workshop. Skilled metalworkers provided the Ur community with the output of their art, of which many items, such as the lead tumblers, found their way into graves of the "Jamdat Nasr cemetery". The first artifacts of frit, occurring in coeval archaeological contexts from Ur, show that not even entirely artificial materials remained unknown to the local consumers. How far the Ur entrepreneurs traded products manufactured there, and especially in the textile-production establishment, into the commercial sphere is hard to say. At any rate, Ur then acted as a port-of-trade and *emporium* from which Sumerian goods travelled to customers outside the land, who paid for such deliveries by their own surplus commodities. The personnel of this port-of-trade, established probably as an agency of the still influential Uruk polity nearby, bought and presumably also sold goods denoted as such by written tags, and kept them in storerooms under their own seal(s). We do not know how far the Ur merchants were already "seafaring adventurers" in those remote days; what seems to be clear was that trade plied from Ur involved not only local, but also transit goods (lapis lazuli or obsidian, for instance).

Some kind of social ranking or even stratification may be inferred on the basis of cosmetic containers of the "Jamdat Nasr cemetery" graves (and their imitations), and of the delightful tiny boar sculpture, once decorating a piece of furniture or a standard, from "kiln stratum 4", but hardly anything more can be said on this.

Nothing of that remote age seemed to herald the power and the glory that awaited the abode of Nannar after the turn of the fourth and third millennium BC. Yet, the Sumerian political establishment threw itself headlong into the third millennium, and things took an unexpected turn.

Two important decisions were made around, and shortly after, 3000 B.C. First and foremost, Ur was singled out at first as a regional-administration focus, and then as a centre of the "City League", a (con)federation of municipal communities of Sumer, replacing the now defunct central administration of the Late Uruk polity.

We may ponder upon the possibility that by the establishment of the "City League", Sumerian elites might have intended to create something that has been achieved, on the other side of the Atlantic, by the well-known Iroquois league, a confederation of kinship-based political units lasting from the 15th century A.D. until today. The latter proved to be eminently successful, giving the member communities stability of public life over centuries and, remarkably, not developing into a state. Reading about this political association, which offered positions of prestige to personages ambitious enough to yearn for public respect, which introduced both the Great Council and the assembly of the warriors, and which took care to transform possible political conflicts into ritual proceedings, we cannot help perceiving a number of traits resembling Sumerian political history of the early third millennium (*Bonhage-Freund – Kurland 1994*, esp. pp. 297, 300; on recent studies of incipient political systems and their economy see a most useful overview in *Blanton et al. 1999*, 111–134, and *Frangipane 2010a*). Yet, the Sumerians did not find theirs a long-term solution, and opted for the state instead.

Second decision: the lower-grade Ur centre which had hitherto served as a purveyor of products and commodities to a major center of social life – Uruk-Warka, in all likelihood – had to acquire a very different character, and rise to a status of a subject of political history. In practice, that meant that Ur had now to obtain administrative and management capacities required for a focus of supra-regional significance.

The first, "trial-and-error" period of this new arrangement, followed in the time marked by deposition of SIS 8-6. The incipient form of the "City League" came to Ur in those times, and it might have already been called EREŠ_2. The seal icons, however, already roughly divided into the AMOR, LABOR, HONOR and DOLOR thematic spheres, show beyond all doubt that the administrative know-how came in as a result of a single will, and reflected a single purpose articulated in visual symbols designed to carry a message aimed at a single goal. In this manner, the "City League" administration, and possibly that of the LUGAL, whom I choose to call the prince of Ur, as he really was the first among his equals (Latin *princeps*, from which the word "prince" comes), emerged together, at a single time, reflecting a singular purpose. It seems conceivable that inscribed seals not expressedly referring to the "City League" fulfilled their function within the administration of this very prince.

This inchoate stage of the Ur administration show some particular features. First and foremost, sealed goods received simple delivery-identifying designations (solidified[?] "soup" = TU_7, or seafood in containers). Other instances probably indicated the supplying agencies of the goods, but we may even have a pisandubba, or description of an archival file, at this early date (my # 1 = *UE III*: 1). At this stage, the socially engineered goods exchange took on a simpler form: in this time, sealings of moveable containers prevailed numerically over those of immovable structures, though the "travelling seals" (same seal marking moveables and immovables) did occur.

The new arrangement of the Ur centre required adjustments, visible, first and foremost, in the economic sphere. Both field management and livestock-keeping showed an effort at a more intense grasp of the resources at hand, rationalization of the production procedures such as shortening of the circuits of goods circulation, for instance. The registrars of archaic Ur seem to have noted down arrears in payment. The arts and crafts did not remain unchanged either; the metallurgists of Ur may have been the first to introduce alloying of copper to bronze in Sumer. Our evidence for trade and exchange activities stays somewhat behind that of the preceding age with its abundant archaeologial sources, but references to "Dilmun axes" and to aromatic substances, likely to have been originating from products imported from the wider Mediterranean area, do not indicate any substantial shortening of circuits of commercial goods. The light grey-brown flint, used for the production of chipped industry of Sakheri Sughir, an ED-I village close to Ur, cannot be traced to any local source and must thus have been introduced from elsewhere.

The "City League" seals reflect a lively exchange- and activity sphere of this political association. Loads of goods of various nature clearly travelled to and fro among the various member communities. These did not always amount to the token quantities recorded in the Jemdet Nasr age. Commodities of all kinds obviously changed hands, sometimes such as were presumably hard to obtain under common everyday circumstances, such as textiles or cords. The "City League" developed an embryonic stage of statehood institutions – it collected some of the goods circulating through its activity sphere as taxes (IL_2), and wielded an elementary administrative apparatus (chancery with an official seal).

A varied social and political structure is revealed by the "City League" seals. A single occurrence of the now traditional NAMEŠDA title, in conjunction with the city of Nippur and equipped with a seal in which his title appeared together with a version of the "City League", throws light on this heritage of Late Uruk administration. No reference to LUGAL appears in the

"City League" seals, but, in addition to glosses referring to him, they attest to the presence of his consort, NIN, albeit rarely. A number of external dignitaries, lands and estates dealt with the "City League", but office-holders of the Ur palace, temple, municipal administration and the city's free citizenry (LU_2) appeared in connection with it as well. We cannot even exclude the possibility that the "City League" sent troops to wage war.

This political association constituted a hotbed of intellectual activities as well. It seems to be clear that its central recording facility, which we may call chancery, operated on the principles of the traditional Late Uruk – Jemdet Nasr written documents. The script of the archaic Ur seals complies fully with the culture of the earlier days, consisting of denotations of "bare necessities" – substantives without grammatical particles, next-to-no adjectives and verbs, with signs written in random sequences. Unlike the written documents of archaic Ur, rendered in Sumerian, the "City League" sealings echoed the habits and customs of the preceding, and now traditional, culture. A good example of this may be seen in the polyvalence of the UR_2 sign. With respect to the varying contexts in which we perceive it in archaic Ur textual material, it may mean the fertility-triggering ceremony; or a temple idol relevant to this; or supplies given in compensation for carrying out this ceremony; or those adressed to specific "entry points" in relation to this ceremony (ALAM); or possibly deliveries of a more general character (on such polyvalence in proto-cuneiform texts see *Friberg 1999*, 135–136; on that of UR_2 recently *Peterson 2007*, 567–571). This makes it likely that the transfer of the "City League" administration to Ur occurred in an early times when the Late Uruk – Jemdet Nasr writing usages still prevailed. In addition to that, the "City League" seals attest to participation of the asociation in cultic and ritual proceedings, furnishing offerings to Ur (and other?) shrines.

To put the matter shortly and succinctly, the "City League" apparently represents a last-ditch attempt at keeping the Late Uruk polity – together with its social, religious and intellectual structures – alive in the Early Dynastic times. It does thus constitute a source of prime importance on how the ancient Late Uruk corporate community had once worked.

The assumption that the "City League" and the LUGAL office of Ur emerged during the same time, and together, has already been advanced. What knowledge do we have of the LUGAL of archaic Ur?

The first thing that he probably had to accomplish was to build himself an official residence. Walther Sallaberger has shown that this is likely to have been erected within the AB precinct of Ur, containing, together with the abode of the LUGAL, the chief temple of the city, and presumably other service- and utility buildings. How far the vestiges of structures assigned by Leonard Woolley to his phases "Archaic 2" and the subsequent "Archaic I" belong to this building complex can hardly be said with certainty. The fact that at least one king of the Ur III-dynasty chose to dwell in a residence situated within the sacred precinct of Nannar's temple (*Frayne 1997*, 329–330, # E3/2.1.4.19, Šusu'en or Šusin) may imply that in this case the scions of Ur-Namma drew on an ancient tradition, but this is pure speculation.

On what spiritual foundations did the prince of Ur erect his legitimacy, and by what means did he convince his fellow citizens that his rule is legitimate? Drawing on my earlier research (*Charvát 1997*, 10–12, 27–28, 57–58, 78–80, 84–85), and on the conclusions reached now by Jakob Andersson (*Andersson 2012*), I believe that this involved a rather complex procedure modifying, to a substantial degree, the elite structures of the preceding Late Uruk times. In short, the most important offices of the Late Uruk culture, those of EN (on him see now *Szarzyńska 2011*) and NIN, derived the anchoring of their dominant social position from the fact that together, they performed the NA_2 ritual, presumably catalyzing fertility and procreative forces of both nature and the human society. They could do this as the EN of Inanna was male and NIN of An female, the personage's sex being always the opposite of the gender of the respective deity (on the NIN of Late-Uruk or Jemdet Nasr times see now a text published by *Monaco 2007*, 14–15). This device worked well at Uruk with its twin shrines of An and Inanna, but ran aground in Ur with its single god Nannar, and, in consequence of that, with its female EN. The EN of Ur had to find somebody else, with whom the local NIN could perform the NA_2 ritual. This led to the emergence of LUGAL who now took his place at NIN's side, and, presumably performing with her the ceremony now referred to as UR_2, rose to the status of a major cultic and social figure assuring abundance and plenty to his subjects by activation of the living world's fecundity, of "all that creepeth on earth, swimmeth in waters and flieth in the air".

The LUGAL of Ur seems to have been primarily a temple official, chosen possibly by a divine omen (*Andersson 2012*, 246), and his first task was to procure subsistence to the community of Ur. The personal names of archaic Ur show eloquently this function of his (in review *Andersson 2012*, 228–229, 238, 245–247). Activating fertility of living beings, the LUGAL was assumed to pass it on to his subjects (*Andersson 2012*, 126–137). In an almost incredible parallel with early medieval Irish usage (see, for instance, *Fischer 2007*, 21–24), the Ur LUGAL "slept with his city" (*Andersson 2012*, 96 – lugal-uru-na-nu_2), perfoming presumably a variant of the "sacred marriage" ceremony (*Andersson 2012*, 150–151). This procedure finds confirmation in a personal name lugal ti-ma-nu_2 = "LUGAL lies down in a sanctuary" (*Andersson 2012*, 158 fn. 915) and in other names of this type (*Andersson 2012*, 224 s. v. nu_2). The LUGAL office, however, linked up also with the divine world, especially in its spheres where humans went after death and from which they burst upon this world, as well as with determination of destinies (see below), and with the Nether world in particular (*Andersson 2012*, 156–157, s. v. lugal-ki-gal-la; *Andersson 2012*, 179 fn.

1084 = lugal ki-nu-gi$_4$ = "LUGAL /in/ the place of no return?"). Much as the moon god, the LUGAL was nevertheless ritually re-born every month (*Andersson 2012*, 172).

The qualities presumed to belong to the competence sphere of the LUGAL included dominion (*Andersson 2012*, table on p. 81, 81–103), protection (*Andersson 2012*, 107–118), wisdom (*Andersson 2012*, 104–107), cosmic order and posssibly decreeing of fates (*Andersson 2012*, 103–104), care of the living and dead (*Andersson 2012*, 126, # 3.1.4.4), sometimes even causing or helping humans to come into this world (*Andersson 2012*, 127–129), and assiduous diligence vis-à-vis the sacred sphere (*Andersson 2012*, 138–158). The Ur citizens expected their LUGAL to be physically perfect (*Andersson 2012*, 159–174).

Thus the link between fertility, the supernatural sphere and especially with the voyages to, and returns from, the Nether world make the ED-I LUGAL of Ur a likely candidate for the terrestrial incarnation of Dumuzi, the "dying god" of fertility, as expressedly denoted on the Mesannepada seal (my # 121 = *UE III*: 518).

A certain amount of later evidence tends to confirm these conclusions. During the third excavation season at Ur, the Woolley expedition found a group of texts datable into the course of the whole third millennium, beginning with a set of ED-III documents, in a levelling layer under the pavement of Room 8 in the Kassite-period Edublalmah shrine. These texts, coming possibly from the temple of Nanna (*Visicato-Westenholz 2005*, 67), were published in a Supplement to the UET-II volume (*Visicato-Westenholz 2005*, 56). In them, the lugal was primarily an agent of the cult. The public brought monthly offerings to his deity (dingir-lugal, *Visicato-Westenholz 2005*, 65), and the lugal office undertook the re-distribution of these offerings to a number of adressees, including, for instance, the city of Eridu (*Visicato-Westenholz 2005*, 63). The number of recipients included a GAL.UKKIN (*Visicato-Westenholz 2005*, 64), and as the UKKIN associated mostly with divine names at Fara (*Krebernik 2002b*, 21), we may suspect a religious character of this delivery as well. Among the suppliers of such offerings we find the Nanna temple of Ekišnugal; animals coming from thither went to the residence of the lugal (é-gal). Obviously, even at the end of the ED-III period, the lugal discharged primarily religious duties, without any political involvement of his office being apparent from the texts (*Visicato-Westenholz 2005*, 68).

Of course, the LUGAL also had to procure the revenues allowing him to carry on with his duties, that is, he had to put into function a scheme for siphoning-off the surplus of the Ur economy. This redistribution system worked presumably along the same lines as that of the "City League", as the administrative artifacts resulting from the activities of both the LUGAL and the "City League" finished in the same discard area, that is, were thrown out into the same rubbish deposits.

He is also very likely to have defended his community as a war leader, as implied by the scenes of military triumph figuring on some seals.

Even though the inscribed seals of archaic Ur give evidence of a determined effort to keep the heritage of the Late Uruk polity alive in the "City League", their iconography tells a different story. The images speak eloquently of the focusing of socially relevant ideas on one single personage, the LUGAL, the prince of Ur. They show him fulfilling his tasks of

- **replenishment** of the society's resources through activation of fertility,
- of **re-assertion** of his community's position in this world through everyday toil but also through its defence against inimical forces,
- of **representation** of his political body vis-à-vis the gods and neighbours,
- and of his **rebirth** as a faithful public servant, giving his bereaved subjects a consolation in the proposition that not even death can prevent him from returning from "over there" to serve his community.

The prince of Ur may thus be perceived as a personage charged with duties of both profane government and supernatural character (destiny-making, Nether world, birth, see above).

At the beginning of the third millennium BC, the LUGALs of the abode of Nannar undoubtedly played a complementary role to the "City League". Fate had deemed, however, that the weight of future public functions shift to the LUGAL office, not to the (con)federation of the municipal communities of Sumer, only a shadow of ages past in later times. And it was also here, in the city of Ur at the onset of the third millennium BC, that the whole arsenal of symbols and emblems pertaining to the royalty of early Sumer took its primeval shape.

In addition to the LUGAL, NIN and their court (however that might have looked like; we only know of NIMGIR, and possibly KISAL = $gipar_x$, *Selz 2011b*, 233 sub # 1: 3?, but not always: *Andersson 2012*, 158 fn. 912, on gipar see also *Lion 2009*, 179; *Westenholz 2013*, 254–256), the municipal community of city of Ur wielded a self-governing agency. This consisted of the PA.SI ($ensi_2$?), most probably a "mayor", or "burgomaster". In carrying out the tasks incumbent in his office, he seems to have been assisted by the AB+$AŠ_2$, "city elders" (congregating in an assembly, UKKIN?). Together, they bore their responsibility before the LU_2, "free-born citizenry". In fact, early Ur might conceivably have been managed by a single social body – a conical clan, for instance – which, monopolizing communication with the supernatural in the temples, rose to a position so prominent in the local community as to appoint even the LUGAL from among its ranks.

We may suppose that the intellectual and artistic creativity, embellishing the public life of Ur and making it more cultivated, also fell to the competence sphere of the LUGAL. The Nannar temple of Ur, built probably on the initiative of, and out of the resources of, the LUGAL (or the community?) was an architectural creation which I have already mentioned. Here also the residence, and the main activity area, of the EN priestess of Ur were to be found. Of the rituals performed under the temple roofs (and on them?) we know little. We can name at least two of them, UR_2 (the fertility-triggering ceremony) and TAK_4 (fertility-transferring ritual?). But in ED-IIIb inscriptions, $SAHAR.DU_6.TAG_4$ may mean "burial tell", with translation of TAG_4 as "leave behind" (*Richardson 2007*, 193–194; *Suriano 2012*, 218 fn. 36, in general 218–219), and there may thus be a connection with burial ceremonies. A most interesting reference links the NIN of Ur, a structure for the UR_2 ceremony and the "sacred" or "primeval hill" in *UE III*: 438 (= my # 102), much in line with the new observations by Gebhard Selz (*Selz 2014a*, 207–212).

This temple hosted a major intellectual centre comprising a school and a scribal centre (*scriptorium*). I have already noticed that unlike the officials of the "City League", the scribes of Nannar's temple rendered their documents in Sumerian, leaving us a testimony of the ascent of that language to the status of an established language of the Ur administration. The abode of Nannar also constituted a centre where both musical and figurative arts were cultivated. Of prose, poetry and the theatrical arts we know next to nothing (save perhaps for the personal name BALAG SI SA_2 in *UET II*: 3: i: 2, and the animal fable of *UE III*: 384)[27]. Yet, a literary tradition must have been cultivated at archaic Ur, as is shown by the "Götterlisten" of Fara, incorporating elements of the Ur pantheon into a set of deities probably of traditional, Late Uruk – Jemdet Nasr character (*Selz 1992a*, 199, sub ## 1 and 2, and 218 sub # 55 = ^{d}nanna, 219 sub ## 62, 63 and 68, 224 sub # 106 = ^{d}su'en?, see also *Cohen 1996*, 10, and *Steible-Yildiz 2008*, 185 s. v. ^{d}zu-en). Four or five examples of the LU_2 A list from the archaic Ur, apparently modernized as against the Uruk predecessor, bear witness to the scientific output of the local intellectual workshop (on similar creative development of the Uruk-III tradition at Kish see *Steinkeller 2013*, 134). In this case the Ur scribes probably established a tradition, as the later versions of this list heed rather to Ur than to an Uruk archetype (*Falkenstein 1937*, 95; *Landsberger 1969*, 4, 8, 10–11; *Lecompte 2013*, 148–149; see also *Johnson 2014a*, 22). One of the texts of archaic Ur might have served as model for the Fara text NTSŠ 168+ (*Johnson 2014a*, 27, in Table 3, Stratum β). Music and dance are amply documented by the iconography of archaic Ur seals. As to the figurative arts, sculpture joined architecture in an effort to provide worthy tabernacles for the worship of supreme powers. The richly documented

27 *Edzard 1987–1990*, 36: text *UET II*: 69 may be of literary character but cannot be interpreted (*Biggs 1974*, p. 29 fn. 8). Who, and where, wrote the diminutive za_3-mi_3 hymn to Nannar attested to at Abu Salabikh (*Cohen 1996*, 9, 12)?

glyptic arts contributed to the solidification of visual forms of communication conveying semantic messages that were soon understood all over Sumer.

We might note that in the time immediately following ED-I, a number of motifs of the SIS glyptic appeared on the so-called bas-relief plaques, which subsequently became the commonly accepted form of temple art of Sumer (*Boese 1971*; for banquet scenes see *Marchetti 2006*, 184–190, esp. p. 186; *Romano 2010a*; *Romano 2010b*). This took up some of the religious charges borne up to that time by cylinder seals, which now became available as vehicles of secular symbolism, advertising especially the prestige of profane leaders.

Two modifications of the use of cylinder seals occurred in consequence of this. First, those bearing figural scenes became integral components of royal administration, an eloquent example being that of the situation at Ebla where figurative seals served the royal administration while seals bearing abstract ornaments denoted goods sent in from outside the palace (*Mazzoni 1992*, 65–66, 184–196; *Mazzoni 2003*, 183). Second, the narrower link between cylinder seals and secular authority resulted in more intense appropriation of such vehicles by power-holders and their officials, and first inscribed seals, revealing the names and/or offices of their proprietors, appeared (*Rohn 2011*).

Those who sweated under the hot sun of southern Mesopotamia, managers and administrators who facilitated the public life of the abode of Nannar, as well as wise men and women who made life worth living for the citizens of Ur at the turn of the fourth and third millennia B.C., did not toil in vain. They were not those who had witnessed the departure of the ship of Mesopotamian statehood from its Late Uruk harbour. Nevertheless, the structures which they erected on foundations laid by their ancestors served the inhabitants of ancient Mesopotamia – and not only them – for the millennia to come. In fact, this edifice, the house of civility, public order, religion, science and the arts has been serving, and is serving, mankind until this very day.

REFERENCES CITED

al-Mutawalli, Nawala A. 2010:
Administrative Cuneiform Texts from Umma in the Iraq Museum - Excavation of Shara Temple (1999–2000), *Sumer* 55, 45–86.

Alberti, Amedeo, Pomponio Francesco 1986:
Pre-Sargonic and Sargonic texts from Ur edited in UET 2, Supplement (Studia Pohl, Series Maior 13), Rome: Biblical Institute Press.

Algaze, Guillermo 1993:
The Uruk World System, Chicago–London: The University of Chicago Press.

Allred, Lance Burris 2006:
Cooks and Kitchens: Centralized Food Production in Late Third Millennium Mesopotamia, A dissertation submitted to Johns Hopkins University in conformity with the requirements for the degree of Doctor of Philosophy, Baltimore, Maryland, October 2006, UMI Microfilm 3240662, Ann Arbor, MI: ProQuest Information and Learning Company.

Alster, Bendt 1974:
The Instructions of Shuruppak - A Sumerian Proverb Collection (Mesopotamia vol. 2), Copenhagen: Akademisk Forlag.

Alster, Bendt 1991–1992:
Early Dynastic Proverbs and other Contributions to the Study of Literary Texts from Abū Ṣalābīkh, *Archiv für Orientforschung* 38–39, 1–51.

Alster, Bendt 1992:
Two Sumerian Short Tales Reconsidered, *Zeitschrift für Assyriologie* 82, 186–201.

Alster, Bendt 1997:
Proverbs of Ancient Sumer - The World's Earliest Proverb Collection I–II, Bethesda, MD: CDL Press.

Amiet, Pierre 1980:
La glyptique mésopotamienne archaïque, 2ème édition, Paris: Editions du Centre national de la recherche scientifique.

Amiet, Pierre 1997:
L'utilisation des sceaux en Iran élamite, in R. Gyselen (ed.), *Sceaux d'Orient et leur emploi* (Res orientales 10), Bures-sur-Yvette: Groupe pour l'Etude de la Civilisation du Moyen-Orient, 11–21.

Andersson, Jakob 2012:
Kingship in the Early Mesopotamian Onomasticon 2800–2000 BCE (Acta Universitatis Uppsaliensis, Studia Semitica Uppsaliensia 28), Uppsala: Uppsala Universitet (reference courtesy Jakob Andersson).

André-Salvini, Béatrice 1995:
Les pierres précieuses dans les sources écrites, in *Tallon* 1995, 71–88.

André-Salvini, Béatrice 2003:
No. 57, Plaque dedicated by a queen of Umma, in J. Aruz, R. Wallenfels (edd.), *Art of the First Cities – The Third Millennium B. C. from the Mediterranean to the Indus*, New York–New Haven–London: The Metropolitan Museum of Art and Yale University Press, p. 78.

André-Salvini, Béatrice 2012:
Un mapa topográfico de los alrededores de la ciudad de Girsu, in *Antés del Diluvio – Mesopotamia 3500–2100 A. C.*, Barcelona: Fundación "la Caixa", 147.

Archi, Alfonso 1990:
Données épigraphiques éblaites et production artistique, *Revue d'Assyriologie* 84/2, 101–106.

Asher-Greve, Julia M. 1995–1996:
Reading the Horned Crown, *Archiv für Orientforschung* 42–43, 181–189.

Attinger, Pascal 1997:
Review of Philadelphia Sumerian Dictionary A II, *Zeitschrift für Assyriologie* 87, 112–122.

Attinger, Pascal 2005:
A propos de l'AK, "faire", *Zeitschrift für Assyriologie* 95, 46–64, 208–275.

Attinger, Pascal 2006:
Aza "ours", *N. A. B. U.* 2/2006 (juin), 33–34.

Attinger, Pascal 2011:
Review of Niek Veldhuis, Religion, Literature, and Scholarship: The Sumerian Composition Nanše and the Birds, with a catalogue of Sumerian bird names, Leiden-Boston: Brill-Styx 2004, in *Archiv für Orientforschung* 52, 222–229.

Attinger, Pascal 2012:
Une nouvelle édition de la correspondence royale d'Ur, *Orientalia* N. S. 81, 355–385.

Attinger, Pascal, Manfred Krebernik 2005:
L'Hymne à Hendursaga (Hendursaga A), in R. Rollinger (ed.), *Von Sumer bis Homer – Festschrift für Manfred Schretter zum 60. Geburtstag am 25. Februar 2004*, Münster: Ugarit-Verlag, 21–104.

ATU 3:
Robert K. Englund, Hans-Jörg Nissen: *Die lexikalischen Listen der Archaischen Texten aus Uruk* (Ausgrabungen der Deutschen Forschungsgemeinschaft in Uruk-Warka, Bd. 13, Archaische Texte aus Uruk Bd. 3), Berlin: Gebr. Mann Verlag 1993.

ATU 5:
Robert K. Englund, Rainer M. Boehmer: *Archaic administrative texts from Uruk – The early campaigns* (Ausgrabungen der Deutschen Forschungsgemeinschaft in Uruk-Warka, Bd. 15, Archaische texte aus Uruk Bd. 5), Berlin: Gebr. Mann Verlag 1994.

Barrett, Caitlín E. 2007:
Was dust their food and clay their bread? Grave goods, the Mesopotamian afterlife, and the liminal role of Inanna/Ishtar, *Journal of Ancient Near Eastern Religions* 7/1, 7–65.

Bauer, Josef 1989–1990:
Altsumerische Wirtschaftsurkunden in Leningrad, *Archiv für Orientforschung* 36–37, 78–90.

Bauer, Josef 2001–2002:
Review of ATU 5, *Archiv für Orientforschung* 48–49, 168–173.

Bauer, Josef 2004:
KU als Berufsbezeichnung, in H. Waetzoldt (ed.), *Von Sumer nach Ebla und zurück, Giovanni Pettinato zum 27. September 1999 gewidmet von Freunden, Kollegen und Schülern*, Heidelberg: Heidelberger Orientverlag, 1–4.

Bauer, Josef 2012:
Drei sumerische Rechtsurkunden der vorsargonischen Zeit aus Umma, *Orientalia* N. S. 81, 56–80.

Beal, Richard 1992:
Is KUŠ$_7$ the Reading of IŠ = *kizû*? *N. A. B. U.* No. 48, 1992, 38–39.

Beaulieu, Paul-Alain 1988:
Swamps as Burial Places for Babylonian Kings, *N. A. B. U.* 3/1988, 36–37.

Behrens, Herrmann 1998:
Die Ninegalla-Hymne (FAOS 21), Stuttgart: Franz Steiner.

Benati, Giacomo 2013:
The "Archaic I" phase of the ziqqurat terrace at Ur: a contextual re-assessment, Mesopotamia 48, 2013, 197–220.

Benati, Giacomo 2015:
Re-*modeling* Political Economy in Early 3rd Millennium BC Mesopotamia: Patterns of Socio-Economic Organization in Archaic Ur (Tell al-Muqayyar, Iraq), in Cuneiform Digital Library Journal 2015:2, 1–37, accessible at the address http://www.cdli.ucla.edu/pubs/cdlj/2015/cdlj2015_002.html [accessed September 21st, 2015].

Biga, Maria Giovanna 1978:
Le attività commerciale e i commercianti nella città di Šuruppak (Fara), *Oriens Antiquus* 17, 85–105.

Biggs, Robert D. 1966:
The Abū Ṣalābīkh Tablets – A Preliminary Survey, *Journal of Cuneiform Studies* 20, 73–93.

Biggs, Robert D. 1967:
Semitic Names in the Fara Period, *Orientalia* N. S. 36, 55–66.

Biggs, Robert D. 1974:
Inscriptions from Tell Abū Ṣalābīkh (OIP 99), Chicago–London: The University of Chicago Press.

Blanton, Richard E. et al. 1999:
Ancient Oaxaca – The Monte Albán State, Cambridge–New York–Melbourne: Cambridge University Press.

Boehmer, Rainer M. 1999:
Uruk – früheste Siegelabrollungen (Ausgrabungen in Uruk-Warka – Endberichte Bd. 24), Mainz am Rhein: Philipp von Zabern.

Boehmer, Rainer M. 2001:
Die Siegelabrollungen auf den archaischen Tafeln der Heidelberger Sammlung, in R. K. Englund, H. J. Nissen, R. M. Boehmer, *Archaische Verwaltungstexte aus Uruk – Die Heidelberger Sammlung (ATU 7 = ADFU 17)*, Berlin: Gebr. Mann Verlag, 11–13.

Boese, Johannes 1971:
Altmesopotamische Weihplatten, Berlin–New York: Walter de Gruyter.

Boese, Johannes 2010:
Die Blau'schen Steine und der "Priesterfürst" im Netzrock, *Altorientalische Forschungen* 37, 208–229.

Bonechi, Marco 2003:
Leopards, Cauldrons, and a Beautiful Stone. Notes on Some Early Syrian texts from Tell Beydar and Ebla, in Paolo Marrassini et alii (edd.), *Semitic and Assyriological Studies. Presented to Pelio Fronzaroli*, Wiesbaden: The Harrassowitz Publishing House, 75–96.

Bonhage-Freund, Mary Theresa, Jeffrey A. Kurland 1994:
Tit-for-Tat among the Iroquis: A Game Theoretical Perspective on Inter-Tribal Political Organization, *Journal of Anthropological Archaeology* 13/3, 278–305.

Boschung, Dietrich, Günther Blamberger (edd.) 2011:
MORPHOMATA – Kulturelle Figurationen: Genese, Dynamik and Medialität, München: Wilhelm Fink Verlag.

Bottéro, Jean 1980:
La mythologie de la mort en Mésopotamie ancienne, in B. Alster (ed.), *Death in Mesopotamia – Papers read at the XXVIe Rencontre Assyriologique Internationale* (Mesopotamia 8), Copenhagen: Akademisk Forlag, 25–52.

Braun-Holzinger, Eva 1993:
Die Ikonographie des Mondgottes in der Glyptik des III. Jahrtausends v. Chr., *Zeitschrift für Assyriologie* 83, 118–135.

Breniquet, Catherine 2008:
Essai sur le tissage en Mésopotamie des premières communautés sédentaires au milieu du iiie *millénaire avant J.-C. (Travaux de la Maison René-Ginouvès* 5), Paris: de Boccard.

Breniquet, Catherine 2010:
Weaving in Mesopotamia during the Bronze Age: Archaeology, techniques, iconography, in C. Michel, M. – L. Nosch (edd.), *Textile Terminologies from the 3rd to the 1st mill. BC in the Ancient Near East and the Eastern Mediterranean Area* (Ancient Textiles Series 8), Oxford: Oxbow Books, 52–67.

Bretschneider, Joachim, Greta Jans 2012:
Checkpoint Room 32912: Inspection of Incoming Goods, Outgoing Wares or Temporary Sealing Disposals in the Early Jezirah Upper City Complex of Tell Beydar?, in Ph. Quenet, M. al-Maqdissi (edd.), *"L'heure immobile" – Entre Ciel et Terre, Mélanges en Honneur d'Antoine Souleiman* (Subartu XXXI), Turhnout: Brepols, 9–19.

Brunke, Hagan 2011:
Zur Rekonstruktion von Speisen in Sumer anhand administrativer Urkunden, in G. Selz, Kl. Wagensonner (edd.), *The Empirical Dimension of Ancient Near Eastern Studies – Die empirische Dimension altorientalischer Forschungen* (Wiener Offene Orientalistik Bd. 6), Wien–Berlin: LIT Verlag, 375–403.

Brunke, Hagan, Walther Sallaberger 2010:
Aromata für Duftöl, in A. Kleinermann, J. M. Sasson (edd.), *Why Should Someone Who Knows Something Conceal It? Cuneiform Studies in Honor of David I. Owen on His 70th Birthday*, Bethesda: CDL Press, 41–74.

Buchanan, Briggs 1981:
Early Near Eastern Seals in the Yale Babylonian Collection, New Haven–London: Yale University Press.

Buckland, Anne W. 1893:
Our Viands, Whence They Come, and How They Are Cooked, London: Ward & Downey, a reedition by Applewood Books, Bedford, Massachusetts.

CAD:
The Chicago Assyrian Dictionary, 26 volumes, Chicago and Glückstadt: The Oriental Institute and J. J. Augustin Verlagsbuchhandlung, 1956–2011, accessible from the address http://oi.uchicago.edu/research/pubs/catalog/cad/ [accessed September 2, 2012].

Campbell, Stuart, Elizabeth Carter, Suellen Cauld 2003:
Elusive complexity: New Data from Late Halaf Domuztepe in South Central Turkey, *Paléorient* 29/2, 117–133.

Carroué, Francis 1981:
Geštinanna à Lagaš, *Orientalia* N. S. 50, 121–136.

Casanova, Michèle 1995:
Le lapis-lazuli dans l'Orient antique, in *Tallon* 1995, 15–20.

Caubet, Annie, François Poplin 2003:
Une statuette sumérienne en ivoire de dugong (note d'information), in *Comptes rendus des séances de l'Académie des Inscriptions et Belles-Lettres*, 147e année, No. 1, 361–373.

Cavigneaux, Antoine 1987:
Notes Sumérologiques, *Acta Sumerologica (Japan)* 9, 45–66.

Cavigneaux, Antoine 1992:
SAHAR = $kuš_7$?, *N. A. B. U.* 4/1992 (décembre), 78–79.

Cavigneaux, Antoine, Manfred Krebernik 1998–2001:
Nin-tur, in *Reallexikon der Assyriologie* 9, Berlin–New York: Walter de Gruyter, 507–508.

CDLI:
Files of the Cuneiform Digital Library Initiative, A joint project of the University of California, Los Angeles, the University of Oxford, and the Max Planck Institute for the History of Science, Berlin, see http://cdli.ucla.edu/ [accessed February 13, 2014].

Charpin, Dominique 1987:
La mise à jour des listes nominatives, *N. A. B. U.* 3/1987 (septembre), 40–41.

Charpin, Dominique 2011:
Zur Funktion mesopotamischer Tempel, in G. Selz, Kl. Wagensonner (edd.), *The Empirical Dimension of Ancient Near Eastern Studies – Die empirische Dimension altorientalischer Forschungen* (Wiener Offene Orientalistik Bd. 6), Wien–Berlin: LIT Verlag, 403–422.

Charvát, Petr 1979:
Early Ur, *Archív Orientální* 47, 15–20.

Charvát, Petr 1982:
Early Ur – War Chiefs and Kings of Early Dynastic III, *Altorientalische Forschungen* 9, 43–59.

Charvát, Petr 1988:
Archaeology and social history. The Susa sealings, Ca. 4000–2340 B.C., *Paléorient* (Paris, France) 14/1, 57–63.

Charvát, Petr 1992:
The token of the covenant: Stamp seal of the ancient Near East, *Archív Orientální* 60, 279–284.

Charvát, Petr 1993:
Ancient Mesopotamia – Humankind's Long Journey into Civilization (Disertationes Orientales No. 47). Prague: Oriental Institute 1993.

Charvát, Petr 1994:
Pig, or, on Ethnicity in Archaeology, *Archív Orientální* 62, 1–6.

Charvát, Petr 1997:
On people, signs and states – Spotlights on Sumerian Society, c. 3500–2500 B.C., Prague: The Oriental Institute, Academy of Sciences of the Czech Republic.

Charvát, Petr 2002:
Mesopotamia Before History, London–New York: Routledge, Taylor and Francis Group.

Charvát, Petr 2005a:
The iconography of pristine statehood – Painted pottery and seal impressions from Susa, southwestern Iran, Prague: Karolinum Press.

Charvát, Petr 2005b:
The backs of some sealings from Nineveh 5, *Iraq* LXVII Part 1, Spring 2005 (Papers of the XLIXe Rencontre Assyriologique Internationale London, 7–11 July 2003, Part Two) (ISSN 0021–0889), 391–397.

Charvát, Petr 2006:
"Hail, Thou son of the Noble", An inscribed sealing from Archaic Ur, in *Studia Hercynia* vol. X, Prague, 7–9 and Pl. VIII.

Charvát, Petr 2007:
Sumeřané erbu prasete divokého. Kančí emblém v počátcích dějin starověké Mezopotámie (Sumerians of the Wild-Boar coat-of-arms, The boar emblem at the beginning of ancient Mesopotamian history, in Czech), in Ľ. Obuchová (ed.), *Lidé a zvířata – Soubor studií pracovní skupiny "Člověk a krajina v dějinách"*, Prague: Česká orientalistická společnost, 63–73.

Charvát, Petr 2010a:
Introduction – Archaeological data concerning the seals and sealings of archaic Ur, in Kateřina Šašková, Lukáš Pecha, Petr Charvát (edd.), *Shepherds of the Black-headed People – The Royal Office Vis-à-vis Godhead in Ancient Mesopotamia*, Pilsen: University of West Bohemia, 15–17.

Charvát, Petr 2010b:
Inscriptions on sealings from archaic Ur, in Kateřina Šašková, Lukáš Pecha, Petr Charvát (edd.), *Shepherds of the Black-headed People – The Royal Office Vis-à-vis Godhead in Ancient Mesopotamia*, Pilsen: University of West Bohemia, 39–73.

Charvát, Petr 2011a:
On Sheep, Sumerians and the Early State, in Luděk Vacín (ed.), *U4 du11-ga-ni sá mu-ni-ib-du11, Ancient Near Eastern Studies in Memory of Blahoslav Hruška*, Dresden: Islet Verlag, 49–60.

Charvát, Petr 2011b:
Zrození státu – Prvotní civilizace Starého světa (The Birth of the State – Pristine Civilizations of the Old World, in Czech), Prague: Karolinum Press.

Charvát, Petr 2012:
From King to God: The NAMEŠDA Title in Archaic Ur, in Gernot Wilhelm (ed.), *Organization, Representation, and Symbols of Power in the Ancient Near East, Proceedings of the 54th Rencontre Assyriologique Internationale at Würzburg, 20–25 July 2008*, Rencontre Assyriologique Internationale – RAI 54, Winona Lake, Indiana: Eisenbrauns, 265–274.

Charvát, Petr 2013:
Three Kings of the Orient in Archaic Ur, in L. Feliu, J. Llop, A. Millet Albà, J. Sanmartín (edd.), *Time and History in the Ancient Near East, Proceedings of the 56th Rencontre Assyriologique Internationale at Barcelona, 26–30 July 2010*, Winona Lake, Indiana: Eisenbrauns, 635–644.

Charvát, Petr 2014a:
Primeval Statesmen: Winnie the Pooh at archaic Ur, in H. Neumann, R. Dittmann, S. Paulus, G. Neumann und A. Schuster-Brandis (edd.), *Krieg und Frieden im alten Vorderasien, 52e Rencontre Assyriologique Internationale, International Congress of Assyriology and Near Eastern Archaeology, Münster, 17. – 21. Juli 2006* (AOAT 401), Münster: Ugarit-Verlag, 215–219.

Charvát, Petr 2014b:
Sumer, obilí a neolit (Sumer, grain and the Neolithic, in Czech, extensive summary in German), in M. Novák, P. Burgert (edd.), *Sborník k poctě Jiřího Kalfersta* (Archeologie východních Čech – supplementum 1), Hradec Králové: The Museum of Eastern Bohemia in Hradec Králové, 114–116.

Charvát, Petr 2014c:
The Deep Well of the Past: Earliest Seal Impressions from the City of Ur, in P. Bieliński, M. Gawlikowski, R. Koliński, D. Ławecka, A. Sołtysiak and Z. Wygnańska (edd.), *Proceedings of the 8th International Congress on the Archaeology of the Ancient Near East 30 April – 4 May 2012, University of Warsaw Volume 1, Plenary Sessions, Township and Villages, High and Low – The Minor Arts for the Elite and for the Populace*, Wiesbaden: The Harrassowitz Publishing House, 603–612.

Charvát, Petr, Petra Maříková Vlčková (edd.) 2010:
Who Was King? Who Was Not King? The Rulers and the Ruled in the Ancient Near East, Prague: Institute of Archaeology of the Academy of Sciences of the Czech Republic.

Chen, Y. S. 2013:
The Primeval Flood Catastrophe – Origins and Early Development in Mesopotamian Traditions, Oxford: Oxford University Press.

Cheng, Jack 2009:
A Review of Early Dynastic III Music: Man's Animal Call, *Journal of Near Eastern Studies* 68/3, 163–178.

Chiodi, Silvia Maria 1997:
Offerte "funebri" nella Lagaš presargonica (MVS 5/I), Roma: "La Sapienza".

Civil, Miguel 1982:
Studies in Early Dynastic Lexicography I, *Oriens Antiquus* 21, 1–26.

Civil, Miguel 1987:
The early history of HAR-ra: The Ebla link, in L. Cagni (ed.), *Ebla 1975–1985*, Naples: University Institute of Oriental Studies, Department of Asian Studies, Series Minor 27, 131–158.

Civil, Miguel 1990:
The verb šu-tak$_4$, "to send", *Aula Orientalis* 8, 109–111.

Civil, Miguel 2013:
Remarks on AD-GI$_4$/A.U.A. "Archaic Word List C" or "Tribute", *Journal of Cuneiform Studies* 65, 13–67.

Cohen, Mark E. 1981:
Sumerian Hymnology: The Eršemma, Hebrew Union College Annual Supplement No. 2, Cincinnati.

Cohen, Mark E. 1993:
The Cultic Calendars of the Ancient Near East, Bethesda, Maryland: CDL Press.

Cohen, Mark E. 1996:
The Sun, the Moon, and the City of Ur, in A. Berlin (ed.), *Religion and politics in the ancient Near East (Studies and texts in Jewish history and culture)*, Bethesda, MD: University Press of Maryland, 7–20.

Collon, Dominique 1981/1982:
Review of Mark Brandes: Siegelabrollungen aus den archaischen Bauschichten in Uruk-Warka, Wiesbaden 1979, *Archiv für Orientforschung* 28, 177–181.

Cooper, Jerrold S. 1999–2002:
1. Sumer et Sumériens: Questions de terminologie, in *Supplément au Dictionnaire de la Bible*, fasc. 72–73, t. XIII – Sumer, Paris: Letouzey & Ané, 87 bd Raspail, 75006 Paris, 78–93.

Cragg, Gene 1969:
The Keš Temple Hymn, in A. Sjöberg, E. Bergmann (edd.), *The Collection of the Sumerian Temple Hymns* (Texts from Cuneiform Sources vol. III), Locust Valley, NY: J. J. Augustin Publisher 1969, 155–188.

Cunningham, Graham 1997:
Deliver me from evil – Mesopotamian incantations 2500–1500 B.C. (Studia Pohl, series maior 17), Roma: Pontifical Biblical Institute.

Dahl, Jacob 2006:
Revisiting B a l a, *Journal of the American Oriental Society* 126.1, 77–88.

Dahl, Jacob 2011:
The statue of Nin-e'iga, in G. Barjamovic, J. Dahl, U. Koch, W. Sommerfeld, and J. G. Westenholz (edd.), *Akkade is King, A Collection of Papers by Friends and ColleaguesPresented to Aage Westenholz on the Occasion of His 70th Birthday 15th of May 2009*, Leiden: Nederlands Instituut van het *Nabije Oosten*, 55–65.

Dalton, George 1969:
Theoretical issues in economic anthropology, *Current Anthropology* 10, 63–102.

De Genouillac, Henri 1934:
Fouilles de Telloh, tome 1, Paris: Paul Geuthner.

De Graef, Katrien 2007:
Another Brick in the Wall – Dūrum in the Old-Elamite Susa Texts, *Akkadica* 128, 85–98.

De Maaijer, Remo, Bram Jagersma 1997–1998:
Review of Philadelphia Sumerian Dictionary vol. A I, *Archiv für Orientforschung* 44–45, 277–288.

De Miroschedji, Pierre 2011a:
A propos d'un fragment d'objet en forme de construction: Un aspect de pratiques cultuelles cananéennes aux âges du bronze et du fer, in F. Wateau (ed.), *Profils d'objets. Approches d'anthropologues et d'archéologues* (Colloques de la Maison René-Ginouvès 7), Paris: de Boccard, 109–120.

De Miroschedji, Pierre 2011b:
At the Origin of Canaanite Cult and Religion: The Early Bronze Age Fertility Ritual in Palestine, in *Eretz-Israel volume thirty (Amnon Ben-Tor Volume)*, 74–103.

De Schauensee, Maude 1998:
The "Boat-Shaped Lyre" – Restudy of a Unique Musical Instrument from Ur, *Expedition* 40/2, 20–28.

Deimel, Anton:
Sumerisches Lexicon:
Bd. I, 1st edition, Roma: Pontifical Biblical Institute 1925, 2nd edition, Roma: Pontifical Biblical Institute 1930;
Bd. II/1, Roma: Pontifical Biblical Institute 1928;
Bd. II/2, Roma: Pontifical Biblical Institute 1930;
Bd. II/3, Roma: Pontifical Biblical Institute 1932;
Bd. II/4, Roma: Pontifical Biblical Institute 1933;
Bd. III/1, Roma: Pontifical Biblical Institute 1934;
Bd. III/2, Roma: Pontifical Biblical Institute 1937.

Deimel, Anton 1950:
Pantheon Babylonicum, Roma: Pontifical Biblical Institute.

Deller, Karlheinz 1991:
On the names of some divine doorkeepers, *N. A. B. U.* 1/1991 (mars), 14–16.

Dittman, Reinhard 2006:
Bemerkungen zu Ur, Pit F, *Baghdader Mitteilungen* 37, 23–44.

Drewniowska, Olga 2012:
Panteony miast regionu Dijali w okresie starobabilonskim (Panthea of the Diyala-region cities in the Old Babylonian period, in Polish), Warszawa: Wydawnictwo Agade.

Durand, Jean-Marie 2003:
*Halhu-sur-Euphrate, *N. A. B. U.* 2003/4, décembre, 122–123.

Edzard, Dietz Otto 1981:
Archivi Reali di Ebla – Testi II, Verwaltungstexte verschiedenen Inhalts aus dem Archiv L-2769, Roma: Missione Archeologica Italiana in Siria.

Edzard, Dietz Otto 1987–1990:
Überblick über die sumerische Literatur, *Reallexikon der Assyriologie* vol. 7, Berlin–New York: Walter de Gruyter, 35–48.

Edzard, Dietz Otto 1993:
Review of ZATU, *Zeitschrift für Assyriologie* 83, 136–141.

Edzard, Dietz Otto 2009:
Geschichte Mesopotamiens, Von den Sumerern bis zu Alexander dem Großen, 2nd edition, München: C. H. Beck.

Englund, Robert K. 1988:
Administrative Timekeeping in Ancient Mesopotamia, *Journal of the Economic and Social History of the Orient* 31, 121–185.

Englund, Robert K. 1990:
Organisation und Verwaltung der Ur-III-Fischerei, Berlin: Dietrich Reimer Verlag.

Englund, Robert K. 1995a:
Regulating Dairy Productivity in the Ur III period, *Orientalia* N. S. 64/4, 377–429.

Englund, Robert K. 1995b:
Late Uruk Pigs and other Herded Animals, in U. Finkbeiner, R. Dittmann, and H. Hauptmann (edd.), *Beiträge zur Kulturgeschichte Vorderasiens – Festschrift für Rainer Michael Boehmer*, Mainz: Verlag Philipp von Zabern, 121–133.

Erarslan, Alev 2009:
Emergence of Local Trajectories in Southeastern Anatolia at the Fourth and the Early Third Millennium B.C., *Akkadica* 130, 189–209.

Falkenstein, Adam 1937:
Review of UET II, *Orientalistische Literaturzeitung* 40, 93–97.

Fenollós, Juan Luis Montero, Ignacio Montero Ruiz 2004:
Los vestigios más antiguos de la actividad metalúrgica en la ciudad sirio-mesopotámica de Mari, Primeros datos, *Aula Orientalis* 22, 229–241.

Fischer, Robert 2007:
Die keltische Religion in Irland und ihre Beeinflussung durch die Christianisierung, Diplomarbeit an der Universität Wien, Wien, im Juni 2007, accessible from the address *www.univie.ac.at/keltologie/diplomarbeiten/diplomarbeit1.pdf* [accessed August 28, 2012].

Forest, Jean-Daniel 1983:
Les pratiques funéraires en Mésopotamie du 5e millénaire au début du 3e, étude de cas, Paris: Editions Recherche sur les civilisations.

Frangipane, Marcella 2010a:
Chapter I – Politics, economy and political economy in early centralised societies. Theoretical debate and archaeological evidence, in M. Frangipane (ed.), *Economic Centralisation in Formative States. The Archaeological Reconstruction of the Economic System in 4th Millennium Arslantepe* (Studi di Preistoria Orientale vol. 3), Roma: Sapienza Università di Roma, Dipartimento di Scienze Storiche Archeologiche e Antropologiche dell'Antichità, 11–22.

Frangipane, Marcella 2010b:
Chapter XV – The political economy of the early central institutions at Arslantepe. Concluding remarks, in M. Frangipane (ed.), *Economic Centralisation in Formative States. The Archaeological Reconstruction of the Economic System in 4th Millennium Arslantepe* (Studi di Preistoria Orientale vol. 3), Roma: Sapienza Università di Roma, Dipartimento di Scienze Storiche Archeologiche e Antropologiche dell'Antichità, 289–307.

Frayne, Douglas 1997:
The Royal Inscriptions of Mesopotamia, Early Periods vol. 3/2: Ur III Period (2113–2004 B.C.), Toronto-Buffalo-London: University of Toronto Press.

Frayne, Douglas 2008a:
The Zagros Campaigns of the Ur III kings, *Journal of the Canadian Society for Mesopotamian Studies* 3/2008, 33–56.

Frayne, Douglas 2008b:
The Royal Inscriptions of Mesopotamia, Early Periods vol. 1: Presargonic Period 2700–2350 B. C., Toronto-Buffalo-London: University of Toronto Press.

Friberg, Jöran 1999:
Counting and Accounting in the Proto-Literate Middle East: Examples from Two New Volumes of Proto-Cuneiform Texts, *Journal of Cuneiform Studies* 51, 107–138.

Friberg, Jöran 2011:
Seven-Sided Star Figures and Tuning Algorithms in Mesopotamian, Greek, and Islamic Texts, *Archiv für Orientforschung* 52, 121–155.

Gelb, Ignace, Piotr Steinkeller, Robert M. Whiting Jr. 1991:
Earliest Land Tenure Systems in the Near East: Ancient Kudurrus, Chicago: The Oriental Institute of the University of Chicago.

George, Andrew R. 1992:
Babylonian topographical texts (OLA 40), Leuven: Departement Orientalistiëk-Uitgeverij Peeters.

George, Andrew R. 1993:
House Most High – The Temples of Ancient Mesopotamia, Winona Lake, Indiana: Eisenbrauns.

Glassner, Jean-Jacques 1984:
La division quinaire de la terre, *Akkadica* 40, 17–34.

Glassner, Jean-Jacques 2000:
Écrire à Sumer – L'invention du cunéiforme, s. l.: Editions du Seuil.

Glassner, Jean-Jacques 2003:
The Invention of Cuneiform – Writing in Sumer (translation of *Glassner 2000* into English by Z. Bahrani and M. van de Mieroop), Baltimore-London: Johns Hopkins University Press.

Glassner, Jean-Jacques 2009:
En-Hedu-Anna, une femme auteure en pays de Sumer au IIIe millénaire?, in F. Briquel-Chatonnet, S. Farès, B. Lion, C. Michel (edd.), *Topoi Orient Occident – Supplément 10, Femmes, cultures et sociétés dans les civilisations méditerranéennes et proche-orientales de l'Antiquité*, Lyon: Maison de l'Orient Méditerranéen – Jean Pouilloux (Institut Fernand-Courby), 219–231.

Good, Irene 2006:
Textiles as a Medium of Exchange in Third Millennium B.C.E. Western Asia, in V. H. Mair (ed.), *Contact and Exchange in the Ancient World*, Honolulu: University of Hawai'i Press, 191–214.

Götzelt, Thomas 1995:
Zur sumerischen und akkadischen Verwandschaftsterminologie, in U. Finkbeiner, R. Dittmann, H. Hauptmann (edd.), *Beiträge zur Kulturgeschichte Vorderasiens – Festschrift für Rainer Michael Boehmer*, Mainz: Verlag Philipp von Zabern, 177–182.

Green, Margaret 1980:
Animal husbandry at Uruk in the archaic period, *Journal of Near Eastern Studies* 39/1, 1–35.

Gubel, Eric 2012:
Relieve en miniatura, in *Antés del Diluvio – Mesopotamia 3500–2100 A. C.*, Barcelona: Fundación "la Caixa", 226.

Hansen, Donald 1998:
Art of the Royal Tombs of Ur. A Brief Interpretation, in Richard Zettler, Lee Horne (edd.), *Treasures from the Royal Tombs of Ur*, Philadelphia: University of Pennsylvania Museum, 43–72.

Haul, Michael 2004:
Lú an-šè ba-e_{11}-dè, Der Mythus von Etana vom 2000 v. Chr., in J.-W. Mayer, W. Sommerfeld (edd.), *2000 v. Chr., Politische, wirtschaftliche und kulturelle Entwicklung im Zeichen einer Jahrtausendwende*, Berlin: Deutsche Orient-Gesellschaft in Kommission bei Saarbrücker Druckerei und Verlag, 237–262.

Heeßel, Nils P. 2001–2002:
"Wenn ein Mann zum Haus des Kranken geht…", *Archiv für Orientforschung* 48/49, 24–49.

Helbaek, Hans 1960:
Irrigation in ancient Mesopotamia, *Iraq* 22, 1960, 186–196.

Hill, Jane A. 2004:
Cylinder-Seal Glyptic in Predynastic Egypt and Neighbouring Regions, BAR International Series No. 1223, Oxford: Archaeopress.

Hookman, Daniel 2008:
Die Warka-Vase – eine neue Interpretation, *Altorientalische Forschungen* 35, 326–336.

Hruška, Blahoslav 1995:
Herden für Götter und Könige. Schafe und Ziegen in der altsumerischen Zeit, *Altorientalische Forschungen* 22/1, 73–83.

Huber, Christian 2000:
$Guru_7$-a im-ùr-ra revisited, in S. Graziani (ed.), *Studi sul Vicino Oriente Antico dedicati alla memoria di Luigi Cagni*, Naples: University Institute of Oriental Studies, 463–495.

Huh, Su Kyung 2008:
Studien zur Region Lagaš, Von der Ubaid-Zeit bis zur altbabylonischer Zeit (AOAT 345), Munster: Ugarit-Verlag.

Hurowitz, Victor (Avigdor) 1992:
I Have Built You an Exalted House. Temple Building in the Bible in Light of Mesopotamian and Northwest Semitic Writings, Sheffield: Sheffield Academic Press.

Hussein, Salim Younis, Mark Altaweel, Zuhair Rejeb 2009:
Report on Excavations at Tell al-Wilaya, Iraq – Further Information on the 1999 and 2000 Seasons, *Akkadica* 130, 3–42 and 113–166.

Inizan, Marie-Louise 1995:
Cornaline et agates: Production et circulation de la préhistoire à nos jours, in *Tallon* 1995, 21–24.

Ishida, Keiko 2006:
Spade tree motif in Near Eastern seals, *Bulletin of the Ancient Orient Museum* 26, Tokyo, 11–25 (English summary on p.11).

Jaques, Margaret 2006:
Le vocabulaire des sentiments dans les textes sumériens (AOAT 332), Münster: Ugarit-Verlag.

Johnson, J. Cale 2014a:
The Origins of Scholastic Commentary in Mesopotamia: Second-Order Schemata in the Early Dynastic Exegetical Imagination, in Sh. Gordin (ed.), *Visualizing Knowledge and Creating Meaning in Ancient Writing Systems* (BBVO 23), Berlin: PeWe Verlag, 11–55.

Johnson, J. Cale 2014b:
The Cost of Cosmogony: Ethical Reflections on Source Extraction, Monumental Architecture and Urbanism in Sumerian Literary Tradition, in N. N. May, U. Steinert (edd.), *The Fabric of Cities – Aspects of Urbanism, Urban Topography and Society in Mesopotamia, Greece and Rome*, Leiden–Boston: Brill, 43–76.

Jones, Philip 2003:
Embracing Inanna: Legitimation and Mediation in the Ancient Mesopotamian Sacred Marriage Hymn Iddin-Dagan A, *Journal of the American Oriental Society* 123.2, 291–302.

Kawami, Trudy S. 2001:
The Cattle of Uruk: Stamp Seals and Animal Husbandry in the Late Uruk / Jemdet Nasr Period, in W. W. Hallo, I. Winter (edd.), *Proceedings of the XLVe Rencontre Assyriologique Internationale Part II: Seals and Seal Impressions*, Bethesda, MD: CDL Press, 31–47.

Keetman, Jan 2010:
Das Ritual in Enḫeduannas Lied "Königin der zahlreichen Me", *Altorientalische Forschungen* 37, 38–48.

Keetman, Jan 2012:
Die Lesung des Wortes UDU "Schaf" im Sumerischen und die akkadischen Vogelnamen arabû und usābu, *N. A. B. U.* 2012 no. 2 (juin), 32–34.

Klein, Jacob 1991:
A New Nippur Duplicate of the Sumerian Kinglist in the Brockmon Collection, University of Haifa, *Aula Orientalis* 9, 123–129.

Krebernik, Manfred 1993–1994:
Review of *Gelb-Steinkeller-Whiting* 1991, in *Archiv für Orientforschung* 40–41, p. 90.

Krebernik, Manfred 1998:
NAĞAR, in *Reallexikon der Assyriologie*, vol. 9, Berlin–New York: Walter de Gruyter, 74–75.

Krebernik, Manfred 2002a:
Geschlachtete Gottheiten und ihre Namen, in O. Loretz, K. A. Metzler, H. Schaudig (edd.), *Ex Mesopotamia et Syria Lux, Festschrift für Manfred Dietrich zu seinem 65. Geburtstag*, Münster: Ugarit-Verlag, 289–298.

Krebernik, Manfred 2002b:
Zur Geschichte des sumerischen Onomastikons, in M. P. Streck, St. Weninger (edd.), *Altorientalische und semitische Onomastik* (AOAT 296), Münster: Ugarit-Verlag, 1–74.

Krebernik, Manfred 2004:
$^{(d)}$PAP.PAP, in *Reallexikon der Assyriologie* vol. 10, Berlin–New York: Walter de Gruyter, 328.

Krebernik, Manfred, John N. Postgate 2009:
The tablets from Tell Abu Salabikh and their provenance, *Iraq* 71, 1–33.

Krecher, Joachim 1983:
Eine unorthographische sumerische Wortliste aus Ebla, *Oriens Antiquus* 22, 179–189.

Krecher, Joachim 1987:
/ur/, "Mann", /eme/, "Frau" und die sumerische Herkunft des Wortes urdu(d), "Sklave", *Die Welt des Orients* 18, 7–19.

Krispijn, Theo J. H. 2008:
Music and Healing for someone far away from home HS 1556, A Remarkable Ur III Incantation, revisited, in R. J. van der Spek (ed.) *Studies in Ancient Near Eastern World View and Society presented to Marten Stol on the occasion of his 65th birthday*, Bethesda, MD: CDL Press, 173–194.

Lafont, Bertrand 1999-2002:
II. La société sumérienne – Institutions, économie et société, in *Supplément au Dictionnaire de la Bible*, fasc. 72–73, t. XIII – Sumer, Paris: Letouzey & Ané, 124–203.

Lafont, Bertrand 2008:
Le prisme cunéiforme conservé au Musée National de Beyrouth, *BAAL* 12, 161–188.

Lafont, Bertrand 2010:
Contribution de la documentation cunéiforme à la connaissance du "Très Long Mur" de la steppe syrienne, *Paléorient* 36/2, 73–89.

LAK:
Anton Deimel: *Die Inschriften von Fara I: Liste der archaischen Keilschriftzeichen*, Leipzig: J. C. Hinrich'sche Buchhandlung 1922.

Lambert, Wilfred G. 1980:
The theology of death, in B. Alster (ed.), *Death in Mesopotamia – Papers read at the XXVIe Rencontre Assyriologique Internationale* (Mesopotamia 8), Copenhagen: Akademisk Forlag, 53–66.

Lambert, Wilfred G. 1981:
Studies in UD.GAL.NUN, *Oriens Antiquus* 20, 81–97.

Lambert, Wilfred G. 1990:
The names of Umma, *Journal of Near Eastern Studies* 49, 75–80.

Lan, Daniel 2012:
Ein älter Frühdynastisches Siegel aus K/L XII/XIII in Uruk-Warka, *Zeitschrift für Orient-Archäologie* 5, 74–88.

Landsberger, Benno (ed.) 1969:
Materialien zum Sumerischen lexicon vol. XII, Roma: Pontifical Biblical Institute.

Ławecka, Dorota 2009:
North-Babylonian Motifs in Early Dynastic Mesopotamian Glyptics, in Olga Drewnowska (ed.), *Here & There Across the Ancient Near East, Studies in Honour of Krystyna Łyczkowska*, Warszawa: Wydawnictwo Agade, 121–148.

Lecompte, Camille 2013:
Temps, mémoire et évolution des cultures aux époques archaiques: écriture du passé et listes lexicales, in L. Feliu, J. Llop, A. Millet Albà, J. Sanmartín (edd.), *Time and History in the Ancient*

Near East – Proceedings of the 56th Rencontre Assyriologique Internationale at barcelona, 26–30 July 2010, Winona Lake, Indiana: Eisenbrauns, 143–158.

Legrain, Leon 1951:
Ur Excavations vol. X: Seal Cylinders, London and Philadelphia, New York: The Trustees of the Two Museums (The British Museum and The University Museum), by the aid of a Grant from the Carnegie Corporation of New York.

Lehmann, Gunnar 1999:
Biblische Landeskunde oder kultur- und sozialgeographische Raumanalyse?, in H. Kühne, R. Bernbeck, K. Bartl (edd.), *Fluchtpunkt Uruk – Archäologische Einheit aus methodischer Vielfalt, Schriften für Hans Jörg Nissen*, Rahden/Westf.: Verlag Marie Leidorf, 95–124.

Lion, Brigitte 2009:
Sexe et genre (2) – Des prêtresses fils de roi, in F. Briquel-Chatonnet, S. Farès, B. Lion, C. Michel (edd.), *Topoi Orient Occident – Supplément 10, Femmes, cultures et sociétés dans les civilisations méditerranéennes et proche-orientales de l'Antiquité*, Lyon: Maison de l'Orient Méditerranéen – Jean Pouilloux (Institut Fernand-Courby), 165–182.

Lupton, Alan 1996:
Stability and Change – Socio-Political Development in Northern Mesopotamia and Southeastern Anatolia, 4000–2700 B.C., BAR International Series 627, s. l.: Tempvs reparatum.

Maekawa, Kazuya 1997:
The Agricultural Texts of Ur III Lagaš in the British Museum (XI), *Acta Sumerologica (Japan)* 19, 113–145.

Mallul, Meir 1989:
Susapinnu = The Mesopotamian paranymph and his role, *Journal of the Economic and Social History of the Orient* 32, 241–278.

Mander, Pietro 1980:
Brevi considerazioni sul testo "lessicale" *SF* 23 = *SF* 24 e paralelli da Abu-Salabīkh, *Oriens Antiquus* 19, 187–192.

Mander, Pietro 1986:
Il panteon di Abu-Ṣālabīkh, Contributo allo studio del panteon sumerico arcaico, Naples: University Institute of Oriental Studies, Department of Asian Studies, Series Minor 26.

Marchesi, Gianni 2004:
Who Was Buried in the Royal Tombs of Ur? The Epigraphic and Textual Data, *Orientalia* 73/2, 153–197

Marchesi, Gianni 2011:
Goods from the Queen of Dilmun, in J. G. Dercksen, J. Eidem, K. van der Toorn, K. R. Veenhof (edd.), *Akkade is King – A Collection of Papers by Friends and Colleagues Presented to Aage Westenholz on the occasion of His 70th Birthday 15th May 2009* (PIHANS CXVIII), Leiden: Nederlands Instituut van het Nabije Oosten, 189–200.

Marchesi, Gianni, Nicolò Marchetti 2011:
The Royal Statuary of Early Dynastic Mesopotamia (Mesopotamian Civilizations vol. 16), Winona Lake, Indiana: Eisenbrauns (reference courtesy Giacomo Benati).

Marchetti, Nicolò 2006:
La statuaria regale nella Mesopotamia protodinastica (Atti della Accademia Nazionale dei Lincei Anno CDIII, 2006, Classe di scienze morale, storiche e filologiche, Memorie, Series IX, Volume XXI, Fascicolo I), con un Appendice di Gianni Marchesi (205–271), Rome: Bardi Editore.

Martin, Harriet P. 1982:
The Early Dynastic cemetery at al-ᶜUbaid, A re-evaluation, *Iraq* 44, 145–185.

Martin, Harriet P. 1988:
Fara: A Reconstruction of the Ancient Mesopotamian City of Shuruppak, Birmingham: Chris Martin & Associates.

Martin, Harriet P., Roger J. Matthews 1993:
Seals and Sealings, in Anthony Green (ed.), *Abu Salabikh Excavations Volume 4, The 6G Ash-Tip and its contents: cultic and administrative discard from the temple?*, London: British School of Archaeology in Iraq, 23–81.

Martin, Harriet P., Francesco Pomponio, Giuseppe Visicato, Aage Westenholz 2001:
The Fara tablets in the University of Pennsylvania Museum of Archaeology and Anthropology, Bethesda, Maryland: CDL Press.

Mařík, Tomáš 2005:
Dvojí hora a jeden pahorek v Mezopotámii (A twin mountain and a single hillock in Mesopotamia, in Czech), in Jana Maříková-Kubková, Tomáš Mařík (edd.), *Hora hor, Sborník příspěvků přednesených na konferenci uspořádané u příležitosti výstavy Aleše Veselého na téma "Hora hor"*, Prague: Institute of Archaeology of the CAS, 31–50.

Matney, Timothy, Algaze Guillermo 1995:
Urban Development at Mid-Late Early Bronze Age Titriş Höyük in Southeastern Anatolia, *Bulletin of the American Schools of Oriental Research* 299/300, 33–52.

Matthews, Donald M. 1997:
The Early Glyptic of Tell Brak – Cylinder Seals of Third Millennium Syria (Orbis Biblicus et Orientalis, Series Archaeologica 15), Fribourg-Göttingen: University Press, Vandenhoeck & Ruprecht.

Matthews, Roger J. 1993:
Cities, seals and writing: archaic seal impressions from Jemdet Nasr and Ur, Materialien zu den frühen Schrifterzeugnissen des Vorderen Orients (MSVO) Bd. 2. Berlin: Gebr. Mann Verlag.

Matthews, Roger J. 2002:
Secrets of the dark mound – Jemdet Nasr 1926-1928 (Iraq Archaeological Reports No. 6), London: British School of Archaeology in Iraq.

Matthews, Roger J., Wendy Matthews, Helen McDonald 1994:
Excavations at Tell Brak, 1994, *Iraq* 56, 177–194.

Mayer, Werner R. 2005:
Lexikalische Listen aus Ebla und Uruk, *Orientalia* N. S. 74, 157–164.

Mazzoni, Stefania 1992:
Le impronte su giara eblaite e siriane nel bronzo antico (Università degli Studi di Roma "La Sapienza", Materiali e studi archeologici di Ebla – MSAE I), Roma: Missione archeologica italiana in Siria.

Mazzoni, Stefania 2002:
The Squatting Woman: Between Fertility and Eroticism, in S. Parpola, R. M. Whiting (edd.), *Sex and Gender in the Ancient Near East, Proceedings of the 47th Rencontre Assyriologique Internationale, Helsinki, July 2–6, 2001*, Helsinki, 367–377.

Mazzoni, Stefania 2003:
Ebla: Crafts and Power in an Emergent State of Third Millennium B.C., *Journal of Mediterranean Archaeology* 16/2, 173–191.

Mazzoni, Stefania 2008:
Seals and jars – The Evidence of Early Interconnections in the Eastern Mediterranean, *BAAL Hors Série VI* (Interconnections in the Eastern Mediterranean, Lebanon in the Bronze and Iron Ages), Beirut, 37–56.

McCaffey, Kathleen 2013:
The Sumerian Sacred Marriage: Texts and Images, in H. Crawford (ed.), *The Sumerian World*, London–New York: Routledge, Taylor and Francis Group, 227–245.

McMahon, Augusta 2009:
The lion, the king and the cage: Late Chalcolithic iconography and ideology in northern Mesopotamia, *Iraq* 71, 115–124.

McMahon, Augusta, Joan Oates 2007:
Excavations at Tell Brak 2006–2007, *Iraq* 69, 145–171.

MEA:
René Labat: *Manuel d'épigraphie akkadienne*, Sixième édition par Florence Malbran-Labat. Paris: Geuthner 1988.

Meyer-Laurin, Vera 2011:
Die "Zeichenpaare" in sargonischen Akkadisch aus sumerologischer Sicht, *Die Welt des Orients* 41, 27–68.

Micale, Maria C., Davide Nadali 2010:
Royal Palace Officials at Ebla in the 3rd Millennium B.C. – Names, Duties and Movement through Their Seal Impressions, *Zeitschrift für Orient-Archäologie* 3, 2010, 8–24.

Michalowski, Piotr 1993:
On the early toponymy of Sumer, in A. F. Rainey et al. (edd.), *kinattūtu ša dārâti – Raphael Kutscher Memorial Volume*, Tel Aviv: Institute of Archaeology of the Tel Aviv University, 119–133.

Michalowski, Piotr 2003:
An Early Dynastic Tablet of ED Lu A from Tell Brak (Nagar), *Cuneiform Digital Library Journal* 2003:3 <http://cdli.ucla.edu/pubs/cdlj/2003/003.html,>, accessed June 22, 2012 (ISSN 1540–8779), 1–6.

Michalowski, Piotr 2013:
Of Bears and Men – Thoughts on the End of Šulgi's Reign and on the Ensuing Succession, in David S. Vanderhooft, Abraham Winitzer (edd.), *Literature as Politics, Politics as Literature: Essays on the Ancient Near East in Honor of Peter Machinist*, Winona Lake, Indiana: Eisenbrauns 2013, 285–320.

Mirelman, Sam, Walther Sallaberger 2010:
The Performance of a Sumerian Wedding Song, *Zeitschrift für Assyriologie* 100, 177–196.

Mittermeyer, Catherine 2005:
Die Entwicklung der Tierkopfzeichen (AOAT 319), Münster: Ugarit-Verlag.

Molina, Manuel 1991:
Tablillas sargónicas del Museo de Montserrat, Barcelona, *Aula Orientalis* 9, 137–154.

Monaco, Salvatore F. 1986:
Parametri e qualificatori nei testi economici della terza dinastia di Ur II. Qualificatori non numerici, *Oriens Antiquus* 25, 1–20.

Monaco, Salvatore F. 2004:
Revisiting Jemdet Nasr Texts: IM 55580+, *Cuneiform Digital Library Bulletin* 2004: 3, 1–5.

Monaco, Salvatore F. 2007:
The Cornell University Archaic Tablets, (CUSAS No. 1) Bethesda, Maryland: CDL Press.

Monaco, Salvatore F. 2009:
Review of R. K. Englund, H.-J. Nissen, Archaische Verwaltungstexte aus Uruk, Die Heidelberger Sammlung (Ausgrabungen der Deutschen Forschungsgemeinschaft in Uruk-Warka 17), Berlin 2001, in *Bibliotheca Orientalis* 66/1–2, 150–152.

Moorey, Peter R. S. 1979:
Unpublished Early Dynastic Sealings from Ur in the British Museum, *Iraq* 45, 105–120.

Moorey, Peter R. S. 1985:
Materials and Manufacture in Ancient Mesopotamia: the Evidence of Archaeology and Art (BAR International Series 237), Oxford: Bar Publications.

Moortgat-Correns, Ursula 1994:
Die Rosette – ein Schriftzeichen?, *Altorientalische Forschungen* 21, 359–371.

MSVO 1:
Robert K. Englund, Jean-Pierre Grégoire, Roger J. Matthews: *The Proto-Cuneiform Texts from Jemdet Nasr I: Copies, Transliterations and Glossary*, (Materialien zu den frühen Schriftzeugnissen des Vorderen Orients Bd. 1), Berlin: Gebr. Mann Verlag 1991.

MSVO 2:
See *Matthews* 1993.

MSVO 4:
Robert K. Englund, Roger J. Matthews: *Proto-Cuneiform Texts from Diverse Collections* (Materialien zu den frühen Schriftzeugnissen des Vorderen Orients = MSVO Bd. 4), Berlin: Verlag Gebr. Mann 1996.

Müller-Karpe, Michael 1990:
Metallgefässe des dritten Jahrtausends in Mesopotamien, *Archäologisches Korrespondenzblatt* 20/2, 161–176.

Müller-Karpe, Michael 1991:
Aspects of early metallurgy in Mesopotamia, *Archaeometry* 90, Basel-Boston-Berlin: Borkhauser Verlag, 105–116.

Müller-Karpe, Michael, Ernst Pászthory, Ernst Pernicka 1993:
Metallgefässe in Iraq (Von den Anfängen bis zur Akkad-Zeit), PBF Part II, vol. 14, Stuttgart: Franz Steiner Verlag.

Nagel, Wolfram, Eva Strommenger 1995:
Sechzig Jahre Forschung zur frühdynastischen Bildkunst und ein neues Denkmal des Urdynastikums, in U. Finkbeiner, R. Dittmann, H. Hauptmann (edd.), *Beiträge zur Kulturgeschichte Vorderasiens – Festschrift für Rainer Michael Boehmer*, Mainz: Verlag Philipp von Zabern, 455–468.

Neumann, Hans 1993:
Handwerk in Mesopotamien, 2nd edition, Berlin: Akademie Verlag.

Nissinen, Martti, Risto Uro (edd.) 2008:
Sacred Marriages – The Divine-Human Sexual Metaphor from Sumer to Early Christianity, Winona Lake, Indiana: Eisenbrauns.

Ó Corráin, David 1995:
Ireland, Scotland and Wales to the early eleventh century, in R. McKitterick (ed.), *The New Cambridge Medieval History vol. II, c. 700 – c. 900*, Cambridge-New York-Melbourne: Cambridge University Press, 43–63.

Otte, Marcel, Manfred R. Behm-Blancke 1992:
Das lithische Inventar: Rekonstruktion technischer Verfahrenswesen, in M. R. Behm-Blancke (ed.), *Hassek Höyük – Naturwissenschaftliche Untersuchungen und lithische Industrie*, Tübingen: Ernst Wasmuth Verlag, 165–176.

Otto, Adelheid 2010:
The iconography and use of the Ur SIS 8-4 seals reconsidered, in Kateřina Šašková, Lukáš Pecha, Petr Charvát (edd.), *Shepherds of the Black-headed People – The Royal Office Vis-à-vis Godhead in Ancient Mesopotamia*, Pilsen: University of West Bohemia, 19–29.

Otto, Adelheid 2013:
Königssiegel als Programm – Überlegungen zum Selbstverständnis altorientalischer Herrscher und zu Deutung der Tierkampfsszene, *Zeitschrift für Assyriologie* 103, 45–68.

Owen, David 1995:
Amorites and the location of BÀD^{ki}, in K. van Lerberghe, A. Schoors (edd.), *Immigration and Emigration within the Ancient Near East – Festschrift E. Lipinski*, Leuven: Peeters Publishers and Department of Oriental Studies, 213–219.

Paoletti, Paola 2012:
Der König und sein Kreis (BPOA 10), Madrid: Consejo Superior de las Investigaciones Científicas.

Perlov, Boris 1980:
The families of the ensí's Urbau and Gudea and their funerary cult, in B. Alster (ed.), *Death in Mesopotamia – Papers read at the XXVIe Rencontre Assyriologique Internationale* (Mesopotamia 8), Copenhagen: Akademisk Forlag, 77–81.

Peterson, Jeremiah 2007:
A Study of Sumerian Faunal Conception with a Focus on the Terms Pertaining to the Order Testudines, A Dissertation in Near Eastern Languages and Civilizations Presented to the Faculties of the University of Pennsylvania in Partial Fulfilment of the Requirement fort he Degree of Doctor of Philosophy 2007, UMI 3260966, Ann Arbor, MI: ProQuest Information and Learning Company.

Peterson, Jeremiah 2009:
Two New Sumerian texts Involving the Netherworld and Funerary Offerings, *Zeitschrift für Assyriologie* 99, 233–246.

Pettinato, Giovanni 2005:
L'economia sumerica. Un dilemma ancora attuale: economia templare o economia palaziale? in *Convegno internazionale – L'economia palaziale e la nascita della moneta: Dalla Mesopotamia all'Egeo* (Academia Nazionale dei Lincei, Anno CDII, 2005, Contributi del Centro Linceo Interdisciplinare "Beniamino Segre" N. 111), Roma, 12–13 febbraio 2002, in collaborazione con la Banca d'Italia, Roma: Academia Nazionale dei Lincei, 51–71.

Pfälzner, Peter, Jochen Schmid 2008:
Das Tempeloval von Urkeš. Betrachtungen zur Typologie und Entwicklungsgeschichte der mesopotamischen Ziqqurat im 3. Jahrtausend V. Chr., *Zeitschrift für Orient-Archäologie* 1/2008, 396–433.

Pientka-Hinz, Rosel 2011:
Bunte Kühe? Zu den frühesten Farbbezeichnungen im Alten Orient, in G. Selz. Kl. Wagensonner (edd.), *The Empirical Dimension of Ancient Near Eastern Studies – Die empirische Dimension altorientalischer Forschungen* (Wiener Offene Orientalistik Bd. 6), Wien und Berlin: LIT Verlag, 325–374.

Pittman, Holly 2002:
Bears at Brak, in Laila al-Gailani Werr, John Curtis, Harriet Martin, Augusta MacMahon, Joan Oates, Julian Reade (edd.), *Of Pots and Plans – Papers on the Archaeology and History of Mesopo-*

tamia and Syria presented to David Oates in Honour of his 75th Birthday, London: NABU Publications, 287–296.

Pollock, Susan 2007a:
Chapter 4: The Royal Cemetery of Ur: Ritual, Tradition, and the Creation of Subjects, in M. Heinz, M. Feldman (edd.), *Representations of Political Power – Case Histories from Times of Change and Dissolving Order in the Ancient Near East*, Winona Lake, Indiana: Eisenbrauns, 89–110.

Pollock, Susan 2007b:
Death of a household, in N. Laneri (ed.), *Performing Death – Social Analyses of Funerary Traditions in the Ancient Near East and Mediterranean* (Oriental Institute Seminars No. 3), Chicago: The Oriental Institute of the University of Chicago, 209–221.

Pomponio, Francesco 1980:
AO 7754 ed il sistema ponderale di Ebla, *Oriens Antiquus* 19, 171–186.

Pomponio, Francesco 1987:
La prosopografia dei testi presargonici di Fara, Roma: "La Sapienza".

Pomponio, Francesco 1991:
Antiche sementi, *Rivista degli Studi Orientali* LXV/3-4, 161–163.

Pomponio, Francesco 1998:
The Exchange Ratio between Silver and Gold in the Administrative texts from Ebla, *Acta Sumerologica (Japan)* 20, 127–133.

Pomponio, Francesco, Giuseppe Visicato 1994:
Early Dynastic Administrative Tablets of Šuruppak, Naples: University Institute of Oriental Studies, Department of Asian Studies, Series Maior 6.

Pongratz-Leisten, Beate 1992:
1. Mesopotamische Standarten in literarischen Zeugnissen, *Baghdader Mitteilungen* 23, 299–340.

Prosecký, Jiří 2008:
L'arche comme *imago mundi*, *Archiv Orientální* 76, 1–14.

PSD:
Pennsylvania Sumerian Dictionary, accessible: http://psd.museum.upenn.edu/epsd/index.html

Quenet, Philippe 2008:
Les échanges du nord de la Mésopotamie avec ses voisins proche-orientaux au IIIe millénaire (ca. 3100-2300 av. J. C.), (Subartu XXII), Turnhout: Brepols.

Racine, Louis 1986:
Les formes élémentaires de la reciprocité, *L'Homme* 99, XXVI(3), 97–118.

Richardson, Seth 2007:
Death and Dismemberment in Mesopotamia: Discorporation Between the Body and Body Politics, in N. Laneri (ed.), *Performing Death – Social Analyses of Funerary Traditions in the Ancient Near East and Mediterranean* (Oriental Institute Seminars No. 3), Chicago: The Oriental Institute of the University of Chicago, 189–208.

Richardson, Seth 2012:
Early Mesopotamia: The Presumptive State, *Past and Present* 215, 3–49.

Rodin, Therese 2014:
Rodin, T. 2014. The World of the Sumerian Mother Goddess, An Interpretation of Her Myths (*Historia religionum* 35), Uppsala: Acta Universitatis Upsaliensis.

Rohn, Karin 2011:
Beschriftete mesopotamische Siegel der Frühdynastischen und der Akkad-Zeit (Orbis Biblicus et Orientalis, Series Archaeologica 32), Fribourg and Göttingen: Academic Press and Vandenhoeck & Ruprecht.

Romano, Licia 2008:
La corona del dio. Nota sull'iconografia divina nel protodinastico, *Vicino Oriente* 14, 41–57.

Romano, Licia 2010a:
The Barber's Gift: Votive Plaques as Expression of Elite's *Pietas*, in P. Matthiae, F. Pinnock, L. Nigro, N. Marchetti, L. Romano (edd.), *Proceedings of the 6th International Congress on the Archaeology of the Ancient Near East, May 5th-10th 2008*, "Sapienza" Università di Roma vol. 1, Wiesbaden: The Harrassowitz Publishing House, 973–981.

Romano, Licia 2010b:
Who was worshiped in the Abu Temple at Tell Asmar? *KASKAL* 7, 51–65.

Rosengarten, Yvonne 1960:
Le concept sumérien de consommation dans la vie économique et religieuse – Etude linguistique et sociale d'après les textes présargoniques de Lagaš. Paris: Editions E. de Boccard.

Rothman, Mitchell 2013:
5. Interpreting the Role of Godin Tepe in the "Uruk Expansion", in Cameron A. Petrie (ed.), *Ancient Iran and Its Neighbours, Local Developments and Long-Range Interactions in the Fourth Millennium BC* (British Institute of Persian Studies, Archaeological Monographs, Series III), Oxford: Oxbow Books,75-91.

Rova, Elena 1994:
Ricerche sui sigilli a cilindro vicino-orientali del periodo di Uruk/Jemdet Nasr (Orientis Antiqui Collectio XX). Roma, Istituto per l'Oriente C. A. Nallino.

Sallaberger, Walther 1993:
Der kultische Kalender der Ur-III-Zeit 1, Berlin – New York: Walter de Gruyter.

Sallaberger, Walther 2006–2008:
Provinz A, in *Reallexikon der Assyriologie* vol. 11, Berlin – New York: Walter de Gruyter, 34–38.

Sallaberger, Walther 2010:
The city and the palace at archaic Ur, in Kateřina Šašková, Lukáš Pecha, Petr Charvát (edd.), *Shepherds of the Black-headed People – The Royal Office Vis-à-vis Godhead in Ancient Mesopotamia*, Pilsen: University of West Bohemia, 31–37.

Sauren, Herbert 1980:
Götter am Eingang zum Totenreich, in B. Alster (ed.), *Death in Mesopotamia – Papers read at the XXVIe Rencontre Assyriologique Internationale* (Mesopotamia 8), Copenhagen: Akademisk Forlag, 91–97.

Scharlach, Toni 2000:
Review of Marcel Sigrist, Texts from the Yale Babylonian Collections: Sumerian Archival Texts Vols. II and III, *Journal of Cuneiform Studies* 52, 131–137.

Schmidt, Conrad 2005:
Überregionale Austauschsysteme und Fernhandelswaren in der Ur III-Zeit, *Baghdader Mitteilungen* 36, 7–155.

Schrakamp, Ingo 2012a:
Zu den vor-Ur III-zeitlichen Keilschrifttexten des Wold Museum, Liverpool, *Journal of Cuneiform Studies* 64, 145–162.

Schrakamp, Ingo 2012b:
Review of M. Maiocchi, Classical Sargonic Texts Chiefly from Adab in the Cornell University Collections, Bethesda 2009, *Bibliotheca Orientalis* 69/3–7, 275–290.

Schrakamp, Ingo 2014:
Krieger und Bauern. RU-lugal und aga/aga$_3$-us$_2$ im Militär des altsumerischen Lagaš", in H. Neumann, R. Dittmann, S. Paulus, G. Neumann, A. Schuster-Brandis (edd.), *Krieg und Frieden im Alten Vorderasien – 52e Rencontre Assyriologique Internationale, Münster 17. – 21. Juli 2006* (AOAT 401), Münster: Ugarit-Verlag, 693–726.

Scott, Sarah Jarmer 2005:
Figure, Symbol and Sign: Semiotics and Function of Early Dynastic I Cylinder Seal Imagery from Ur, A Dissertation in The History of Art Presented to the Faculties of the University of Pennsylvania in Fulfilment of the Requirements for the Degree of Doctor of Philosophy, Philadelphia, January 2005 (reference courtesy Sara Jarmer Scott).

Selz, Gebhard J. 1992a:
Enlil und Nippur nach präsargonischen Quellen, in M. deJ. Ellis (ed.), *Nippur at the Centennial – Papers Read at the 35th Rencontre Assyriologique Internationale, Philadelphia 1988*, Philadelphia: Occasional Publications of the Samuel Noah Kramer Fund, 189–225.

Selz, Gebhard J. 1992b:
Eine Kultstatue der Herrschergemahlin Šaša: Ein Beitrag zum Problem der Vergöttlichung, *Acta Sumerologica (Japan)* 14, 245–268.

Selz, Gebhard J. 1993:
Altsumerische Wirtschaftsurkunden aus amerikanischen Sammlungen 2 (FAOS 15.2), Stuttgart: Franz Steiner.

Selz, Gebhard J. 1995:
Untersuchungen zur Götterwelt des altsumerischen Stadtstaates von Lagaš (UGASL), Philadelphia: Occasional Publications of the Samuel Noah Kramer Fund.

Selz, Gebhard J. 1998a:
Über Mesopotamische Herrschaftkonzepte – Zu den Ursprüngen mesopotamischer Herrscherideologie im 3. Jahrtausend, in M. Dietrich, O. Loretz (edd.), *dubsar anta-men, Studien zur Altorientalistik, Fetschrift für Willem H. Ph. Römer zur Vollendung seines 70. Lebensjahres mit Beiträgen von Freunden, Schülern und Kollegen*, Münster: Ugarit-Verlag, 281–344.

Selz, Gebhard J. 1998b:
Du$_{11}$-ga-ni-mu-gi-na, aber steht die Lesung von URU+KA-gi-na(k) fest?, *Altorientalische Forschungen* 25, 312–327.

Selz, Gebhard J. 2000:
Schrifterfindung als Ausformung eines reflexiven Zeichensystems, *Wiener Zeitschrift für die Kunde des Morgenlandes* 90, 169–200.

Selz, Gebhard J. 2003:
Who is Who? Akka, König von Ĝiš(š)a: zur Historizität eines Königs und seiner möglichen Identität mit Aka, König von Kiš, in G. Selz (ed.), *Festschrift für Burkhart Kienast zu seinem 70. Geburtstage dargebracht von Freunden, Schüler und Kollegen* (AOAT Bd. 274), Münster: Ugarit-Verlag, 499–518.

Selz, Gebhard J. 2004a:
"Tief ist der Brunnen der Vergangenheit". Zu "Leben" und "Tod" nach Quellen der mesopotamischer Frühzeit – Interaktionen zwischen Diesseits und Jenseits, in F. Schipper (ed.), *Zwischen Euphrat und Tigris – Österreichische Forschungen zum Alten Orient* (Wiener Offene Orientalistik Bd. 3), Wien und Berlin: LIT Verlag, 39–60.

Selz, Gebhard J. 2004b:
Early Dynastic Vessels in 'Ritual'Contexts, *Wiener Zeitschrift für die Kunde des Morgenlandes* 94, 185–224.

Selz, Gebhard J. 2008:
The Divine Prototypes, in N. Brisch (ed.), *Religion and Power – Divine Kingship in the Ancient World and Beyond* (The Oriental Institute of The University of Chicago – Oriental Institute Seminars No. 4), Chicago: The University of Chicago, 13–31.

Selz, Gebhard J. 2010:
"He put in order the accounts..." – Remarks on the Early Dynastic Background of the Administrative Reorganization of the Ur III State, in L. Kogan et al. (edd.), *Proceedings of the 53e Rencontre Assyriologique Internationale, Volume 2: City Administration in the Ancient Near East* (Babel und Bibel 5), Winona Lake, Indiana: Eisenbrauns, 5–30.

Selz, Gebhard J. 2011a:
Reconstructing the Old Sumerian Administrative Archives of the é-mí – é ^{d}ba-ba$_6$ – Institution, in J. G. Dercksen, J. Eidem, K. van der Toorn, K. R. Veenhof (edd.), *Akkade is King – A Collection of Papers by Friends and Colleagues Presented to Aage Westenholz on the occasion of His 70th Birthday 15th May 2009* (PIHANS CXVIII), Leiden: Nederlands Instituut van het Nabije Oosten, 273–286.

Selz, Gebhard J. 2011b:
Zur Holzwirtschaft im altsumerischen Lagaš, in L. Vacín (ed.), *U4 du11-ga-ni sá mu-ni-ib-du11, Ancient Near Eastern Studies in Memory of Blahoslav Hruška*, Dresden: Islet Verlag, 213–246.

Selz, Gebhard J. 2011c:
Staat A., in *Reallexikon der Assyriologie* 13 – 1/2, Berlin–New York: Walter de Gruyter, 23–32.

Selz, Gebhard J. 2011d:
"Medium and Message": Beyond the Written Text, in *Sapienza Università di Roma: Scienze dell'Antichità* 17, 283–295.

Selz, Gebhard J. 2012:
Götter der Gesellschaft – Gesellschaft der Götter, Zur Dialektik von Abbildung und Ordnung, in H. Neumann, S. Paulus (edd.), *Wissenskultur im Alten Orient – Weltanschauung, Wissenschaften, Techniken, Technologien*, 4. Internationales Kolloquium der DOG, 20.–22. Februar 2002, Münster–Wiesbaden: The Harrassowitz Publishing House, 61–86.

Selz, Gebhard J. 2014a:
Dumuzi(d)s Wiederkehr?, in L. Sassmannshausen, G. Neumann (edd.), *He Has Opened Nisaba's House of Learning, Studies in Honor of Åke Waldemar Sjöberg on the Occasion of His 89th Birthday on August 1st 2013*, Leiden–Boston: Brill, 201–215.

Selz, Gebhard J. 2014b:
The tablet with "Heavenly Writing", or How to become a star, in A. Panaio (ed.), *Non licet stare caelestibus – Studies on Astronomy and its History offered to Salvo De Meis*, Milano-Udine: MIMESIS, 51–67.

SF:
Anton Deimel: *Schultexte aus Fara* (Wissenschaftliche Veröffentlichungender Deutschen orient-Gesellschaft 43), Leipzig: J. C. Hinrich'sche Buchhandlung 1923.

Spada, Gabriela 2011:
A Handbook from the Edubba'a: An Old Babylonian Collection of Model Contracts, *Zeitschrift für Assyriologie* 101, 204–245.

Stauder, Wilhelm 1970:
Die Musik der Sumerer, Babylonier und Assyrer, in H. Hickmann, W. Stauder (edd.): *Orientalische Musik, Handbuch der Orientalistik I: Der Nahe und Mittlere Osten, Ergänzungsband IV*, Leiden–Cologne: E. J. Brill, 171–244.

Steible, Horst 1991:
Die neusumerischen Bau- und Weihinschriften 2 (FAOS 9.2), Stuttgart: Franz Steiner.

Steible, Horst, Fatma Yildiz 2008:
Die Listen mit Abgaben an Götter aus Šuruppak, *Mitteilungen der Deutschen Orient-Gesellschaft zu Berlin* 140, 151–204.

Steinkeller, Piotr 1981:
Studies in Third Millennium Palaeography I: Signs TIL and BAD, *Zeitschrift für Assyriologie* 71, 19–28.

Steinkeller, Piotr 1989:
Sale Documents of the Ur III Period (FAOS 17), Wiesbaden: Franz Steiner Verlag.

Steinkeller, Piotr 1995:
Review of *ZATU*, *Bibliotheca Orientalis* 52/5-6, 689–713.

Steinkeller, Piotr 2002a:
Archaic City Seals and the Question of Early Babylonian Unity, in Tzvi Abusch (ed.), *Riches Hidden in Secret Places, Ancient Near Eastern Studies in Memory of Thorkild Jacobsen*, Winona Lake, Indiana: Eisenbrauns, 249–257.

Steinkeller, Piotr 2002b:
More on the Archaic City Seals, *N. A. B. U.* 2/2002 (juin), 29.

Steinkeller, Piotr 2004:
On the Writings of *bēlum* in Sargonic and Earlier Sources, *N. A. B. U.* 1/2004 (mars), 12–14.

Steinkeller, Piotr 2010:
More on the Archaic Writing of the Name of Enlil/Nippur, in A. Kleinermann, J. M. Sasson (edd.), *Why Should Someone Who Knows Something Conceal It? Cuneiform Studies in Honor of David I. Owen on His 70th Birthday*, Bethesda: CDL Press, 239–244.

Steinkeller, Piotr 2013:
An Archaic "Prisoner Plaque" from Kiš, *Revue d'Assyriologie* 107, 131–157.

Steinkeller Piotr, John N. Postgate 1992:
Third-Millennium Legal and Administrative Texts in the Iraq Museum, Baghdad, Winona Lake, Indiana: Eisenbrauns.

Stol, Marten 1989:
Malz, in *Reallexikon der Assyriologie* vol. 7, Berlin–New York: Walter de Gruyter, 322–329.

Stol, Marten 2012:
Bitumen in ancient Mesopotamia. The textual evidence, *Bibliotheca Orientalis* 69/1–2, 48–60.

Sumner, William M. et al. 2003:
Early Urban Life in the Land of Anshan: Excavations at Tal-e Malyan in the Highlands of Iran (University Museum Monograph 117), Philadelphia: University of Pennsylvania Museum of Archaeology and Anthropology.

Suriano, Matthew J. 2012:
Ruin Hills at the Threshhold of the Netherworld, *Welt des Orients* 42, 210–230.

Sürenhagen, Dietrich 1999:
Untersuchungen zur relativen Chronologie Babyloniens und angrenzender Gebiete von der ausgehenden 'Ubaidzeit bis zum Beginn der Frühdynastisch II-Zeit 1, Studien zur Chronostratigraphie der südbabylonischen Stadtruinen von Uruk und Ur, Heidelberg: Heidelberger Orientverlag.

Szarzyńska, Krystyna 1992:
Names of Temples in the Archaic texts from Uruk, *Acta Sumerologica (Japan)* 14, 269–287.

Szarzyńska, Krystyna 1993:
Archaic Sumerian signs indicating successive days, in J. Zabłocka, St. Zawadzki (edd.), *ŠULMU* IV, Poznań: Adam Mickiewicz University Press, 273–285.

Szarzyńska, Krystyna 1994:
Archaic Sumerian Tags, *Journal of Cuneiform Studies* 46, 1–10.

Szarzyńska, Krystyna 1996:
Some Comments on Individual Entries in the Uruk Sign-List *ZATU*, *Acta Sumerologica (Japan)* 18, 235–242.

Szarzyńska, Krystyna 2011:
The Urukean Archpriest EN in the Archaic period. A Few Remarks on his Functions, *Palamedes* 6, 5–15 (reference courtesy Małgorzata Sandowicz).

Šašková, Kateřina, Lukáš Pecha, Petr Charvát (edd.) 2010 :
Shepherds of the Black-headed People – The Royal Office Vis-à-vis Godhead in Ancient Mesopotamia, Pilsen: University of West Bohemia.

Tallon, Francoise 1995:
Les pierres précieuses de l'Orient ancien, des Sumériens aux Sasanides, Paris: Réunion des Musées Nationaux.

Tinney, Steve 1999:
Ur-Namma the Canal-Digger: Context, Continuity and Change in Sumerian Literature, *Journal of Cuneiform Studies* 51, 31–54.

Thalmann, Jean-Paul 2013:
Le lion, la chèvre et le poisson – A propos d'une jarre à empreintes de sceaux-cylindres de Tell Arqa (Liban), *Syria* 90, 255–312.

Thorn, Brett, Dominique Collon 2013:
Dr. Lee's Collection of Cylinder Seals, *Iraq* 75, 119–142.

Trigger, Bruce G. 1998:
Writing systems: A Case Study in Cultural Evolution, *Norwegian Archaeological Review* 31/1, 39–62.

Tsouparopoulou, Christina 2012:
The "K-9" Corps of the Third Dynasty of Ur: The Dog Handlers at Drehem and the Army, *Zeitschrift für Assyriologie* 102, 1–16.

Tunca, Önhan 1984:
L'architecture religieuse protodynastique en Mésopotamie (Akkadica Supplementum II) I–II, Leuven: Peeters.

UE III:
Leon Legrain: *Ur Excavations volume III: Archaic Seal Impressions*, London and Philadelphia: The Trustees of the Two Museums (The British Museum and The University Museum), by the aid of a Grant from the Carnegie Corporation of New York 1936.

UET II:
Eric Burrows: *Ur Excavations, volume II: Archaic Texts*, London and Philadelphia: Trustees of the two Museums (The British Museum and The University Museum, University of Pennsylvania, Philadelphia) 1935.

Van de Mieroop, Marc 1999–2000:
An Accountant's Nightmare: the Drafting of a Year's Summary, *Archiv für Orientforschung* 46–47, 111–129.

Van Ess, Margarete 2012:
Stiftmosaik, in M. P. Streck et al. (edd.), *Reallexikon der Assyriologie* vol. 13, Berlin–New York: Walter de Gruyter, 184–186.

Vandiver, Pamela et al. 1993:
Thermoluminiscence dating of a crucible fragment from an early tin processing site in Turkey, *Archaeometry* 35/2, 295–298.

Veldhuis, Niek 1995:
Review of R. K. Englund, H. J. Nissen, Lexikalische Listen (ATU 3), *Bibliotheca Orientalis* 52, 433–440.

Veldhuis, Niek 1997:
Elementary Education at Nippur – The Lists of Trees and Wooden Objects, Proefschrift Doctoraat Letteren aan de Rijksuniversiteit Groningen, Groningen: Universiteit.

Veldhuis, Niek 2006:
"How did they learn cuneiform?" in P. Michalowski, N. Veldhuis (edd.), *Approaches to Sumerian Literature: Studies in Honour of Stip (H. L. J. Vanstiphout)*, Leiden–Boston: Brill, 181–200.

Ventura, Agnès Garcia 2008:
Neo-Sumerian Textile Wrappings, Revisiting some Foundation Figurines from Nippur, *Zeitschrift für Orient-Archäologie* 1/2008, 246–254.

Ventura, Agnès Garcia 2012:
The Emperor's New Clothes: Textiles, Gender and Mesopotamian Foundation Figurines, *Altorientalische Forschungen* 39, 235–253.

Visicato, Giuseppe 1989:
Fara ed Ebla – Nuove prospettive storico-politiche nel periodo protodinastico, *Oriens Antiquus* 28, 169–176.

Visicato, Giuseppe 1991:
Unia di misura di capacità a Fara: bariga e gur-mah, *N. A. B. U.* 3/1991, 53–54.

Visicato, Giuseppe 1994:
Un testo di assegnazioni d'orzo ad Abu Salabikh, *N. A. B. U.* 4/1994, 87–89.

Visicato, Giuseppe 1995:
The Bureaucracy of Šuruppak – Administrative Centres, Central Offices, Intermediate Structures and Hierarchies in the Economic Documentation of Fara, Münster: Ugarit-Verlag.

Visicato, Giuseppe 1997:
Indices of Early Dynastic Administrative Tablets of Šuruppak, Naples: University Institute of Oriental Studies, Department of Asian Studies, Series Maior 6 A.

Visicato, Giuseppe 2000:
The Power and the Writing – The Early Scribes of Mesopotamia, Bethesda, MD: CDL Press.

Visicato, Giuseppe 2008:
Gestione e sfruttamento dei terreni agricoli nella Babilonia dal periodo tardo-Uruk al periodo sargonico, in M. Perna, Fr. Pomponio (edd.), *The Management of Agricultural Land and the Production of Textiles in the Mycenaean and Near Eastern Economies*, Naples (diffusion: de Boccard, Paris), 9–31.

Visicato, Giuseppe, Aage Westenholz 2000:
Some unpublished sale contracts from Fara, in S. Graziani (ed.), *Studi sul Vicino Oriente Antico dedicati alla memoria di Luigi Cagni*, Naples: University Institute of Oriental Studies, 1107–1133.

Visicato, Giuseppe, Aage Westenholz 2005:
An Early Dynastic Archive from Ur Involving the lugal, *KASKAL* 2, 55–78.

Volk, Konrad 1990:
Zur Lesung von teme (NAGA-inversum) und téme (NAGA), *N. A. B. U.* 2/1990 (juillet), 37–38.

Waetzold, Hardtmut 1995:
DUB.NAGAR in Ebla, *N. A. B. U.* 1995 p. 102.

Waetzold, Hardtmut 2001a:
Wirtschafts- und Verwaltungstexte aus Ebla Archiv L.2769 (Materiali epigrafici di Ebla = MVN 7), Rome: "La Sapienza".

Waetzold, Hardtmut 2001b:
Eine Perle mit Inschrift des Königs Kurigalzu, *N. A. B. U.* 2001/2, juin, 41–42.

Wasserman, Nathan 2013:
Treating Garments in the Old Babylonian Period: "At the Cleaners" in a comprative view, *Iraq* 85, 255–277.

Weadock, Penelope N. 1975:
The Giparu at Ur, *Iraq* 37, 101–128.

Wengrow, David 2014:
The Origins of Monsters – Image and Cognition in the First Age of Mechanical Reproduction, Princeton –Oxford: Princeton University Press.

Westenholz, Aage 1987:
Old Sumerian and Old Akkadian Texts in Philadelphia 2, Copenhagen: Museum Tusculanum Press.

Westenholz, Joan Goodnick 1997:
Legends of the Kings of Agade, Winona Lake, Indiana: Eisenbrauns.

Westenholz, Joan Goodnick 2013:
In the service of the gods: The ministering clergy, in H. Crawford (ed.), *The Sumerian World*, London–New York: Routledge, Taylor and Francis Group, 246–274.

Wilcke, Claus 1988:
Anmerkungen zum Konjugationspräfix /i/ und zur These von "silbischen" Charakter der sumerischen Morpheme anhand neusumerischer Verbalformen beginnend mit ì-íb, ì-im und ì-in, *Zeitschrift für Assyriologie* 78, 1–49.

Wilcke, Claus 1991:
Zur Herstellung von Reflexbögen, *N. A. B. U.* 1/1991 (mars), 14.

Wilcke, Claus 1996:
Neue Rechtsurkunden der altsumerischer Zeit, *Zeitschrift für Assyriologie* 86, 1–67.

Wilcke, Claus 2006:
Die Hymne auf das Heiligtum Keš - Zu Struktur und "Gattung" einer altsumerischen Dichtung und zu ihrer Literaturtheorie, in P. Michalowski, N. Veldhuis (edd.), *Approaches to Sumerian Literature - Studies in the Honour of Stip (H. L. J. Vanstiphout)*, Boston-Leiden: Brill, 201-237.

Wilkinson, Tony 2003:
Archaeological landscapes of the Near East, Tucson: The University of Arizona Press.

Wilson, Anne C. 1991:
Food and Drink in Britain: From the Stone Age to the 19th Century, Chicago: Academy Chicago, accessible from the address http://www.foodtimeline.org/foodsoups.html#portable [accessed September 7, 2013].

Winter, Irene 2007:
Representing Abundance: A Visual Dimension of the Agrarian State, in Elizabeth Stone (ed.), *Settlement and Society - Essays Dedicated to Robert McCormick Adams*, Los Angeles-Chicago: Cotsen Institute of Archaeology, UCLA and The Oriental Institute of the University of Chicago, 117-138.

Woods, Christopher 2005a:
On the Euphrates, *Zeitschrift für Assyriologie* 95, 7-45.

Woods, Christopher 2005b:
A Unique Writing for Sippar at Abū Salābīkh. ^{d}UD.KIB^{ki} (Addendum to ZA 95 [2005], 7-45), *N. A. B. U.* 3/2005 (septembre), 73-74.

Woolley, Ch. Leonard, et al. 1934:
Ur Excavations, volume II, The Royal Cemetery, A Report on the Predynastic and Sargonid Graves Excavated between 1926 and 1931, London and Philadelphia: Joint Expedition of the British Museum and of the University Museum, University of Pennsylvania.

Woolley, Ch. Leonard 1955:
Ur Excavations volume IV: The early periods, A report on the sites and objects prior in date to the Third dynasty of Ur discovered in the course of the excavations, London and Philadelphia: Trustees of the two Museums by the aid of a grant from the Johnson Fund of the American Philosophical Society, Philadelphia.

Wright, Henry T. 1969:
The administration of rural production in an early Mesopotamian town (Anthropological Papers, Museum of Anthropology, University of Michigan No. 38), Ann Arbor: The University of Michigan.

Yıldız, Fatma, Gomi Tohiru 1993:
Die Umma-Texte aus den archäologischen Museen zu Istanbul III, Bethesda, Maryland: CDL Press.

Yoshikawa, Mamoru 1988:
Telicity and Momentariness in the Sumerian verb, *Zeitschrift für Assyriologie* 78, 50-75.

Zaccagnini, Carlo 1988:
Terms for Copper and Bronze at Ebla, in Hauptmann, H., Waetzoldt, H. (edd.), *Wirtschaft und Gesellschaft von Ebla - Heidelberger Studiem zum Alten Orient Bd. 2, Akten der Internationalen Tagung Heidelberg 4. - 7. November 1986*, Heidelberg: Heidelberger Orientverlag, 359-360.

ZATU:
Hans-Jörg Nissen, Margaret Green, Peter Damerow, Robert K. Englund: *Zeichenliste der archaischen Texte aus Uruk*, Berlin: Gebr. Mann Verlag 1987.

Zettler, Richard 1989:
Pottery Profiles Reconstructed from Jar Sealings in the Lower Seal Impression Strata (SIS 8-4) at Ur: New Evidence for Dating, in A. Leonard, Jr., B. B. Williams (edd.), *Essays in Ancient Civilizations Presented to Helene J. Kantor* (SAOC 47), Chicago: Oriental Institute of the University of Chicago, 369–387.

Zettler, Richard 2007:
Clay sealings from the ED-I levels of the Inanna temple at Nippur: A preliminary analysis, in M. Roth, W. Farber, M. Stolper and P. von Bechtolsheim (edd.), *Studies presented to Robert D. Biggs, June 4, 2004*, Chicago: The Oriental Institute of the University of Chicago, 343–362.

Zgoll, Annette 1997:
Der Rechtsfall der En-hedu-Ana im Lied nin-me-šara (AOAT 246), Münster: Ugarit-Verlag.

Zgoll, Annette 2006:
Review of Yitschak Sefati, Love Songs in Sumerian Literature, Ramat Gan: Bar Ilan University Press 1998, *Zeitschrift für Assyriologie* 96, 109–119.

Electronic sources

Buckland 1893: accessible from the address http://books.google.de [accessed March 1, 2012].
Chicago Assyrian Dictionary online: http://oi.uchicago.edu/research/pubs/catalog/cad/ [accessed September 2, 2012].

Fischer, Robert 2007:
Die keltische Religion in Irland und ihre Beeinflussung durch die Christianisierung, Diplomarbeit and der Universität Wien, Wien, im Juni 2007, accessible from the address www.univie.ac.at/keltologie/diplomarbeiten/diplomarbeit1.pdf [accessed August 28, 2012].

Philadelphia Sumerian Dictionary: http://psd.museum.upenn.edu/epsd/nepsd-frame.html [accessed October 6, 2014].

Wilson, Anne C. 1991:
Food and Drink in Britain: From the Stone Age to the 19th Century, Chicago: Academy Chicago, accessible from the address http://www.foodtimeline.org/foodsoups.html#portable [accessed September 7, 2013].

CONCORDANCE OF EXCAVATION NUMBERS OF OBJECTS INCLUDED IN THE TEXT OF THIS BOOK

U = field number of objects excavated at Ur by the expedition of the British Museum (London) and University Museum of Archaeology and Anthropology of the University of Pennsylvania (Philadelphia) in 1922–1934.

UE III = Leon Legrain: *Ur Excavations volume III: Archaic Seal Impressions, London and Philadelphia: The Trustees of the Two Museums (The British Museum and The University Museum), by the aid of a Grant from the Carnegie Corporation of New York 1936.*

UM = designation of objects deposited in the collections of the University Museum of Archaeology and Anthropology of the University of Pennsylvania at Philadelphia.

U 11 680 = UM 31-16-630 = UE III: 416 = my # 78

U 12 776 = UM 31-17-351A = UE III: 483 (reference p.)

U 12 776 = UM 31-17-351P = UE III missing (reference p.)

U 12 776 = UM 31-17-351S = UE III: 481 (reference p.)

U 12 776 = UM 31-17-351T = UE III missing (reference p.)

U 12 778 = UM 31-17-352B = UE III: 480 = my # 119

U 12 778 = UM 31-17-352R = UE III: 480 = my # 120

U 13 607 = UM 31-16-677 = UE III: 518 = my # 121

U 13 912 = UM 31-16-675 = UE III: 424 = my # 86

U 13 933 = UM 31-16-645 = UE III: 418 = my # 80

U 13 943 see U 20 083

U 13 969 = UM 31-16-644 = UE III: 442 = my # 106

U 13 972 = UM 31-16-674 = UE III: 404 = my # 67

U 14 115 = UM 31-16-651 = UE III: 432 = my # 97

U 14 163 = UM 31-16-672 = UE III: 304 = my # 44

U 14 586 = UM 31-16-602 = UE III: 398 = my # 62

U 14 589 = UM 31-16-646 = UE III: 134 = my # 26

U 14 594 = UM 31-16-640 = UE III: 417 = my # 79

U 14 643 = UM 31-16-673 = UE III: 43 = my # 9

U 14 813 = UM 31-16-652 = UE III: 114 = my # 23

U 14 825 = UM 31-16-671 = UE III: 281 = my # 42

U 14 841 = UM 31-16-642 = UE III: 119 = my # 25

U 14 878 = UM 31-16-680 = UE III: 80 = my # 13

U 14 883 = UM 31-16-653 = UE III: 433 = my # 98

U 14 896A = UM 31-16-604 = UE III: 431 = my # 93

U 14 896B = UM 31-16-654 = UE III: 431 = my # 94

U 15 045 = UM 31-16-676 = UE III: 427 = my # 89

U 18 394 = UM 33-35-263 = UE III: 77 = my # 10

U 18 394 = UM 33-35-264 = UE III: 81 = my # 14

U 18 394 = UM 33-35-265 = UE III: 105 = my # 22

U 18 394 = UM 33-35-266 = UE III: 85 = my # 17

U 18 394 = UM 33-35-267 = UE III: 79 = my # 12

U 18 394 = UM 33-35-268 = UE III: 91 = my # 20

U 18 394 = UM 33-35-269 = UE III: 90 = my # 19

U 18 394 = UM 33-35-270 = UE III: 474 = my # 118

U 18 394 = UM 33-35-271 = UE III: 117 = my # 24

U 18 394 = UM 33-35-274 = UE III: 84 = my # 16

U 18 394 = UM 33-35-276 = UE III: 83 = my # 15

U 18 394 = UM 33-35-277 = UE III: 89 = my # 18

U 18 394 = UM 33-35-278 = UE III: 78 = my # 11

U 18 394 see U 18 407

U 18 397 = UM 33-35-290 = UE III: 395 = my # 57

U 18 397 = UM 33-35-291 = UE III: 395 = my # 58

U 18 397 = UM 33-35-292 = UE III: 395 = my # 59

U 18 397 = UM 33-35-293 = UE III: 429 = my # 91

U 18 397 = UM 33-35-294 = UE III: 436 = my # 100

U 18 397 = UM 33-35-296 = UE III: 397 = my # 61

U 18 398 = UM 33-35-297 = UE III: 431 = my # 95

U 18 398 = UM 33-35-298 = UE III: 431 = my # 96

U 18 399 = UM 33-35-301 = UE III: 155 = my # 28

U 18 399 = UM 33-35-404 = UE III: 396 = my # 60

U 18 401 = UM 33-35-314 = UE III: 460 = my # 113

U 18 402 = UM 33-35-324 = UE III: 275 = my # 41

U 18 404 = UM 33-35-338 = UE III: 349 = my # 51

U 18 404 = UM 33-35-343 = UE III: 349 = my # 52

U 18 404 = UM 33-35-350 = UE III: 239 = my # 36

U 18 407 = U 18 394 (2 fragments) = UM 33-35-358 = UE III: 238 = my # 35

U 18 407 = UM 33-35-366 = UE III: 239 = my # 37

U 18 407 = UM 33-35-370 = UE III: 257 = my # 40

U 18 407 = UM 33-35-373 = UE III: 254 = my # 39

U 18 407 = UM 33-35-374 = UE III: 234 = my # 34

U 18 409 = UM 33-35-381 = UE III: 463 = my # 115

U 18 409 = UM 33-35-383 = UE III: 447 = my # 109

U 18 409 = UM 33-35-385 = UE III: 329 = my # 49

U 18 413 = UM 33-35-399 = UE III: 202 = my # 31

U 18 413 = UM 33-35-423 = UE III: 405 = my # 68

U 18 413 = UM 33-35-425 = UE III: 296 = my # 43

U 18 413 = UM 33-35-430 = UE III: 252 = my # 38

U 18 490 = UM 33-35-465 = UE III: 1 = my # 1

U 18 550 = UM 33-35-467 = UE III: 34 = my # 7

U 18 550 = UM 33-35-469 = UE III: 25 = my # 5

U 18 550 = UM 33-35-474 = UE III: 26 = my # 6

U 18 550 = UM 33-35-477 = UE III: 35 = my # 8

U 18 550 = UM 33-35-478 = UE III: 24 = my # 4

U 20 083 = (U 13 943 in UE III) = UM 35-1-671 = UE III: 401 = my # 64

U 20 083 = (U 14 618 in UE III) = UM 35-1-672 = UE III: 454 = my # 110

U 20 083f = UM 35-1-707 = UE III: 559 = my # 123

U 20 083h = UM 35-1-709 = UE III: 556 = my # 122

U missing = UM 31-16-613 = UE III: 411 = my # 74

U missing = UM 31-16-614 = UE III: 402 = my # 65

CONCORDANCE OF MUSEUM NUMBERS OF OBJECTS INCLUDED IN THE TEXT OF THIS BOOK

U = field number of objects excavated at Ur by the expedition of the British Museum (London) and University Museum of Archaeology and Anthropology of the University of Pennsylvania (Philadelphia) in 1922–1934.

UE III = Leon Legrain: Ur Excavations volume III: Archaic Seal Impressions, London and Philadelphia: The Trustees of the Two Museums (The British Museum and The University Museum), by the aid of a Grant from the Carnegie Corporation of New York 1936.

UM = designation of objects deposited in the collections of the University Museum of Archaeology and Anthropology of the University of Pennsylvania at Philadelphia.

UM 31-16-602 = UE III: 398 = U 14 586 = my # 62

UM 31-16-604 = UE III: 431 = U 14 896A = my # 93

UM 31-16-613 = UE III: 411 = U missing = my # 74

UM 31-16-614 = UE III: 402 = U missing = my # 65

UM 31-16-630 = UE III: 416 = U 11 680 = my # 78

UM 31-16-640 = UE III: 417 = U 14 594 = my # 79

UM 31-16-642 = UE III: 119 = U 14 841 = my # 25

UM 31-16-644 = UE III: 442 = U 13 969 = my # 106

UM 31-16-645 = UE III: 418 = U 13 933 = my # 80

UM 31-16-646 = UE III: 134 = U 14 589 = my # 26

UM 31-16-651 = UE III: 432 = U 14 115 = my # 97

UM 31-16-652 = UE III: 114 = U 14 813 = my # 23

UM 31-16-653 = UE III: 433 = U 14 883 = my # 98

UM 31-16-654 = UE III: 431 = U 14 896B = my # 94

UM 31-16-671 = UE III: 281 = U 14 825 = my # 42

UM 31-16-672 = UE III: 304 = U 14 163 = my # 44

UM 31-16-673 = UE III: 43 = U 14 643 = my # 9

UM 31-16-674 = UE III: 404 = U 13 972 = my # 67

UM 31-16-675 = UE III: 424 = U 13 912 = my # 86

UM 31-16-676 = UE III: 427 = U 15 045 = my # 89

UM 31-16-677 = UE III: 518 = U 13 607 = my # 121

UM 31-16-680 = UE III: 80 = U 14 878 = my # 13

UM 31-17-351A = UE III: 483 = U 12 776 (reference p.)

UM 31-17-351P = UE III missing = U 12 776 (reference p.)

UM 31-17-351S = UE III: 481 = U 12 776 (reference p.)

UM 31-17-351T = UE III: missing = U 12 776 (reference p.)

UM 31-17-352B = UE III: 480 = U 12 778 = my # 119

UM 31-17-352R = UE III: 480 = U 12 778 = my # 120

UM 33-35-263 = UE III: 77 = U 18 394 = my # 10

UM 33-35-264 = UE III: 81 = U 18 394 = my # 14

UM 33-35-265 = UE III: 105 = U 18 394 = my # 22

UM 33-35-266 = UE III: 85 = U 18 394 = my # 17

UM 33-35-267 = UE III: 79 = U 18 394 = my # 12

UM 33-35-268 = UE III: 91 = U 18 394 = my # 20

UM 33-35-269 = UE III: 90 = U 18 394 = my # 19

UM 33-35-270 = UE III: 474 = U 18 394 = my # 118

UM 33-35-271 = UE III: 117 = U 18 394 = my # 24

UM 33-35-274 = UE III: 84 = U 18 394 = my # 16

UM 33-35-276 = UE III: 83 = U 18 394 = my # 15

UM 33-35-277 = UE III: 89 = U 18 394 = my # 18

UM 33-35-278 = UE III: 78 = U 18 394 = my # 11

UM 33-35-290 = UE III: 395 = U 18 397 = my # 57

UM 33-35-291 = UE III: 395 = U 18 397 = my # 58

UM 33-35-292 = UE III: 395 = U 18 397 = my # 59

UM 33-35-293 = UE III: 429 = U 18 397 = my # 91

UM 33-35-294 = UE III: 436 = U 18 397 = my # 100

UM 33-35-296 = UE III: 397 = U 18 397 = my # 61

UM 33-35-297 = UE III: 431 = U 18 398 = my # 95

UM 33-35-298 = UE III: 431 = U 18 398 = my # 96

UM 33-35-301 = UE III: 155 = U 18 399 = my # 28

UM 33-35-304 = UE III: 396 = U 18 399 = my # 60

UM 33-35-314 = UE III: 460 = U 18 401 = my # 113

UM 33-35-324 = UE III: 275 = U 18 402 = my # 41

UM 33-35-338 = UE III: 349 = U 18 404 = my # 51

UM 33-35-343 = UE III: 349 = U 18 404 = my # 52

UM 33-35-350 = UE III: 239 = U 18 404 = my # 36

UM 33-35-358 = UE III: 238 = U 18 407 = U 18 394 (2 fragments) = my # 35

UM 33-35-366 = UE III: 239 = U 18 407 = my # 37

UM 33-35-370 = UE III: 257 = U 18 407 = my # 40

UM 33-35-373 = UE III: 254 = U 18 407 = my # 39

UM 33-35-374 = UE III: 234 = U 18 407 = my # 34

UM 33-35-381 = UE III: 463 = U 18 409 = my # 115

UM 33-35-383 = UE III: 447 = U 18 409 = my # 109

UM 33-35-385 = UE III: 329 = U 18 409 = my # 49

UM 33-35-399 = UE III: 202 = U 18 413 = my # 31

UM 33-35-423 = UE III: 405 = U 18 413 = my # 68

UM 33-35-425 = UE III: 296 = U 18 413 = my # 43

UM 33-35-430 = UE III: 252 = U 18 413 = my # 38

UM 33-35-465 = UE III: 1 = U 18 490 = my # 1

UM 33-35-467 = UE III: 34 = U 18 550 = my # 7

UM 33-35-469 = UE III: 25 = U 18 550 = my # 5

UM 33-35-474 = UE III: 26 = U 18 550 = my # 6

UM 33-35-477 = UE III: 35 = U 18 550 = my # 8

UM 33-35-478 = UE III: 24 = U 18 550 = my # 4

UM 35-1-671 = UE III: 401 = U 20 083 = (U 13 943 in UE III) = my # 64

UM 35-1-672 = UE III: 454 = U 20 083 = (U 14 618 in UE III) = my # 110

UM 35-1-707 = UE III: 559 = U 20 083f = my # 123

UM 35-1-709 = UE III: 556 = U 20 083h = my # 122

CUNEIFORM TEXTS CITED HEREWITH

CT – abbreviation for texts deposited in the collections of the British Museum, London.

SF: Anton Deimel: Schultexte aus Fara (Wissenschaftliche Veröffentlichungender Deutschen orient-Gesellschaft 43), Leipzig: J. C. Hinrich'sche Buchhandlung 1923.

VAT – abbreviation for finds deposited in the collections of the Vorderasiatisches Museum, Berlin.

W – prefix preceding excavation numbers of texts found at Uruk/Warka.

SUMERIAN SIGNS AND NAMES

AKKADIAN WORDS AND PHRASES

EBLAITE PHRASES

HURRIAN WORDS

REGISTER OF ANEPIGRAPHIC SEALS PUBLISHED IN *UE III* AND REFERRED TO IN THIS BOOK

REGISTER

The following captions are not included in this Register: cylinder seals; ED; Mesopotamia; seal impressions; SIS; Sumer; Sumerian; Ur.